Debunk

Geno
M

Debunking the Genocide Myth

A Study of the Nazi Concentration Camps and the Alleged Extermination of European Jewry

Paul Rassinier
Introduction by Pierre Hofstetter
Translated from the French by
Adam Robbins

The Noontide Press
Los Angeles, California

PUBLISHER'S NOTE

The publication of this edition which embodies the major portions of *Le Passage de la ligne, Le Mensonge d'Ulysse, Ulysse trahi par les siens,* and *Le Drame des Juifs européens* in a single volume has been authorized by Madame Jeanette Rassinier, the widow of the author, and it constitutes the only authorized edition available in the English language.

Library of Congress Catalog Card Number: 78-53090
ISBN 0-911038-24-8

Copyright ©1978 by the Noontide Press

The Noontide Press, P.O. Box 1248
Torrance, California 90505

Manufactured in the United States of America

Table of Contents

About The Author

Paul Rassinier was born on March 18, 1906, in Beaumont, a small village near Montbéliard, the son of a farmer. He received his formal education in the schools of the area and passed the necessary examinations which allowed him to teach history and geography at the secondary school level and to use the title of "professor." He taught in the secondary school at Faubourg de Montbéliard where students were prepared to take the "*brevet*," an examination that is somewhat inferior to that examination which is taken by students in the *lycées* who desire to matriculate at the university. It was at this school that he was arrested by the *Gestapo* in October 1943.

Having joined the Socialist Party, SFIO, in 1934, Paul Rassinier became the head of that party in the Belfort area when the war broke out in 1939. Following the German occupation of France, he participated in the founding of the "*Libre-Nord*" organization which became involved in various forms of "passive resistance," including the smuggling of Jewish refugees over the Franco-Swiss border into Switzerland in cooperation with the Swiss Jewish Committee. Rassinier's activities eventually came to the attention of the German authorities who caused him to be arrested and to be deported to the concentration camp at Buchenwald. Later he was sent to the camp at Dora where he was incarcerated until the end of the war.

Upon his liberation in 1945, he returned to France where he was elected to the *Assemblée Nationale* as a Socialist deputy. He served for one year and then retired. He was awarded the highest decoration which the French government bestowed for service in the wartime resistance movement. Due to his frail health, a consequence of his two years of imprisonment at Buchenwald and Dora, he retired from teaching and received a small pension from the French government. He died on July 29, 1967, at his home in Paris-Asnieres. He is survived by his wife, Jeanette, and his only son, Jean-Paul, who is a practicing physician.

Introduction

In every respect, Paul Rassinier was a remarkable man of his time — out of the ordinary, we are tempted to write — a man to whom can be immediately attributed these three essential qualities, all of which are rather rare today in a single person: courage, honesty and ability.

As a professor of history and geography, he could have had a brilliant and lucrative career in these disciplines if he had confined himself to the "official history" — i.e., the "official false history that is taught *ad usum Delphini*" and of which Balzac spoke — and if he had not opted for historical revisionism by beginning to study carefully the "hidden history" wherein lies the true causes of events, in short, the "shameful history." He devoted the last twenty years of his life to the debunking of the historical orthodoxy that surrounds World War II and produced a shelf full of books which culminated in the remarkable work, insufficiently known, entitled *Les Responsables de la seconde guerre mondiale*[1], which was published shortly before his death in July 1967.

Paul Rassinier also could have made a name for himself in politics if, when he was a socialist representative in 1946, he had submitted to the oppressive climate of that period in France and had accepted open collaboration with the Communist Party. But, he refused such collaboration, and that party did all that it could to defeat him in his bid for re-election. As a matter of fact, the Communists always did want Paul Rassinier's "hide" in both the literal as well as the figurative sense. A confirmed, total pacifist, Rassinier, in 1922 at the age of 16, under the influence of the anarchist Victor Serge, had been drawn into the Communist Party from which, having later gone to the opposition, he was quickly excluded. He joined the Socialist party in 1936, where he made himself known particularly in the pacifist wing that was opposed to the French policies that led to the 1939 war. Then, after France was occupied by the German army, he was one of the earliest resistants to this occupation and helped to found the "*Libre-Nord*" movement, but, unlike the murderous guerrilla bands and the "shadow assassins," he tried to inculcate into these Resistance movements "the idea of nonviolence and the principles of total pacifism." Such an attitude succeeded in getting him "condemned to death" by the Communist resistance (which had arrived on the scene late following the German attack on the U.S.S.R. in June 1941) and in putting him on the receiving end of the ritual "little warning coffin" effigy. It is bitter irony that this man – deported to Buchenwald and to Dora, where he endured frightful suffering for nearly two years – should later concede that he only escaped from the rain of Communist machine gun fire thanks to his arrest by the *Gestapo* on October 30, 1943, and his subsequent deportation to Germany.

Liberated in 1945, returned to France on a stretcher, and declared to be a severe invalid, Paul Rassinier could have, once again, had a lucrative and successful career in what was called *"resistantialisme,"* that is to say, the shameless, continuous, and highly advantageous exploitation – "make room for us!" – of the events of the "resistance," real or imaginary. However, in Belfort, his native city, he began with a nearly naive honesty to proclaim vociferously that he had never met in the Resistance most of the men who were speaking in its name, which was, in itself, already a bold step. But, he went even further, and, with the exceptional courage of an honest man who was sickened by the flood of lies that flowed before his eyes, he began to denounce exaggerations of every kind concerning

German war crimes, while maintaining that there had been as many war crimes committed on the Allied side as on that of the Axis and that they were all of a similar horrible nature.

Indignant. Paul Rassinier was thoroughly indignant, this former deportee, about the whole avalanche of questionable and often fanciful literature about the German concentration camps that passed before him. In the preface of Rassinier's *Le Parlement aux mains des banques*[2], the dramatist and screenwriter Henri Jeanson described Paul Rassinier's indignation as follows:

> I like Rassinier very much. I like him very much because, without losing his composure, without grandiloquence, quite simply Rassinier lived, in the word of Zola, "indignant." Indignant, but calm because he was sure of his facts. Indignant, but imperturbable. Indignant since the age of sixteen.
>
> The indignation of Rassinier does not make itself known through spectacular temper tantrums. He does not at all become carried away and avoids all invective. From these traits stem his strength and perfect aim. He does not belong to that race of congestive polemists who rid themselves in one article — whew — of their scrupulosity or their bad temper and who write like someone purging himself. Once the article has been published, he does not consider himself released from duty as concerns himself and does not move to another sort of exercise. No, he carries on with a good faith that no one dreams of reproaching him for, with the exception, of course, of these national organizations in which authentic resistance fighters and deportees innocently allow themselves to be duped by the profiteers of the crematoriums. And these profiteers do exist. They have always existed. No one is unaware that the ossuary of Verdun, for example, has become a circus attraction and an excellent business whose profits are all the greater since the merchandise is never replenished. It is always the same skeletons which are used. The remains are not a loss for everyone.

Indignant; Paul Rassinier began, then, almost immediately upon his return from Buchenwald, to do battle against the numerous concentration camp legends, as a free spirit and a scrupulous historian. There were then published in succession *Le Passage de la ligne*[3], an impartial and lucid account of his life as a deportee, *Le Mensonge d'Ulysse*[4], a critical look at the orthodox concentration camp "literature," and *Ulysse trahi par les siens* [5], a companion work to *Le Mensonge d'Ulysse*. The bulk of these three works makes up the first eleven chapters of this present edition; some redundant material — i.e., overlapping material which appears more than once in the original French editions — has been removed from the present English language edition, which combines the three books, in an effort to retain the readability of the original works and to reduce the production costs of this edition. Naturally, the scope and the meaning of the original editions have not been altered by this editing.

On the subject of atrocity propaganda, Paul Rassinier, as the reader will discover when he reads the chapters which follow, minces no words:

> The atrocities and those responsible for them are clearly inseparable. Moreover, I shall perhaps astonish you. I forego, as a matter of fact, either giving you a list of these atrocities or decrying them to you. You have already heard far too much on the subject. The atrocity proves nothing, moreover, in history, either against he who commits it or in favor of he who is subjected to it. We have all too many examples of a world where today's victim is tomorrow's executioner and vice versa. It will be enough then for me to tell you that the concentration camps were a world of horrors. And if anything ought to be added, it would be this: in spite of this, just about all those who have spoken of them have overdone it and particularly their explanations have little in common with the truth . . . . Concerning figures, the "witnesses" have said and written the most improbable things. Concerning the implementation of the means of killing, also. Concentration camp literature on the whole has the appearance of a collection of contradictory pieces of ill-natured gossip.

With such a view on the worth of concentration camp literature, it is no surprise that Paul Rassinier began to question the central tenet of the concentration camp orthodoxy, to wit: the claim of Jewish genocide. On this subject, the authoritative work of Paul Rassinier clearly remains his *Le Drame des Juifs européens*[6] in which he examined, with the care of the scrupulous historian that we know him to be, the documents, the statistics, and the census figures that are related to the alleged holocaust. The translation of this study is found in the final four chapters of this volume. Without question, it is an authoritative work in its genre. And, as such, it has been circulated widely through Europe during the past decade. Moreover, *Le Drame* — as well as Rassinier's numerous other works — has inspired an ever-growing library of other "revisionist" works on the subject, including the excellent study by Arthur R. Butz, *The Hoax of the Twentieth Century*[7].

Paul Rassinier's contentions that there was no Nazi policy of Jewish genocide, that there were no officially sanctioned "exterminations by gas" and that there were no six million Jewish deaths at the hands of the Nazis have, naturally, bothered greatly the "court historians," caught with their hands in the cookie jar, so to speak, with their dishonest scholarship, as well as the entire Zionist establishment which has built the State of Israel on the "myth of the six million." In fact, the post-war politics of the Soviet Union, of the Bonn government in West Germany, and of the United States with regard to its "Cold War" policies have been justified, to a large extent, by the pointing to the alleged Nazi wartime atrocities, with the expressed hope that the given policy under consideration will prevent what the Nazis "did" from ever occurring again, *et caetera, ad nauseam*. Thus, it should be no secret why historical revisionism in this area of study has been greeted with such hostility from "official quarters" on both sides of the "Iron Curtain."

Notwithstanding his iconoclastic contentions, Paul Rassinier kept things in balance. In the chapter concerning the "Jewish question" in his *Les Responsables de la seconde guerre mondiale,* he argued that ". . . even stripped of all the exaggerations that have falsified its meaning, Hitler's policy against the Jews was an unquestionable attack on human rights and was, according to the sanctioned expression 'more than a crime, a transgression.' " But, he hastens to add that to a certain extent the misfortunes of the Jews during that period were a consequence of their own doing:

> Let us recognize that [the Jewish] claim to wanting to be in Germany — as in every other country that they regard as a "land of welcome" — a national minority was scarce-

ly tenable either. It was up to themselves to admit that they were foreigners in Germany and to surrender any right to protest if, in his turn, Hitler treated them like foreigners. The other governments of the world were free to accept this claim of the Jews; it was a problem of domestic policy which was none of Hitler's affair. Let the Jews of Germany go settle elsewhere, he said. The Third Reich was a totalitarian state, and, in its bosom, there was no room for a national minority.

The only problem with Hitler's plan was that the other sovereign states wanted nothing to do with these Jews, at least in appreciable numbers. "Even had they wanted to deal with them, Hitler's policy would have remained, without any doubt, a blow to human rights," Rassinier remarked further, "but it would have remained such only from the point of view of principles and, on the practical level, it would have not taken on [the subsequent] inhuman turn of events. The matter could have been resolved by the expedient of a transfer of the population accompanied by a transfer of personal property, the likes of which history offers us many an example. That is what Hitler was proposing."

In spite of the outbreak of hostilities in September 1939, this policy of population transfer remained the ultimate goal of the Hitler government, and, as the study that is printed in the final four chapters of this book demonstrates, such a population transfer actually did take place for the vast majority of European Jewry, although admittedly it occurred under inhumane and brutal conditions which caused numerous casualties. But, as the study also shows, such deaths were an unfortunate coincidence and were not the result of a deliberate policy of "genocide."

As an important revisionist historian in the tradition of the late American historian Harry Elmer Barnes — through whose efforts, incidentally, this translation was commissioned — Paul Rassinier left an impressive body of work, without doubt indispensable to a complete understanding of the events of the Twentieth Century. Among his works which have not been mentioned previously, is a large volume, rich in documentary material of prime importance and analyzed with his customary lucidity, concerning that gross example of "kangaroo justice" known as the Jerusalem Tribunal which passed judgment on

Adolf Eichmann; it is entitled *Le véritable procès Eichmann ou Les Vainqueurs incorrigibles.*[8].

Other works that should be noted include his *Candasse ou Le Huitième péché capital*[9], a "story beyond time" that is told a bit in the manner of Anatole France, and, above all, his *L'opération "Vicaire"*[10] in which he admirably exposes the political operation which consisted, in conjunction with the play "The Deputy," in charging Pope Pius XII with the crime of "having favored Nazism," and, in doing so, having favored the anti-Jewish persecutions conducted by the Nazis, whereas, to the contrary, the Pope condemned those policies. Interestingly, as if by chance, there were found in rather great numbers in the gaggle of the Pope's accusers people who had helped Hitler to come to power.

To the everlasting credit of Paul Rassinier is the fact that with his *L'opération "Vicaire"* he undertook the defense of the "highest moral authority on earth" in spite of the fact that he was a professed atheist. It was likewise honorable for this former deportee, the poor victim of the hell of the concentration camps, to refrain from capitalizing on his experiences as a camp inmate and, instead, to put himself at the service of historical truth concerning the German camps and the "Jewish holocaust." Clearly, Paul Rassinier belonged, as his friends and admirers were always able to appreciate, to this elite of men whose sole ambition is never to repudiate themselves and to conserve an unswerving allegiance to the principles they have chosen to serve.

PIERRE HOFSTETTER
July, 1977

FOOTNOTES

1 *Those Responsible for the Second World War* (Paris: Nouvelles Editions Latines, 1967)

2 *The Parliament in the Hands of the Banks* (Paris: Contre-Courant, 1955)

3 *The Crossing of the Line* (Paris: Editions Bressanes, 1950)

4 *The Lie of Ulysses* (Paris: La Librairie Francaise, 5th ed., 1961)

5 *Ulysses Betrayed by his Own* (Paris: La Librairie Francaise, 1961)

6 *The Drama of the European Jews* (Paris: Les Sept Couleurs, 1964)

7 (Richmond, Surrey: Historical Review Press, [1976]). See pages 9-13 for a bibliographical essay concerning other "revisionist" titles as well as other source material.

8 *The Real Eichmann Trial or the Incorrigible Victors* (Paris: Les Sept Couleurs, 1963)

9 *Candasse or the Eighth Capital Sin* (Paris: L'Amitie par le Livre, 1955)

10 *Operation "The Deputy,"* (Paris: La Table Ronde, 1965)

PART I
The Author's Experience

Chapter One

Prologue

It rained a fine, cold, icy April rain; steady, relentless, and inexorable. It had rained for two days and the third night was beginning.

The train, a long line of cars grinding along the rails, slowly disappeared into the blackness. The engine, a locomotive of another era, sweated, blew and strained, coughed and spat, slipped and back-fired. A hundred times it hesitated, and a hundred times it seemed to refuse to make the effort expected of it.

It rained unceasingly. In the gondola car, open to the sky, were eighty huddled cringing bodies, intertangled, on top of each other. Were they living? Were they dead? No one could say. In the morning they woke once more, frozen in their miserable rags; they were emaciated and hollow with their eyes staring out, feverish and dazed. With a superhuman effort they shook themselves. They were aware of the daylight. They felt the rain — the stinging slashes of the rain — go through their ragged clothing, to their thin and hardened flesh, reaching to the very bone. They arched their backs with an imperceptible shudder. Perhaps, they were just beginning to make those thousands of instinctive, waking up movements, when they saw themselves reflected in each other's eyes. Through the fog of fever and the sheet of water falling from the skies, they noticed the men in uniform, armed to the teeth, planted in the four corners of the car, impassive but vigilant. Then they remembered. They realized their destiny, and with a start, dejected and overwhelmed, they fell back into that half sleep, that half life, that half death.

It rained, and rained, on and on. A heavy fetid air rose from the mass of bodies, and disappeared into the cold wetness of the night.

When they had left there were a hundred of them. They had been collected together in a hurry, with dogs at their heels and thrown pell-mell in groups into the train, under blows and shouted commands. They were horror stricken when they found themselves about to leave from the small platform, without provisions for the journey. Suddenly they understood that a great ordeal was beginning.

"Achtung, Achtung!" they were warned. "On your feet during the day; sit down during the night! . . . *Nicht Verschwinden*! Any breaking of the rule, *sofort erschossen*! understand?"

The open car, the cold, and the rain, that was one thing; that had been seen before. But, nothing to eat; nothing to eat!

To cap their misery, for weeks there had not been an ounce of bread in the camp, and they had had to make do with supplies from the storage pits: plain soup of rutabaga, a quart, sometimes half a quart, and small potatoes, in the evening, after a long, hard day of work. Nothing to eat. Everything else vanished before this menace. The sound of the Americans seven and a half miles away barely reached them.

Standing during the day, sitting down at night . . . ! Before the end of the first night, three or four of them who had shown too precipitately a desire to satisfy a pressing need, were seized by the collar, smacked brutally against the high wall of the car and executed point blank: Craa-ack! against the wood, craa-ack! They did it in their pants, cautiously at first, holding themselves so as to soil themselves as little as possible; then, progressively they gave up.

Three or four others who had fallen down with exhaustion during the following day, were coldly finished off with a bullet in the head. Craa-ack! against the floor, craa-ack! The bodies were tossed out, as the train rolled along, after the registration numbers were removed. At the beginning of the third night, the ranks were considerably thinned, and fear gave way to terror, and terror to complete resignation. Abandoned was any urge to escape this hell, any urge to live; they let themselves die in their own excrement.

And still it rained, on and on and on. A little breeze riffled across the convoy, and the bit of canvas, that make-shift shelter under which in each corner the guard passed his long hours of watch, was lifted. It was as if the miasma were blown away, and the S.S. man, nervous at first, fussing about although in a determined way, suddenly became concerned. For some time, fewer rifle shots were heard, and there was less machine gun chattering. The dogs themselves – oh those dogs! – barked and yelped less at the numerous stops. In 48 hours, due to the constant changing of direction from side-track to side-track, the train was less than twelve and a half miles from where it started. Late in the afternoon it set off toward the southwest, after having tried the north, the south, and east in vain. If this track was cut like the others, it would mean that we were trapped and that we would be taken. The S.S. guards frowned, and then passed the news on from car to car, throughout the length of the train. "We are trapped; we will be captured!" They were completely bowled over. They were going to be captured, and all of these half conscious prostrate bodies were going to come back to life, rise up to accuse them; they would be caught red-handed.

Still, during the morning we heard them frequently calling out questions to each other with guttural voices, cracking jokes, and laughing coarsely at the sad and disabused girls who all along the right of way gave them back only occasional and melancholy encouragement. Now they were silent, only the click of a lighter, or the red end of a cigarette, from time to time broke this death-like silence, or disturbed the thick and humid obscurity of the night.

It rained endlessly, on and on. On top of this, the wind had become stronger. It began to whistle sharply between the boards, and the water came down in torrents. The canvas cover over one S.S. guard ballooned up, and its props gave way. Suddenly, the tent cloth began to flutter like a flag and to flap against the wall of the car. The S.S. swore. Then, grumbling and swearing, he tried in vain to repair the damage. If he got it attached on one side, the wind tore it off on the other! *"Gott Verdammt!"*

After two futile attempts he gave up. Suddenly, he turned toward the nearest of the miserable creatures, and gave a few shoves with his knee. *"Du,"* he cried. *"du ... Du. blöder Hund!"* *Blöder Hund?* The man heard, understood where the cry came from, automatically collected all the strength left in him, and got up frightened. When he saw what he was expected to do, he felt a little reassured. He raised himself onto the top of the wooden side of the car where he balanced on his hands and knees. Then, very carefully so as not to fall over the other side onto the road bed, he brought in the canvas, and helped the guard to fix the corners onto the supports.

"Fertig?" (Finished?) *"Ja, Herr S.S."*

And, then an extraordinary thing happened. He came to his senses all of a sudden. All of a sudden the thought came to him that he was on his knees on the top edge of the wall, that his two legs were turned toward the outside, that the train was not moving very fast, that it was raining, that the night was black, and that the Americans were perhaps seven or so miles away, that freedom . . . Freedom, oh liberty! With that evocation, a sudden madness filled him who just a little while before was afraid of falling − oh irony − a light filled his brain, flooded his whole being: *"Ja . . . "* he repeated; then cried, *"Ja! Ja! Ja! . . .a . . .a . . . ah!"*

Before the S.S. guard even had time to register surprise, the man, the half-dead skeleton, tightened his muscles in one supreme effort, propped his poor thin arms on the edge of the board, and threw himself backward. He heard the crackling of gunfire ringing in his head, and he still found the strength, the astonishing lucidity, to realize that he had fallen into a spot that was out of the line of fire. He felt himself caught there, body and soul, and he collapsed into the nothingness of unconsciousness. A machine gun continued to fire: Tch!. . . Tch! . . . Clac! . . . Tcheretchstche! . . . Clac! . . . Tch! . . . Clac! Taratatata! . . . Tche! . . . Tche! . . . Tche! . . . Tche! . . . The locomotive sweated and blew, hesitated, slid and back-fired, and the trian moved on. The guns stopped spitting death. Little by little the great indifferent silence of nature asleep closed over the drama going on, disturbed only by the hissing of the rain that now became steady with the dying of the wind. It rained on and on and on.

* * *

It was no longer raining. Hours had gone by, two, three, four, perhaps. The heavens had finally given up. In the thick and spongey night something next to the iron rail moved.

First, two eyes tried to open, but the heavy eyelids sank down in a sudden reflex, as though the head were under water.

His dry throat contracted to salivate and brought up the taste of earth on his tongue. An arm sketched a movement which was paralyzed in mid air by a sharp pain in the elbow, dull at the shoulder. Then, nothing more; the man lost himself again in a strange sense of well-being, and actually thought that he was falling asleep.

Suddenly, a shiver came over him and enveloped him. His chest was bared of its wet covering, brrr! . . . He wanted to curl himself up to get warm. Then, he tried to wake up, his eyelids fluttered nervously, and he forced them to stay open. He stared into the opaque blackness.

A desire to cough rose up from his lungs and shattered him. He had the feeling that his body was acting in sections, independently and aching, in the dripping grass, and on the muddy ground.

He tried to think. Like a knock in his head came the thought "The dogs." This time he did wake up. He reviewed everything. A flood of experiences assailed him, one after the other: the loading, the train, the hell of the railroad car, the cold, the hunger, the canvas, the wind, the jump into the night. The train; what if it should come back over the same way once again? The dogs! Oh! Any death but that.

He wanted to flee; there was nothing else to do, but the pieces of his body were riveted there. He wanted to gather himself together; he heard his bones grating against each other. But, he had to get away from there, at any cost.

His reasoning took another turn: a railway line was a military objective for the attackers and a defensible breastwork for those attacked. The Germans would return to make use of it as a defensive line, and they would find him.

To flee! To get a few hundred yards from the railway right of way and wait there would be a little safer. The Amercans would eventually come. "But, first, stand up! First, stand up." He was thinking out loud and the murmur from his lips brought forth from his mouth gritty bits of earth. He sputtered.

With infinite carefulness he moved his arms one after the other; the left seemed all right, but from the right came that pain in the elbow and shoulder. "Well, well, it seems to be going away." He repeated the motion, and it was true; the pain grew less as he moved his muscles and joints. Nothing was broken. He breathed easier. Now the legs. Gently he moved his muscles. He felt no pain; nothing was broken there either — at least it did not seem so. He became calmer.

He managed to sit up. His bruises became more painful, and his wet sticking clothes became more icy. He shivered. In the pit of his stomach he felt a round ache. He was hungry, and that was a good sign. He was surprised that he had not felt this hunger before. He put his hand to his head; his prison beret was still in place. This fact made him laugh. He thought of his clogs which he had lost during his jump; never mind. He felt all over himself: he was covered with mud and was rolled up in a tangle of wire from which he at once tried to extricate himself. He turned and got on all fours; one more effort and he would be standing up . . . .

On his feet; he was standing; he *would* get away; the Germans could double back, cling to the railway . . . not so fast; his head was spinning. He felt like vomiting. He felt himself tottering, about to fall. He stiffened, held himself upright as long as he could, and saw that he was going to collapse and that he might hurt himself in the fall. So, gently and very carefully, he crouched down. If he could not walk, he would drag himself, but he would not stay there; no, he would not stay there. He thought of the train, the dogs, and the Germans who would be coming back. And, he thought of the Americans . . . "To think that they are there seven miles away. No, it would be too stupid."

On his hands and knees, crawling like a huge tormented worm, he managed to go down a slope, to cross what seemed to be a ditch, full of gluey water, and to slither along a newly ploughed section of an adjacent field where the earth came up in hunks and stuck to his knees, his legs and his elbows. He stopped and got his breath back.

Meanwhile, the night had become less black, and the sky was higher. Already the shapes of the hedges and the single trees around him could be made out in the thinning fog. Day was about to break and that was another danger. A few hundred yards away on a little rise of ground he made out a dark mass; woods, no doubt.

He made it his first objective to reach them before dawn. He started to move again. The struggle had warmed his body, had loosened his muscles and his joints, and had localized the pain down the whole length of his right side. He succeeded in standing up, in staying up, in putting one foot before the other, and in walking. He walked slowly because his right leg pulled and his shoulder was very painful. But, he was walking, and he made progress. Bent over, dead beat, broken, twisted, he pulled himself toward the woods. He straightened up, forced himself, and kept hold of himself. He would be there before dawn, and would take cover there; the Americans would come, and he would be saved. The rest took place in a dream — a long, dead tired, slow-motion dream.

* * * *

When he arrived at the edge of the woods, he gave up the idea of hiding deep inside, which could prove treacherous, and decided it was wiser to sit down there, partially concealed in the low brush from which he could observe all sides.

Day broke. The ground which sloped down from his feet gradually appeared out of the darkness; the indistinct checkerboard pattern of fields and meadows became more outlined; the railroad tracks down below stood out like a long ribbon. In between two distant hills, a church spire rose among little wisps of smoke rising straight up from invisible chimneys. Very quickly the radiant spot in the still grey sky, which announced the sun piercing the clouds, was high in the sky. The country-side was animated here and there with yokes of oxen peacefully going and coming. A man, a civilian too, but whose brassard could be distinguished, had nonchalantly begun to do his stint along the tracks.

The sight evoked in him the image of a similar corner of the earth — in similar weather, under the same sky, and with the same checkerboard of fields and meadows, the same woods, the same isolated trees, the same church steeple, and the same railroad — somewhere in the vicinity of Alsace and Franche-Comte.

It occurred to him that if his mother could see this scene at this very hour, she would certainly have commented that the sky was "washing itself" or that the weather was "drying itself off." For a long time he watched two horses about five

hundred yards away who were pulling a sort of harrow, over a
square of meadow, to "scatter" the mole hills; the old man
guiding them, surely that was father Tourdot, and that good
little girl pulling on a rope attached to the back of the harrow,
that was his granddaughter, whose father, Tony, was a prisoner
in Germany! In an association of ideas he saw the worried face
of his wife bending over a little bit of a fellow two years old . . . .
Then, the reality of his present situation came to him with a
start of anxiety.

No, no, it was a trap! The Americans couldn't be seven miles
away because everything was too quiet. Nothing in these fields
and meadows and these woods gave a sign of war, much less of
a complete collapse. He was crushed; what was going to become
of him? He could not approach those people in his prisoner's
clothing! He was hungry, very hungry, and thirsty, and he picked up a twig which he put into his mouth; that was another
remedy of his mother's, when he had cried into her skirts with
thirst in the hot afternoons during the harvest. It took his mind
off it.

The hours went by; the sun managed to pierce the greyness
and to clear up the sky. A church bell rang; noon it was. The
afternoon went by in the same way. The teams of animals became more numerous under a hotter sun which completely
dried his garments. A man went by near him, a hoe over his
shoulder, and almost brushed against him. He didn't move a
muscle, but he realized that he couldn't stay there much longer
without being discovered. The next day was Sunday; he had no
trouble deciding that since they had left the camp on a Wednes-
day evening. So, in the morning he would be all right, but in the
afternoon he would have a lot to worry about, since the Germans, large and small, liked to walk in the woods.

Evening came, then the night. The moon, a huge moon, the
color of embers, shed its strange light over the country. The
guard on the tracks was still going back and forth. There had
been no alert; in fact, there had not been the least little noise of
an airplane motor in the sky during all day long. But, now he
heard heavy thuds sounding in the distance. He thought, "They
are still twenty-five or thirty miles away. The dogs, if they are
set after me, will find me before the Americans get here. I must
go, go toward them, but which way first?"

He was about to despair of everything when the sound of

aircraft gave him back his courage. Airplanes wheeled above him and dropped their bombs in the immediate vicinity, without in the least being disturbed by anti-aircraft fire. Then they went away, and others came; a continual coming and going until dawn.

Daylight came, and the fog quickly broke up under a bright sun. All at once the day became clear. It was a beautiful spring-time Sunday morning that gave no hint of what was to come. It might have been ten o'clock when the great upheaval finally came. Tac! . . . . Tac! . . . . Tacatacatacatac!. . . . Tac! He esti-mated the distance: two to three miles at the most. It came from the direction of the church and a little beyond. Tac! Tac!. . . . tac tac tac!. . . . Tac!

The machine gun persisted, and another replied. Toc! Toc! . . . . toc toc! Toc toc!

Then a great uproar: Boom! boom! Boom!. . . Boom! The projectiles did not fall far away, but still on the other side of the village. Boom! Boom! . . . boom, boom . . . . A pause, Boom! . . . boom! . . . Another pause. Boom! Boom! Boom! . . . Boom! Boom! . . . Boom! They came right at him; the discharge was regular, sharp, ringing. It would soon be time to do something, but what? A formidable explosion tore the air behind him; a shell had almost fallen on top of him. Brr. . . oom! Then another. Brr. . . oom! His ear drums were bursting with it! Brr. . . oom! Br. . . oom! It didn't stop, and was echoed from behind. Boom! . . . Boom! . . . Boom! . . . Boom! . . . The countryside was de-serted, and the man with the brassard had disappeared. He was alone. Brr . . . oom! . . . Boom, boom, boom, Brou . . . Brr . . . oom!

He was on the axis of a trajectory that was cut almost at right angles by the rail tracks, along which the Germans were doub-ling back. They would try to defend it, but they could not hold out for long in the face of the artillery fire; they would then retreat into the woods, where they would find him. "No, he must not stay there!"

He got up. He went down the slope, veering toward the left to get out of the line of the trajectory. His leg hardly dragged any more, the earth was dry, the ground was hard, and he was in possession of all his faculties. The last act of the tragedy was about to be played, and no false step must be made. "Not too near the tracks, not too near the forest," he decided.

The artillery duel continued: Boom! . . . Boom! . . . Boom! . .
Boom! . . . The shells came down again; they were hitting the
tracks. He saw the earth explode in a long line which cut obli-
quely across the tracks. He could smell the burning explosives.
"The Devil! Get down!" He would have liked to go farther on,
but . . . . He saw a single bush that was near by: a poor shelter.
He preferred a deep trough which separated two farm plots; he
threw himself down in it.

ZZ . . . . Boom! . . . . ZZ . . . . Boom! Just in time! The shell
whistled over his head and fell near him. The thunder behind
him, which had ceased, began again; the sounds were heavier,
and farther away. They were drawing back!

While the Americans lengthened their fire, the Germans
shortened theirs, following their withdrawal step by step.
Suddenly, he found himself in the very center of a terrifying
earthquake, a cloud of smoke, iron, earth. He was almost
buried in earth and wondered what miracle had saved him from
being pulverized.

As the dust settled, he risked taking a look around him. He
could see forms in field grey who were crossing the tracks, one
after the other, in rapid spurts between bursts of machine gun
fire. They flattened themselves against the embankment; a burst
of fire! They were up and moving again. Down again, another
burst of fire! They retreated toward him, trying to get out of
the open, to make it to the woods. Down . . . a burst of fire;
fifteen steps back, a burst of fire . . . down again. "Let's hope
that one of them doesn't throw himself down next to me!" he
thought. A shot rang less than fifteen feet on his left, another
less than five on his right. He could not see anyone. "What are
they shooting at, Good Lord?"

The exploding artillery shells, little by little, reached the
woods, and the chattering of machine gun fire raked it. More
grey forms climbed up over the tracks and withdrew into the
woods from which they directed their fire: Clac! . . . Clac! . . .
Clac! . . . Clac! . . . Clac! . . . But, in the face of the brisk
artillery fire, the reports from the forest grew weaker, and
finally stopped altogether.

Suddenly there was a great clamor. It came from all corners
of the horizon and echoed nearer and nearer, never ending.
Suddenly, a host of men began to appear with rifles and
machine guns in hand. While those who, a short while ago, had

crossed the tracks amounted to a few dozen men, a hundred at the most, there were at least a thousand of these. They all seemed to be converging on the same point. Soon they were everywhere, walking and running. Not one of them saw him, which was just as well since one never knew what might happen at moments like these. He was careful not to make his presence known too soon. He waited for the excitement to subside. Finally he dared to move.

He sat up. About three hundred yards away some fifteen very nervous men, with their hands above their heads, were slowly emerging from the woods under the watchful eyes of guards, with their machine guns on the alert. In front of them, their backs to the woods, other men were already lined up, their hands resting on their heads, rigid. Finally others with their arms raised high appeared one by one; they threw their guns to the ground, took off their equipment, and took their places in the line-up.

"Jump to it!" One of them, too slow, was reminded of his new status with a well placed kick. Another received a blow with a gun-butt. A third tried to argue; Cra-a-ac! A machine gun was fired point blank at his chest. A few more blows, kicks, and slugs with the gun-butt, and the column was ready. "Get marching, toward the church!"

The group passed him at a distance of about seventy-five yards. The prisoners, in rows of five, completely stripped of equipment, jackets unbuttoned, and hands behind their heads shuffled by, awkward, silent and docile. On both sides an armed cordon of seven or eight men showered them with insults and warnings. He decided that it was time to show himself, and he rose up with a leap. "Hey! . . . Hey! . . . " he shouted, and he raised one arm in a gesture of appeal.

Without delay, the group halted, four men detached themselves on the run, and before he had time to realize what was happening to him, the barrels of four machine guns were pressed against his chest and back. "Like this, at least, I know they won't shoot!" he thought. The questions all came at once, menacing, and in a language that he did not understand.

"French man," he said. It was all the English that he knew and he wasn't sure that was right. They looked at him round-eyed, astonished and mistrustful. He was obviously not understood. Then, he said, *"Francaise!"* This was not understood either. He tried his last resource: *"Französiche Häftling!* · · · *Franzous!"* This time it worked; one of the machine guns was lowered.

"Was?" He briefly explained, in broken phrases, and he saw that he was in the presence of a German, two Spaniards and a Yugoslav, whose *lingua franca* was Italian. They had understood, all the machine guns were lowered, and a canteen was offered to him. He drank a bitter cold drink, which he wanted to spit out. He grimaced. *"Koffé,"* said the German, *"gut Koffé."* They got out dry biscuits, hard, hard, oh how hard, chocolate, tins, cigarettes . . . . Cigarettes! First a cigarette . . . . But, they must not waste time. *"Schnell,"* said the German, *"Wir müssen . . . "* (Hurry . . . . we have to . . . .) They saw what condition he was in. Two of them hoisted him onto their shoulders, and like a living trophy took him, laughing, to the group which was waiting. *"Sin-Sin?"* asked one of the fellows of the escort. "Yes," he answered. But, the others said nothing. There was only one Englishman — or an American — in the company . . . which was a kind of international brigade, and he thought of the Spanish War.

As evening fell, the little column resumed its march toward the church, with the emaciated figure keeping his balance with difficulty on the shoulders of the two men, while nibbling slowly, his mouth watering copiously, on the biscuits and the chocolate. The sarcastic comments, the warnings, and the oaths, continued to rain on the prisoners, who, always docile, moved along, awkwardly in the unlaced shoes, their heads hung down, their two hands crossed at the nape of their necks. *"Porco Dio!* . . . *Gott Verdammt!!"* From time to time the German spoke up: *"Du!* . . . *Blöder Hund!* . . . *Du!!"* And, he pointed to a prisoner. Then, taking his revolver out of its holster, he asked him, *"Muss ich erschiessen?"* (Shall I shoot?) The prisoner rolled his frightened and pleading eyes, waiting for the answer — a neutral, resigned smile. *"Du hast Glück!* . . . *Mensch! Blöder Hund!"* (You're lucky . . . stupid dog . . . .) he said and spat contemptuously, *"tt!* . . . *Lumpe."* The roles were reversed.

From insult to insult, gibe to gibe, and threat to threat, the column of triumphant conquerors and disappointed losers made their entrance into the village just before midnight. They were past a station, very small, just like others that he knew, in Franche-Comté and Alsace. On the front he read "Munschof" in

Gothic lettering. They set him down on the ground and the column rested. Then, slowly they started up again, amidst the deafening noise of the imposing war machines which at full speed went through the deserted but intact village on to new positions. Sometime later, the column reached the headquarters encampment.

* * * *

An odd little fellow was the Commanding Officer: English, German, Italian, French; he seemed to be familiar with all languages. And, then there was that tone, that manner:

"First, find a place to stay, my friend, eat, get your strength back, rest, a good bed. Then, we will see . . . . Knock at the first door that strikes you as a good place . . . . No, no, not with my men, they haven't the time, the hell with them now. Knock; if they open the door to you, ask for something to eat, hot, you need something hot. You will get a little something extra, from us, cold of course . . . . If they don't open, go in just the same, whether there is someone there or not; make yourself at home; all these people are our servants, it is their turn . . . . All they have to do is behave properly. No, no, don't be afraid, at the slightest lack of respect . . . . Come back to see me tomorrow. Until then . . . . Not wounded? Not sick? . . . Yes, of course, weak, just weak. Until tomorrow then. And try to find another pair of shoes there . . . and another dinner jacket!"

The next day he went back. The Commanding Officer was sitting in an armchair on the porch, playing around with two very pretty persons, laughing out loud, who seemed to be quite ready "to behave properly" in the military sense of the phrase as applied to civilians of the opposite sex. "The female always submits to the conqueror with smiles," he thought. In France, in 1940 . . . . All of them, girls from Colas Breugnon.

But, the Commanding Officer said at once: "Ah, there you are! You know, since last evening I have been handed quite a lot of people like you. Since dawn my men haven't stopped bringing them to the *Arbeitsdienst* camp. What am I going to do with them, Good Lord? There is a train load of them, a train! And me, I haven't any way to transport them to the rear! . . . They are all going to die; they'll all die! What sort of a place was it that you were in. Ah! the skunks! Well, don't worry about it, old boy, these two girls . . . ."

"Good," he began again, "You can walk? . . . Then, don't go
to the *Arbeitsdienst* camp . . . . Go West, my friend, toward the
West. Escapee, get there on your own, on friendly ground . . . .
Hague Convention, deportee, priority . . . . Signal the first
ambulance you run into. In eight days you'll be in Paris. All the
laws, I'm telling you . . . . We'll see that you have something to
eat to take with you. Really, is that all you have found since
last evening? You'll give a fright to the girls all the way, old
boy. Wasn't there anything where you spent the night? We won
the war, in God's name! . . . She's pretty good that one! Ah,
these French, you can't ever teach them anything . . . . *Frantz*!"

Then he added in a few words in Anglo-German lingo:

"*Also*, bye, bye! Follow the guide, he's going to give you
something to take along. Good luck, but . . . try to do better
the next time!"

Well weighed down with canned food, sugar, chocolate, biscuits and cigarettes, among other things . . . which he didn't
know where to put, he found himself outside. He wanted to see
the train from which he had escaped, and he turned toward the
station.

People, civilians and soldiers, were busily going back and
forth along the platforms. They made room for him as he came
along: the clothes that he wore gave him a sort of respect.
Gangs of men were pulling from the cars, the half clothed
bodies, in rags, lank, dirty, bearded, and muddy! Some civilians
were helping and watching them, full of pity, horrified. The
dead bodies were lined up along the edge of the tracks, after
their numbers, if there were any on their rags, were taken down.
He looked to see if he could find anyone he knew among the
dead . . . . Two men, two German civilians, arrived carrying a
big thin body. "*Kaput?!*" one of them said. "*Nein,*" answered
the other, "*atmet noch.* . . . " (Finished . . . . No, he's still
breathing.) He recognized Barray; Barray!

Barray was an engineer from St. Etienne. In camp they had
slept together on the same straw mat for three weeks and had
become friends. They had promised to write to each other if
they got out. He learned from one of the survivors that the poor
man had gone down under the blows of some German prisoners
for having, in the delirium of hunger, cold and fever, begun to
sing the *Marseillaise*. The S.S. guards had stood by unconcerned
during the show. "Barray!" . . . . "It's all over," he said to himself.

And, he went away thinking that there was a fatality in things that some premonitions did come about in life: for fifteen days, at least, Barray had been swearing by all the Gods that they would be freed on Quasimodo (Low) Monday . . . . He promised himself to write to his widow and two children about whom they had so often talked before they went to sleep.

A survivor told him what had happened to the convoy. A mile and a quarter beyond the station, it had been brought to a halt, very early Saturday morning. The S.S. guards had hurriedly made all of the able-bodied men get down from the cars and had formed them into a long endless line, which trailed away into the landscape, accompanied by the howling of the dogs and the sound of gun shots. The S.S. had left – on the train – the dead, the dying, and all of those who, taking advantage of the general confusion, were lucky enough to pass for dead, Obviously, there were too many of them, and there wasn't time to kill them one by one – nor was there the desire to do so. (Since this was written, it has been determined that there was no order to kill the prisoners, either.)

He continued his inspection. In one wide open car that no one was paying any attention to, the surviving prisoners shivered in spite of the full sun; they crawled out from under the pile of dead bodies; they huddled together to protect themselves from a cold that they alone felt. "What are you waiting for?" "Well . . . waiting to die, can't you see?" "What?" "There are still fourteen of us living; all the rest are dead; we are waiting our turn. . . . " He could not understand how they could be so little concerned with the saving of their lives. "They have given up," he thought; "It is not worthwhile to bother with them. They are already 'dead' and are satisfied. To force them back to life would be to inflict a kind of punishment on them . . . . "

And, he went on, with a feeling of indifference. He had known many prisoners in the camp who had been burdened with a sort of "death wish" and whom one could never meet without thinking that they were already dead, but that their bodies, in some manner, had survived them . . . . They were the ones who never missed a chance to announce, to drum it into one, that the war would be over in two months, that the Americans were here, that the Russians were there, that Germany was in revolution, and so forth. They were irritating, and they exhausted one's patience. Then, one fine day they were seen no more. The two months — or whatever — had gone by, and, since nothing had happened, they had just "let go of the railing," as it was said, and had let themselves die on the appointed date. These prisoners had let go of the railing right at the winning post; the two months had ended there, and the day of liberation had arrived! He knew from experience that there was nothing to do. But, two steps farther on a feeling of remorse overcame him. "Don't stay like that; get out of there; the Americans are here; they are emptying the next car, and they will get to you soon. They will give you something to eat; there is a hospital in the village." They did not believe him, but he had made peace with himself.

At the end of the train was a boxcar that was filled with supplies; sacks of peas, flour, canned goods, packages of every sort of ersatz goods imaginable, liquor, beer, liqueurs, suits of clothes, shoes, accessories, and equipment. He took a soldier's nap sack and a pair of Italian shoes, with cloth sides and low-heels, which fitted his feet wonderfully. Then he left, eager to leave behind all that misery.

But, he still wanted to see the *Arbeitsdienst* camp where the Commanding Officer had told him that the Americans were taking those inmates who were still living. On the mustering grounds, surrounded by wooden buildings, living skeletons were coming and going, and corpses lay crumpled here and there . . . There were some five or six hundred men milling about. Well-wishing nurses — attached to the American army — busied themselves among them, running from one to another. The nurses did their utmost in vain to try to get the inmates to understand that they should stay inside the barracks and rest on the straw mattresses. Few among them had in their hearts any desire to live. Those who might have been saved began to die of dysentery because they had, disregarding all warnings, stuffed themselves too greedily with all of the food that was so profusely distributed among them. They ate, then felt a great need for air, and then went outside to die in the yard. No, no, this was no place for him. In the first place, he was too near the front lines; one could still hear the cannon fire all too sharply. He thought of Ulysses' return.

He made his way toward the villa where he had slept the night before and where another tug at his heart awaited him. On the way, he found an American soldier who wanted to shave him, amused.

To tell the truth, it was not a villa but the modest house of an engineer or a retired person — just like so many in France — with an iron fence and a garden all around. The evening before he had found it empty with all the doors open. In the kitchen, the table had not even been cleared; a white cheese was on one plate, and jam was on another. In the dining room, the doors of a cupboard were swung open, and the linen and various other things were piled up on the sofa, on the table, and on the chairs, without thought. A trunk with its top gaping open sat waiting. The bedroom was in perfect order. He felt there the pressing distress of a comfortably well-off family who had hoped to the end and had waited until the last minute before leaving. "They aren't far away," he had thought, "They will come back any minute."

He had slept in the big bed in the bedroom; he had laid there lazily in the morning smoking a cigarette. He had stretched himself out under the warmth of the covers, under a wide beam of sunshine which shone on the polished furniture. Leaving this house, to go to the Commanding Officer's about ten o'clock in the morning, he had thought of what had happened to him in 1940 when, turning back into Alsace, he had wanted to go home one last time. He had caught himself holding a pencil to write a note which he would have stuck on the door if at the last moment a sort of pride, which he had always felt was misplaced, had not restrained him: "Make use of everything, steal nothing, break nothing. Do not take vengeance on things for what you reproach people for. Do not make individuals pay for what you believe is the error of the whole community." And so he had taken out of the linen cupboard only what was indispensable: a shirt, a pair of under shorts, a handkerchief, and — from under the kitchen sideboard — the pair of imitation leather sandals that had made the Commanding Officer laugh so much . . . He had even resisted the very strong temptation, when passing in front of the garage, to borrow the magnificent Opel that was parked there.

Now everything had disappeared, the magnificent Opel was gone, the cupboards were emptied, the linen was stolen, and the dishes were broken. "And I who was so conscientious," he thought. "The war, ah the war!" On the night table, an alarm clock that he had noticed the night before was still there by some miracle. It pointed to 6:30. He threw himself, still all dressed, onto the bed and went to sleep.

* * * *

Early the next morning, when the sun was already high, he set off. The thunder of cannon was still rumbling in the distance, and behind him the mighty war machines rolled toward the front. At the edge of the village, in front of a house a little apart, some civilians were cooking something in a kettle balanced on two stones; there were about half a dozen of them, badly clothed, unwashed, unshaved, dirty, and he noticed that one of them kept the fire going with books which he picked up in bundles. He approached, curious. They were Belgian and Dutch laborers — volunteers who had worked in the factories in the area. The books were those from the *Hitler-Jugend-Bucherei* of the village.

He glanced at the titles: *Kritik über Feuerbach; Die Räuber* of Schiller; *Kant und der Moral.* Goethe, Holderlin, Fichte, Nietzsche, and others, were all there as if at a tragic rendezvous, and they were waiting for their fate to be decided by less noble lords, the Goebbeles and the Streichers. The paper was fine, the bindings were unpretentious, and the workmanship was good. He had always had a weakness for books of any kind. He spotted one, *Du und die Kunst* by one of National Socialism's leaders. He opened it mechanically, and he saw a colored reproduction of *"La Liberté guidant le peuple,"* by Delacroix. He leafed through it more attentively: Monet's flowers, a detail from Renoir, *la Joconde, Mme. Récamier, le Martyr de Saint Sébastien.* This sharp contrast with the hell out of which he had just come made him ill. He asked if he could take this book away with him, as a souvenir of that civilization that had been so cruel to him, and which would astonish and shock the world for years to come. Permission to take the book was given with a smirk and a sneer. Of course it was difficult for them to understand.

He turned west again, with the feeling that he would never come upon an ambulance and that he would continue to the end on foot . . . . All of a sudden, he felt that he was on the threshhold of a new adventure, and that he would have liked to have it resemble, although in other times and under a different sky, that of Ulysses of whom he had thought the day before.

Before him he saw roads, the peasants in the fields, the hedges in bloom, the trees budding, the farms, the people who asked about him and to whom he gladly told his story, and the never ending roads. And, there at the end of this mirage-like horizon, a small house with arbor vitae, on the outskirts of a small village. In the little yard, a little boy always two years old playing in the sand, who raised astonished eyes at seeing him arrive in his prison clothes . . . On the tip of his tongue he was about to ask, "What's your name? Little fellow? Where is your mama?" He wept.

* * * *

Chapter Two

Swarms of Humanity at the Gates of Hell

The time was about six o'clock in the morning, but I could only guess. There were about twenty of us of all ages and backgrounds, all French, all dressed in the most unlikely rags, and all quietly sitting around a large table set on trestles. We did not know each other, and we made no attempt to become acquainted. Silent, or just about, we tried to read each other's expressions, and, although without much interest, to size each other up. We had the feeling that, united in a common fate, we were destined to live through some painful experience together and that we must therefore resign ourselves to the idea of depending on each other. But we acted as though we wanted to put that idea off until the last possible minute; it was not easy to break the ice.

Each man was absorbed in his own thoughts; we were trying to buck ourselves up and to understand what had happened to us: for three days and three nights, one hundred of us per car, hunger, thirst, madness, death, the unloading at night, in the snow, with the howling of men and the barking of dogs, with blows from some and swipes from others; the shower, the disinfection, the "gasoline tank," and so forth. We were all stupefied by what had happened. We had the feeling that we had just crossed a no-man's land and that we had been in a more or less mortal obstacle course which had been carefully graduated and organized in every detail.

After the trip, and without any transition, we encountered a long string of halls, offices and underground corridors, each filled with strange and menacing people, who had their no less strange and humiliating specialties. Here, your wallet, wedding ring, watch, fountain pen; there, your jacket, trousers, shorts, socks, shirt; in the last place, your name. They had stolen everything from us. Then came the barber who shaved us bald, the cresylic bath, and the shower. Finally, the whole process was repeated in reverse: at one window, a shirt that was falling to pieces; at another shorts with holes; at another pants with patches; and so on to the wooden clogs and the strip of cloth with the registration number. A frock coat thrown away, a military blouse no longer used, a Russian cap, a Bersagliers hat made up our clothing. We were not given back our wallets, wedding rings, fountain pens or watches.

"Just like Chicago," someone said, showing his number and joking, "there they go into the factory as pigs and come out as cans. Here we go in as men and come out as numbers." Nobody laughed; between the pig and the can in Chicago there is surely not much difference than between what we were and what we had become.

When we arrived in that large, light and clean hall, well aired and comfortable at first glance, we felt a sort of relief; the same feeling, doubtless, that Orpheus felt coming out of Hades. Then we withdrew into our own preoccupations, to the one which dominated and checked any desire for inner speculations and which could be seen in the eyes of all: "Will we get anything to eat today? When will we be able to sleep?"

We were at Buchenwald, Block 48, Wing A. It was six o'clock in the morning at a guess. And it was Sunday—Sunday, January 30, 1944. A dark Sunday.

**

The building which housed Block 48 was made of stone and had a roof that was covered with tiles; and, unlike almost all of the other buildings which were made of lumber, it had a ground floor and one story. There were toilets and washrooms on both floors; the washrooms had two large circular basins with places for ten or fifteen, and a stream of water coming down like a shower; the W.C.'s had six places for sitting and six for standing. On each side, with a space between, was a *Esszimmer* (refectory) with three large trestle tables and a *Schlafsaal* (dormitory) with thirty or forty bunk beds. One *Esszimmer* and one *Schlafsaal* in pairs, made up a wing, or *Flügel*; the four *Flügel*, consisted of "A" and "B" on the ground floor and "C" and "D" on the first floor. The building covered about one hundred and twenty to one hundred and fifty square yards; twenty to twenty-five yards long and five to six yards wide; the design was intended to provide a maximum of comfort in a minimum of space.

In preparing for our arrival the day before, the camp authorities had emptied Block 48 of its prior occupants. Only the administrative personnel who were attached to it remained: the *Blockältester* or the Block Chief; his *Schreiber* or bookkeeper; the barber, and the *Stubendienst* or barracks men. There were two *Stubendienst* per wing. In all, eleven persons ran the block.

Our group, which was the first to arrive, was housed in the Block Chief's *Flügel*. Little by little others came in. And, little by little the atmosphere livened, too, as tongues became loosened. Fellow countrymen who had been arrested at the same time, or in the same operation, met each other again. As for me, I had found Fernand again, who came to sit next to me.

Fernand was a former student of mine, a solid and conscientious worker, who was twenty years old. During the occupation he had just naturally turned to me. We made the trip to Compiègne chained together, and already at Compiègne we made a nice little island among the seventeen who were arrested in the same operation that had netted us. To tell the truth, we had decided to ignore them. First, there was the one who had set himself down at the interrogation table, then the inevitable career non-com who had become an insurance agent, and who, upon decorating himself with the Legion of Honor, had felt that it was indispensable to his dignity to promote himself to the rank of Captain. Then there were the others, steady and serious, whose silence and whose every look betrayed their awareness of the seriousness of their plight. The insurance agent, especially, annoyed us with his megalomania, his grandiloquent manners, his air of being in on God's secrets, and the stupidly optimistic exaggerations which he incessantly imposed on us. "Come on," Fernand had said to me, "they're not our kind of people."

At Buchenwald, where we had arrived in the same railroad car, we once again stuck together, and took advantage of a moment of inattention on the part of the group to slip away and to present ourselves, one behind the other, for what can only be called prison registration formalities. Separated for an instant, we again found ourselves together with the group.

At eight o'clock in the morning, there wasn't room left to break an egg around the tables, and the chattering that went on was so noisy that it disturbed the Block Chief and the *Stubendienst.* Introductions, occupations, and positions that had been held in the Resistance were shouted back and forth over the heads: bankers, big industrialists, twenty year old commanding officers, colonels hardly any older, the big chiefs in the Resistance, all having the confidence of London and in possession of military secrets, especially the landing date. In addition, there were a few professors, a few priests who timidly kept apart, and a few who said that they were simply job holders or workmen. Aside from these few, everyone wanted to have a social position more enviable than that of his neighbor's; above all, one that included having been entrusted by London with a mission of the greatest importance. You could not count the number of brilliant feats. We two unpretentious people found ourselves crushed. "Upper crust, upper ten . . . Crud," Fernand whispered into my ear in a very, very low voice.

After a quarter of an hour, really tormented, we felt an irresistible urge to urinate. In the hallway which led to the WC, an animated conversation among five or six persons was in progress. As we went by, we heard talk about millions of dollars. "God, what sort of a crowd have we fallen into?"

All the places were occupied in the WC; there was a line-up, and we had to wait. On the way back, a good ten minutes later, the conversation was still going, and it still concerned millions. It was a matter then of some fourteen million. We wanted to find out what it was all about and stopped. It was a poor old fellow who was lamenting over the fabulous sums that the time he would spend in camp would cost him. "But then, sir," I ventured, "what do you do in civilian life that would cause you to handle such large sums of money? You must have quite a position." And, I assumed an air of admiring commiseration when I said that. "Ah, don't talk about it." And, he showed me the wooden clogs he had on. I couldn't keep from laughing out loud. He did not understand and started to tell his story again for my benefit.

"You understand, first the Germans ordered a thousand pairs of them from me, which they came to get without checking either the number or the invoices. Then another thousand pairs, then two thousand, then five thousand, then . . . Lately the orders were pouring in. And, they never checked them. So I began to cheat a little on the quantity, then on the prices. What else can you do? The more money you take from them the weaker they get, and the job gets easier for the English. *Sales boches,* just the same! Then, one fine day they compared the invoices with the reports of their receiving clerks; you can expect anything from people like that. They found they had been robbed of about 10 million. And, so they sent me here. Directly. And, without any trial, Sir. But, can you see – me, a thief? Ruined, I am going to be ruined Sir! And without any trial . . ."

He was truly shocked. Quite sincerely, he was under the impression that he had indisputably performed a patriotic service, and that he had been, although with so many others, the victim of an injustice. Another fellow nearby, without batting an eye began to explain, "That's just like me, Sir, I was a business manager in . . ." "O.K. Come on," Fernand said to me, "You see!".

* * * *

The days went by, and we familiarized ourselves, insofar as we could, with our new life. First, we learned that we were there to work, that we would soon be assigned to a *Kommando,* probably outside the camp, and that we would then go out "in transport." Meanwhile, we would remain in quarantine for three to six weeks, depending on whether or not an epidemic sickness broke out among us.

Then, the camp administration let us know something about the provisory regime that we would be required to follow. During the quarantine, we were absolutely forbidden to leave the Block or its small yard; in any case, it was surrounded with barbed wire. Every morning, we were roused at half past four, "with bugle," by the *Stubendienst*, with a rubber truncheon in hand for those tempted to lag behind; we washed on the run, and then received our food distribution for the day: 250 grams of bread; 20 grams of margarine; 50 grams of sausage or white cheese or jam, and a pint of ersatz coffee without sugar. Roll-call was held at half past five and lasted until half past six or seven. From seven to eight, we cleaned the block. At about eleven we got a quart of rutabaga soup and at about four o'clock the *café-trink.* At six o'clock there was another roll-call which could last until nine o'clock, rarely longer, but usually ended at eight. Then to bed. In between times, we were left to ourselves, sitting around the tables, and if we weren't too noisy about it, we could tell our little stories, our discouragements, our fears, our apprehensions, and our hopes. In fact, from morning to night, the talk centered around the date of the eventual end of hostilities and how they would end; the general opinion was that the war would be over in two months with one of us having gravely announced that he had received a secret message from London giving the beginning of March as the sure date for the landing.

Gradually Fernand and I became acquainted with the others in our group, while keeping our distance and remaining on our guard. In two days, we were sure that at least half of our companions in misery were not there for the reasons that they gave, and, in any case, they had had practically no connection with the Resistance. Most of these internees seemed to have been arrested for black market activities.

It was more difficult to adjust to the rhythm of things. Through the intermediary of a Luxemburger who knew hardly any French, the Block Chief made speeches to us explaining things every evening during roll-call; but, needless to say, it was hard to understand. The Block Chief was the son of a former Communist delegate to the *Reichstag,* who had been assassinated by the Nazis. He was a Communist and didn't conceal it, a fact which surprised me. The main gist of all of his palaver was that the French were dirty, that they talked like magpies, and were lazy, that they didn't know how to wash themselves, and that those listening to him had the double good luck of having arrived at a moment when the camp had become a sanitorium and of having been assigned to a Block whose Chief was a political and not a common criminal. One could not say that he was a bad fellow; he had been in prison for eleven years and had acquired the ways of the establishment. Rarely did he strike one; his displays of violence generally consisted of vigorous *"Ruhe!"* cutting across our talk, which were followed by imprecations in which there was always something about a crematorium. We were afraid of him, but we were much more afraid of the Russian and Polish *Stubendienst.*

We knew nothing, or almost nothing, about the rest of the camp because of our confinement to the four *Flügel* of the Block. We sensed that there was work going on around us and that the work was hard, but we had only scuttle-butt to give us any idea of the nature of it. On the other hand, we knew very quickly about every nook and cranny of our Block, as well as the life stories of the occupants who lived there. There was a little of everything there: adventurers, people whose social origin and standing were very ill-defined; genuine Resistants; serious minded people; Cremieux, the attorney to the Belgian King, among others. It is hardly necessary to say that neither Fernand nor I felt any desire to attach ourselves to any one of the groups that formed.

*   *   *   *

The first week was especially distressing. Among us were the cripples, the maimed with only one leg or with both legs gone, and the congenitally disabled, who had to leave their canes or their crutches or their artificial limbs at the entrance along with their wallets and jewelry. They dragged around miserably, and we helped them or carried them. There were also the very seriously ill from whom had been taken away the indispensable medicines which they always carried on their persons; these persons died slowly. Then, there was the shock that is produced in all organisms by a brutal change in diet, both as to its quality and quantity. Then, all of our bodies began to suppurate; and the Block soon became a vast carbuncle which *ex tempore* doctors, or doctors without any supplies, tried to treat. Finally, on the moral level, various unexpected incidents made even more insupportable the promiscuity that had been imposed on us: the business manager,

who had claimed the rank of Colonel, was caught stealing
bread from one of the sick men whose nurse he had volunteered
to be; a violent quarrel pitted the attorney to the King of the
Belgians against a doctor over the division of a piece of bread;
a fellow, who went around from group to group claiming that
he was going to be a magistrate after the Liberation, was surprised in the act of stealing for himself some extra food from
the general rations, etc . . . We were in the Court of Miracles.
All this stirred up the philanthropists. There is no Court of
Miracles without philanthropists, and France, copiously endowed with them, perforce exported some to this place, who
asked only to have their devotion noted and, if possible, to be
remunerated. One fine day they cast a haughty glance of
commiseration on this mass of men in rags and tatters, abandoned to all of the machinations of the mind and possible
victims of all of the perversions. The level of our morale seemed
in danger to them, and they flew to its assistance, because in a
situation like this, the factor of morale was essential. So it is in
life; there are those who grudge you your bread, others your
freedom, and others your morale.

A man from Lyon, who said he was editor-in-chief of *l'Effort;*
a Colonel, if my memory is good; a big supply official; and a
lame man who called himself a Communist, but whom the
people of Toulouse accused of having betrayed them to the
Gestapo during his interrogation, got underway a program of
regular singing and a series of lectures on various subjects.
During the week, we heard a discourse on syphilis among dogs,
another on the world petroleum production and the role of
petroleum after the war, and a third on comparative labor
organizations in Russia and America.

On Sunday afternoon, there was a continuous program from
three to six, with a stage-manager. A dozen volunteers gave
impromptu performances. The most mixed feelings arose from
the depths of their souls, and the most varied personalities
displayed themselves: from the *Violon brisé* to the *Soldatal-
sacien,* and through *G.D.V., Margot reste au Village* and *Coeur
de Lilas.* In addition the most daring broad jokes were told
along with the most comical monologues. These clownish
actions clashed with the place, the audience, the spot we were
in, and with the preoccupations which should have occupied
our minds. Definitely, the French well deserve the reputation
for levity that the world has attributed to them.

Finally, an intelligent, handsome young man, twenty years old, with a warm voice, sang *La petite Eglise* by Jean Lumiere and made everyone homesick. *"Je sais une église au fond du hameau . . ."* Everyone had tears in his eyes, faces resumed a human look, and the unbalanced became men again. I understood what *"le lent Galoubet de Bertrandou, le Fifre ancien berger"* meant to the Cadets of Gascogne de Cyrano de Bergerac. I forgave the philanthropists and, then and there, vowed eternal gratitude to Jean Lumiere.

* * * *

A change of scene the second week revealed still more formalities that had to be carried out. On Monday morning, medical orderlies burst into the block with hypodermic syringes in hand to administer vaccinations. On the way to the *Esszimmer*, everyone was caught in the corridor and was given one hypo after another. This operation was repeated three or four times with a few days in between. In the afternoon it was the *politische Abteilung* that descended on us and proceeded to conduct a detailed interrogation of one's civilian standing, profession, political convictions, reasons for having been arrested and deported. These interrogations took up three or four days and were conducted in between the vaccinations. And, then, there was the "m . . . duty".

The "m . . . duty": ah! my friends! All the defecations of some 30 to 40 thousand inhabitants of the camp converged into a cone of excrement on a lower level. Since nothing was to be wasted, every day a special *Kommando* spread this precious commodity on the gardens attached to the camp which produced the vegetables for the S.S. and the foreign civilian workers who worked in and around the camp. Ever since the convoys of foreign prisoners began to provide a continuous supply of new manpower, the German prisoners, who were in charge of the administration of the camp, decided that they could have this work done by the new arrivals; it took the place for them of the traditional farce played on the recruits in the casernes in France, and it amused them enormously. This duty was the most painful one.The prisoners were harnessed in pairs to a *Trague* (a wooden basket in the shape of a pyramid with a rectangular base) which contained the stuff;

they then went back and forth from the reservoir to the gardens, like horses in a circus, for twelve consecutive hours, in the cold and in the snow. In the evening they returned to the Block dog-tired and stinking.

One day we were told, without even being detailed to a *Kommando,* that our Block was to quarry rock each morning and each afternoon during the rest of the quarantine period. The Block Chief had decided that instead of sending out groups of a hundred men who would work in relays for a period of twelve hours, it would be easier on us for all of us to go at once, that is, all four hundred, and to stay out only two hours for each shift. Everybody agreed. From that day on, every morning and every evening we filed across the camp to get to the *Steinbruch* where we picked up a stone whose weight was what our strength could manage. We dragged it back to the camp where gangs broke it up for street pavement. Then we went back to the Block. This work was light, particularly in comparison with that of the quarry workers who excavated the stone under the insults and the blows of the *Kapos,* the abbreviation for *Konzentrationslager Arbeitpolizei,* or police in control of labor.

Four times a day we passed close to villas where rumor had it that Leon Blum, Daladier, Reynaud, Gamelin and Princess Mafalda, daughter of the King of Italy, were imprisoned. We all envied the lot of those privileged people. Everytime we passed, I heard comments: "Wolves don't eat each other!" "All depends on whether we are powerful or miserable . . . " "The big shots, old boy, you break your neck for them and they bow to each other." "Hitler's race laws apply to all Jews but one." And, the like.

In our ranks there was a former prime minister of Belgium, a former French minister, and other personages, more or less important. They were more mortified than we at the treatment enjoyed by the inhabitants of the villas. It was said that each of them had two rooms, a radio, German and foreign newspapers, and three meals a day. Moreover, we were sure that they didn't have to work. Leon Blum[1] was especially envied. Chance had it that during one trip, Fernand and I, who never left each other, found ourselves next to the French minister. "Why Leon Blum and not me?" he said to us. Judging by the tone of his voice, we gathered that he did not find it at all strange that we should be detailed to those low jobs fit for slaves, but for him, really, a former minister! Fernand shrugged his shoulders. I was puzzled.

Another day, instead of taking us to the *Steinbruch,* we were taken to the criminal anthropometry department where our photographs, face and profile, and our finger prints were taken. Coarse, fat, well-fed individuals, but prisoners just like ourselves, each with a brassard on the arm of some authority or other, and each with a rubber truncheon in the hand to back it up, yelled at our heels. In front of me were Dr. "X" and the little Communist cripple who was in the good graces of the Block Chief and who was considered by the French to be his confidential agent. I listened to their conversation. Doctor "X," whom everyone knew had been several times a candidate for the U.M.R. in various elections, was explaining to the cripple that he was not a communist, but not an anti-Communist either, far from it. The war had opened his eyes, and, perhaps, when he had time to assimilate the doctrine . . . For two days a possible move to Dora had been talked about, and Doctor "X" was beginning to lay the ground work so that he could stay at Buchenwald. Misery!

Suddenly I felt a terrible blow. Absorbed in reflections that had been stimulated by this conversation, I must have strayed a little from the ranks. I turned around and got an avalanche of insults in German of which I made out *"Hier ist Buchenwald, lumpe schau mal, dort ist Krématorium!"* (This is Buchenwald, take a look you, there is the Crematorium.) That was all I was to know about the reason for the assault. By the way of explanation, and to justify it, the little cripple turned to me and said, "You could have been more careful; that's Thaelmann!"

We arrived at the entrance to the anthropometry department where somebody else with brassard and truncheon pushed us brutally in line against the wall. This time it was the little cripple who got a blow and who was soundly imprecated. The storm passed, and he turned to me, and said, "That doesn't surprise me coming from that S.O.B.; that's Breitscheid." I did not in the least care who in the world these two fine fellows were. But, I smiled at the thought that the Communists had finally realized that unity of action that they had talked about so much before the war, and I admired that acute sense of difference which the little cripple felt even in his reflexes.

* * * *

I was a pessimist; at least, that was my reputation. First, I refused to take seriously the optimistic news that Johnny reported each evening to the Block. Johnny was a Negro. The first time that I saw him was at Compiègne where I heard him say, with a strong American accent, that he was a Captain of a Flying Fortress and that during a raid on Weimar, when his aircraft was hit, he had had to parachute. When he got to Buchenwald he began to talk French fluently and called himself a doctor of medicine. He spoke two other languages almost as well as French: German and English. Thanks to this advantage, to his imagination, and to the fact that he was undeniably cultivated, he managed to get assigned as a doctor in the *Revier* (sick ward) even before quarantine was ended. The French prisoners were sure that he was no more a doctor than he was a captain of a Flying Fortress, but they acknowledged the skill with which he took care of himself. Every evening he was mobbed by news hungry inmates: the *Revier* was supposed to be the only place from which reliable news came. Besides, in spite of his reputation for talking big, Johnny was listened to seriously when he spoke about events in the war. One evening he came back with the story of revolution in Berlin; another evening with the revolt of the troops on the Eastern front; a third time with the landing of the Allies at Ostende; a fourth with the International Red Cross taking all of the concentration camps over. Johnny was never short of good news, with the result that every evening, in February 1944, the war was going to be over in two months. He exhausted my patience, and that of others, too. To those who came up to me with the assurance that had been fed to them by Johnny, I was in the habit of answering that as far as I was concerned, I did not think that the war would be over for another two years. Moreover, since I was one of the very few who did not believe in the fall of Stalingrad, just on the face of things as it were, and I admitted it after it happened, I was immediately pigeon-holed as a pessimist. In fact, I listened to everything with unshakable skepticism: the most refined horrors that were told about the history of the camps; the optimistic assumptions about the future conduct of the S.S. who felt, it was said, the wind of defeat blowing over Germany and who wanted to redeem themselves in the eyes of the coming conquerors; and the reassuring rumors about our ultimate assignment. I did not even fly in the face of facts. For example, the famous inscription which was on the wrought iron gate which closed the entry to the camp read: *Jedem das Seine*. With my little knowledge of the German language, I translated it as *A chacun sa destinée*. (To each his destiny.) All of the French prisoners were convinced that it was a translation of the celebrated phrase which Dante had put on the gate to Hell: *Vous qui entrez ici abondonnez tout espoir*[2]. That was the limit, and I the nonbeliever.

* * * *

The Block was divided into two antagonistic groups: on one side were the newly arrived prisoners, and on the other side were the eleven individuals – Block Chief, Secretary, Barber, and *Stubendienst*, German or Slav – who constituted its administrative backbone. There was a sort of solidarity which eliminated all of the differences of background or ideology, and yet bound together the first in reprobation against the second. The latter, prisoners like ourselves, but for a much longer time, knew all of the dodges of prison life, acted as though they were our actual masters, and controlled us with abuse, threats, and beatings. It was impossible for us not to consider them to be *agents provocateurs* or sycophants of the S.S. I saw at last what the *Chaouchs* – the prisoner trustees who are referred to in French literature about penitentiaries of all kinds – really were. From morning to night, our *Chaouchs*, throwing out their chests, plumed themselves on the power that they said that they had to send us to the *Krêmatorium* for the least indiscretion and with a single word. Also from morning to night, they ate what they stole, to our certain knowledge, from our rations: quarts of soup, bread and margarine, and potatoes fricasseed with onion or paprika. Moreover, they did not work. They were fat. They revolted us. Among these fellows I met Jircszah.

Jircszah was a Czech and a lawyer. Before the war he had been the assistant Mayor of Prague. The first thing that the Germans did when they occupied Czechoslovakia, was to arrest and deport him. He had been moved from camp to camp for four years. He knew them all: Auschwitz, Mauthausen, Dachau, Oranienburg. A commonplace accident had brought him to

Buchenwald, among a transport of the sick. When he arrived, one of his compatriots got him the job of general interpreter for the Slavs. He hoped to be able to hold that position until the end of the war which he did not think was very near, but which he felt would come finally. He lived with the *Chaouchs* of Block 48, who considered him to be one of themselves, but his attitude immediately set him apart from the others and made us consider him to be one of us; among other things, he was more generous with the rations that he distributed, and he got hold of and lent us books.

With our arrival in the camp, Jircszah came into contact for the first time with Frenchmen. He looked at us with curiosity and with pity, too. So that's what the French are? So that's the culture they told him so much about when he was a student? He was disappointed; he couldn't get over it.

My skepticism and the way I kept myself apart from the noisy life of the Block drew him to me. "Is that what it is, the Resistance?" he asked. I did not answer. To reconcile him to France I introduced him to Cremieux.

He certainly did not approve of the conduct of the *Chaouchs*, but he was no longer shocked, and he did not even despise them. "I have seen worse," he said. "You mustn't expect men to have too much imagination along lines of what is right; when a slave gets power without changing his station, he becomes more tyrannical than the tyrants."

He told me the story of Buchenwald and the other camps. "There is a lot that is true in all that is said about the horrors for which they are the setting, but there is a lot of exaggeration, too. You have to reckon with the complex of Ulysses' lie, which is everyone's, and so it is with all of the internees. Human beings need to exaggerate the bad as well as the good and the ugly as well as the beautiful. Everyone hopes and wants to come out of this business with the halo of a saint, a hero, or a martyr, and each one embroiders his own Odyssey without realizing that the reality is quite enough in itself."

He did not hate the Germans. To his mind, concentration camps were not specifically German and did not reveal propensities that were unique to the German people. "The camps — *Les Lager*," as he said, "are an historical and social phenomenon through which all peoples go as they reach the idea of Nation and State. They were known in Antiquity, the Middle Ages, and in modern times. Why should the contemporary epoch be different? Long before the birth of Jesus Christ, the Egyptians could find no other way than this to neutralize the commercial threat that was presented by the Jews, and Babylon reached its marvelous apogee thanks to persons in concentration camps. The English, themselves, resorted to them with the unfortunate Boers, after Napoleon who invented Lambessa. As a matter of fact there are some in Russia which are nothing to be envied when they are compared to the German ones. Moreover, they exist in Spain, in Italy, and even in France[3]; you will come across Spaniards here and you will see what they have to say about camp Gurs, in France, for example, where they were stuck right after Franco's triumph."

I ventured a remark. "In France, all the same, it is done out of humanity." In response, Jircszah, countered: "The Germans, when they speak of the institution, use the word *Schutzhaftlager*, which means 'camp for protected prisoners.' When the Nationalist Socialists came to power, they decided, in a gesture of compassion, to put all of their adversaries in a place where they could not hurt the new regime and where they could be protected from the public anger. In other words, the National Socialists wanted to put an end to assassinations and to beatings on street corners and, at the same time, wanted to rehabilitate the strayed sheep and to bring them back to a healthier concept of the German community, of its destiny, and of the role that the individual was to play within it. But, National Socialism was overtaken by events and, particularly, by its agents. It is something like the story of the eclipse of the moon that is told in the barracks. The Colonel says one day to his Adjutant that there will be an eclipse of the moon and that the officers and noncoms should see to it that the soldiers see the phenomenon and that they have it explained to them. The adjutant then passed the word on to the Captain, who, in turn, passed it on down the ranks, and the news got to the soldiers via the Corporal in this form: 'By order of the Colonel, there will be an eclipse of the moon this evening at 23:00; all those not present will get four days guard duty.' And, so it is in the concentration camps: the ruling powers within the National Socialist regime thought them up and, then, set up regulations by which former unemployed illiterates run them through the assistance of *Chaouchs* who are selected from among us. In France, the democratic government of Daladier had established the camp at Gurs and had fixed the regulations for its operation, with the result being much the same as that that is found in the German camps. The implementation of those regulations was delegated to gendarmes and to militia whose power to interpret them was very limited.

"It is Christianity which introduced into Roman law the humanitarian nature that is given to punishment in the West and which assigned to it, as its first objective, the rehabilitation of the delinquent. But, Christianity failed to account for human nature, which cannot come to terms with itself, except on a basis of perversity. Believe me, there are three kinds of people who have remained the same throughout all of recorded history: policemen, priests, and soldiers. Here, we have to deal with policemen."

Obviously, here it was a matter of policemen. I never had had any trouble with any other than the German police, but I had often read and heard it said that the French policemen do not distinguish themselves for any special consideration. I remember that at this moment in my conversation with Jircszah, I brought up the Almazian affair. But, Almazian was involved in a crime of common law, and we were political prisoners. The Germans did not seem to distinguish between common prisoners and political prisoners, and this fact accounted for the commingling of the two groups in the camps. . . .

"Come, come," Jircszah said, "You seem to forget that it was a Frenchman, an intellectual of whom France is proud, a fine scholar, a great philosopher, Anatole France, who wrote: 'I am a supporter of the suppression of the death penalty in a matter of common law and of its reinstitution in political law.'"

By the end of the quarantine — since the S.S. never meddled with the camp life itself, which thus seemed to be left the master of its own laws and rules — I believed that Jircszah was more or less right; the National Socialists had resorted to this classic method of coercion, and it was the prisoners themselves who had made it still worse.

We hashed over other problems together, especially the war and the post-war period. Jircszah was middle class, a democrat, and a pacifist. "The last war left the world divided into three rival blocks," he said. "The Anglo-Americans, the traditional capitalists, the Soviets, and the Germans, the latter supported by Italy and Japan. There is one too many. The post-war period will find a world divided in two, and the democracies will make no headway and the peace will be no less precarious. The Allies think that they are fighting for liberty and that the Golden Age will rise from the ashes of Hitler. It will be terrible afterwards; the same problems will lie before two powers instead of three in a world that will be ruined materially and morally. Bertrand Russell was right when he said during his courageous youth, 'No ill that war claims to do away with is as bad as war itself.' " I shared that view, and even cherished it. As time went on, I thought often of Jircszah.

* * * *

It was March 10th, at about three o'clock. An officer of the S.S. entered the Block and shouted, *"Raus, los! Raus, raus!!"* (Everybody out. Out!) We began to assemble in the yard. We were going to leave, and the formalities were about to begin. For about a week, a rumor about this move had been going around, and guesses ran riot: to Dora, some said; to Cologne to clear up the rubble from the bombings and to salvage what could still be used, said the others. The latter guess carried the day. Those well-informed persons felt that the National Socialists — seeing that the war was lost — were abandoning the *Kommando* at Dora, considered to be the hell of Buchenwald, and were not sending anyone there any more. They added that, even though given the dangerous work of clearing ruins, we would be well treated at Cologne. Maybe we would run the risk of setting off an unexploded bomb at any moment, but we would get all that we wanted to eat; first, we would receive the camp ration; then, we could have whatever we might find in the cellars, some of which would certainly be full of food supplies.

We did not know what Dora was. Not one of those prisoners who had been sent there had ever returned as far as we knew. It was said to be an underground factory, constantly being enlarged, in which secret weapons were being manufactured. One lived there, ate there, slept there, and worked there without ever seeing the light of day. Every day trucks brought full loads of dead bodies from Dora to be cremated at Buchenwald, and it was from the presence of these corpses that the horrors of the camp were deduced. Fortunately, we were not going there.

Four o'clock: we were still standing in front of the Block, at attention *(Stillgestanden)* under the eyes of the S.S. guards. The Block Chief went down the ranks and the old men, the cripples, and the Jews were taken out. Cremieux, who filled all three of these categories by himself, was one of them. The little cripple—as well as a few others who did not seem to be either old men, cripples, or Jews, but whom we knew were in the good graces of the Block Chief since they passed for, or actually were, Communists—was also removed.

Half past four: we were marched to the infirmary for a medical checkup—"checkup" was just a figure of speech. An S.S. doctor who was smoking a huge cigar and who was flopped in an armchair conducted the examination, so to speak. We passed in front of him in a single file, and, generally, he did not even bother to look up.

Five thirty: next we went to the *Effectenkammer,* where we were given clothing—striped trousers, jacket and coat—and shoes (leather with wooden soles) to replace the wooden clogs which were not fit for labor.

Six thirty: we had to stand for a roll call which lasted until nine o'clock. After that, before we could go to bed we still had to sew our numbers on to the clothing that we had just been issued; the stips of cloth on which numbers had been stenciled had to be sewn on the left side chest on the jacket and coat, and on the right pocket of the trousers.

On March 11th reveille came at half past four, and the roll-call lasted from five-thirty until six. Ah! those roll-calls! In March, in the cold, whether it rained or the wind blew, we had to stand for hours and hours being counted and re-counted! This last one was a general roll-call of all of those prisoners—regardless of the Block that they belonged to—who were destined for the transport, and it took place on the mustering grounds in front of the guard tower.

At eleven o'clock we were given our ration of soup. Then at four o'clock, there was another roll-call which lasted until six or seven; we lost track of how long it lasted.

On March 12th, we got up at the usual reveille, and the roll-call lasted from half past five until ten. Roll-call, and again the roll-call. They wanted to drive us crazy. At three o'clock, we left Block 48 for good, and, after a wait for some time on the grounds, we were sent to the Block where the movie theater

was, where we spent the night, with the lucky ones sitting down
and with the rest of us standing up.

The next morning, reveille was sounded at half past three, an
hour earlier than usual. The guards led us under the tower
where we waited, in the dark and in the cold, with nothing in
our stomachs since the day before at eleven, to be loaded onto
a train. It was sometime between seven and eight o'clock when
we got into the cars.

The trip was uneventful. We had elbow room, and we talked
mainly about where we were going. The train was going in a
westerly direction. To Cologne, that was it. We were right! At
about four o'clock, the train stopped in the middle of no-
where, at a sort of railroad switchyard, where, floundering in
the mud and the snow, miserable men, who were haggard and
dirty, and who wore striped rags of the same kind as our new
clothes, unloaded the cars, dug ditches, and cleared away rubble. Men with brassards and numbers—who were well clothed
and full of health—pushed them on with threats, insults or the
blows of truncheons. We were forbidden to speak to them.
Passing next to them, if by chance they were out of eye and
ear shot of the guards, we questioned them in as low a voice
as possible: "Say, where are we?" "At Dora, old boy, haven't
you finished . . . yet?" Fernand and I looked at each other.
We had only with difficulty just come to believe the optimistic
rumors about Cologne. Now, we felt terribly discouraged, our
shoulders sagged, and we felt the shadow of death pass over
us.

* * * *

FOOTNOTES

[1] [Leon Blum was imprisoned at Buchenwald at about the same time that Professor Rassinier was there. Several interesting references to Blum's stay at Buchenwald are found in his biography by Louise Dalby. One of them confirms the camp rumors which Professor Rassinier mentions:

> Occasionally visits to Blum were restricted and letters censored, but he suffered very little while in France. His quarters at Buchenwald were reasonably comfortable, but his diet was poor and contributed greatly to his ill health. He resented most of the restrictions on his privacy, and the annoyance of being disturbed every two hours as guards thoroughly inspected his quarters. He was allowed to take a servant to care for him, he was permitted a radio by which he could occasionally get the B.B.C., although this was forbidden, and he received most of the food parcels sent him.
> (Louise Elliott Dalby, *Leon Blum*, New York: Yoseloff, 1963, pp. 418-419.)]

[2] This phrase translates: "Abandon all hope, ye who enter here." Immediately after my liberation, in May 1945, when I was still in Germany on my way home, I heard a talk over the radio by a deportee—Gandrey Retty, if my memory holds—who gave this translation. This is how tall stories are born.

[3] [The fact should be noted that the United States also had its concentration camps during this period. Best known, in spite of the repeated efforts of the liberal establishment to sweep all memory of the matter under the rug, are the so-called "relocation camps" where Americans of Japanese ancestry were interned during World War Two. This sordid episode, although officially justified as being necessary in the interest of national security, seems to have had as its real impetus certain racial and economic motives. Clearly, the relocation of the prosperous Japanese-American community away from the West Coast afforded numerous bargain conscious Californians, among others, the opportunity of purchasing Nisei and Issei businesses and properties at "fire sale" prices, a fact which, without doubt, was on the minds of many of those persons who applauded the prompt action of General John DeWitt. For a general discussion of these "relocation camps", see, Allan R. Bosworth, *America's Concentration Camps* (New York: W.W. Norton, 1967). Not so well known are the numerous concentration camps that were spread across the United States from the Carolinas to the Dakotas where German and Italian nationals—many of whom had been long time residents of the U.S.— were incarcerated. Following the outbreak of formal hostilities in

December 1941, these German and Italian nationals were declared to
be "enemy aliens", were rounded-up by the American version of the
Gestapo, i.e., the Federal Bureau of Investigation, and were confined
behind barbed wire for the duration of the war.]

Chapter Three

The Circles of Hell

On June 30, 1937, Buchenwald was only what its name means, a forest of beech trees, a place perched on a foot hill of the Harz mountains, five and a half miles from Weimar. One reached it by a stony, winding path. One day some men came by car to the foot of the hill. They climbed to the top on foot, as though it were an excursion. They carefully inspected the area. One of them pointed out a clearing; then they returned after having had a good luncheon at Weimar.

"Unser Führer wird zufrieden werden," they said. (Our Fuhrer will be pleased).

Sometime later others came. They were chained together by fives, one to the other and constituted a detachment of a hundred men, surrounded by about twenty S.S., guns in hand. There was no more room in the German prisons. They climbed up the path as best they could, sworn at and kicked. When they reached the top exhausted, they were put to work without any delay. A group of fifty put up tents for the S.S., while the other group put in place a circle of barbed wire, three strands high and about a hundred yards in diameter. The first day that was all that could be done. They ate a meagre meal in a hurry and almost without stopping work and, very late in the evening, they went to sleep right on the ground, wrapped in thin coverings. The next day, the first group of fifty unloaded all day long construction materials and sections of wooden barracks which heavy tractors managed to bring about half way up the hill; they carried this material the rest of the way up on their backs and placed it inside the barbed wire. The second group cut down trees to clear the area. They did not eat that day because they had started off in the first place with food for one day only. But, they slept better that night in the shelter of the branches and among the piles of boards.

Beginning with the third day, sections of barracks began to arrive at a faster rate and began to pile up half way up the hill. There were also a kitchen outfit, quantities of striped clothing, some tools, and some supplies. The S.S. stated in their daily report that with one hundred men they could not keep up with material delivered. Others were sent them. The rations then were insufficient. At the end of the week, some fifty S.S. struggled with about a thousand prisoners who they did not know where to put at night, who they could barely feed, and who overwhelmed their ability to supervise. The prisoners were made up into several groups, or *Kommandos*, each detailed to a particular job: the kitchen for the S.S., the orderlies for their camp, the kitchen of the prisoners, the construction of the barracks, the transport of material, the administration accounting. All of these operations were called *S.S. Küche, Häftlingsküche, Barrakenkommando Bauleitung, Arbeitsstatistik*, etc., and on paper, in reports, it looked like a simple and methodical organization. But it was, in fact, a complete mess, a horrible swarming of men who went through the motion of eating, who worked haphazardly, and who barely slept covered in a jumble of branches and boards. Since it was easier to keep them under surveillance when they were working than when they were sleeping, the days were twelve, fourteen or sixteen hours long. Since there were not enough guards, they were forced to select a complement of trustees out of the whole lot of the prisoners on appearances alone, who, since they had uneasy consciences, created a reign of terror by way of excusing and justifying themselves. Blows rained, not just insults and threats.

The bad treatment, the poor and insufficient food, the superhuman work, the lack of medicines, and the pneumonia created conditions that caused this gang of men to die at an alarming rate, endangering the general health. The S.S. had to think of another way to get rid of the bodies other than by burial which took too much time and which was too often repeated: so they had turned to cremation, a procedure that was much faster and in conformity with Germanic traditions. Another *Kommando,* in its turn, became indispensable, the *Totenkommando,* and the construction of a crematorium was put on the list of "urgent" work to be done. Thus it happened that a place was built for men to die in, before the place was built for them to live in. Everything is linked together: evil attracts evil, and when one is caught in the mesh of evil forces . . . .

Moreover, the camp was not conceived in the minds of the National-Socialist authorities to be just a camp, but a community working under supervision for the building of the Third Reich, just like the other individuals of the German community who remained in relative liberty. As a consequence, after the crematorium came the factory, the *Guzlow.* So it is seen that the order of precedence for all the installations was determined first by the need to keep everything well under guard, second by hygienic requirements, and third by the demands of work that constituted the *raison d'etré* for the camp. Everything was subordinate to the collective interest which trampled down and crushed the individual.

Buchenwald was thus, during the period of the first installations, a *Straflager* (punishment camp) where only those considered incorrigible in other prisons were sent. Then, from the moment that the factory, the *Guzlow,* was ready to go, an *Arbeitslager* (labor camp) with *Strafkommandos.* Finally, it was transformed into a *Konzentrationslager* (concentration camp) which is what it was when we knew it, a camp equipped with all the amenities of a small city, where everyone was sent without discrimination. Around the central camp there were satellite camps, which it kept supplied with human material. All the camps went through these three stages successively. Unfortunately, with the war breaking out, prisoners from all places, of all kinds, in for all kinds of reasons, and under all kinds of disciplinary punishment, were haphazardly, because of the disorder of the circumstances, and indiscriminately sent to a *Straflager,* an *Arbeitslager,* or a *Konzentrationslager.* The result was a frightening mixture of all kinds of humanity which resembled, under the sign of the truncheon, a gigantic basket of crabs, over which National-Socialism, so sure of itself and so methodical in its operations, but overwhelmed on all sides by events which were beginning to master it, threw an immense Noah's mantel.

Dora was born under the sponsorship of Buchenwald and in the same way. It grew and prospered following the same process.

In 1903, German engineers and chemists had discovered that the stone of the Harz mountains in that area was rich in ammonia. Since no private company was willing to risk capital in its extraction, the Government undertook it. Germany did not possess, as did her neighbors, colonies that were able to put at her disposal men from Cayenne or Nouméa. Because of this fact, together with the fact that she was obliged to keep her convicts inside the country, they were imprisoned in certain places where they were used for especially disagreeable labor. As a consequence, a convict prison, like all convict prisons in the world, except for a few minor differences, was created at Dora. In 1910, for reasons unknown, but most likely because the yield of ammonia was much smaller than was anticipated, quarrying the stone was stopped. It was resumed during the war of 1914-1918, as a sort of punitive camp for prisoners of war at a time when Germany was already beginning to think of going underground to escape some of the devastation of bombing. Again the operation was interrupted by the Armistice. Between the two wars, Dora was completely forgotten: wild tangled growth masked the entrance to the excavations and, all around, vast fields of suger-beets were cultivated to supply the sugar refinery at Nordhausen, three and a half miles away.

It was into these beet fields that on September 1, 1943, Buchenwald disgorged a first well escorted *Kommando* of two hundred men. Germany, again feeling the need to go underground or at least to put her war industries underground, had taken up the project of 1915 again. Construction of the S.S. camp and of the crematorium was begun, underground the factory was set up, and the kitchens, showers, the *Arbeitsstatistik*, the *Revier*, or infirmary, were built, last of all. So long as the underground work existed, the S.S. delayed as long as possible, putting off always a little longer, the unprofitable work of constructing Blocks for the prisoners, preferring instead to dig the gallery of the tunnel farther in, and to make it possible to get as many factories as possible under protection from the ever increasing threats from the open sky. When we arrived at Dora, the camp was still in the *Straflager* stage. We made an *Arbeitslager* out of it. When we left it with its 170 Blocks, its infirmary, its theater, its brothel, and with all its installations in place and its tunnel completed, it was on the point of becoming a *Konzentrationslager*. Already, at the other end of the double tunnel, there was another camp, Ellrich, its offspring, and which was itself in the *Straflager* stage. There could be no break in the descending curve of human misery.

But, the English and Americans and the Russians had decided otherwise, and, on April 11, 1945, they came to free us. Since then the penitentiary system of East Germany has been in the hands of the Russians who haven't changed things a fraction. Tomorrow, it will be in the hands of . . . who knows? Since there must be no gap in history.

* * * *

A concentration camp, when it is completely set up, is a regular city which is isolated from the outside world which conceived it, which is surrounded by fences of electrified barbed wire, and which is guarded with special guards every fifty yards on platforms, armed to the teeth. To make the screen between the two even more dense, an S.S. garrison bordered the camp and at a distance of three or four miles all around sentinels were encamped. Thus, anyone trying to escape would have a certain number of obstacles to overcome, or perhaps it would be better to say that any attempt would be doomed to failure. This isolated city had its own laws and its own particular social phenomena. Any ideas born there, individually or collectively, were stopped at the barbed wire and remained unsuspected by the rest of the world. By the same token, almost everything that took place in the outer world, was unknown on the inside, any penetration being made almost impossible by that screen.[1] Newspapers came in; but, they were carefully selected and said nothing but those things that had been especially printed for the inmates in the concentration camp. It did happen in wartime that the "news" for the concentration camp inmates was the same as that which the Germans were supposed to take as gospel, and that is why the newspapers were the same for both, but it was pure chance. Use of the radio was punishable. It follows that camp life, organized on other moral and sociological principles, had quite a different orientation from that of normal life. As a consequence, it revealed aspects that could not be judged by standards common to mankind in general. But, it was a city, and a human city.

Inside – or on the outside, but near by – a factory was the reason for its existence and its means of existence: at Buchenwald, the *Guzlow;* at Dora, the Tunnel. The factory was the keystone of the entire edifice, and its needs, which had to be satisfied, were the iron laws. The camp was made for the factory, and not the factory to keep the camp busy.

The most important department of the camp was the *Arbeitsstatistik,* which kept a strict accounting of the entire population, and kept track of each man day after day in his work. At the *Arbeitsstatistik* the personnel could tell you at any moment whatsoever of the day what each prisoner was doing and where he could be found. This department, like all the others, too, was entrusted to prisoner trustees and kept busy a considerable and privileged number of them.

Then came the *Politische-Abteilung,* which kept track of the political aspects of the camp and which was able to give for any prisoner any information wanted about his previous life, his moral conduct, the reasons for his arrest . . . It was the department of anthropometry of the camp, its *Sicherheitsdienst* (security police), and employed only those prisoners in whom the S.S. had confidence. Once again the privileged.

Then the *Verwaltung,* or the general administration, which kept track of everything that came into the camp: food, material, clothing, etc . . . It was the quartermaster of the camp. Those prisoners employed in office work always occupied a privileged position.

These three big departments ran the camp. They had at their head a *Kapo* who ran them under the supervision of a noncommissioned officer of the S.S., or *Rapportführer.* There was a *Rapportführer* for all the key services, and each one of them reported every evening to the *Rapportführer-general* of the camp, who was an officer, generally an *Oberleutnant.* This

Rapportführer-general communicated with the prison camp through the intermediary of his subordinates and of the *Lagerältester,* or the doyen of the prisoners, who was responsible in general for the camp and who answered for its smooth running even with his life.

Similarly, the departments of the second level: the *Sanitatsdienst,* or health service, which included doctors, male nurses, disinfection, infirmary and crematorium services; the *Lagerschutzpolizei,* or camp police; the *Feuerwerk,* or fire protection; the *Bunker,* or jail for those prisoners caught breaking the rules of the camp; the *Kino-Theater,* or movie, and the brothel, or *Pouf.*

There were also the *Küche,* or kitchen; the *Effecktenkammer,* or clothing store, which was attached to the *Verwaltung;* the *Häftlingskantine,* or canteen, which supplied the prisoners with extra food and drinks in exchange for the coin of the realm; the *Bank,* where the special money good only in the camp was issued.

And, now to describe the mass of workers . . . They were divided up into Blocks constructed on the same plan as that of Buchenwald 48, but of wood, and with only one floor. They lived there only at night. They returned there at night after rollcall at about nine o'clock, and they left every morning before dawn, at half past four. They were supervised by the Block Chiefs who were surrounded by their *Schreiber, Friseur, Stubendienst,* who were veritable satraps. The Block Chief governed life in the Block through the supervision of an S.S. soldier, or *Blockführer,* who reported to the *Rapportführer-general.* The *Blockführer* were only rarely seen; generally they confined themselves to one friendly visit with the Block Chief during the day, that is, when the prisoners were away, so that it was the latter who was in effect the only authority, and practically all of his exactions were without appeal.

During the day, that is, during the period of actual work, the prisoners were caught in the meshes of another group of prisoner trustees and camp officials. Every morning those who worked only during the day were divided up among *Kommandos,* each with a *Kapo* for chief, assisted by one, two or several foremen or *Vorarbeiter.* Each day, beginning at four thirty, the *Kapos* and the *Vorarbeiter* were at the mustering grounds, in a designated place—always the same, and formed their respective *Kommandos* which they conducted in marching time to the place where they were to work. There a *Meister* or a civilian supervisor informed them of the job that they were to have their men get done during the day. The *Kommandos* which were used by the factory did two twelve hour shifts rather than the usual three eight hour shifts. They were divided into two teams or *Schicht:* There was the *Tageschicht* which came before the *Kapos* and *Vorarbeiter* at nine o'clock in the morning, and the *Nachtschicht* at nine o'clock in the evening. The two *Schicht* alternated one week of day labor and one week of night labor.

That was the Buchenwald which we knew. Life was bearable there for the prisoners who definitely were assigned to the camp; it was a little harder for those who were destined to stay there only for the quarantine period. It must have been the same in all of the camps. Unhappily, when mass deportations of foreigners into Germany were taking place, few camps were ready, aside from Buchenwald, Dachau, and Auschwitz. Consequently, almost all of the deportees knew the camps only during their construction, as *Straflager,* and *Arbeitslager,* but not *Konzentrationslager.* Unhappily, too, even in camps that were ready, all responsibilities were given to German prisoners at first, to facilitate relations between the *Häftling* people and those of the *Führung,* and to the survivors of the *Straflagers* and the *Arbeitslagers* afterward, who could not imagine the *Konzett,* as they called it, without the horrors that they had themselves suffered there. This latter group constituted a much greater obstacle to any humanizing of the camps than did the S.S. The "Do not do unto others what you do not want others to do unto you" is a concept of another world, which had no meaning in the concentration camp. "Do unto others what has been done to you" was the motto of all the *Kapos,* who had spent years and years in *Straflagers* and *Arbeitslagers,* and in whose minds the horrors that they had lived through had created a tradition, which, by an understandable distortion, they felt obliged to perpetuate. If by chance the S.S. forgot to mistreat us, these prisoners took care to make up for the slip.

* * * *

The population of the camp, its social composition, and its origins were also elements that were de-humanizing. I have already remarked that National-Socialism drew no distinctions between political crime and common crime, and that consequently, there was in Germany no distinction between the civil and the political regime. As in the prisons of most civilized nations, there was something of everything in the camps—of everything and something else besides. All of the prisoners, whatever social or criminal element they came from, lived together, under the same regulations. The only thing that distinguished them was the colored triangle on their prison clothing which was the insignia of their classification—i.e., their reason for being there.

Red was reserved for political crimes. For common crimes, there was a green triangle; it was plain for *Verbrecher,* or petty crimes; it was embellished with an "S" for *Schwerverbrecher,* or serious crimes, and a "K" for *Kreigsverbrecher,* or war crimes. Thus, a gradation was made from common crimes, such as a simple theft, to murder and to the theft of supplies or armaments.

Between these two extremes, there was a whole series of intermediary crimes: the black triangle (professionally unemployed); the pink triangle (pederasts and homosexuals); the yellow triangle reversed over a red one so as to form a star (Jews); purple triangle (conscientious objectors).2 In addition, those who had done a certain term in prison, and then, following their release, were incarcerated again for committing new crimes wore instead of the triangle a black circle on white background with a large "Z" in the center, which stood for those freed from the *Zuchthaus* or prison. And, finally, those who wore a red triangle with the point up had committed minor crimes in the army and had been sentenced by a court-martial.

To these were added a few special ones: the red triangle with a transverse bar for those sent to the *Konzett* for the second or third time; three black dots on a yellow and white brassard for the blind; the *Wifo,* the same circle as for the *Zuchthaus* people with the "Z" replaced by a "W." These latter had originally been volunteer workers. They had been employed by the *Wifo* firm which had been the first to try to achieve the *Vergeltungsfeurer,* the famous V1 and V2 rockets. One fine day, and for no apparent reason, they got the striped clothes and were put into concentration camps. The secret of the VI and V2 having gone through the trial period and into the intensive production stage was not to be freely circulated, even among the German people. In other words, they were interned for reasons of State security. The *Wifo* were the most unfortunate people in the camp: they continued to be paid their salary, half of which was paid them in the camp itself, the rest being sent to their families. They had the right to keep their hair and to write whenever they wanted to, on condition that they said nothing about what had happened to them; and since they were the best off, they introduced the black market into the camp and raised the exchange.[3]

As far as the population was concerned, the concentration camps were regular towers of Babel in which personalities clashed because of differences of origin, of their sentences, and previous social standing. The common law offenders hated the political criminals whom they didn't understand, and the latter returned the feeling. The intellectuals looked down on the manual laborers, and the latter rejoiced to see the former "working at last." The Russians wrapped the whole of the West in the same icy contempt. The Poles and the Czechs couldn't stand the French, because of Munich, etc . . . On the nationality level, there were enmities between Slavs and Germanic people, between the Germans and the Italians, between the Dutch and the Belgians, or between the Dutch and the Germans. The French, who came last and began to receive the most magnificient parcels of food, were looked down on by everybody except the Belgians, who were pleasant, frank, and good. France was regarded as a land of milk and honey, and her inhabitants as sybaritic degenerates, who were incapable of work, who ate well, and who were occupied only with making love. To these sentiments the Spaniards added the concentration camps of Daladier. I remember having been accosted in Block 24 at Dora by a vigorous: "Ah! The French; now you know what a *Lager* means. No harm, it'll teach you!"

It was one of the three Spaniards (there were 26 in all at Dora) who had been interned at Gurs in 1938, enrolled in labor companies in 1939, and sent to Buchenwald after Rethel. The three maintained that the only difference between the French and the German camps was the work; all other things, treatment, food, being just about the same. In fact they added that the French camps were dirtier.

Oh, Jircszah!

* * * *

The S.S. guards lived in a parallel camp. In general, they were a company. At first, this company was a training unit for young recruits, and only Germans were in it. Later on, the S.S. became more international in composition: Italians, Poles, Czechs, Bulgarians, Rumanians, Greeks, among others filled the ranks[4]. The necessities of war had compelled the Germans to send the young recruits to the front, often with limited military instruction, or even without any special preparation, and the young were replaced by the old, those who had already served in the war of 1914-1918, on whom National Socialism had made scarcely any imprint. They were less hard. In the last two years of the war, when there were not enough S.S., the rejects from the *Wehrmacht* and the *Luftwaffe*, who couldn't be used for anything else, were assigned as guards to the camps.

All the services of the camp had their parallel in the S.S. camp where everything was centralized, and from which daily or weekly reports were sent directly to Himmler's offices in Berlin. The S.S. camp was, therefore, the administrator of the other. When the camps were just beginning during the *Straflager* period, they were administered directly; afterwards, and as soon as possible, the S.S. carried on the camp administration only through the prisoners themselves as intermediaries. One would think that this arrangement was used out of sadism, and, after the war was over, that is what was said. But, it was really out of the necessity to economize personnel that the system was used, and for that reason, in all prisons in all countries, the same situation holds. The S.S. itself only administrated the camp when it was impossible for them to do otherwise. We knew what self-government by the prisoners in the camps was. All of the old hands who have experienced both systems are unanimous in recognizing that the former was in principle the better and the more humane, and that if it was not in fact, it was because wartime circumstances and the pressure of events did not permit it. I believe it; it is better to deal with God than with the saints.

So the S.S. guarded the perimeter of the camp, and it can be said that we hardly ever saw them inside the camp, except when they simply went through to take the salute of the prisoners, the famous *"Mützen ab"*. They were helped in their guard duty by a company of marvelously trained dogs, always ready to bite and capable of hunting out an escaped prisoner tens of miles away. Every morning, the *Kommandos* that were to work outside the camp, often they traveled three or four miles on foot — when they had to go farther, they used trucks or trains— were accompanied, according to their importance, by two or four S.S., guns in hand, each with a muzzled dog on a leash. This special guard, which complemented the surveillance of the *Kapos*, just kept watch from afar, and did not intervene in supervision of the prisoners unless a show of force was called for.

In the evening, at the roll-call by Block, when everyone was there, at a whistle, all the *Blockführer* turned toward the Block for which they were responsible, counted those present, and then went back to report. During this operation non-coms went around the Blocks to enforce silence and attention. The *Kapos,* Block Chiefs, and *Lagerschutz*[5] greatly helped them in making this task easy. From time to time an S.S. man stood out from the others for his brutality, but it was rare; and in no case was he ever more inhuman than the prisoner trustees who filled the positions that are mentioned in the preceding sentence.

* * * *

The problem of the *Häftlingsführung* dominated the life of the concentration camps, and the way it was handled deter-mined their evolution in so far as the welfare of the common prisoners was concerned.

At the inception of every camp there was no *Häftlingsführung*[6] ; there was just the first convoy of prisoners which arrived out in the open, guarded by the S.S. who themselves assumed all responsibility, directly and in detail. And that's the way it remained until the second, third, or fourth convoy arrived. The direct supervision of the S.S. could last six weeks, two months, six months, a year. But, as soon as a camp grew to a certain size, since the number of S.S. personnel could not be indefinitely expanded, they were obliged to take from among the prisoners the additional manpower necessary to keep watch over the mass of prisoners. One has to have experienced concentration camp life and have assimilated their history really to understand this phenomenon and the form it took in practice. When the camps were originated in 1933, the German state of mind was such that opponents of National Socialism were considered the worst of brigands. With this attitude in the popular mind, the new masters easily succeeded in indoctrinating the masses to accept the idea that there were no crimes or offenses against common rights or political rights, but only and simply crimes and offenses. As a result, the distinction between the two became unclear and in many instances it took very little to make the second, to all appearances, more odious than the first in the eyes of a youthful fanatic, enrolled in the S.S. and entrusted with carrying out the project! Now put yourself in the place of the fifty S.S. soldiers at Buchenwald, on the day when, deluged by a thousand prisoners and a huge mass of materiel, they had to select the first trustees from among their prisoners, and appoint the first *Lagerältester*. Between a Thaelmann or a Breitscheid, whose recalcitrance was especially brought to their attention, and the first criminal they came across who had murdered his mother-in-law or raped his sister, but who was just as dull and docile as you please, they did not hesitate; they chose the second. He, in his turn, appointed the *Kapos* and the *Blockältesters*, and naturally he picked them from his kind of people, that is, from the common criminal, the "greens".

It was only after the camps had developed up to a certain point that they became real ethnographic and industrial centers, and that men of some moral and intellectual caliber were really needed to give efficacious assistance to the *S.S.-Führung*. The latter perceived that the common criminals were the dregs of the population, in the camp as elsewhere, and that they were quite beneath what was required of them. Then the S.S. turned for help to the political criminals. One day a "green" *Lagerältester* had to be replaced by a "red," who at once began to get rid of the "greens" in all positions, in favor of the "reds." And, so arose the struggle which rapidly became a permanent one between the "greens" and the "reds." And, that explains why old camps like Buchenwald and Dachau were in the hands of the politicals when we were there[7] while the newer ones, still at the

Straflager or *Arbeitslager* stage, except for miraculous variations, were always in the hands of the "greens."

An attempt has been made to claim that the struggle between the "greens" and the "reds", which only very late in the day extended beyond the German contingent in the camps, was the result of a coordinated effort on the part of the second against the first: this assertion is incorrect. The politicals, distrusting each other, not knowing where to turn, had only very vague and tenuous solidarity among themselves. But, on the side of the "greens," it was quite different: they formed a compact block, firmly held together by that instinctive confidence which always exists among criminals, recidivists and convicts. The triumph of the "reds" was due only to chance, to the incompetence of the "greens," and to the discernment of the S.S.

It was also said that the politicals — and especially the German politicals — had organized revolutionary committees, had held meetings in the camps, had stocked arms, and had secret correspondents on the outside. This is pure legend. It is possible that some happy concurrence of circumstances made it possible, on occasion, for an individual to write to the outside, or to another prisoner in another camp, under the nose of the *S.S-Führung*. Or, someone who was released from a camp might carry, with great precaution, news from a prisoner to his family or a political friend; maybe someone who had just arrived might do the same thing in reverse. In fact, a transport of prisoners sometimes became a means of communication from one camp to another. But it was extremely rare, at least during the war, for a prisoner to be discharged from a camp and, as for the transports, no one in the camp, not even most of the S.S., knew what their destination was to be before they got there. Generally one only learned that a transport had taken place several weeks or months after its departure, and that it had arrived at Dora or Ellrich, through the sick, who sometimes came back from them. More often, this information was learned through the dead, who were returned to the camp to be cremated, and on whose chests their numbers and places of origin could be seen. But to say that these communications were premeditated, organized, and carried through, is pure fantasy. As for the stocking of arms: in the final days of Buchenwald, thanks to the chaos, some of the prisoners were able to filch pieces of guns, and even whole weapons from the manufacturing that was going on, but to state that such activity was a systematic practice is ridiculous. And, as for the revolutionary committees, and the meetings held: I had a good laugh, when, after the liberation, I heard of a committee for French interests at Buchenwald being talked about. Three or four vociferous Communists, including Marcel Paul[8] and the famous Colonel Manhes, who had managed to escape from the evacuation transports, evoked this committee in the vacuum between the departure of the S.S. and the arrival of the Americans. They succeeded in making others believe that this committee had long been organized[9], but the existence of this committee is a pure invention, and the Americans did not take it seriously. Their first action, when they came into the camp, was to ask the trouble-makers to be quiet and the crowd that was getting ready to listen to them to go back quietly to the Blocks. In short, everybody was required to submit from the start to a discipline of which they alone intended to remain the masters. After order was restored, they took care of the sick, the feeding of the prisoners, and the organization of the repatriation efforts, without taking any notice of the advice and suggestions which the several last minute VIP's tried in vain to impress upon them. And, that was all to the good: it cost Marcel Paul a lesson in humility, and a certain number of lives were saved.

Finally, it was said that the politicals, when they had the upper hand in the *H-Führung*, were more humane than the common criminals. And, this claim was said to be supported by the experience at Buchenwald[10]. It is true that Buchenwald was, when we arrived there, a relatively comfortable camp for those prisoners who were definitely free of any threat of being transported to any of the satellite camps. But, the bearable situation at Buchenwald was due more to the fact that it had completed its evolution and had become a *Konzentrationslager*, than because it had a political *H-Führung*. In the other camps which were behind it in development, the distinction between the "greens" and the "reds" were hardly discernible. It could have been that contact with the politicals might have improved the moral standards of the criminals; but, the opposite took place, and it was the criminals who corrupted the politicals.

* * * *

FOOTNOTES

1 It is said that the German population was almost totally ignorant of what went on in the camps during the war, and I believe it. In fact, the SS personnel who lived near the camps and who guarded their perimeters were, for the most part, ignorant of—or, at least, did not learn of—certain happenings until long after they were past. If the reader finds this contention hard to believe, permit me to ask the following question: who in France knows any of the details about the life of the prisoners at French penal institutions at Carrere, La Noe, and other places? [And, for the American reader: how many Americans really know what goes on in the thousands of jails, penitentiaries, and prison farms that exist throughout the United States?]

2 [For a scathing description by an English prisoner of the Jews—as well as others—who were interned at Buchenwald, see Christopher Burney, *The Dungeon Democracy* (New York: Duell, Sloan, & Pearce, 1946).]

3 ["Black markets" seem to have been a common feature throughout the German concentration camp system. For a detailed discussion of how this kind of *sub rosa* economic activity worked in a German P.O.W. camp, see R. A. Radford, "The Economic organization of a P.O.W. Camp," *Economica*, (November 1945), pp. 189-201.]

4 [By the end of the war, nationals of virtually every country in Europe —including, even, Turkey—were fighting along side the Germans. A kind of "pan-Europeanism" in the face of the possible annihilation of European culture at the hands of the Russians seems to have been a primary motivational factor for some of these volunteers. For a general discussion on the foreign volunteers from German occupied Europe who fought on the German side—generally in units of the *Waffen-SS*— see David Littlejohn, *The Patriotic Traitors* (Garden City: Doubleday, 1972). As a general rule, most of the foreign volunteers fought in combat units on the Eastern Front against the Russians. Some, however, were assigned to other duties such as the guarding of concentration camps. Littlejohn mentions, for example, that while the bulk of the Dutch and Flemish SS volunteers were transferred to the *Waffen-SS* following June 22, 1941, some of them were retained in Holland where, among other things, they guarded the concentration camps at Westerbork, Vught, and Amersfoort (p. 99).]

5 All of these administrative positions within the camp were filled by prisoners who had been selected for the jobs by the SS guards.

6 *"Häftlingsführung"* means the "self-government" or the direction of the day to day operation of the camp by the prisoners themselves.

7 [Following the liberation of Buchenwald by American troops, a U.S. Army report was prepared in which it was stated that " . . . the prisoners themselves organized a deadly terror within the Nazi terror . . . " with German communist inmates running things. This report formed the basis of an article by a former U.S. Army officer who was present at Buchenwald following the capture of the camp and who interviewed many of the prisoners. In his article, he presents a story of how the communists ran the camp which corroborates many of the details which Professor Rassinier mentions in the text. Among other things, he says that " . . . on the day Buchenwald was liberated, the Army intelligence men were astounded to note that the 300 surviving German communists [who were running the camp from the inside] were dressed like 'prosperous business men'." See, Donald B. Robinson, "The Communist Atrocities at Buchenwald," *American Mercury* (October, 1946), pp. 397 - 404. See, also, R.H.S. Crossman, "Buchenwald," *Nation* (July 30, 1945), pp. 123-125, in which the author reports on an interview with an Austrian inmate who describes at length how the communists ran Buchenwald from the inside.]

8 Marcel Paul was a *Stubendienst* in Block 56, and later he was assigned to Block 24 where the parcels that were sent to prisoners by their relatives were received.

9 There was only one "committee" of long standing in the camps, and this "committee" was the loose association of thieves and pillagers, composed of either "reds" or "greens", who had been given the levers of command by the SS. At the liberation—in order to save their own necks—they tried to put everyone off the track by claiming that they had represented organized prisoner resistance to the Germans, and to a large measure they have succeeded in this objective.

10 Although to this camp was due all the notoriety about the "human skin lamp-shades" for which Ilse Koch, called the "Bitch of Buchenwald", today remains *solely* responsible, the question still remains: did the wife of the *Lagerkommandant* walk around the camp looking for handsome tattooing, and herself pointing out their unfortunate owners for death? I can neither confirm nor disprove it. Nevertheless, I can point out that from February through March 1944, rumors in the concentration camp accused the two *Kapos* of the *Steinbruch* and the *Gartnerei,* of that crime, already carried out by them, with the complicity of almost all their "colleagues." The two buddies had made a

business of the death of tattooed prisoners, whose skins they sold to Ilse Koch in exchange for a variety of favors, and to *others*, though the intermediation of the *Kapo* and the SS of the Crematorium service. So, the contention of the accusation, if it has any basis in fact, is very fragile. [For a further discussion of the Ilse Koch matter, see Arthur R. Butz, *The Hoax of the Twentieth Century* (Richmond, Surrey: Historical Review Press [1976]), pp. 42-43.]

Chapter Four

Charon's Bark

We were received at Dora according to the customary routine: Out of the rail cars, a frantic race across the rubble, in the mud up to the ankles, under melting snow, insults, shouted threats, barking, blows.

Across the *S.S.-Lager:* about fifty buildings were spread around, with no paved walks going from one to the other; just muddy paths through fields.

Entrance to the *H-Lager:* two blocks of wooden buildings, one on each side of a wire tangle that opened in front of us. We were counted. "*Zu fünf! Zu fünf! Mensch Blöder Hund!*" Wham, a blow from a fist. Wham, a kick.

On the other side of the wire fence was the camp itself. Ten or so square blocks of wooden buildings, a dozen at the most, were laid out haphazardly with no visible coordination. On the way we could read from a distance the numbers on the Blocks: 4, 35, 104, 17. Where are the other Blocks?

A muddy track, marked out by many tramping feet, led away from the entrance and climbed the hill, with nothing to indicate that it led anywhere. The guards had us take it and we came to the *gemeinde Abort* (public toilet) where we were penned in, waiting for orders. The *gemeinde Abort* was a Block in which there were only toilets, urinals, and wash basins. It was impossible to sit down or to stretch out, and going outside was forbidden. We were tired and famished, too. Toward six o'clock, a bowl of soup, 300 grams of bread, a piece of margarine and a slice of sausage were served to us. We noticed that the rations were ampler than at Buchenwald. A breath of optimism blew over us. "We shall be working, but at least we shall eat," was whispered among the group.

Men with brassards appeared at eight o'clock: a table was set up; a clerk sat down. One by one we passed in front of the table where we stated our registration number, name, and profession. The men with brassards were Czechs and Poles who had been interned for a variety of offenses. They were heavy handed and made generous use of the rubber truncheons with which they were armed. *Hier ist Dora! Mensch! Blöder Hund!"* and wham, wham.

At midnight, the business was finished. Everyone was ordered outside. We retraced our path, in the dark this time, always surrounded by *Kapos* and S.S. Suddenly we found ourselves in front of an immense excavation which opened on the hill side: the Tunnel. Two enormous iron folding doors opened: this was it, we were going to be buried; nobody had any idea that these iron doors would ever open again to liberate us. The horrors that we had heard about this "underground" installation while we were at Buchenwald worried us.

We entered the Tunnel and were confronted with a Dantesque scene: outside, all was darkness; inside, we were in full light. Two parallel railroad tracks were set a yard apart; so trains shuttled back and forth in the belly of the monster? A string of cars loaded and covered with tarpaulin shrouded torpedo shapes, immense shells longer than the cars which carried them, was sitting on one of the tracks. They were the famous V1 and V2 rockets. By their looks, their diameter was greater than a man's height, and they appeared to be more than 40 feet long. "That must have quite an effect where it falls!"

Talk started to turn to the mechanical details and the launching method of the V1 and V2 which we had heard about and which we saw now for the first time. To my great amazement, I found that there were some persons among us who seemed to be very well informed, and who with the greatest seriousness provided the most precise details, but who later turned out to be the most fanciful story-tellers.

We kept going farther inside. On each side of the main tunnel were offices and caverns that had been fixed up as work shops. We came to a portion of the Tunnel which was still being worked on: gaunt, thin, diaphanous shadows of men perched on scaffolding all over, against the walls like bats, were boring into the rock. On the ground, the S.S. guards walked around, guns in hand; the *Kapos,* in all the coming and going, bawled out the poor men who were carrying tools or were pushing wheel barrows full of the excavated material. The noise of machinery was deafening, and dead bodies were sprawled along the passageways.

One cavern was fixed up as a living Block; we were ordered to stop.

At the entrance were two garbage cans and fifteen or so corpses. Inside, men were running around like madmen between the tiers of bunks, three, four and five layers. Brawls erupted between two or in a group now and then. Among them, serious and imposing, were the *Stubendienst* who tried in vain to restore order. That was where we were to spend the night. The *Stubendienst* interrupted their police work to take care of us. *"Los! Los! Mensch! Hier ist Dora!"* The rubber truncheons began to dance on their new targets. The Block Chief, a big German, looked on, amused, mocking, and threatening at the same time. We quickly saw that this Block was occupied by Russians whose day gang was off work. Still dressed we threw ourselves down on the straw pallets assigned to us. At last! Hours later, we woke up: all our shoes and what was left from the food distribution the evening before had disappeared. Even our pockets had been emptied. We admired the dexterity of the Russians who had accomplished this general pillage without waking us up. Only two or three were caught in the act. The victims took them to the Block Chief and were themselves brought back to their straw mattresses, with blows of the rubber truncheon, by their *Stubendienst* accomplices. *"Hier ist Dora, mein Lieber!"* We had fallen for sure into the lair of brigands whose only law is that of the jungle.

As soon as we were awake, we were brought back up to the daylight. We breathed easier; so we were not to be buried indefinitely. The morning was spent standing in front of the

Arbeitsstatistik, stamping around in the mud and the snow; we were freezing cold and hungry again. In the afternoon, we were divided up into *Kommandos:* Fernand and I were landed in the *Strassenbauer 52* (road builders). Right away they put us to work, and until the evening roll-call we carried fir trees on the run, from the camp to the railway station.

At six o'clock, the roll-call: it lasted until half past eight. At nine o'clock we were ordered to Block 35. This time we were sure that we were not going to be put underground in the Tunnel. But, we learned that quite a few among us had claimed to be skilled in all kinds of specialized technical professions so that they would be employed in the factory and so that they would not have to come up again in all probability until the liberation.

The Chief of Block 35 was a Czech; the *Stubendienst,* too, naturally. The Block itself was still bare of furnishings. We slept piled together, right on the floor, without covers, in our clothes. But first, in an indescribable scuffle, they gave us a quart of rutabaga soup which we ate while standing; that was all we had to eat that day. At ten we went to sleep, certain now that we were an integral part of Dora. Dora!

* * * *

The first day of work . . .

Half past four: a gong sounded four times in that shell of a camp. The Block lights went on, the *Stubendienst,* rubber club in hand, burst in to the *Schlafsaal.* *"Aufstehen! Aufstehen! Los Waschen!"* Then, with pause, *"Los, Mensch! Los, Waschen!"*

The two hundred men got up as one, crowded through the *Esszimmer,* bare to the waist, and in the passage between came to the door of the wash room at the same time as the two hundred from the other *Flügel.* The wash room could hold twenty persons. At the entrance two *Stubendienst,* hose nozzle in hand, held back the invasions. *"Langsam! Langsam! . . . Langsam, Lumme!"* At the same time the hose went into action. The poor fellows fell back . . . Meanwhile, two other *Stubendienst* having anticipated the water spray, forced them on:

"Los! Los! Schnell, Mensch! Ich sage: waschen!" And, the truncheons rained down pitilessly on the thin bare shoulders.

Every morning it was the same tragi-comedy. It didn't stop
there, however. After washing came the distribution of food for
the day. We went single file holding in hand the chit that had
been handed out in the wash room (you could not get your food
until you had shown that you had washed) and which had to be
given to a *Stubendienst*. Another solid crush of humar.ity. The
hour allowed by the rules to accomplish this double formality
was soon over.

Half past five: the *Kapos*, warmly clothed, were there on the
mustering ground waiting for the arrival of the human tide. It
came pouring out toward them from all the Blocks; men running
in the icy morning while still dressing and swallowing the last
mouthful of the meager portion of the daily ration that had
been handed out for breakfast. The *Kapos* proceeded with the
assembling of the *Kommandos* and called the roll of their men;
blows and insults rained down. With the roll-call over, the
Kommandos started out at a predetermined pace according to
the distance they had to go; some had to go as far as three and
a half to five miles, and they left first. Then came those who
had only an hour's march, and finally those with only half an
hour's walk. *Kommando 52* was twenty minutes away. It left
at six thirty. At exactly seven o'clock everyone was where he was
to work. The Tunnel *Kommandos* were run on another schedule:
reveille at seven in the morning for the day shift, seven in the
evening for the night shift, and all of the preliminaries for the
work took place in the Tunnel itself.

At seven o'clock *Kommando 52* was at the embankments,
having arrived there after having completed the washing and the
feeding operations, after having waited shivering in ten inches
of mud at attention for an hour and ten minutes, and after
having marched the mile and a quarter or so from camp to
work. The men were already exhausted long before the work
began.

The purpose of the work was to construct a road bed from
the station to the camp. An ellipse of narrow-gauge railway
track, whose greatest diameter was perhaps 800 yards, was
used in the construction. Two trains of eight dump cars each,
pulled by gasoline-powered engines, made a perpetual circuit
over the tracks. While 32 men—four per car—loaded the train
up at one end, 32 others unloaded the other one at the far
end, being careful to spread the rock level. When the empty

train arrived, the other had to leave filled; this was supposed to happen every twenty minutes. Generally, the first train left in the time prescribed. However, with the second, there were delays which provoked growls from the *Meister*, the *Kapo*, and the *Vorarbeiter*. On the third circuit, the empty train had already been waiting for five minutes and another five were needed before it was ready to leave. The *Meister* smiled ironically and shrugged his shoulders, the *Kapo* shouted, and the *Vorarbeiters* lashed at us; no one escaped being hit. The delay was increased by the amount of time that it took three men to beat thirty-two, and from then on the time lost was never made up, and the work was off schedule for the rest of the day. On the fourth trip, there was a further delay; more blows rained down. On the fifth, the *Kapo* and *Vorarbeiter* grasped the fact that nothing could be done, and they gave up beating us. In the evening, instead of the thirty-six trips planned at the rate of three per hour, only fifteen or twenty had with difficulty been achieved.

Noon: a pint of hot coffee was distributed right where we worked. We drank it standing up while eating the remains of the bread, margarine and sausage given out in the morning.

Twelve thirty: we began work again. During the afternoon the work dragged. The men, hungry and frozen, had just enough strength to keep standing. The *Kapo* disappeared, the *Vorarbeiter* calmed down, the *Meister* himself seemed to recognize that there was nothing more to be got from such rags as we were, and he gave up. We kept up an appearance of working; but that was hard, too. We had to rub our hands and stamp our feet for the cold. From time to time, an S.S. guard went by. The *Vorarbeiter*, on the lookout, saw him coming from way off and gave the signal. When he reached the *Kommando*, everybody was busy at his job. He tossed out a word to the *Meister*, *"Wie geht's?"* (How's it going?) A discouraged shrug of the shoulders answered, *"Langsam, langsam, Sehr langsam! Schauen Sie mal diese lumpen: Was machen mit?"* (Slow, slow, very slow. Just look at these no-goods. What can you do with them?) The S.S. guard shrugged his shoulders, too, grunted and went on, or else, depending on his humor, gave vent to insults, handed out a few blows of his fist, threatened with his revolver, and left the area. Once he was outside of earshot the *Kommando* relaxed again. *"Aufpassen! Aufpassen!"* said the *Meister* almost paternally.

Six o'clock came, and everybody slackened off. *"Feierabend,"* (Knock off) said the *Meister.* The *Kapo,* who had returned a few minutes before, had his men stack the tools, shouted a few insults which stimulated the *Vorarbeiter,* and distributed a few cuffs; a return to discipline through the use of terror.

Six forty: the *Kommando* started the march back to the camp in fives. At seven o'clock, organized by Block, and not by *Kommando,* we once again waited shivering, feet in the mud, for these gentlemen to finish counting us; that job took two or three hours.

Between eight and nine o'clock we got to the Block. A *Stubendienst,* rubber truncheon in hand, was stationed at the entrance. We had to take our shoes off, wash the wooden soles and enter with them in our hands; and then only if they passed as really cleaned were we allowed to go in. On the way to the *Esszimmer* we put them down in rows; then we held out tin bowls into which theoretically a quart of soup was poured, which we ate standing up in an indescribable jostling. When these various formalities were over, a third *Stubendienst* gave us permission to make for the *Schlafsall,* where we simply fell in a heap on a little straw that had been brought in during the day. Half past ten. We were dead tired, hungry, and cold. We felt that the work forced on us counted for very little in contributing to our fatigue.

The next morning, it all began again at four-thirty. During the night, the Russians stole the *Holzschuhe* which we had so carefully lined up in the *Esszimmer* at the command of the *Stubendienst.* Thus, in addition to the washing and the distribution of food, we had to locate another pair before running outside, while still dressing and swallowing the last mouthful of the meager breakfast, into the cold night to reach the mustering grounds where the *Kapos* were waiting. By the end of the week we had become shadows of our former selves.

* * * *

There were worse *Kommandos* than ours: the Ellrich *Kommando,* the *Transport Eins*, and all the transport *Kommandos, Steinbruch, Gartnerei . . .,* etc.

At the other end of the Tunnel, camp Ellrich was being built. A very important *Kommando* of about a thousand men went there every morning on a ballast train which left the station at Dora at half past four. There were three miles to go. On foot it would only have been necessary to leave at half past five to get there by seven o'clock, but that would have been too simple. The S.S. authorities decided to show that they had some human feelings and, to spare the *Kommando* the fatigue of the march, they ordered the prisoners to be transported to work by the train. As a consequence, the Ellrich *Kommando* was awakened at three; the men washed, got rations and were at the mustering grounds at four. Then came the departure from the station. The train which was due at four-thirty was never less than an hour late, and the *Kommando* had to wait. At six at the earliest, half past six at the latest, it arrived at Ellrich. The work consisted of digging all day. The work stopped at six. Theoretically, the prisoners should have gotten on the train at half past six, but like the morning train, it was never less than an hour late. They had to wait again. At about half past eight, at the best, but often nine or even ten, they returned to Dora where they had to observe all of the formalities of going into the Block, the shoe washing, and the distribution of soup. At about eleven they could lie down and sleep; five hours of sleep and up again, assembly, departure, waiting. The grind of the days was merciless; the steps that the S.S. took, or pretended to take, to improve things turned into an additional torment. The very travel back and forth was more killing than the work itself. Added to that fact was the fact that the *Kapos* of the Ellrich *Kommando* were the worst of brutes, whose blows rained down upon the prisoners without pity. Then, too, the work was rigorously supervised; in short, it was the *Kommando* of death, and every night corpses were brought back.

In the camp itself there was *Transport Eins.* The men of *Transport Eins* began their day in the same way and at the same time as all the others: they unloaded cars and carried on their backs heavy loads from the station to the tunnel, or from the station to the camp. We saw them from morning to evening working like circus horses in fours with large boards, by twos with railroad ties, by lines of eight or ten with rails, and singly with bags of cement. They moved slowly under the weight of their burden. Their *Kapo* was a Pole with the red triangle who went from one group to the next swearing, menacing, striking.

The *Gartnerei*, or garden *Kommando* also worked in teams like *Transport Eins*, but they carried human excrement instead of building material. The *Kapo* was a "green" who used the same methods as the Pole of *Transport Eins* with the same results.

The *Steinbruch*, the famous quarry for all of the camps, supplied rock building material. Stone was excavated and loaded on wagons which were pulled or pushed to the places where the stone was broken up to be used as surfacing for the camp roads. The people at the *Steinbruch* had the additional bad luck of having to work on the slope of the hill at the opening of the quarry where the beatings by the *Kapos* often caused them to lose their footings and to fall to the bottom of the quarry where they were killed. Every day the dead were brought back to the mustering grounds. Four men carried each body by the arms and legs. *"Ein, zwei, drei, vier,"* the *Kapo* at the head of the column called out to set the pace; ploc, ploc, ploc, the heads of the dead men knocked against the ground. From time to time we heard that some poor devil at the *Steinbruch*, having been hit with a truncheon tottered and fell into the stone-crusher, or the concrete-mixer, without anyone trying to stop him.

There were also *Kommandos* that were better. Among them were all those that made up the camp administration: the *Lager Kommando,* the *Holzhof,* the *Bauleitung,* the *Schwung.*

At the *Effektenkammer,* an account was kept of the clothing that had been taken away from the prisoners when they came into the camp; that was an easy job. It was lucrative, too. From time to time a pair of pants could be stolen, or a watch, or a fountain pen, all of which were valuable exchange goods for food. At the *Wäscherei,* the underwear which the prisoners were supposed to change every two weeks was washed. There it was sheltered and warm. Also quite a few opportunities presented themselves to obtain food. At the *Schusterei,* the shoes were repaired, at the *Schneiderei,* clothing was repaired and underclothing mended, and at the *Küche* . . . .

The best *Kommando* was without question the kitchen or *Küche Kommando.* The food was not rationed to those who prepared it, and the work was not difficult. First they got the ration that was given to everyone at the Block before starting for work. When they got to the kitchen or place where they worked, they received a supplementary ration officially. Then, whenever they were hungry they could help themselves from the provisions that they were preparing. In addition, they stole food in order to provide themselves with exchange for tobacco, socks, clothes, and favors. On top of that, they were exempt from the roll-call. They lived the life of regimental cooks. A certain amount of influence was necessary to get into the *Küche Kommando*; the French did not have it; and, as a result, the positions were reserved for Germans, Czechs and Poles. On a par with the *Küche* were the *Arbeitsstatistik* and the *Revier*. There was no roll-call either. Blows were not the usual practice. At the *Arbeitsstatistik,* the work was office work, and one could obtain as much food as one wanted because those who were assigned to the better *Kommandos* by the personnel there paid in kind: clothing, food, tobacco, etc. I know two Frenchmen who had managed to get themselves into the *Arbeitsstatistik;* all the rest were Germans, Czechs, and Poles, as in the kitchen service.

In the *Revier,* there were doctors, *Pflegers,* and *Kalifaktors.* The *Pflegers,* or nurses of sorts, took care of the patients, and the *Kalifaktors* were responsible for the cleanliness of the hospital. In addition, there were a lot of clerks, who ate their fill; you could hardly say that they worked, and they were not beaten.

Then came the *Lagerkommando*, or the *Kommando* responsible for the maintenance of the camp. All those prisoners in delicate health were assigned there, in principle. Actually only those prisoners with pull, with friends among the *Kapos* and *Lagerschutz,* with influential friends in the *Revier* or the *Küche*, or with relatives who sent good parcels were assigned to the *Lagerkommando.* The *Lagerkommando* supplied crews for light janitorial work, cook-house work for the S.S., the *Häftling,* and the volunteer foreign workers who worked in the factories at the camp, and for the care of the *Altverwertung,* the place where things were repaired. At the beginning, when the camp was still small, it was a very much sought after spot. Later on, when the *Kommando* had grown to include hundreds and hundreds of individuals, the personnel were periodically screened for manpower to fill out other *Kommandos* without enough men, a fate which was escaped only by those with pull.

Two other *Kommandos* were also sought after: the *Tabak-fabrik* and the *Zuckerfabrik*. They both went to Nordhausen to work, and they were transported in trucks. Each evening, the first group came back with pockets full of tobacco which they exchanged for bread and soup, and the others did the same with sugar. Afterwards, a third *Kommando* was assigned to the slaughter houses at Nordhausen, and they introduced meat barter into the camp.

To get a good or a bad *Kommando* was a matter of chance, which connections with someone in the *Arbeitsstatistik* could decisively influence. The constant preoccupation of all the prisoners was to get into a good *Kommando*, and this over-riding objective was pursued by any means regardless of how incompatible it might be with human dignity.

* * * *

The Tunnel *Kommandos* were considered both the best and the worst. They were formed into a single *Kommando*, called *Zavatsky*, after the name of the supervisor who ran the Tunnel operations.

They had at their head a *Kapo* general—the great Georges—who had under his orders a whole team of *Kapos* in charge of prisoners according to their specialties. To be assigned to a *Kommando* working in one of the ten or twelve factories sheltered in the Tunnel was to be guaranteed light labor, and to be protected from the wind, the rain, and the cold. All this was a very great advantage. Such an assignment also guaranteed being free of the roll-calls, since there were no roll-calls for the Tunnel people. But, it was also a certainty that the tunnel workers never came up into the daylight, and had to breathe in galleries that were badly ventilated. Consequently, they were afflicted with miasmas of all sorts, and dust for months on end, and they risked dying before they were liberated. But, on the road building, for example, one worked in all kinds of weather: rain, snow, wind, or hot sunshine. In other words, the work never stopped. Nor were the roll-calls cancelled or shortened. During the rainy season it happened that for weeks on end we could never get the rags that served us for clothing dry. In the evening, coming back to the Block, we put our

clothes under the straw mattresses in the hope that the heat
of our bodies would evaporate the dampness. The next morning we put them on warmed, but wet, and we went out once
again into the rain. Simple or double pneumonia was endemic
among the road workers, and many ended up in the crematorium, but at least we were living out in the open. And,
during the good weather . . . Opinion was divided between
wanting to work in the Tunnel or on the roads. "One should be
able to get in the Tunnel during the winter, and come out
during the summer," Fernand said to me. That solution was
obviously impossible, and I was not sure that in the end that it
would be a good solution.

What was called the Tunnel was a system of two parallel
galleries going through a mountain from one side to the other.
At one end was Dora, and at the other was the hell of Ellrich.
These two main galleries, each about three miles long, were
connected by about 50 transverse galleries or halls each about
200 yards long, 8 yards wide, and 8 yards high. Each one of
these halls contained a work shop. In April 1945 the Tunnel
was all finished and if it had not been for the sabotage would
have produced at maximum capacity. It was estimated that
at that time there was a total of eight to ten miles of galleries,
excavated and fitted out, as against the five to six in existence
in August 1943, when Dora was just started. These figures
give an idea of how hard the prisoners were made to work.
It should also be noted that the two camps, Dora and Ellrich,
together, could never handle more than 15,000 men, who had,
in addition, to build barracks, as well as to produce a certain
number of V1 and V2 rockets, or airframes and secondary
weapons. And, that if one wants to calculate the cost of this
work, one must add to the francs or marks, the 20,000 to
25,000 human lives it cost in less than two years.

Twice every day, at seven in the morning and at seven in the
evening, the *Kommandos* of the Tunnel, who slept in the
galleries, or in those parts of the galleries fixed up as Blocks,
were awakened by shifts. They had less water; consequently
the hygiene was deficient, and fleas and lice abounded. At nine
in the morning and at nine in the evening, depending on the
Schicht to which they belonged, they were at work.

There were also bad *Kommandos* in the Tunnel. Those digging the galleries, and those who were assigned to the transportation of drilling tools and the excavated material had a

bad time. Those *Kommandos* were veritable chain gangs whose members died like flies, their lungs poisoned by the ammonia laden dust. But, most of the Tunnel *Kommandos* were good.

In the factories, scientific management was carried to an extreme: one *Kommando* spent its time sitting in front of drills punching out holes one after the other; another inspected gyroscopes; a third assembled electrical switches; a fourth polished sheet metal; a fifth was made of turners or fitters. And, there were some jobs that were neither good nor bad like those involved in the assembly of the V1 and V2 rockets. Generally speaking, the productivity was not very good: ten men were employed at a job, against their will, which one or two could have done if they had had the incentive. The most difficult things were always to pretend to be working, to be standing up all the time, to seem to be very busy, and, above all, to live in that noise and miasma, getting hardly any air from the outside, through the few and inefficient air ducts.

Toward the middle of March, at the request of Zavatzky, who wanted to eliminate one of the main causes which he thought was responsible for the poor output, they began to take the Tunnel *Kommandos* up into the open air to have their camp soup, instead of taking the soup down to them. By the end of April, the construction gangs had finished just about all of the Blocks that had been planned: 132 of them. It was decided that no one would sleep in the Tunnel any more. So, all the *Kommandos* after that date only went underground to work, that is, for twelve hours a day.

To give the whole picture, it must be said that civilians, too, were used in the various factories in the Tunnel. In April 1945, there were six to seven thousand of them. They included the Germans who were *Meister*, and the S.T.O., or volunteers, from all over Europe. They, too, were grouped in *Kommandos*, but they lived in a camp about a mile from Dora, worked ten hours a day, got good wages, and ate fairly monotonous food, but which was healthful and plentiful. Besides, they were free to move about within an 18 mile radius; in order to go beyond that, they needed special papers. Among them were many Frenchmen who kept themselves at a distance from us, and in whose eyes one always saw the fear that they had that they might someday have to share our lot.

The date was March 31, 1944. For the past week the *Kapos*, the *Lagerschutz*, and the Block Chiefs had been particularly on edge. Quite a number of prisoners had died from blows; lice were found not only in the Tunnel, but even among the *Kommandos* outside; and the *S.S.-Führung* laid the responsibility for this state of affairs on the *H-Führung*. On top of that, the weather the whole day long was terrible: it was colder than usual, and an icy rain mixed with hail came down without any let-up. In the evening, we got to the muster grounds, frozen, soaked, and hungry beyond belief. How we hoped the roll would not last too long! But, there was no such luck. At ten o'clock we were still standing at attention under the rain of hail, waiting for the order *Abtreten* (break ranks!) which would liberate us. Finally it came, and we could go and eat the hot soup in a hurry and fall onto the straw. We got to the Block and began the shoe cleaning. But, then, gesturing that we should stay outside, the Block Chief, standing framed in the entrance, announced that since lice had been found, the whole camp was going to be disinfected. It was to begin that night. Five of the 35 Blocks were picked for *Entläusung* (delousing) that night. Consequently, that night there was no soup until that was over. The delousing process then began: *"Alles da drin!"* (Everybody in there!) We went into the *Esszimmer* with our shoes in our hands. *"Ausziehen!"* (Undress!) We took our clothes off, wrapped them in a bundle with the number on top. *"Zu fünf!"* (By fives!) That frightened us. *"Zu fünf!"* We form into lines. With the *Stubendienst* carrying our clothes on blankets, surrounding us, all naked, in the cold, in the rain and the snow, we went in the direction of the building where we were to be deloused. There were about 800 yards to cross.

When we got there, the four other Blocks, naked like us, were already pushing against the entrance. We felt Death in our presence. How long would it last? There were about a thousand of us, all naked and shaking in the wet and the cold which penetrated to our very bones, pushing at the doors. There was no way to get in. Only forty at a time could go in. The scene was hideous. At first we tried to force our way in, but the delousing men kept us back with water hoses. Then we wanted to go back to the Block to wait our turns; but that was impossible since the *Lagerschutz*, truncheons in hand, surrounded us. So we had to stay there, crowded together, between the water and the truncheons, soaked and beaten. We pressed together. Every ten minutes, forty of us were allowed to enter the delousing chamber in a crush that was a life and death struggle. Elbows went into play; there were fights, and the weaker were mercilessly trampled underfoot, and their bodies were found at dawn. At about two in the morning, I succeeded in getting inside, Fernand behind me, where we received a haircut, cresyl, and shower. At the exit we were given a shirt and a pair of shorts which we wore when we went out into the night to return to the Block. I felt as though I had accomplished some act of heroism. When we came to the Block, we went into the *Esszimmer* where a *Stubendienst* handed us our clothes which had been disinfected. Next came soup and bed.

At reveille, the sinister comedy was just barely finishing. At least half of the Block got back only just in time to get dressed, get soup, get the daily ration, and hurry to the grounds to go to work. And, there were a number missing: those who had died during the execution of this sorry business. Others survived it only for a few hours or for two or three days and were carried away with the inevitable double pneumonia. The job itself probably killed as many men as it did lice.

How did it happen? The *S.S.-Führung* was responsible only for the decision to disinfect five Blocks per day, and the *H-Führung* was left in complete control of how it was to be carried out. A schedule could have been set up: at eleven, Block 35, at midnight, 24, at one, number 32, etc . . . The Block Chiefs could have, within this frame-work, sent us in groups of one hundred at twenty minute intervals, for example, and in our clothes. But no, that would have been too simple.

When what took place on the night of March 31st reached the ears of the *S.S.-Führung,* the latter itself set up an exact schedule the next morning for the Blocks that remained to be disinfected.

* * * *

April 2, 1944: Easter. The *S.S.-Führung* decided on a twenty-four hour rest period which was not to be disturbed except by a general roll-call, that is, the Tunnel people as well as the quarry workers would be present. The weather was magnificent, a radiant sun in a pure calm sky. Joy; the Gods were with us! We got up at six instead of four-thirty: washing and food distribution was done at a slower pace.

Nine o'clock. All the *Kommandos* were on the grounds at attention. The *Lagerschutz* went in and out among the groups; Block Chiefs were at their stations. The *Lagerältester* chatted familiarly with the *Rapportführer*. He had a paper in his hand: a detailed list of the camp personnel drawn up by the *Arbeitsstatistik*. About thirty S.S. in helmets, their pistols in holsters, were assembled at the entrance to the camp: the *Blockführer*. It looked as though all were going to go well.

A whistle blew, and the *Blockführer* spread out fan-wise, each toward the Block which it was his responsibility to oversee. Each one made his count and compared his figure with that which the Block Chief handed him. *"Richtig."* (Correct.) One by one the *Blockführer* came to report to the *Rapportführer* who waited, pencil in hand, and who wrote down the figures as they were given him.

There was not one discordant note; the roll-call would not last long. The S.S. wanted to take advantage of this Sunday and were moving fast. We were exultant: one day of rest with nothing to do but to eat our soup and to stretch out in the sun.

Just a minute! The total number of prisoners which the *Rapportführer* had did not tally with the figure given to him by the *Arbeitsstatistik;* there were twenty-seven fewer men on the grounds than on the paper. Question: what had become of them? The *Kapo* of the *Arbeitsstatistik* was sent for in a hurry. He was asked to go over his figures right away. One hour later he came back, with the same figure. Perhaps, then, the S.S. had made a mistake. The count was made again, and the *Rapportführer* came up with the same figure. They searched through the Blocks, they searched through the Tunnel; they found none of the missing prisoners.

It was noon. The ten thousand or so prisoners were still on the grounds waiting for the figures of the *Arbeitsstatistik* and of the *S.S.-Führung* to agree. Time dragged; some men fainted; those whose turn it was to die fell down, never to get up again; those with dysentery relieved themselves as they stood; the *Lagerschutz* felt that things were getting slack and began to lay about. The S.S. guards whose Sunday was threatened were furious. They went off to eat, but we stayed there. At two o'clock they came back.

Suddenly the *Kapo* of the *Arbeitsstatistik* came running: he had come up with another figure. A murmur of hope rose from the crowd. The *Rapportführer* looked over the new figure and became violently angry: there were still eight men missing. The *Kapo* of the *Arbeitstatistik* went away again. He came back at four. Now no more than five men were missing. At eight only one was still missing, and we were still there, pale, drawn, and exhausted, after having stood for eleven hours, with empty stomachs. The S.S. decided to send us to eat. We left. Behind us the *Totenkommando* picked up some thirty dead.

At nine, it all began again, in an attempt to find the missing man. At eleven forty-five, after various comings and goings, this missing man was found, too; the *S.S.-Führung* and the *Arbeitsstatistik* were in agreement. We went back to our Blocks and were able to go to bed, again leaving behind us ten or more dead.

There you have the explanation of why the roll-calls took so long. Those employed in the *Arbeitsstatistik,* illiterate or nearly so, had been made bookkeepers only as a favor, and they were incapable of adding up at the first count the number of men present. The concentration camp was a world where every man's place was determined by his connections and his cunning and not by his abilities. Accountants were made masons, carpenters became accountants, wheelwrights became doctors, and doctors became fitters, electricians or road graders.

* * * *

Every day a railway car, full of packages from every western European country, except Spain and Portugal, arrived at the Dora station. With a few exceptions, these packages were intact. However, by the time that a package was given to the one to whom it was addressed, it had been three quarters pilfered. In many cases, one got nothing but the sticker listing the contents: shaving soap, or shaving brush, or a comb, etc . . . A *Kommando* of Czechs and Russians were detailed to unload this car. From there, the package was taken to the *Poststelle* where the *Schreiber* and *Stubendienst* of each Block went to take delivery. Then the Block Chief himself gave it to the addressee. It was during this chain of distribution that the packages were plundered.

The way the pillage was worked was simple. First, it was the French parcels, known for the wealth of their contents, which got all the attention. Right where the parcels were unloaded, under the eyes of an S.S. guard in charge of the operation, they were passed through three hands: at the car, a Czech passed it to a Russian standing outside, who had to catch it in air and toss it to another Russian or Czech, whose job it was to stack it onto a wagon. From time to time, the Czech at the car said *"Franzous,"* and the Russian spread wide his hands; the parcel fell to the ground where it broke open, the contents spilling all over. The Russians and Czechs filled their pockets or musette bags. If something from the parcel pleased the S.S. guard, he held out his hand, and thus was his complicity bought. When the wagon was full, pulled by six men, it rumbled off toward the *Poststelle;* during this brief trip, a number of parcels disappeared or also broke open.

Regulations required that at the *Poststelle* the parcels were to be carefully examined, and that medicines, wine, any alcohol, and weapons or various things that could be used as weapons, be removed. This official search was made by a team of prisoners, Germans or Slavs, under the surveillance of two or three S.S. and provided another opportunity for more filching. The S.S. guards themselves were tempted occasionally by a piece of bacon, a bar of chocolate which a girlfriend liked, a package of cigarettes, or a lighter. They made sure that the prisoners would not talk by closing their eyes to the thievery that was committed by the latter. From the *Poststelle* to the Block, the *Schreiber* and *Stubendienst* arranged things between them so that a third pilfering took place, and at the end of the distribution chain, there was the Block Chief who did the fourth and last and who gave what was left to the addressee.

There was something grotesque about the ceremony of handing over the remains to the party concerned. The prisoner was summoned by his number and invited to present himself to the Block Chief. On the latter's desk lay his parcel, open and contents listed. By the desk was a large basket surmounted by a placard labelled *"Solidarität."* Each prisoner was morally obliged to drop in a little something of what he had received for those who never received anything—in particular the Russians, the Spaniards, the young, and the disinherited of all nationalities who had no relatives or whose relatives did not know where they were.

This is what was supposed to happen in theory; in practice, the Block Chief, after each distribution, simply appropriated what was in the basket and divided it with his *Schreiber* and the *Stubendienst*. After every load was received, the *Kapos*, the *Lagerschutz*, the *Blockältester*, and all those with any rank at all in the *S.S.-Führung* were amply supplied with French provisions, a fact which convinced me that the pillaging was done by an organized gang.

I received my first parcel on April 5, 1944: all the underclothing, a bar of chocolate, I think, and a tin of jam were missing, but there were still three packs of cigarettes, a good two pounds of bacon, a tin of butter and various other eatables. We had changed Blocks two days before, and we were now in 11. Our Block Chief was a German with a black patch. I asked him what he would like. *"Nichts, geh mal."* (Nothing, get going.) Resolutely I held out a package of cigarettes to him, then pointing to the *"Solidarität"* basket, I questioned with my eyes. *"Brauchst nicht! Geh mal, Blöde Kerl!"* (Don't bother, get going, you dumb ass!).

I had guessed correctly. The day after the next, I was called up again. I had three parcels this time. Of one nothing was left but the label; but the two others were more or less intact and in one there was a huge hunk of bacon. *"Dein Messer,"* (Your knife) I said to the Block Chief. I cut off a good half which I handed him and then I went off without asking whether I should leave something in the *"Solidarität"* basket. He watched me go with gaping eyes. The French had a reputation, which was deserved, of being very tight with their parcels and not very generous. Suddenly he called me back. *"Dein Nummer?"* (Your number?)

He wrote it down, and then, said to me, *"Höre, mal, Kamerad, deine Paketten werden nie mehr gestollen werden. Das sage ich. Geh mal jetzt!"* (Listen, your parcels won't be pilfered any more. That I can tell you. Now get going!")

Indeed, from that day on my parcels were given to me just about intact. The Block Chief had passed my number on to the various stations in the chain of distribution, implying an order "do not touch". And, it was to that fact that I owe my life since the parcels which came from France, aside from the fact that they contained food supplements to the camp diet, were a precious exchange currency with which exemptions from work, extra clothing, and light jobs could be bought. They made it possible for me to spend eight months in the infirmary, when others, just as sick, spent the same time working until they died.

Concerning the parcels, another tragic phenomenon took place. Most of the French, even those from very comfortable families, received one parcel three quarters plundered; then they received nothing more. It was only after the liberation that I got an explanation. On arrival at the camp the prisoners wrote to their families, saying that they had the right to write twice a month. The family sent a parcel, and, since it was the first, before sending another they waited for an acknowledgment of receipt, which never came, because, except for the first, only one out of ten letters that we wrote arrived at its destination. In the camp, the prisoner who wrote regularly wondered what was the matter. And, while he was dying of starvation, his family in France was convinced that it was not worth while to send a second package because, since he had not acknowledged reception of the first, he must surely be dead. My wife, who regularly sent me a parcel every day, told me that she did it for her conscience's sake and against all hope; my mother herself was of the opinion that she was sending them to a dead man and that, in addition to the mourning, she was throwing her money away.

* * * *

On June 1, 1944, the camp was unrecognizable. Since March 15, convoys of 800, of 1,000, of 1,500 prisoners kept coming and coming once or twice a week. And, the population grew to about 15,000 individuals. If the population did not climb beyond this figure, it was because the death rate came very close to the arrival rate. Every day fifty to eighty bodies were carried out in the direction of the crematorium. The *H-Führung* itself made up one tenth of the total number in the camp. Fourteen to eighteen hundred men with soft jobs, all powerful and full of their importance, ruled over the *valgum pécus.* With cigarettes in their mouths, plenty of soup in their stomachs, and with beer to quench their thirsts, they almost lived in another world.

Block 141, destined to be the movie theater, was under construction and the brothel was ready to receive the women. All of the Blocks, geometrically and agreeably set out on the hill were connected with concrete streets. Cement staircases with railings, led up to the higher Blocks. In front of each of them were pergolas with climbing plants and little gardens with carpets of flowers; here and there were cross roads with a fountain or statue. The mustering yard, which covered about half a square mile, was entirely paved, and was so clean you could not lose a pin on it. With a swimming pool that was fitted with a diving board in the center, a sports field, and shaded areas nearby, Dora was a regular resort camp for anyone who might happen in, when the prisoners were not there. In fact, such visitors would go away under the impression that a pleasant life was led there, not to be compared to the war risks which free men were running. The S.S. authorized the establishment of a music *Kommando*. After that, every morning and evening, a band of wind instruments, supported by a bass drum and cymbals, gave rhythm to the march of the *Kommandos* going to and from work. During the day they practiced and deafened the immediate area with the most extraordinary sounds. On Sunday afternoon they gave concerts in the midst of general apathy while members of the prisoner elite played football or did acrobatics on the diving board.

Although the appearances had changed, the realities were the same. The *H-Führung* was still what it had always been, except that the politicals had worked their way in in appreciable numbers and the prisoners, instead of being brutally treated by the "greens" got the same from the Communists or so-called Communists. Every person regularly received a wage, of two to five Marks per week. These wages were collected by the *H-Führung* who distributed them usually on Saturday evening in *Arbeitsstatistik* square. But, the distribution was done in such a way that chaotic mobs were created which made any attempt to get them tantamount to offering yourself for the crematorium. Very few prisoners were bold enough to claim their share. The *Kapos*, the Block Chiefs, and the *Lagerschutz*, divided up among themselves what they were relieved of having to pay out. Cigarettes, too, were distributed — twelve cigarettes every ten days—for about 80 *Pfennig* on the average. We had no money to pay for them, and the Block Chiefs in charge of dividing them

up exacted from those who did have some money such standards of cleanliness and order that it was just about impossible to
get possession of one's ration. Finally, beer was distributed, in
principle, to everyone. But, there again one had to be able to
pay. The families of the prisoners were allowed to send them 30
Marks a month, which they no more received than their weekly
wage, or their cigarettes, and for the same reason. And, all in
keeping with this, one day the *H-Führung* people decided to divide up the clothing and the various other things that had been
taken away from us when we arrived at Buchenwald.

It can be added that for things to have reached that stage,
thousands and thousands of prisoners had died as a result of natural causes, as a result of the life they were forced to lead, or as
a result of their summary execution for various other reasons,
especially for sabotage and were no longer around to claim their
property that was stored in the *Effektenkammer*. From March
1944 to April 1945, not a week passed when I did not see three
or four men hanged for sabotage. Toward the end, they were
being hanged by tens and twenties, right in front of each others'
eyes. These executions took place on the muster grounds in
front of everyone. A gallows was set up, the condemned men
arrived, a gag in the shape of a bridle-bit was placed in their
mouths, and their hands were tied behind their backs. They
climbed onto a stool, and their heads were put into the hanging
noose. With a kick, the *Lagerschutz* knocked the stool over. No
sudden jerk; it took the poor people four, five or six minutes to
die. One or two S.S. guards supervised. When the job was done,
the whole camp filed past the bodies strung up on their ropes.

On February 28, 1945, thirty men were hanged in groups of
ten. The heads of the first ten were placed into the nooses. The
next ten were waiting their turn, at attention, near the stools;
the following ten were standing five steps away, waiting for
their turn. The following March 8th, nineteen men were
hanged. This time the job took place in the Tunnel, and only
the *Kommandos* of the Tunnel were witnesses. The nineteen condemned men were lined up in front of Hall 32. A huge pulley, to
which nineteen ropes were attached, was slowly lowered above
their heads. The *Lagerschutz* handed out the nineteen nooses;
then the pulley raised up slowly, slowly. Oh! How the eyes of the
poor fellows grew large, and how their poor feet searched to
keep some contact with the ground! On Palm Sunday, fifty-
seven were hanged, just eight days before the liberation, when

we had already heard Allied cannon fire very close and when the issue of the war could no longer be in any doubt for the S.S. But this was the way it was: the S.S. themselves discovered a certain number of cases of sabotage (in 1945, and since the middle of 1944, it had become impossible for anyone in the camp, or even on the outside to live without sabotaging); however, the *H-Führung*, without any mercy, pointed out to them an even greater number.

It is almost impossible to grasp the cost of this undertaking in human lives. On June 1, 1944, the population of the camp was almost exclusively made up of people who had arrived in March of that year or later. There were still seven prisoners whose numbers ranged between 13,500 and 15,000; at least 800 of them had arrived on July 18, 1943. There were about a dozen left in the 20,000 to 22,000 range; they had arrived in a group of about 1,500 in October, 1943. Of the 800 included in the 30,000 to 31,000 group, who arrived in December-January, there remained about fifty; of the 1,200 taken from the 38,000 to 44,000 group, who came in February-March, three or four hundred survived. Those prisoners who wore numbers 45,000 to 50,000 and who arrived during May 1944, were still more or less all there; but not for long.

Chapter Five

Port of Grace; Anteroom of Death

On July 28, 1943, when the first convoy arrived in the beet fields in front of the Tunnel, there was no question of any *Revier*. They had sent only those prisoners from Buchenwald who were supposed to be in good health, and it was not anticipated that they might fall sick right away: but, should this happen, the S.S. had orders to pay attention only to serious cases, to report them by mail, and to wait for instructions. Naturally, the S.S. never discovered anyone seriously sick; anyone who has been a soldier will easily understand that.

The weather was beastly that year. It rained and rained. Pneumonia and pleurisy ran rampant, and made great inroads among those who were weak and badly treated, who were wet all day long, and who had to sleep at night in damp caves in the rock. In eight days, those unfortunates were doubled up with what the S.S. called a little fever, which seemed to worsen, but they didn't know why. The regulations were that one was not sick unless one had a temperature of more than 39.5° C. (103° F.), in which case one could get a *Schonung*, or work exemption. Until you had such a fever you had to keep on working, and when you did have such a temperature it meant death.

Then there was what we called dysentery, but which was in reality uncontrollable diarrhea. One fine day, for no clear reason, one was overcome with digestive troubles which rapidly developed into an inability to tolerate anything. There was no remedy: one had simply to wait for it to stop, without eating anything. It lasted eight, ten, fifteen days, depending on the resistance of the sick man, who got weaker, who finally began to fall down, without any strength left to move, even to take care of his needs, and who then succumbed to the fever that accompanied it. This sickness, fortunately easier to detect than pneumonia or pleurisy, led the S.S. to take steps, with what means they had available, to check it. They ordered the construction of a *Bud*, where, without regard for their temperatures, those with diarrhea were admitted on showing the proper paper and so long as there was space available.

The *Bud* could hold thirty people. Very soon there were fifty, a hundred, and more, their number ever growing as new convoys arrived from Buchenwald and as the camp grew larger. Generally, the diarrhetics were sent there only in the last stages of the illness, and then only to die there. They were piled together right on the ground, packed like sardines, unmindful of what was under them; it was an epidemic. It got to such a point that for health reasons the S.S. had the first *H-Führung* pick out a *Pfleger*, or nurse, to keep order among the sick and help them to keep themselves clean. The job was given to a "green" (naturally!), a carpenter by trade, who had been sentenced for murder. A fine job was done . . . !

All the day long people were lined up at the entrance to the *Bud*. The *Pfleger*, truncheon in hand, calmed down the impatient ones. From time to time a corpse was brought out of the stench, and a space was made which was jumped at. The number of diarrhetics only increased. When the S.S. saw that the *Pfleger* was not up to the task, the latter pointed out that he had a lot of work to do all alone, and he was given an assistant of whom the S. S. required that he know his business. The job fell to a Dutch doctor who had been employed, until then, in the work of transporting goods from the station to the Tunnel. From that moment on the *Bud* became humanized, the *Pfleger* became *Kapo*, and the Dutchman worked under his orders, exercising prodigious diplomacy. He managed to save one diarrhetic, whose cure he was careful to conceal in order to keep him by his side as a nurse. With the help of a big supply of charcoal, the diarrhea was checked, the S. S. declared themselves satisfied, and the *Bud* could be used for something else. The first *Revier* was born.

In fact, the Dutchman was able to fix it so that as places were left available by the diarrhetics, those with pneumonia and pleurisy with temperatures of 38° C. (102° F.) and up could be admitted. But, this practice aroused the resentment of his *Kapo*! He even began to claim that with a little charcoal it would be possible to care effectively for the diarrhetics without hospitalizing them, if they were caught soon enough, and that, therefore, there would be more room for those with pneumonia and pleurisy. The duel was Homeric. An S.S. doctor, who had been assigned to the camp and who had arrived in November along with the officers of a convoy, after having remained indifferent to this conflict for a long time, ended by backing up the Dutchman. And, the building of a Block was begun, the *Bud* having rapidly become too small.

Then it was the turn of those with nephritis. Nephritis was inherent in the life of the camp: under-nourishment, too many hours standing up, the effects of bad weather, pneumonia, pleurisy, the rock salt — the only kind there was in Germany — which the cooks used immoderately, and which, it seems, was harmful because it contained no iodine. Cases of edema were legion; everybody had legs more or less swollen.

"It goes away," they said, "it's the salt that does it." And no more attention than that was paid to it. When it was an innocuous edema, it did sometimes disappear! When the edema was the outcome of nephritis, one was carried away, one fine day, with an attack of uremia. The Dutchman succeeded in getting those with nephritis hospitalized, too. Another Block had to be built. Then it was the turn of those with tuberculosis, and so on. The expansion continued to such an extent that on June 1, 1944, the *Revier* was composed of Blocks 16, 17, 38, 39, 126, 127, and 128, grouped around the top of the hill. Fifteen hundred patients could be put there, at one person per bed, or a tenth of the camp's population. Each Block was divided into wards, where related sicknesses were assigned.

Block 16 was the administrative center of the whole structure. The Dutchman was promoted to the rank of Head Doctor. Meanwhile, the S.S. replaced the "green" *Lagerältester* with a "red," and there was a great commotion in the *H-Führung.* The *Kapo* of the *Revier* was the first victim of the new *Lagerältester.* A plan was set up to catch him in the act of stealing the food destined for the sick. He was sent to the Ellrich camp by way of punishment, and he was replaced by Pröll.

* * * *

Pröll was a young German, about 27 or 28 years old. In 1934, he had intended to take up medicine. But as the son of a Communist and as a Communist himself, he was arrested when he was still only a child. He spent the next ten years in various camps. First, he was sent to Dachau where it was due only to his youth that he survived the rigors of that budding camp. Neither the S.S. nor the adult prisoners had their knives out for the youngsters: the first because of a kind of respect for real innocence; the second because of a special tenderness which nourished in them the hope of seeing the youngsters become affectionate later. Thanks to these two circumstances, Pröll managed to get into the *Revier* as a *Pfleger* and to stay there for several years. Then, he was sent to Mauthausen in that capacity. The "green" *Häftlingsführung* of Mauthausen got rid of him by sending him to Auschwitz, where he was included in the first convoy that was sent to Natzweiler. It was at Natzweiler that he spent his longest time. There he was promoted to *Kapo* of the *Lagerkommando* and was attached to the *Lagerältester.* The few prisoners who knew him in that camp were unanimous in saying that they never had seen such a brute. A palace revolution in the *H-Führung* of Natzweiler caused his removal to Buchenwald, from whence he was sent to Dora as a confidant of the Communists and *Kapo* of the *Revier.*

At Dora, Pröll behaved like all the other *Kapos* — neither better nor worse. He was intelligent and organized the *Revier* along the lines laid down by the Dutchman whom he considered, in spite of everything, a valuable assistant because he was competent. To be sure, he did not always follow the moral commandments of medicine. He was brutal, and in making up the army of *Pfleger* that he needed to carry out the job he gave preference to the politicals before the professionals. That is how the blacksmith Heinz, who was a Communist and who had managed to get himself into the *Revier* under the regime of the "green" *Kapo* as *Oberpfleger* (head nurse), was completely trusted by him against the advice of all the other medical people. That is also why, to a medical student whose political opinions he knew did not agree with his, he always preferred any lout, German, Czech, Russian or Polish. He had a great admiration for the Russians, and a weakness for the Czechs, who in his eyes had been abandoned to Hitler by the English and the French of whom he was contemptuous. But, he was an organizer of the first order.

In less than a month, the *Revier* was organized on the lines of the big hospitals: in Block 16, the administration, admissions and emergencies; in 17 and 39, general treatment, the kidney cases and those with neuritis; in 38, surgery; in 126, pneumonia and pleurisy; in 127 and 128 the tubercular. In each Block there was a doctor in charge, assisted by an *Oberpfleger;* in each ward, a *Pfleger* for nursing and a *Kalifaktor* for other duties. For the sick two-bunk beds only, one above the other, with a mattress stuffed with wood shavings, sheets and blankets. There were three diets: the *Hauskost,* or food in every way like that given out in the camp, for those whose digestive tracts were not affected; the *Schleimkost,* or thin semolina soup (no bread, no margarine, no sausage), for those who required a low diet; the *Diatkost,* which every day consisted of two soups, one sweetened, and white bread, margarine and jam, for those who needed building up.

In cannot be said that one was very well taken care of in the *Revier.* The *S.S.-Führung* dispensed very little medicines and drugs, and Pröll filched from the lot all that was necessary for the *H-Führung,* letting only that which they didn't need filter through to the sick themselves. But, the beds were clean; one rested; and the food ration, although not of better quality than for the rest of the camp, was still more abundant. Pröll himself limited his activities as *Kapo* to one visit which each day was accompanied with shouts and some generously bestowed blows on the personnel and the sick who had been caught disobeying *Revier* regulations. Life there would have been a contrast to the prevailing conditions in the rest of the camp if the *Pfleger* and *Kalifaktor,* as much out of zeal and loyalty to tradition as out of fear of the *Kapo,* had not been bent on trying to make it intolerable.

* * * *

Every night after roll-call, a mob collected at the entrance to Block 16. Block 16 included, aside from the administration office for the *Revier*, an *Aussere-Ambulanz* and an *Innere-Ambulanz*. The first took care of the immediate needs of all those who, sick or having met with an accident, did not meet the requirements for being hospitalized; the second determined, after examination, those who should or should not be hospitalized.

Aside from the *H-Führung*, everyone in the camp was sick, and, under conditions which prevail in the normal world, everyone would have been hospitalized without exception and without delay, even if only on account of their extreme debility. In the camp, the situation was quite the opposite. There, general debility did not count; only those conditions which exceeded such debility were taken care of, and then only under certain extra-therapeutic circumstances or when nothing else could be done. Every prisoner was, therefore, more or less a candidate for the *Revier*. They had to make a rule that one could apply for admission every four days, on an average.

First of all there were the boils. The whole camp had suppurative furunculosis, the result of the lack of meat and roughage in the food. It was endemic just like the benign edema and the nephritis. There were the sores on the hands or feet or both. Finally, there were cut fingers, arms or legs broken, and the like. They made up the patients of the *Aussere-Ambulance* and from June 1, 1944, were in the hands of the Negro, Johnny, whose incompetence as a doctor had finally been recognized at the Buchenwald *Revier*. In spite of the political pledges that he had given, he was sent to us in a transport, as a doctor, naturally, but with a note stating that it would be more prudent to use him as a nurse. Pröll thought that he was just right for the *Aussere-Ambulanz*, and put him in charge. I learned afterwards that he had been astute enough to get the protection of Katzenellenbogen, that prisoner who called himself an American by origin, who was the general physician of the camp, and who committed so many extortions that he was considered a war criminal after liberation.

Johnny had under him a whole company of *Pfleger*, Germans, Poles, Czechs or Russians, who knew nothing whatever of the job they were charged with; they put on dressings, took them off and put them on again when it struck their fancy. For boils or wounds, there was only one remedy: ointment. Those gentlemen had before them pots of ointments of all colors. On the same sore, they one day put the black salve and another day put the red or the yellow, and there was no guessing what determined their choice. Luckily, all of the ointments were antiseptic!

To the *Innere-Ambulanz* went everybody who hoped to get hospitalized. Every night there were five or six hundred, each one just as sick as the other. Sometimes there were ten or fifteen beds available. Put yourself in the place of the doctor who had to choose which ten or fifteen . . . The others were sent back with or without *Schonung.* They appeared the next day and every day until they had the luck to be admitted. Uncounted were those who died before they made it.

I knew prisoners who never went to take a shower because they they were afraid that gas would come out of the pipes instead of water.[1]   And, then, during the weekly inspection by the nurses of the Block, lice were found on them. Then they had to go through a disinfection treatment that killed them.

I also knew prisoners who never went to the infirmary. They were afraid of being used as guinea pigs of some kind in the medical experiments that rumor had said were being conducted by the S.S. or of being given poison injections. Consequently, they held out and held out against all advice, and one evening a *Kommando* brought their corpses back to the camp.

At Dora, no medical experiments were performed on the prisoners, and poison injections were not administered, at least not to the common prisoners. Generally, in all of the camps, injections of poison were not used against the general run of the prisoners, but they were used on occasion by one of the two *H-Führung* cliques against the other; the "greens" used this method as an elegant means of getting rid of a "red" whose star they saw was rising in the eyes of the S.S. staff, or the other way around.

* * * *

A fortunate circumstance allowed me to get into the *Revier* on April 8, 1944. For fifteen days I had been dragging around the camp with a feverish body that was visibly swelling. The swelling had begun in the ankles. *"Ich auch, Blöder Hund!"* my *Kapo* said, *"du bist verrücht! Geh mal zu Revier!"* (You–you're crazy! Get on to the *Revier!*) And, he punctuated this order with several fist blows. It was April 3rd. At the *Revier* I was caught in the mob. After waiting for an hour my turn came to go before the doctor. "You have only 37.8° (99° F), impossible to hospitalize you; three days of *Schonung*. Rest stretched out in the Block with your legs up, it will go away. If it doesn't go away, come back again."

As for the rest, for three days I was put at Block cleaning by the merciless *Stubendienst*. At the end of the period I presented myself again in a noticeably worse state.

"Of course you will have to be hospitalized," the doctor said to me, "but there are only three vacant places and there are at least three hundred of you, some of them worse off than you are. Another three days of *Schonung;* then come back . . ."

I began to have a presentiment of the crematory. With resignation, I went back to the Block where my first parcel was waiting for me, thanks to which I got the *Stubendienst* to allow me to stretch out on my bed instead of making me work.

On April 8, when my turn came, a package of Gauloise cigarettes got me among the three or four chosen ones. And what was bad about it was that I saw nothing irregular in the bribe.

Before getting to the bed assigned me, I still had to leave at the entrance my clothes and my shoes, which were naturally stolen while I was there, and to go under an individual shower which a Polish *Kalifaktor* kept just as cold as he could.

The shower was the last thing that had to be done. It was supposed to be hot, but when it was not a Czech or a Pole, or a German, the *Kalifaktor* swore to heaven that the thing was out of order. The number of those hospitalized for pneumonia or pleurisy who died of that treatment is incalculable.

I was in the *Revier* six times: from April 8th to the 27th; from May 5th to August 30th; from September 7th to October 2nd; from October 10th to November 3rd; from November 6th to December 23rd; and from March 10, 1945 to the liberation. At the first, I lost track of Fernand, who was sent in transport to Ellrich were he died. I was sick, that fact was quite plain. In fact, I was gravely ill because I still have not fully recovered, but . . .

* * * *

Life in the *Revier* was regulated in detail. We were up at half past five every day, one hour later than the reveille of the rest of the camp. Then came the washing: no matter what the reason was for one's hospitalization, with a fever of 40º C. (104º F.) or 37º C. (98.5º F.), one had to get up, go to the sink, wash, and, on returning, one had to make one's bed. In principle, the *Pfleger* and the *Kalifaktor* were supposed to help those who could not do it themselves, but, with rare exceptions, they simply got the patients to do the chores themselves, with the help of blows. With these chores done, the *Pfleger* took temperatures, while the *Kalifaktor* washed down the ward with a hose.

At about seven o'clock, the Block doctor went among the beds, looked at the temperature charts, heard the comments of the *Pfleger*, the complaints of the sick, said a word to each one, and gave orders for particular treatment or medicines that were to be administered during the day. If he was not Polish, German, or Czech, the doctor was usually a good and understanding man. Perhaps, he trusted the *Pfleger* a little too much, with the latter treating the sick according to their political views, their nationality, their profession or trade, or their generosity with the parcels that they received. Nevertheless, the doctor very rarely allowed himself to be influenced in a bad sense. Rather, his decisions were almost always well intended.

Once in a while someone who was very sick would dare to ask him, *"Krématorium?"* The doctor might answer: *"Ja, sicher . . . Drei, vier Tage."* ("Yes, that's certain . . . in three or four days.") There was a laugh. He then went on without any consideration of the effect that his reply had on the one concerned. After he finished with the last bed, he left the ward; it was all over. He would not be seen again until the next day.

At nine o'clock, the distribution of medicine. It went very fast since the medicine was generally either rest or diet. From time to time, an aspirin or pyramidon was given out very parsimoniously.

At eleven, soup. The *Pfleger* and the *Kalifaktor* ate heartily, served themselves at each issuance and gave the remainder to the sick. It wasn't too bad; there was enough left over to give an honest regulation helping to everyone, with even a little supplement for one's friends.

In the afternoon, a nap until four o'clock, after which lots of talk until the temperatures were taken and the lights put out. The conversations were only interrupted when our attention was drawn to a long line of cadavers which, right under our windows, the *Totenkommando* people were carrying to the crematorium.

Some favored ones, of which I was one, received parcels: they were a little more pilfered than in the camp because they had to go through another pair of hands before they reached the addressee. The tobacco they contained was not replaced; that was deposited at the entrance, but the *Pfleger* were obliging, and with a good hand-out, a fair share, one could also get one's tobacco and permission to smoke secretly. In the same way, by sharing the rest, the *Pfleger* could be gotten to hike-up the temperature readings, and one's stay in the *Revier* was prolonged.

In summer, the afternoon siesta took place in the open air, under the beech trees. The *Kommandos* working inside the camp looked at us with envy, and we grew apprehensive of the time when we would be cured and back among them.

* * * *

In October 1944, only very rarely were diarrhetics admitted to the *Revier*. Every night they came to Block 16, and they were stuffed with charcoal and sent back. Sometimes the trouble disappeared, but it also persisted beyond the calculated eight days and was complicated by some kind of a fever, and then they were hospitalized with all sorts of conjectures as to what it was.

They were collected in Block 17, Ward 8, whose *Pfleger* was the Russian, Ivan, who said that he was a *"Docent"* on the medical faculty at Karkhov, and whose *Kalifaktor* was the Pole, Stadjeck. Ward 8 was the hell of the *Revier*. Every day it supplied two, three or four corpses to the crematorium.

For every diarrhetic admitted, the doctor prescribed, in addition to the charcoal, a supervised diet: very little to eat, if possible nothing at all, and nothing to drink. He advised Ivan to give nothing the first day, to divide a quart of soup among two or three the next, and so on; a return to a normal diet being determined by the disappearance of the sickness. But Ivan considered that he was there as *Pfleger* to take care of himself and not the sick men; to look after them was work too hard for him, and, in any case, out of place in a concentration camp. He found it simpler to administer the absolute diet, to divide with Stadjeck the rations of the patients, to feed themselves amply, and to do some bartering with the rest. The poor men had nothing to eat, absolutely nothing. On the third day, with very rare exceptions, they were in such a state that they could no longer get up, and they had to take care of their needs right where they were, since Stadjeck had other things to do than to bring them the bedpan when they asked for it. From that moment on they were doomed . . . .

Stadjeck started to inspect very carefully the bed of the unfortunate man to whom he had just refused to bring a basin. All of a sudden he got the smell and went into a rage. He began by giving the offender a good beating, pulled him out of bed, pushed him to the adjoining lavatory, and there gave him a good cold shower, since the *Revier* must always be a clean place and patients who didn't want to wash themselves, well, they had to be washed . . . . Then, shouting out curses, Stadjeck took off the sheet and cover from the bed and changed the straw mattress. Hardly stretched out again, the patient would be seized with grips, would ask for the bedpan again which was again refused, would discharge in the bed, and would be taken once more to the cold shower, and so on and on. Usually, twenty-four hours later, the patient was dead.

From morning to night the cries and pleadings of the poor men who were put under the cold shower by the Pole, Stadjeck, could be heard. Two or three times the *Kapo* or a doctor happened to pass near during this operation. They opened the door; Stadjeck explained, *"Er hat sein Bett ganz beschiessen . . . Dieser Blöder Hund ist so faul . . . . Keine warme Wasser."* (He completely dirtied his bed, the stupid dog is so lazy . . . . and there is no warm water.) The *Kapo* or the doctor would close the door again and go away without saying a word. The explanation was, of course, unassailable; those patients unable to wash themselves had to be washed, and when there was no hot water . . . .

In the *Revier* one was kept pretty well informed about the way the war was going. German newspapers, in particular the *Volkische Beobachter*, were delivered, and everyone regularly listened to the radio. Of course there was only official news, but that came rapidly, and that was something.

We also knew what was going on in the other camps; the poor men who had already been through two or three camps before ending up at Dora, recounted the whole day long the experiences they had lived through. That was how we learned about the horrors of Sachsenhausen, Auschwitz, Mauthausen, Oranienburg, etc. And, that was also how we learned that there were very decent camps.

In August, for ten days, the German, Helmuth, was my bed neighbor. He had come straight from Lichtenfeld near Berlin. There were 900 in that camp, and under *Wehrmacht* guard they carried on the work of clearing the bombed suburbs: twelve hours of work, as everywhere, but three meals a day, and three good meals (soup, meat, vegetables, often wine), no *Kapos*, and no *H-Führung,* consequently no beatings. A hard life, but bearable. One day they asked for specialists: since Helmuth was a fitter, he stood up; he was sent to the Dora Tunnel, where they put rock drilling equipment in his hands. Eight days later he was spitting blood.

Before that, I had next to me a prisoner who had spent a month at Wieda, and who had told me that the 1,500 occupants were not too badly off. Naturally, they worked and had little to eat, but they led a kind of family life: on Sunday afternoons, the villagers came to dance at the outskirts of the camp to the music of the prisoners' accordions, exchanged friendly small talk with them, and even brought them things to eat. It seems that that did not last; when the S. S. noticed it, Wieda became as hard and as inhuman as Dora.

But, most of those who came from other camps had only hair-raising things to tell, and the accounts of Ellrich were the most horrifying. They were in an incredible state when they arrived among us, and just one look at them was enough to prove that they were inventing nothing . . . In speaking of bad concentration camps, Buchenwald, Dachau, and Auschwitz are cited, and that is an injustice: in 1944-1945, it was Ellrich that was the worst of all. There, one was without a billet, not given clothing, not fed, without a *Revier*, and all the work consisted of digging under the supervision of the scum of the "greens," the "reds," and the S. S.

It was in the *Revier* that I got acquainted with Jacques Gallier, called Jacky, clown at Medrano. He was as tough as they came. When anyone complained of the hardships of camp life, he invariably answered, "Me, you know, I've done two and a half years at Calvi: I'm used to it." And he went on, "Listen, at Calvi, it was just the same, same work, never enough food, only we didn't get hit so much, but there were irons and solitary, so . . . ."[2]

Champale, the sailor from the Black Sea who had done five years at Clairvaux, didn't contradict him, and as for me, who had earlier witnessed the life of the Joyeux in Africa, I wondered if they weren't right.[3]

* * * *

On December 23rd I left the *Revier* with the firm intention never to set foot there again. Several things had happened.

In July, Pröll gave himself a shot in the arm of potassium cyanide. No one ever found out why, but rumor had it that he had been just about to be arrested and was in danger of being hanged for conspiracy. He was replaced by Heinz, the Communist blacksmith.

Heinz was a brute. One day he caught a fever-case, who had been forbidden any water, in the act of moistening his lips, and he beat him up so hard that he died as a result. He was said to be capable of everything: in the surgery Block, he undertook an appendicitis operation – without the surgeon in charge, the Czech Cespiva, knowing about it. The story was told that in the first days of the *Revier*, under the rule of the "green" *Kapo*, he had given his attentions to an Algerian whose arm had been crushed between two carts in the Tunnel: he disjoined the shoulder, just as a butcher does with a ham, and instead of anesthetizing the victim, he first beat him up with his fists. . . A year later, the whole *Revier* still resounded with the wails of the unfortunate fellow.

Lots of other things were told, too. The patients never felt safe with him. As far as I was concerned, one day at the end of

September, he came near my bed with Cespiva, and he decided that to cure me, the right kidney would have to be removed. I at once begged one of my comrades, who had another disease, to give a urine specimen for me, and thus got a negative analysis, which allowed me, as I had wanted, to be sent back to the *Kommando*. Being incapable of doing the work, I presented myself at the *Revier* a few days later — just time enough for the storm to have passed — and I got in easily.

Everything went well until December, at which date Heinz was arrested, in his turn, for conspiracy, like his predecessor, and he was replaced by a Pole. Caught in the same net by the S.S. were Cespiva, a certain number of *Pfleger,* among them the lawyer Boyer from Marseille, and some others from the camp. We never learn why about this either, but it is probable that it was for having circulated news about the war which they said they got from foreign broadcasts, listed to in secret, and which the S.S. considered subversive.

With the new *Kapo*, the *Revier* was overrun with Poles, and new doctors were put at the head of the Blocks; ours was an illiterate Pole. When he arrived, he decided that nephritis was caused by bad teeth, and gave an order to have all the teeth of all the nephritis cases pulled. The dentist was sent for at once and began to carry out the order without knowing what it was about, but showing his astonishment and protesting. In order to save my teeth, I arranged once more to get out of the *Revier*, with a paper which certified me for *leichte Arbeit* (light labor). An exceptionally favorable set of circumstances occurred which made it possible for me to serve as the *Schwung* (batman) to the S.S. *Oberscharführer* who was in charge of the company of guard dogs which patrolled the perimeter of the camp. I found that the camp had changed considerably when I got back.

* * * *

FOOTNOTES

1.The gas chambers which some of the S.S. denied existed and which others attested to with the logic of Mme. Simone de Beauvoir did not exist at Dora. Nor did they exist at Buchenwald. I note in passing that of all those who so minutely described the horrors of this form of execution (which, incidentally, is a perfectly legitimate form of execution in the United States) not one was an eyewitness, as far as I know. The only possible exceptions are Rudolf Hoess, Miklos Nyiszli, and Kurt Gerstein. The former was *Lagerkommandant* at Auschwitz; his testimony is unreliable both on the grounds of the atrocious conditions under which it was written down and of the fantastic circumstances under which it was published, as will be discussed further on in this book. The testimony of the latter two is obviously false, a fact which will be discussed in the following chapters.

2. For a comparison of prison life in French prisons — during about the same period — I have included four descriptions which are found in Appendix A at the end of this book.

3. In *La Lie de la Terre*, Arthur Koestler gives a picture of the life in a French concentration camp which confirms my point of view. Another account which also confirms my view is that of Julien Blanc under the title *Joyeux, fais ton fourbi.*

Chapter Six

Shipwreck

What happened next is of not great interest. In December 1944 Dora was a large camp. It was no longer a satellite of Buchenwald, but, rather Ellrich, Osterrod, Harzungen, and Illfed, all in the construction stage, were dependents of it.[1] Convoys of prisoners arrived there directly, just as they had earlier at Buchenwald, where they were disinfected, numbered, and divided up among the satellite camps. The numbers that the new prisoners wore now were beyond the 100,000s . . . Every night, trucks brought back corpses from the satellite camps to be burned in the crematorium.

Block 172 was finished; there was a movie theater, as well as a library, functioning for the people of the *H-Führung* and their protégés; the women who had been installed for several months in the brothel also served their needs. The Blocks were comfortable; there was running water; and there were even radios! The beds were set up, without sheets but with straw mattresses and with blankets. The period of great hurry was over; the S.S. were less exacting; their object, which was to get the camp set up, had been accomplished. But, on the other hand, they paid more attention to the political life, got excited about all sorts of imaginary conspiracies, and hunted out acts of sabotage, which, indeed, were real and numerous.

All of these material betterments, nevertheless, did not bring the general mass of prisoners the welfare that might have been expected. The mentality of the *H-Führung* had not changed. It was as though the prisoner bureaucracy tried to make us live the life of savages, but in buildings instead of caves, so hard did they try to retain the atmosphere of the *Straflager* along with its hardships and cruelties.

During the night of December 23-24, some *Kommando,* motivated by cudgels, set up on the grounds a gigantic Christmas fir tree, the erection of which was completed by five thirty the next morning in time for the roll-call before leaving for work and which was resplendent with multi-colored lights. From that day on and until Epiphany we had to listen every night at roll-call to *O Tannenbaum,* played by the *Musik-kommando,* before breaking ranks . . . One was obliged to listen with evident enjoyment or one risked getting hit.

Concerning the matter of prisoner welfare, two unexpected elements had to be considered: the joint advance of the Russians and of the English and Americans forced the evacuation of the camps in the East and the West and the transfer of prisoners to Dora and the more and more intensive bombing from the air that interrupted the normal flow of supplies into the camp.

After January 1945 there was no end to the convoys that arrived; often the prisoners were in an indescribable state. The camp which was planned to hold about 15,000 persons sometimes had 50,000 and more. They were bunked two or three to a bed. There was no more bread since flour was no longer delivered. Instead, one got two or three tiny potatoes. The ration of margarine and sausage was cut in half. As the storehouses were emptied as a consequence of the increased population and of the bombings, only a pint of soup instead of a quart, was distributed. There was no more clothing to replace what could no longer be used; Berlin was unable to send more. No more shoes; one made the best of the old ones. And, the same shortages existed with everything else.

On the work level the whole camp became riddled with sabotage. Raw materials no longer arrived at the Tunnel, and the work was slowed. It was winter. It was useless to ask for window glass to replace what was broken because there was not any to be had; but any prisoner could secretly steal a pane at the Tunnel. There wasn't any paint, either. The Block Chief who needed some had it stolen from a Zawatsky warehouse by one of his protégés. One day there was no electric wire for the V1 and V2 rockets; all of the prisoners who were working in the Tunnel had stolen a yard each to use for shoelaces. Another time, a supplementary stretch of railroad track was to be laid down. For at least a year, the necessary wooden ties had been there, piled up around the station. The *S.S.-Führung* supposed they were still there and gave the order to build the line since they had no choice. It was noticed then that the ties had disappeared, and an investigation revealed that at the beginning of winter the civilian workers had had them sawed up one by one by the prisoners and had taken them away little by little in their *Rücksacks* to supplement the shortage in their fuel rations. A few persons were punished, more ties were requested, and a few days later some gyroscopes were received.

In the Tunnel the acts of sabotage were beyond counting. It took the S.S. months to catch on to the fact that the Russians were making a large number of V1 and V2 rockets perfectly useless by urinating over the wireless equipment. The Russians were master pillagers, and master saboteurs, and they were stubborn; nothing stopped them. They also made up the largest contingent of those hanged. But this was for another reason; they thought they had worked out a plan of escape . . .

Very few prisoners had any idea of escaping from Dora, and those who tried it were all recovered by the dogs. Once back in camp they were usually hanged, not for the attempted escape, but for a war crime, since it was rare indeed that they could not be charged with some theft or other crime in one of the places that they had gone through. . .

Sabotage seems to have extended into even very high circles: the V1 and V2 rockets, before being used, had to be tested, and those that were not right were sent to Harzungen to be dismantled and checked. At Harzungen, they were dismantled, and the various defective parts were put into special packing cases which were then sent back again to Dora where they were assembled again in the same improper way. As a consequence, there were always about thirty V1 and V2 rockets that were being shuttled back and forth between Harzungen, Dora and the testing place. Even the administration at Dora was snowed under in confusion. At the entrance to the Tunnel, there was a sort of stockroom where all the parts that could not be used were collected: nuts, bolts, pieces of sheet-metal, screws of all kinds, etc. A special *Kommando,* detailed for light work, was in charge of sorting all these pieces: into one box went the bolts, into another the screws, in a third the odds and ends of sheet-metal. When all of the boxes were full, the *Kapo* would give the order to empty them all together into a rail car. When the car was full it was attached to a train which went off to an unknown destination; then, two days later it ended up at the entrance at Ellrich where it had been sent to be unloaded and sorted. The *Kommando* in charge of this work at Ellrich sent to the storeroom at Dora all of the pieces that they had sorted out and had dumped in a heap. Thus was a whole lot of scraps being endlessly sorted at the opposite ends of the Tunnel. And so, from incident to incident, from bombings to diminishing food supplies, from virtual conspiracies to sabotage and hangings, we reached the liberation.

During all this period I lived as batman to the *Oberscharführer* in command of the company of dogs; it was easy work which included the polishing of his boots, the brushing of his uniforms, the making of his bed, the keeping of his room and his office meticulously clean, and the fetching of his meals from the S.S. canteen. Every morning at about eight my stint was done. I spent the rest of the time talking here and there, warming myself near the fire, reading newspapers, and listening to the T.S.F. When the S.S. cook gave me food for my *Oberscharführer* at each meal, he surreptitiously gave me just as much for myself. In addition, the thirty S.S. men who lived in the Block gave me various jobs from time to time; they had me wash their mess kits, wax their boots, sweep out their rooms, etc . . . In return, they gave me their left-overs, which every night I took to friends. It was the good life.

This direct contact with the S.S. personnel made me see them in quite a different light than that in which they were universally seen in the camp. There was no possible comparison: in public they were brutes; taken individually, they were lambs. They looked at me with curiosity; they asked questions; they spoke on familiar terms with me; they wanted to know how I thought the war would turn out and took my opinion seriously. They were all men—former miners, factory workers, plasterers—who had been unemployed in 1933 and who the regime had taken out of their misery by giving them what they thought of as a bridge of gold. They were simple, and their intellectual level was extremely low. In exchange for the well-being that the regime had brought them, they carried out its more ignoble deeds and were at peace with their consciences, with morality, with the German fatherland, and with humanity. Although they were very sensitive to the bad luck that had befallen me when I was sent to Dora, they, nevertheless, went among the prisoners in their charge with their heads high, haughty, unbending and without pity. Not once did the idea occur to them that the other prisoners were people like themselves, or even . . . like me!

The anomalies in the camp administration were not generally obvious to them, and when by chance they did notice them, they quite sincerely attributed them to the *H-Führung*[2] or to the general prisoner population. They did not understand how we could be so thin, so weak, so dirty, and so badly clothed. The Third Reich, after all, had furnished us with everything we needed: food, everything necessary to keep us perfectly clean, comfortable lodging in a camp as modern as possible, health recreations, music, lectures, sports, a Christmas tree, and so forth. And, we did not know how to take advantage of it. That was proof that Hitler was right and that, with very rare exceptions, we belonged to a physically and morally inferior part of humanity! The idea never occurred to them that they might be responsible as individuals for the wrongs that were done under their eyes, or with their cooperation, unconscious or active. They were victims of the environment—of that special environment—in which, while breaking collectively with the restraints of tradition, all peoples, without distinction as to regime or nationality, founder periodically.

On March 10th, a group of female *Bibelforscher* (Baptists, Jehovah's Witnesses, and conscientious objectors) arrived at Dora, followed by an order from Berlin stipulating that these women—there were twenty-four of them—were to be put to light work. Henceforth the *Schwung* work was turned over to them. I was removed and sent back to camp. To escape a bad

Kommando, I thought it wiser to take advantage of my state of health and to get hospitalized in the *Revier;* from the hospital windows I watched the bombardment of Nordhausen on April 3 and 5, 1945, two days before being taken in the evacuation transport, the account of which is included in the Prologue.

FOOTNOTES

1. The *Häftlingsführung* of these satellite camps was in the hands of the "greens" which the "red" *H-Führung* of Dora sent there to get rid of them and to prevent their return to power.

2. The majority of the prisoners also felt that the *H-Führung* was much more to blame than was the S.S. for the kind of life that they were forced to lead.

PART II
The
Experience of
Others

Chapter Seven

Concentration Camp Literature

When the time came for me to draw a parallel between my own experience and that of others, as they described it, I found myself in a state of mind which the reader will easily understand.

While we were in the camp, all of our conversations during rare moments of respite, were centered around three things: when the war was likely to end and our individual or collective chances of surviving to see that end, the food that we were going to eat after we were freed, and what might be called camp "gossip," although the word "gossip" seems inappropriate in view of the tragic reality of camp life. None of these topics offered much possibility for escaping from the actual situation of the moment. All three, on the other hand, separately or collectively, depending on the amount of time that we had to discuss them, brought us right back to the present with the use of a phrase like, "When we tell them about that . . .," said with such a tone and such a sinister look that it frightened me. Recognizing that I was powerless to do anything about these pangs of conscience, given the atmosphere of the place, I retired within myself and became an obstinately silent witness.

Instinctively I recalled the aftermath of the First World War: the veterans, their stories and all of their writings. There was no doubt in my mind that the coming post-war period would have, in addition, veteran prisoners and deportees who would go back to their homes with even more horrible memories than those of veteran soldiers. But, instead of merely telling their stories, the way seemed to be open for these veterans to vent their feelings in a spirit of hatred and vengeance. To the extent that I was able to distinguish my personal lot in the great drama that was being played, all the Montagues, all the Capulets, all the Armagnacs, and all the Burgundians of history, taking up all their quarrels from the beginning, began to dance, before my eyes in a frenzied saraband, on a stage enlarged to the size of Europe. I could not convince myself that the spirit of hatred, being kindled before my eyes, could be harnessed no matter how the conflict came out.

When I tried to envision the consequences of this smoldering hatred and when I remembered that I had a son, I had to ask myself whether it would not be better if no one returned. And, I even hoped that the higher authorities of the Third Reich would realize in time that they could only be pardoned by offering, in a gigantic and frightful holocaust, all that remained of the inmates in the camps, as a redemption for so much evil. In that state of mind, I had decided that if I ever got back from the camps, that I would practice what I preached, and I swore never to make the slightest reference to my experience in the camps.

For what seemed to me to be a very long time after my return to France, I stuck to my decision; but it was not easy to do.

First, I had to struggle against a natural inclination to want to tell my story. For example, I shall never forget a demonstration that, in the very first days, the deportees had arranged at Belfort to mark their return. The whole town had gathered itself together to listen to their message. The great hall of the *Maison du Peuple* was full to bursting. Outside the square was thronged with people. Loud-speakers even had to be set up out in the street. My health did not permit me to be present at this demonstration, either as a speaker or listener, and I was very disappointed. But, my disappointment was even greater the next day when the local papers reported all that had been said; it was impossible to discern any statement of objectivity. My apprehensions about the hate-filled and distorted stories of the camp veterans had been confirmed. The crowd, however, was not fooled; never again could the same mass of people be gathered together for such a purpose. I had also to struggle against others. Wherever I went, over a glass of wine or a cup of tea, there was always a distinguished parrot in the grip of emotion, who was discussing the deportation, or a well-wishing friend who thought he was doing me a favor by drawing attention to me by turning the conversation to the subject: "Is it true that . . .?" "Do you think . . .?" "What do you think of the book by . . .?" All these questions irritated me. When they were not inspired by a perverse curiosity, they betrayed an uncertainty and a need to be reassured. Systematically I cut the talk short, a practice which sometimes provoked severe criticism.

I resented such criticism, and I blamed it upon my fellow deportees and their never ending publication of their stories, often imaginary, in which they gave themselves the airs of saints, heroes, or martyrs. As their writings collected on my desk like so many entreaties, I was sure that the time was coming when I would be forced to abandon my reserve and to relate my memories of my experiences as a deportee. Hence, I was not surprised when more than once I thought that the saying, attributed to Riera, that after every war all of the veterans should be killed without pity, was more than just a clever remark.

Then one day I realized that a false picture of the German camps had been created and that the problem of the concentration camps was a universal one, not just one that could be disposed of by placing it on the doorstep of the National Socialists. The deportees—many of whom were Communists— had been largely responsible for leading international political thinking to such an erroneous conclusion. I suddenly felt that by remaining silent I was an accomplice to a dangerous influence. And, at one sitting, without paying attention to literary style and in as simple as possible a form, I wrote my *Le Passage de la ligne* in an attempt to put things into proper perspective and in an attempt to bring people back to a sense of objectivity and, at the same time, to a better conception of intellectual honesty.

Next, the idea occurred to me that future discussions about
the problem of concentration camps would benefit by starting
with a general reconsideration of those things that were attributed to the German camps, drawn from the mass of testimonies
that former prisoners have brought forth. As a consequence, I
have gathered together the first elements of this reconsideration.
This is the explanation and the justification for the *Regard sur
la Littérature concentrationaire* (Survey of concentration camp
literature) which is found in Chapters Eight through Eleven.

* * * *

The experience of the ex-service men, still so fresh from the
1914 war, offers another parallel which I believe to be pertinent.
They came back with a great desire for peace, swearing by all
the saints that they would do everything possible to achieve it;
that this was the "war to end all wars." They were shown
gratitude, appreciation and a certain admiration. With joy,
hope, and enthusiasm, the whole French nation received them
with affection and confidence.

On the eve of the 1939 war, however, their opinions were
very much questioned. Their experiences and the lessons from
them were fully commented on in various ways, and the best
that one can say is that public opinion was not kind to them.
It sneered at their public statements, saying that they were
in their dotage—that was the word used—and that their memories crowded into every conversation. The leaders of the
national veteran associations, whose mission seemed to be
limited to demands for fatter pensions, were also criticized.
Concerning the writings of the veterans, public opinion was just
as categorical, and there was only one testimonial that it would
acknowledge: *Le Feu* by Barbusse. When, in rare moments of
good-will, public opinion made an exception, it was for Galtier-
Boissiere and for Dorgeles, but on other grounds: for the
mocking obdurate pacifism of the one, and what it thought
was the realism of the other.

Who can say what the real reasons were for this reversal of
opinion? As I see it, the reasons all belong within the frame-
work of this general truth: men are much more preoccupied
with the future that they face than they are with the past
from which there is nothing more to be gained. Consequently,

it is impossible to center people's lives around any event, no matter how extraordinary, especially a war, a phenomenon which tends to become commonplace and whose particular characteristics very rapidly become obsolete. On the eve of 1914, my grandfather, who had not yet digested the war of 1870, used to talk about it interminably to my father, who yawned with boredom. On the eve of 1939, my father had not yet finished telling about his war, and, every time that he brought it up, I could not help thinking that Du Guesclin, rising up among us, full of pride in his deeds with his cross-bow, could hardly have been more ridiculous. Thus are generations opposed to each other in their ideas. They are also opposed in their interests. Between the two wars, the rising generations had the feeling that it was impossible for them to make any attempt to realize their own destiny without coming up against the ex-service men, their pretensions, and their preferential rights. They had been given "rights over us." And they took advantage of it and kept pressing for more. But, there are rights which even the fact of having suffered through a long war and having won it, do not confer, particularly that of being the only ones fit to construct a peace, or, more modestly, the right to positions regardless of merit, whether they be in a tobacconist's shop, in a rural police station, or in a teaching post.

The divorce between the public and the veterans took place during the economic crisis of the Thirties. The rift was aggravated, about 1935, when the veterans forgot about the vows that they had made on their return from the battlefield and so easily accepted the possibility of another war, and when, at the same time, the public sentiment was for peace. It is another law of historical evolution that the young generations are pacifist, that through them, over the centuries, humanity progressively becomes firmer in its search for universal peace, and that war is always, in a certain measure, the rancor of old age.

In any case, there is one thing due the ex-service men of that war as well as of the last one: they told about their wars as they were. Almost every word, to read them or to listen to them, rings profoundly true, or, at least convincing. But this cannot be said of the deportees.

The deportees came back with hatred and resentment on their tongues and in their pens. They were not tired of war; rather they had an axe to grind and they demanded vengeance. Moreover, since they suffered from an inferiority complex—there were only some 30,000 of them out of a population of 40 million inhabitants—they wantonly created a story of horror for a public that always clamored for something more sensational in order the more surely to inspire pity and recognition.

The inflammatory fabrications of one deportee soon inspired similar stories by others, and they progressively were caught on a treadmill of lies. Although some deportees were duped by others in this process, most of them managed quite consciously to blacken the picture even more in their zeal to hold the limelight. So it was with Ulysses who, during the course of his voyage, each day added a new adventure to his Odyssey, as much to please the public taste of the times as to justify his long absence in the eyes of his family. But, if Ulysses succeeded in creating his own legend and in fixing the attention of twenty-five centuries of history on it, it is no exaggeration to say that the deportees failed to do so.

Everything was fine for the deportees during the very first days of the Liberation. One could not, without risk of being branded a "collaborator" question what they had to say, even if one would have felt like it. But slowly, the truth took its revenge. With the passage of time, with a return to freedom of speech, and with conditions more and more normal, it burst forth into the light. For example, one could write, sure of expressing the common uneasiness and of not being incorrect, that "Travelers from afar can lie with impunity . . . . I have read many accounts by the deportees and always I felt the reserve, or the pressure. Even David Rousset, at moments, misleads us; he explains too much." (From a letter by Abbé Marius Perrin published in *La Pays Roannais*, 27 October 1949), or that "*La derniére Etape* is an imbecilic film that amounts to nothing." (From a letter by Robert Pernot published in *Paroles francaises*, 27 November 1949.)

It was fifteen years before the military veteran of World War Two lost prestige in the eyes of the public; it took less than four years for the deportees. Except for that difference, their political destiny was the same. Such is the importance of truth in history.

* * * *

I would like to cite a personal story which is typical in that
it shows the relative worth which one must accord to all accounts in general.
The scene takes place in a law court, in the fall of 1945.
A woman is seated on the defendant's bench. The Resistance,
which suspected her of collaboration, had not succeeded in
killing her before the arrival of the Americans. Her husband,
however, fell in a burst of machine gun fire, at the corner of
a dark street one night in the winter of 1944-45. I never learned
what the couple actually did, although I had heard, before my
own arrest, the most improbable tales. In order to get to the
bottom of it, I went to the hearing.
There is not much in her record. The witnesses are the more
numerous and the more merciless. The principal one among
them is a deportee, a former group leader of the local Resistance—so he says! The judges are plainly embarrassed by
the accusations whose substance seems to them to be very
questionable.
The principal witness arrives. He explains that members
of his group had been informed against to the Germans and that
it could only have been by the accused and her husband who
lived in their circle and knew their activities. He adds that he
himself has seen the accused in friendly, possibly amatory,
conversation with an officer of the *Kommandantur,* who lived
over a court behind his parents' shop; that they exchanged
papers, etc. The defense attorney then begins his cross-exam-
ination:

Attorney: "You used to go to this shop then?"
Witness: "Yes, just to keep track of this business."
Attorney: "Can you describe the shop?"

(The witness describes the counter, the shelves, the window
at the back, gives the approximate dimensions, etc . . .)

Attorney: "It was through the window at the back which
looks out on the court that you saw the accused and the
officer exchange papers?"

Witness: "Yes."

Attorney: "Then, you can describe just where they were when you saw them, and where you were in the shop?"

Witness: "The two of them were at the foot of a stairway which led to the officer's room, the accused with her elbows on the railing, and the other one very near her . . ."

Attorney: "That's enough. (Turning to the court and holding a paper) Your Honor, there is no spot from which the stairway in question can be seen: here is a floor plan of the place drawn up by a draftsman."

(The Chief Judge examines the document, passes it to his colleagues, and admits the evidence.)

Chief Judge: "Do you adhere to your statement?"

Witness: "Well, that is . . . It wasn't I who saw . . . It was one of my agents who gave me the report at my request . . ."

Chief Judge: "You may step down."

The rest of the affair has no importance at all, since the witness was not arrested on the spot for perjury and since the accused, having admitted that she had attended some courses at the Franco-German Institute, which, as she said, brought about a certain number of friendly relationships between herself and certain officers of the *Kommandatur,* was in the end sentenced to a term in prison for a number of things in which she was only implicated.

Even if the witness had been cross-examined further, such questioning would probably have revealed that the agent he claimed to have sent to make a report was non-existent and that his statement consisted of nothing but those "they says" which poison the atmosphere in those small towns where everybody knows everyone else.

It is not my intention to compare all of the writings that have appeared on the German concentration camps to this experience. My only object is to show that some were no better, even among those which were most popular. And that, aside from good or bad faith, there are so many imponderables which influence the witness that one must always distrust History as it is told, especially when it is still warm.

Les jours de notre Mort, which established the prodigious talent of David Rousset, and which is discussed further in Chapter Ten, is, for example, a collection of the "they says" which ran through all of the camps and which could never be verified. It is upon this kind of questionable testimony that the author has culled the facts upon which he bases his particular interpretation. In this present work, which is concerned with truth and not with virtuosity, no extracts from it will be found.

* * * *

In 1950, I put the witnesses who had testified as to their experiences in the concentration camps into three categories: first, those who were not intellectually able to be careful witnesses, or accurate observers, and whom I called, without any pejorative intention, minor witnesses; second, the psychologists, victims of a bias, to my mind a little too subjective; and, third, the sociologists, or those claiming to be. I had found no historians, at least none worthy of the name.

On guard, so as not to fall into the error for which I was blaming others of talking about things a little too removed from my own experience, I deliberately gave up presenting a complete list of concentration camp literature of the time. Moreover, the number of witnesses was necessarily limited in each of the above-mentioned categories so as to keep this study in a manageable form: three minor witnesses (Abbé Robert Ploton; Frére Birin of the *Ecoles chrétiennes d'Epernay;* and Abbé Jean-Paul Renard); a psychologist (David Rousset); and a sociologist (Eugen Kogon). In addition, there is a witness who defies classification: Louis Martin-Chauffier. With the exception of one of them, their experiences had to do with the same camps where I had been imprisoned.

Since 1950, sustained and encouraged by the political policies which underpin the so-called "cold-war," concentration literature, which in turn supports those policies, has only grown and blossomed. For example, it is no secret that there are certain features of the foreign policy of the United States which are expressly designed to prevent any serious breakdown of relations with the Soviet Union; the contrived danger of a re-birth of Naziism and Fascism in Europe is one of them. Both Stalin and Truman fully exploited this myth, the former to keep Europe from achieving economic and political unity and from integrating Germany into such a European community, and the latter to justify in part the huge cost of maintaining an army of occupation in Germany. And, Khrushchev continues to play the same game that Stalin played with Truman with Kennedy . . . but, with a little less luck?

About 1950, the idea was revived among many Europeans that Europe – as a political entity – did exist. Formerly brought about by the haunting memory of the Franco-German wars, this pan-Europeanism was this time provoked by another obsession with two complementary aspects: on the one hand, the near certainty that, divided against itself, Europe was an easy prey for Communism; on the other hand, that no United Europe was possible without the integration of Germany. In Moscow and in Tel-Aviv, it was felt, from the first breath of this revival of pan-Europeanism that if it grew into a tempest, it could not fail to end in a united Europe, which would mean the political isolation of Russia and the end of the so-called reparation payments paid out by Germany to Israel. The counter-attack was not long in coming: two attacks, as remarkably synchronized as if they had been planned together ahead of time, were spear-headed by two propaganda organizations, the one with the title *Comité pour la recherche des crimes et des criminels de guerre,* located at Warsaw, and the other called the *World Center of Contemporary Jewish Documentation,* whose two most important branches are in Tel-Aviv and in Paris. The target was Germany. The theme was that the horrors and atrocities that had been committed during the Second World War by the Nazis were a natural vocation of Germany. Therefore, in order to prevent a re-emergence of this horrible propensity, the Germans had to be kept under severe control and very carefully segregated. The first result of this policy of defamation was, so far as I know, the publication of *Documentation sur l'extermination par les gaz* (1950) by Helmut Krausnik; the second, was *Médecin à Auschwitz* (1951) by a certain Dr. Miklos Nyiszli, a Hungarian Jew who was deported to that camp in May

1944, and the third was *Le Bréviaire de la Haine* (1951) by Leon Poliakov. Since then the deluge has not stopped: every time that the least sign of rapprochement between Germany and the other European countries is seen (e.g., C.E.C.A., Common Market, Franco-German Treaty, etc . . .) we get, with the stamp of the Warsaw Committee or of an important member of the *World Center for Jewish Documentation,* or again, of the Munich *Institut für Zeitgeschichte,* which is associated with the two, a study that each time amounts to an accusation more terrible than the last one. And, each time, the world press supports the defamation with a spectacular publicity campaign. Thus have three publications appeared one after the other: *Le Troisième Reich et les Juifs* (1953) by Leon Poliakov and Josef Wulf; *l'Histoire de Joël Brand, un echange de 10,000 camions contre un million de juifs* (1955); and *Le Lagerkommandant d'Auschwitz parle, Mémoires de Rudolf Hoess* (1958). These volumes are among the best known; to cite them all, just a list without commentary, would require an entire book. Recently, an anthology of this literature was compiled by a *Comité d'étude de la seconde guerre mondiale,* whose head office is in Paris and among whose directors are a woman by the name of Olga Wurmser of the *World Center of Jewish Documentation,* and a re-nowned unknown, who can put his hand to anything, by the name of Henri Michel. It contains excerpts from 208 author-witnesses, and I can add that it cites only those authors who strictly followed the Zionist and Communist lines because on the shelves of my library there are almost as many books which are not cited, although they are often just as accusatory, often more intelligently, and although they often have the same lack of respect for historical truth. Naturally, I was not included in this anthology which is entitled *La Tragédie de la Déportation* (1962). What makes one despair is that there are historians who are intellectually dishonest enough to support these works with their authority: Labrousse and Renouvin in France, and Rothfels in Germany, among others . . . From the United States has come Raul Hilberg, whose book, *The Destruction of the European Jews* (1961), is surely the most important of all the works that have been published on the question and the one that has best succeeded in giving the appearance—the appearance only—of being a serious and objective study. Because of its importance, I have devoted the third section of this work to an examination of *The Destruction of the European Jews,* as well as other historical studies. Finally, to be thorough one should also cite the films, whose purpose is to condition public opinion, that have been taken from this literature: *La Derniére Etape, Kapo,* the *Nuremberg Documents,* etc. . .

The reader may be tempted to place this survey of the concentration camp drama, with regard to its over-all tragic consequences alone, on the human plane, and perhaps to find that I included too much detail. If I point out that the deportation trains from France to Germany carried a hundred persons per car in cars that were intended to hold forty at a maximum, and not a hundred and twenty-five as some have claimed, it will be observed that the fact scarely mitigates the conditions of the trip. If I point out that a camp bore the name Belsen-Bergen and not Bergen-Belsen, that fact certainly does not alter the lot of those who were interned there. If I claim that the word *Kapo* is derived from the first letters of the German phrase *Konzentrationslager Arbeitpolizei,* instead of coming from the Italian *Il Capo,* that fact does not excuse the brutalities that were committed by the prisoner police. And, the bad working conditions, the hunger, the tortures, etc . . ., whether they took place in one camp or in another, whether the one reporting them saw them or not, whether they were the acts of the S.S. themselves or carried out by the prisoner trustees whom they chose at random from among the inmates, were still inhuman and brutal treatment.

I would like to make the observation, in my turn, that a whole is composed of details, and that an error of detail, whether made in good or bad faith, regardless of whether it is of a kind that is intended to mislead the observer, must logically make the observer doubt the reliability of the whole; and if there are many errors in detail . . .? And if they are almost all shown to be made in bad faith . . .?

I shall make myself better understood by referring to a news item that filled all of the papers a few years ago. Just before the outbreak of the 1939 war, a foreign student, taking advantage of a momentary distraction on the part of the guards, stole a painting by Watteau called *l'Indifférent* from the Louvre. A few days later the painting was recovered, but the student, in the meantime, had made a slight modification to it: disturbed by that hand raised in a gesture which all of the experts said was something that had been left unfinished by the artist, the student had rested it on a cane that he had added. This cane did nothing to change the figure. On the contrary it harmonized marvelously with the pose. But, it emphasized the figure's indifference, and noticeably changed the interpretation one could place on his reasons for it and his purposes. Moreover, one could argue that quite another interpretation could have been made if, instead of the cane, a pair of gloves had been put into the figure's hand, or if a bouquet of flowers had negligently been dropped from it. In spite of the fact that no one could swear that Watteau had not intended that the cane be included in the picture, the cane was effaced and the painting was put back in its place. If the curators had let the cane remain, no one would have noticed anything amiss either in the painting itself or in the general appearance of the painting galleries of the Louvre. But, if, instead of confining himself to correcting *l'Indifférent,* our student had taken it into his head to eliminate all of the enigmas of all of the other paintings, if he had put a velvet mask over the smile of the *Joconde,* rattles in all the outstretched hands of the little Jesuses lying astonished on the knees and in the arms of spell-bound Virgins, spectacles on Erasmus; and if all that had been allowed to remain, one can imagine how all of those little changes would have changed the general appearance of the entire Louvre collection!

The errors that can be found in the testimonies of the deportees are of the same kind as the cane of *l'Indifférent:* without modifying noticeably the picture of the camps, they have falsified the sense of History. Moreover, by taking these errors collectively, the viewer is confronted with a distorted picture of a similar magnitude as if he had gone through the Louvre's collection of paintings, after they had been thoroughly corrected.

The same will hold true for the reader if he will reserve his judgment, both on the secondary works and the documents which I indict and on the conclusions which certain historians, who are obviously in the service of a cause, have drawn from them, and if he will ask himself apart from all other considerations whether these documents and interpretations could be upheld in their entirety before a properly constituted court of law, that is, one that is not a kangaroo court like the Nuremberg Tribunal![1]

FOOTNOTE

1. [This view is not unique to Paul Rassinier. For example, William O. Douglas, former Associate Justice of the U.S. Supreme Court, observed that he ". . . thought at the time and still think [s] that the Nuremberg trials were unprincipled. Law was created *ex post facto* to suit the passion and clamor of the time . . . ." For additional strong "anti-Nuremberg" views by numerous notables who were in the highest echelons of the Allied governments during World War Two, see, H.K. Thompson, Jr. and Henry Strutz, eds., *Doenitz at Nuremberg: A Re-appraisal* (New York: Amber Publishing, 1976).]

Chapter Eight

The Minor Witnesses

These witnesses recount only what they saw or what they claim to have seen, without much comment. Criticism here pertains only to details, which are often small. While the great enigmas of the concentration camp problem can only be approached through the major witnesses, the others cannot be overlooked.

I. Frére Birin

Frére Birin, whose real name is Alfred Untereiner, published a chronological account of his experiences at Buchenwald and Dora entitled *16 mois de bagne* (Reims: Matot-Braine, 1946). In the prologue, he relates the circumstances that led to his arrest and deporatation. He was arrested in December, 1943, was deported to Buchenwald on January 17, 1944, and was transferred to Dora the following March 13th. We were in the same deportation convoy and in the same transport from Buchenwald to Dora. Our registration numbers were also close together: 43,642 for him, and 44,364 for me.

We were liberated together. But, inside the camp we fared differently: Thanks to the perfect knowledge that he had of

the German language, because of his Alsatian origin, he managed to get himself assigned as secretary of the *Arbeitsstatistik*
(work statistics office), a particularly privileged position,
while I shared the common lot until sickness interrupted. As
secretary of the *Arbeitsstatistik* he rendered innumerable
services to a large number of prisoners, especially to the French.
His devotion was without limits. Implicated in a plot which
I have always believed was without substance, he was incarcerated in the camp's prison for the last four or five months
of his deportation. He is presently teaching, if I am not mistaken, in the *écoles chrétiennes* at Epernay.

Frére Birin claims that *16 mois de bagne* is a faithful account.
"I wish nevertheless only to give an account of what I have
seen," writes the author (page 38). Perhaps indeed he believes
this quite sincerely. But, we shall see how faithful it really is.
He writes that in the deportation train from the Compiegne
station "They made us get into an '8 *chevaux* 40 *hommes'*
car . . . but 125 of us." (page 28)

What really happened when we left the Royallieu camp
was this: the guards lined us up in columns of fives and in
groups of 100, each group destined for one rail car. Fifteen
or twenty sick men had been brought to the station by automobile, and they had a rail car all to themselves. The last
group in the long line, which that morning was strung out
along the streets of Compiègne, between heavily armed German
soldiers, was short of men. It consisted of some forty persons
who were disbursed among all the cars, after all of the complete
groups had boarded. We got three in our car which brought our
number to one hundred and three. I doubt that there were
any special reasons why the car in which Frére Birin found
himself should have taken on twenty-five. At any rate, even
if that were the case, he should in all honesty have shown it
to be an exception.

He describes our arrival at Buchenwald as follows:

> Everyone arriving had to be disinfected. First of all, the shear-
> ing, where *ex tempore* barbers, amused at our confusion, and
> at the gashes which in haste or carelessness they gave us, mock-
> ed us. Like a flock of sheep shorn of their fleece, the prisoners
> rushed pell-mell into a big tank of water strongly dosed with
> Cresyl. Streaked with blood, dirty with filth, this bath served
> the entire detachment. *Harried with clubs,* heads had to be
> plunged under the water. At the end of each session, drowned

bodies were dragged out of that despicable basin. (Page 35, emphasis added.)

The reader, not forewarned, will not fail to think that these *ex tempore* barbers who mocked and gashed us were the S.S., and that the clubs that beat the heads were held by the same. Not at all, they were prisoners. And, since the S.S. were absent from this operation, which they only supervised from a distance no one made the prisoner barbers behave the way they should have. But, because this detail is omitted, the entire responsibility seems to fall on the S.S. This confusion, which I shall not point out again, is maintained all through the book, and in the same way.

Concerning the camp schedule, Frére Birin writes:

> Very early rising, food clearly insufficient for twelve hours of work: one liter of soup, two to two hundred and fifty grams of bread, twenty grams of margarine. (Page 40)

Why did he forget, or neglect to mention, the half-liter of coffee each morning and night, and the round of sausage or the spoon of cheese or jam which regularly came with the margarine? The fact that the food was insufficient would not have been lessened and the honesty of the information given would have suffered less. He then goes on to say:

> Since March, twelve hundred French, I among them were designated for an unknown designation. Before our departure we were issued convict's clothes, striped blue and white: *Jacket and trousers* only which could not protect us from the cold. (Page 41, emphasis added.)

I was in that convoy. Everyone was issued, in addition, an overcoat. If this clothing could not protect us from the cold it was not because there were not enough pieces but because the pieces were badly worn.

He describes the Dora camp as follows:

> The installation of the camp at Dora began in November 1943 . . . (Page 40)

Actually, the first convoy arrived there on August 28, 1943, exactly. Concerning our reception at Dora, he writes:

> There, as at Buchenwald, the S.S. were waiting for us at the unloading of the cars. A road furrowed with ruts full of water led to the camp. We ran along it at race speed. The Nazis, with big boots on, chased us and *let their dogs loose on us* . . . This

new style of "corrida" was punctuated with many gun shots
and inhuman yells . . . (Pages 43-44, emphasis added.)

I have no recollection that dogs were set on us or that any guns
were fired. On the contrary, I remember very well that the
Kapos and *Lagerschutz* (camp police composed of prisoners)
who came to take charge of us were much more aggressive and
brutal than the S.S. who had convoyed us.

Before going on to the serious errors, I would like still to
point out two more which are not so serious but which expose
the lack of accuracy of Birin's testimony, all the more so when
one recalls that the author was, through his duties in the camp,
in control of job placement, which eliminates any excuse:

> I will only mention that good old doctor Mathon, nick-named
> Papa Girard . . . (Page 81)
> For ten months I always carried on my person the Holy Res-
> ervation. Priests, constantly risking death, kept me always
> replenished. I should mention here Abbé Bourgeois, the R.P.
> Renard, Trappist, and that dear Abbé Amyot d'Inville. (Page
> 87)

For one thing, there was at Dora a doctor Mathon and a doctor
Girard. The latter was very old, and it was he who we had
nicknamed "good Papa Girard." For another, Abbé Bourgeois
died in the second month after he came to Dora, between the
10th and the 30th of April, 1944, before the departure of a
transport of the sick, among whom he was supposed to have
been included. He, therefore, could not have kept Frére Birin
supplied for ten months. One might also add that if the priests
were maltreated for the same reasons as the other deportees,
and even more because of their religious calling, they still
were not risking death by keeping in their possession the
Holy Reservation.

Now to turn to the serious errors that Frére Birin includes
in his account. He writes that:

> The wives of the S.S. also picked out their victims, and with
> even more cynicism than their husbands. What they wanted
> were fine human skins, artistically tattooed. To humor them
> an assembly was ordered on the parade grounds, Adam naked
> was the rule. Then, these women went up and down the ranks,
> as if at a style show, and made their choices. (Pages 73-74)

It is not correct to say that these things took place at Dora.
There was one case of a lamp shade made of tattooed human

skin at Buchenwald. It figures in the case of Ilse Koch, who was called "the Bitch of Buchenwald." And, even at Buchenwald, Frére Birin could not have been present at the selection of the victims, as is claimed in his statement that is already cited from page 38, since these incriminating activities took place before we arrived at Buchenwald, if, in fact, they ever did take place at all. He gives to this selection of victims the feeling that it was something that happened regularly and as a matter of course and that his description is quite precise. If the person, who had placed the event at Buchenwald, in the first place, from having seen evidence of the crime (the lamp shades in question), did so in the same fashion, how can one avoid thinking that the accusation against Ilse Koch rests on very fragile grounds?[1]

To conclude the matter, I shall point out that from February through March 1944, a camp rumor at Buchenwald maintained that two *Kapos,* one from the *Steinbruch* (quarry) and the other from the *Gärtnerei* (garden) were responsible for that crime, which earlier had been perpetrated by them with the complicity of almost all of their colleagues. The two comrades had, it was said, made a business of the killing of tattooed prisoners, whose skins they sold for various favors to Ilse Koch and others, through the intermediary of the *Kapo* of the crematorium service and of some S.S. personnel who looked the other way. But, did the wife of the commandant of the camp, and the other wives of officers, walk around the camp looking for fine tattoo specimens, whose owners they themselves designated to be killed for their skins? Did they organize roll-calls in the nude to facilitate this search? These allegations I can neither confirm nor deny. All that I can say is that, contrary to what Frére Birin attests, these things never took place at Dora, nor at Buchenwald, during our common internment there.

> Where there was a sure case of sabotage, the hanging was carried out in a more cruel fashion. Those about to be executed were lifted up from the ground very slowly by an electric winch. Not getting the fatal jerk that kills the victim and often breaks his neck, the poor men went through all the stages of agony . . .

> Other times a butcher's hook was placed under the jaw of the condemned man who was thus hung in that barbarous manner. (Page 76)

It is true that at the end of the war—i.e., between the end of
1944 and the end of the spring of 1945—acts of sabotage
became so numerous that groups of guilty men were hanged
at a time. The S.S. took to holding executions in the Tunnel
itself, with the use of a pulley worked by a winch, and not
just on the parade grounds with gallows that looked like the goal
posts on the ends of football fields. On March 8, 1945, nineteen condemned men were hanged in this way, and on Palm
Sunday fifty-seven were executed. Palm Sunday, incidentally,
was eight days before the Liberation, when we could even
hear the Allied cannon very near and when the outcome of the
war could not have been in any doubt in the minds of the
S.S.! But, the story of the butcher's hook, which was told
about Buchenwald, where the instrument was found in the
crematory oven, was unlikely to have been true of Dora. In
any case, I never heard anything about it in the camp itself,
and it did not fit in with the way things were done at Dora.

> On the instigation of the notorious *Oberscharführer* Sanders,
> S.S., with whom I had something to do, other methods of
> execution were used for the saboteurs.
>
> The unfortunates were made to dig narrow ditches, in which
> their comrades were forced to bury them up to the neck.
> They were left for a certain length of time. After that an
> S.S. with a long handled axe cut off their heads.
>
> But the sadism of some of the S.S. led them to discover
> an even more cruel death. They ordered other prisoners to
> pour barrow loads of sand over their poor heads. I am still
> haunted by the looks, etc . . .   (Page 77)

This, too, was never done at Dora. But the story was told to
me in almost the same words, in that camp, by prisoners who
had been transferred there from other camps and who all
claimed to have been present at the scene: Mauthausen, Birkenau, Flossenburg, Neuengame, etc . . . Back in France I came
across references to it by various writers; but none concerned
Buchenwald or Dora because it was not desirable to place the
story, in a written testimony, at a camp where it did not take
place. French public opinion, catching an author in a deliberate
error, would have become suspicious about all the accounts
concerning all of the camps, and German public opinion also
would have made an issue of the lie.

Concerning the fate of the deportees, Frére Birin reports as follows:

> As *Geheimnisträger* (those who knew the secret of the V1 and V2) we knew we were condemned to death and destined to be massacred as soon as the Allies approached. (Page 97)

Here it is not a question of a fact but of speculation. Such speculation was engaged in by all the writers of memoirs about the camps up to and including Leon Blum in *Le Dernier Mois.* Blum found some semblance of justification for his speculation in the drownings in the Baltic of some deportees who a short time before Liberation were loaded onto boats which were set adrift and which were allegedly sunk from the shore by gunfire. In addition, he pointed to the statement of an S.S. doctor at Dora who confirmed the existence of secret orders to that effect, and who, in so doing, saved his own life.

In any case, the *Geheimnisträger* at Dora were not massacred; nor was anyone in the evacuation convoy in which Leon Blum was included. For a long time it was maintained that the absence of massacres, which was the case in all the camps, resulted solely because, in the turmoil of the German collapse, the S.S. had neither the time nor the means to carry out their sinister execution plans. Then one day, January 6, 1951, light was thrown suddenly on the worth of that assumption. On that day, in *Le Figaro-littéraire,* Mr. Jacques Sabille, of the *Center of Jewish Documentation* at Paris wrote under the title *"Un Juif négocie avec Himmler"* that:

> It was thanks to pressure from Günther, put on Himmler through the intermediary of Kersten (his personal physician), that the fratricidal order to sack the camps at the approach of the Allies—without sparing the guards—remained a dead letter.

This means that this order, supposedly received by everyone, and brandished with such forceful indignation against the accused at Nuremberg, although not one of the prosecutors could produce a copy of it, was never given by anyone who had the authority to issue it. In 1960, in the *Les Mains du Miracle,* a study by Dr. Kersten, Joseph Kessel confirmed this account unreservedly.

For having testified that the order actually did exist, Dr. Piazza, the S.S. physician at Dora, saved his life, and a number of good marks were awarded him, among them the following statement, made on the 25th day of June, 1954, at the Struthof Trial, by Dr. Bogaerts, Major-Doctor at Etterbeek (Belgium):

> I had managed to get myself detailed to the infirmary of the camp, and there I was under S.S. Doctor Piazza's orders, the only man at Struthof with any humane feelings.

Now at Dora, where this Dr. Piazza assumed the position of head doctor of the camp, opinion was unanimous in putting the responsibility on him for all that was inhuman in the diagnosis and treatment of illness in the camp. The reports from the *Revier* (infirmary) were crammed with his misdeeds, which, it was said, his assistant Dr. Kuntz was only able to mitigate with great difficulty. Those who knew him at Struthof spoke of him in horrifying terms. I personally had contact with him and agree with all those in the same position: he was a brute among brutes. Back in France, I was surprised to see so many certificates of good behavior given—by privileged prisoners, true—to a man whom everyone at the camp, even the better disposed, wanted to see hanged. I could only understand it after I had learned that he had been the first, and for a long time the only one, to attest to the authenticity of the order to destroy all of the camps on the approach of the Allies, and to murder all of their occupants, guards included. It was his reward for false testimony; the worth of which at the time could not be known, but which was indispensable for the fabrication of a theory itself indispensable to a policy!

As for the drownings in the Baltic, it has long been a question as to whether they were an isolated instance, due to the excessive zeal of underlings, or whether they were part of a general plan drawn up in various departments on the initiative of Himmler, head of the German Police, and later Minister of the Interior. In reality, this is what took place: On the 3rd of May, 1945, in the roads at Neustadt near Lubeck, three ships that were loaded with deportees, who, by an agreement between Himmler and Count Folke Bernadotte, were to be transported to Sweden and from there repatriated to their various countries, were waiting for the order to sail; they were the *Cap Arcona,* the *Deutschland,* and the *Thielbeck.* On that same day, the three ships were attacked by British aircraft, which persisted for hours in the attack, even though the people on the ships hoisted up, from the moment of the first bomb, white flags, and spread out on the decks all the linen, towels, sheets, etc. that they had. But, nothing worked, and the attack was not ended until the pilots decided that no one was left alive on board. There were 7,000 dead, buried in a cemetery especially made for them. Most of the victims were of foreign nationalities and came from thirty different countries. However, prior to the burial, the mass of bodies that had been taken out of the smoldering ships was piled up on the shore. Photographs and films made of the corpses—piled like so much cordwood— were circulated all over the world, and the commentaries of many journalists made them appear as a new atrocity to add to Germany's charge. This was all the easier since the shore batteries of the German D.C.A. had opened fire on the British warplanes, and that fact provided a perfect occasion for spreading the word that the Germans had fired on the three ships, under orders.

The mystery has been cleared up for almost ten years now. It is known that the three ships were destroyed by an attack of British warplanes. This fact is admitted by historians all over the world, even those of the *World Center of Jewish Documentation* and the *Institut für Zeitgeschichte* at Munich. But in *La Tragédie de la Déportation* (1962) Madame Olga Wurmser and Mr. Henri Michel still maintain that the drownings in the Baltic were the work of German artillery which had fired on the three ships from the shore. And, no one contests their error— not even the *Center of Jewish Documentation* or the *Institut für Zeitgeschichte* of Munich, which not only let it stand but which continue to give praise to that "remarkable work."

II. Abbé Jean-Paul Renard

Deported with registration number 39,727, Abbé Jean-Paul Renard preceded Frére Birin and myself by several weeks to Buchenwald; it was Dora where we met him again. He published a collection of poems inspired by a sometimes moving mysticism with the title *Chaines et Lumières.* These poems consist of a series of spiritual reactions rather than any attempt at objective testimony. One of them, nevertheless, enumerates some facts: *J'ai vu, j'ai vu, et j'ai vécu . . .* Frére Birin published it in an appendix to his own work, which has been discussed in the first section of this chapter. One of the poems reads:

> "I saw going into the showers thousands and thousands of
> persons over whom poured out, instead of liquid, asphyx-
> iating gases. I saw those who were unfit for work injected
> in the heart."

Actually, Abbé Jean-Paul Renard saw nothing of the kind
because gas chambers did not exist either at Buchenwald or
at Dora. As for the injections, it was not done at Buchenwald at
the time he went through there. When I pointed that fact out
to him at the beginning of 1947, he answered, "Right, but
that's only a figure of speech . . . and since those things existed
somewhere, it is of no importance."

I found his reasoning delightful. At the moment I did not
dare to retort that the Battle of Fontenoy was also an historical
reality, but that was no reason for saying, even as a figure of
speech, that he had been present. Nor did I say that, if twenty-
eight thousand survivors of the Nazi camps had claimed that
they had been present at all of the horrors set forth by all of
the testimonies, the camps would assume, in the eyes of history,
quite a different image than if each survivor had confined himself to telling only what he had actually seen. Nor did I mention
that it was in our interest that not one of us should be guilty
of lying or exaggeration.

When, in July 1947, *J'ai vu, j'ai vu et j'ai vécu* appeared in
Chaines et Lumières, I had the satisfaction of noting that,
although the author had allowed his testimony on the injections to remain in its entirety, he had nevertheless honestly
attributed his statement on them as well as on the gas chambers
to another prisoner, who, in turn, had laid the responsibility
on still another deportee.

III. Abbé Robert Ploton

Abbé Robert Ploton was curé at the *Nativité* at St. Etienne
and presently is Curé at Firminy. He was deported to Buchenwald with the number 44,015, in January, 1944, in the same
convoy with me. We ended up together in Block 48, which we
left, also together, for Dora. His account of his deportation,
entitled *Montluc á Dora*, was published by Dumas in March,
1946 at St. Etienne.

Montluc à Dora is an unpretentious testimony of 90 pages. Abbé Ploton states the facts simply, as he saw them, without going into much detail and often without checking himself. Manifestly he is quite sincere, and if he sins, it is out of a natural predisposition for the superficial, heightened by the eagerness with which he recounts his memories. For example, when the German collapse came, he was sent to Bergen-Belsen. But, he writes "Belsen-Bergen" throughout the chapter in which he tells about this, so that one cannot think that it was a mere typographical error. And he misses other facts: In Block 48, at Buchenwald, he heard someone say, "We are under the orders of a German prisoner, Communist ex-deputy of the *Reichstag*," (Page 26), and he accepted that statement as being fact. Actually, the particular Block Chief in question, Erich, was only the son of a Communist deputy.

As concerns the camp food, it is doubtless in the same manner that he writes:

> On principle, the daily menu consisted of a liter of soup, 400 grams of a very heavy bread, 20 grams of margarine extracted from coal, and a dessert which varied: sometimes a spoon of jam, sometimes white cheese, or again some ersatz sausage. (Page 63-64)

So many people have said that the margarine was made from coal, and without being questioned, that the exact origin of that product is no longer brought up. After all, Louis Martin-Chauffier did even better in writing that:

> It seems that nothing pleases them [the S.S.] unless it is artificial; and the margarine that they stingily distributed to us derived all its flavor from having been a product made from coal. [The cardboard box was labelled "Guaranteed to contain no fat."] (*L'homme et la bete,* Page 95)

When Abbé Ploton undertakes to speak of the categories of prisoners he finds eight classifications, without realizing that there were in reality thirty and when he talks about the camp regime, he writes:

> One of the most effective and ignoble ways to moral degradation, *inspired by the instructions in "Mein Kampf,"* is to charge a few prisoners, chosen almost exclusively from the Germans, with the policing of the camp. (Page 28, emphasis added.)

He does not know that this ignoble procedure is used, precisely because it is effective, in all the prisons of the world, and that that was the case long before Hitler wrote *Mein Kampf*.[2] Shall we recall that *Dante n'avait rien vu,* by Albert Londres, establishes France in the application of this system in her prisons and jails?

On the duration of the roll-calls, which plagued all of the prisoners, here is the explanation that he gives:

> We wait for the count to be verified, a laborious job *the length of which depends on the humor of the S.S. Rapport-Führer.* (Page 59, emphasis added.)

The length of the roll-calls, if it depended on the humor of the *Rapport-Führer,* also depended upon the competence of those persons who were in charge of establishing every day the number of the men present. Among them there were S.S. personnel who generally knew how to count, but there were also illiterate, or almost so, prisoners who had become clerks in the *Arbeitsstatistik* only as a favor. It must not be forgotten that the employment of each prisoner in a concentration camp was determined by his ability to get around and not by his ability to do the job. At Dora, as everywhere else, it happened that masons became accountants, accountants became masons or carpenters, wheelwrights became doctors or surgeons, and it could even happen that a doctor or a surgeon became a fitter, an electrician or an earth-works laborer.

Concerning the injections, Abbé Ploton sides with the general view:

> Meanwhile the infirmary had to be expanded and an increasing number of its barracks were built on the hillside. Those with incurable tuberculosis ended their poor existence there as a result of a euthanasia injection.

This practice, as I have explained in earlier pages, is not true.

With the exception of these remarks, this witness is not tainted by a mania for exaggeration. He is simply crushed by an experience which was too much for him. And the inaccuracies of which he is guilty are only minor when compared with those of Frère Birin; they also carry much less influence. But, a concern for objectivity, nevertheless, requires that they be noted.

FOOTNOTES

1. So fragile was the case against Ilse Koch that the Augsburg Court of Assizes, dealing with the case, refused to hold her for trial due to the lack of evidence.

2. See Appendix A to this volume: *La discipline a la Maison centrale de Riom*, in 1939, by Pierre Bernard, who was interned there, and *Dans les prisons de la "Liberation,"* a testimony given by A. Paraz.

Chapter Nine

Louis Martin-Chauffier

He falls between the lesser witnesses, whom he surpasses due to his effort to explain in a learned way the experiences which he lived through, and the great tenors like David Rousset, whose power of analysis he lacks, or like Eugen Kogon, whose exactness and attention to detail he lacks. Given that, and taking into account the place that he occupies in post-war literature and journalism, he cannot be classified with either the first or with the second.

Martin-Chauffier is a writer by profession. He belongs to that class of writers called "committed." He is committed, but he frees himself often enough—in order to re-commit himself, since commitment is second nature to him. He has been known as a fellow-traveler, and he is now an anti-Communist. Probably, moreover, for the same reasons and under the same circumstances—i.e., it is the thing to do. He could not fail to give his testimony on the concentration camps for a couple of reasons: First, because his profession is writing. Second, because he had to get straight for himself what had happened to him. The others profited by him. Doubtless, he did not realize that he was saying just what everybody else said, although he expressed it differently. The title of his testimony is *L'Homme et la Bete* (1948, Gallimard). As far as originality is concerned, he saw the cardboard boxes, which contained the margarine—made of coal, of course—which were given to us with the label "Guaranteed to contain no fat." Other than that, his testimony is a long chain of reasoning based on facts which the author has isolated from all moral or other reflections.

I. The Line of Argument

Before he was deported to Neuengame, Louis Martin-Chauffier was for a while at Compiègne-Royallieu. He knew Captain Douce there, who was then camp elder. Here is his opinion of him:

> Captain Douce, "doyen" of the camp and zealous servant of those who had put him in that position, perched on a table, doing his figures out loud, chain-smoking the cigarettes which had been refused to us, against regulations. (p. 51).

At Neuengame, he knew Andre who was one of the important inmates in the camp, an official with authority, chosen from the prisoners by the SS. This is the portrait he gives of him:

> Narrowly watched by the S.S., a most suspicious sort, he was forced, in order to keep the role he had chosen and gotten with difficulty, to speak roughly to the prisoners, to make a show of being without feeling, unbending, and brutal in his language. He knew that the least sign of weakness would inexorably bring denunciation down on him, and his immediate dismissal. Nearly everyone was taken in by his manner, believed him to be working with the SS, their creature, our enemy. Since he was responsible for the sorting out and allocation of posts, he was blamed for all those he sent to the *Kommandos,* with apparent indifference, deaf to prayers, pleas, recriminations . . . When a thousand deportees were to go to the *Kommandos,* and only about 990 were piling into the cattle cars, no one realized how many ruses Andre had used, all the risks he had run, to preserve ten men from probable death . . . He knew that he was universally detested or suspect. He had chosen it that way, preferring the service he could render to esteem. . .

As I saw Andre, he accepted in the same spirit the menacing cordiality of the SS, the corresponding servility of the *Kapos* and the Block chiefs, the hostility of the mass. I think that he had risen above humilation, substituted a glacial purity for his own inner courage, a stranger even to himself. He had renounced his being, in favor of a duty which in his eyes was deserving of this submission. (Pages 167-168-169.)

Thus of the two men fulfilling the same function, one gets the laconic severity and contempt of the author, while the other enjoys not only his approving indulgence, but even his admiration. When one examines this inconsistency further, one learns, during the course of reading the work, that Andre rendered considerable service to Martin-Chauffier in circumstances when his life was in danger. I did not know Captain Douce at Compiègne, but it is very likely that, compared with Andre, his only mistake was in not knowing how to choose the people for whom he did favors—since he, too, certainly had his favorites—and in having too limited a familiarity with literature to know that there was in his realm a certain number of Martin-Chauffiers, and even Martin-Chauffier himself. And it is not beside the point to add that this kind of reasoning leads to:

I have always admired, with some fear and some repulsion THOSE who, in order to serve their country or a cause they consider just, are willing to face all the consequences of duplicity: the contemptuous defiance of the enemy employing them, and his confidence when HE deceives THEM; and the disgust of his comrades in battle who see in HIM a traitor; and the abject comraderie of the real traitors or those who have simply sold themselves, who seeing HIM doing the same thing, consider HIM as ONE of them. It requires a self-renunciation that is beyond me, a guile which confounds me and goes against my grain. [1] (Page 168)

One wonders whether Pétain's attorneys might not make use of this kind of argument, whose pungency comes from having issued from the pen of one of crypto-Communism's finest ornaments. If Pétainism becomes fashionable again, Martin-Chauffier, in any case, will have reason to be proud of it, and perhaps to profit from it . . .

II. Another Line of Argument

In the camp the author was talking with a doctor who said to him:

> There are at present in the camp three times as many sick people as I can take care of. The war will be over in five or six months, at the latest. It is up to me to see to it that the greatest possible number hold out. I have decided. You and others, you will get better slowly. If I send you back to the camp in this state and at this season (we were at the end of December) you will be dead in three weeks. I am going to keep you here. And—listen carefully—I am going to bring in those who are not so seriously afflicted, those that a stay in the *Revier* can save. Those who are lost, I am going to reject.[2] I cannot afford the luxury of letting them in just to give them a peaceful death. What I can assure is the care of the living. The others will die eight days sooner: in any case, they would die too soon. It can't be helped, I am not here to be sentimental, but to be effective. That's my job. All my colleagues are in agreement, that's the right thing to do . . . Everytime that I refuse to let in a dying man, and he looks at me with stupor, fear, with reproach, I would like to explain to him that I am exchanging his lost life for a life that can be saved. He would not understand, etc. . . (Page 160)

As far as admittance into the infirmary is concerned, I had the experience that one could get into the *Revier* and be cared for (in a loose manner of speaking) for reasons among which sickness or infirmity were sometimes only secondary; know-how, pull, politics and bribery were the common reasons for getting a hospital bed. I attributed this fact to the general conditions of concentration camp life. Further, if some prisoner doctors behaved the way Martin-Chauffier says this one did, that conduct should be recorded as both a philosophical argument and as a causal element, side by side with the "sadism" of the SS, in explaining the large number of deaths. For it takes a great deal of knowledge, confidence, and also presumption, for a doctor to determine in a few minutes who can be saved and who cannot. And, I am very much afraid that if such were the case generally among doctors, then once having taken this first step toward a new code of professional conduct, they might progressively arrive at another by asking themselves no longer who *could* be saved but who *ought* to be saved and who *ought not* and by resolving this problem of conscience on grounds that have nothing to do with therapeutics.

III. The Regime of the Camps

The treatment inflicted on us by the S.S. was the execution of a plan worked out in high places. It could have refinements, embellishments, flourishes, due to the initiative, the imagination, the tastes of the head of the camp; sadism has nuances. The overall plan was fixed. Before killing us or making us die, we had to be debased. (Page 85)

During the occupation, there existed in France an Association of the Families of Deportees and Political Internees. If a family sent an inquiry to the Association for information about what had become of its deportee, it received, in the return mail, a report coming from those German "high places." Here is this report:[3]

Weimar camp. —The camp is situated 9 km. from Weimar and is connected to it with a railroad. It lies at an altitude of 800 m. It consists of three enclosures of concentrically strung barbed wire. In the first enclosure, the prisoners' barracks, between the first and the second, the factories and the workshops where T.S.F. accessories are manufactured, pieces of machinery, etc . . . Between the second and the third lies an area not yet built upon, which has just been cleared of trees, and where they are laying out camp streets and a small railroad.

The first enclosure of barbed wire is electrified and is marked out with a great many watch towers, on top of which there are three armed men. No sentinels in the second and third enclosures, but within the area of the factories there is an SS caserne; during the night they patrol with dogs, likewise in the third enclosure.

The camp spreads over 8 km. and contains about 30,000 internees. At the beginning of the Nazi regime, its enemies were interned there. The population is partly French, partly foreign, anti-Nazi Germans, but who remain Germans, and who make up most of the Block chiefs. There are also Russians, among them officers of the Red Army, Hungarians, Poles, Belgians, Dutch, etc . . .
The camp regulations are as follows:
4:30—Rise, wash, under surveillance, stripped to the waist; washing the body is obligatory.

5:30—a half liter of soup or coffee, with 450 gr. of bread (at times they have less bread, but they have an abundant ration of potatoes of good quality), 30 gr. margarine, a slice of sausage or a piece of cheese.
12:00 noon - coffee.
18:30 - a liter of good thick soup.

In the morning at six, leave for work. Assembly is by job, factory, quarry, woodcutters, etc . . . In each detachment the men line up in rows of five, holding each other by the arm so that the ranks are well aligned and separated. Then they leave, with music at the head (70 or 80 musicians from among the prisoners, in uniform: red pants, blue jackets with black trimming.)

Sanitation in the camp is very good. At the head of this is Professor Richet, deportee. Medical checkup every day. There are numerous doctors, an infirmary and a hospital, just as for a regiment. The internees wear the costume of German convicts made of artificial cloth, relatively warm. Their underclothing has been disinfected on arrival. There is one blanket for two men.

There is no chapel in the camp. There are, however, a number of priests among the internees, but they generally have concealed their calling. These priests gather together the faithful for talks, recitation of the rosary, etc . . . Free time — Complete liberty in the camp on Sunday afternoon. This afternoon is enlivened by a theatrical group organized by the prisoners. Cinema, once or twice per week (German films), radio in each barrack (German news). Fine concerts are given by the orchestra made up of internees.

All the prisoners agree that they are better off at Weimar than they were at Fresnes or in the other French prisons.

We call attention to the families of the deportees that the Allied bombardment of the factories at Weimar toward the end of August did not find a single victim among the deportees of the camp.

Jean Puissant, who quoted the above, followed it with this appraisal: "a monument of deceit and lies."

Self-evidently, it is written in a benevolent style. It does not say that in the workshops of Buchenwald the pieces of machinery being made were weapons. It does not speak of the hangings for sabotage, the numerous roll-calls, the conditions of work, or the physical punishments. It does not point out that the Sunday afternoon liberty was subject to limitations which depended upon what went on in the place; nor does it say that if the priests gathered together their faithful for talks and prayers, that such gatherings were clandestine and were held at the risk that they might be taken for a meeting of conspirators. It even lies when it says that the deportees thought they were better off than in French prisons, that the August 1944 bombardment had no victims among the internees, and that most of the trains leaving Compiègne or Fresnes at that date were headed for Weimar.

But, such as it is this text is closer to the truth than the testimony of Frére Birin, particularly with regard to the food. And, it still is a resumé of the regulations of the camps as they were established by the higher levels of the Nazi government. That these regulations were not applied often at the local level is certain. History will tell why. Probably, it will consider the war as the major cause as well as the principle of camp administration by the prisoners themselves. The deterioration which, in a hierarchical administration, all orders undergo as they are handed down from the top to the bottom will be listed also. This deterioration can be seen, for example, in a regiment where the orders of the colonel are delivered by the lieutenant to the sergeant who has the responsibility for their execution. Everyone knows that in a caserne it is the sergeant who is dangerous, not the colonel.

For my part, I am convinced that, within the constraints imposed by the condition of total war, there was nothing to prevent the prisoners who administered over us, who commanded us, who supervised us, and who cadred us, from making life in a concentration camp something resembling closely the picture that the Germans presented to the families of prisoners.

IV. Mal-Treatment

I saw my unfortunate comrades, guilty only of not having strong enough arms, die under blows lavished on them by German political prisoners promoted to overseer, who had become the accomplices of their former enemies. (Page 92)

Those brutes, while striking, did not at first intend to kill; nevertheless they did kill in an access of joyous fury, eyes bloodshot, face scarlet and foam on their lips, because they could not stop themselves; they had to go to the very end of their pleasure.

Here we have a deed which, for change, is imputed to the prisoners without any qualifications. One never knows: it is possible that there are people who kill "in an access of joyous fury" and whose only purpose is "to go to the very end of their pleasure." In the normal world, there are abnormal people; likewise, there can also be some in a world where everything is abnormal, such as a concentration camp. But, I am rather led to think that if a *Kapo*, a Block Chief, or a camp elder let himself go to that extent, it was for motives arising from more likely reasons: the need for revenge; the desire to please the masters who had given him his choice post; the desire to hold onto it at any price, etc. I believe that even if they had resorted to the brutality which is described above, they usually stopped short of killing a man, since his death might have gotten them in trouble with the SS, at least at Buchenwald and Dora.

In spite of this explanation, Martin-Chauffier must be forgiven for having cited two more actions whose criminal nature can in no way be considered the result of the execution of a plan "worked out in high places":

> Each week the *Kapo* of the *Revier* made his rounds (he was completely ignorant about it), examined the temperature charts whose margins were covered with remarks about a disturbing diagnosis, looked at the sick: if he didn't like their looks, he stated that they were to leave, whatever condition they were in. The doctor tried to forestall or influence his decision, which was difficult to foresee, since the *Kapo* whose impressions took the place of knowledge was a lunatic, besides. (Page 185).

> The frigid draft, the obligatory washing stripped to the waist, were hygienic provisions. Each killing process was thus cloaked in the guise of sanitation. This proved to be most efficacious. All those who suffered from some chest ailment were carried out in a few days. (Page 192).

Nothing obliged the *Kapo,* the *Stubendienst,* or the *Pfleger* of the *Revier,* to let a draft of ice cold air through, to make the unfortunate patients in their care wash bare-chested in cold water, or to render medical decisions without the concurrence of the treating physicians. Nevertheless, they did do it, with the aim of pleasing the SS, who most of the time knew nothing about it, and of holding on to the positions which saved their lives. One would like to have seen Martin-Chauffier direct his

accusations against them with as much vigor as he has done
against the SS, or—at least—divide the responsibility between
them.

V. A Qualified Witness?

The following is an account of Martin-Chauffier that was
written by Dominique Canavaggio (former editor-in-chief of
Temps de Paris and son-in-law of Pastor Boegner):

> Louis Martin-Chauffier—who later was to be arrested by the
> *Gestapo* and sent to Auschwitz—was a contributor to *Sept
> jours,* a weekly newspaper of Jean Prouvost. One morning
> when I was in Lyon he visited me. His face was distorted with
> anxiety. He said, "My daughter has tuberculosis; her condition
> is very serious. I have tried to have her treated in France. It
> is impossible: nowhere here does one find combined the
> necessary altitude, comfortable accommodations and board;
> only a sojourn in Switzerland could save her. Do you think
> that she could obtain a travel pass from Laval?"
>
> I promised him even to attempt the impossible, and upon my
> return I went immediately to see the head of the government
> in Vichy. Impossible was truly the right word, for since
> November 1942 the Germans tightly controlled all travel in
> and out of France at the Swiss frontier; they allowed, prac-
> tically, no one to cross the border except some official persons.
> Besides, the name of Martin-Chauffier was already at that time
> suspected by Laval and was not likely, for that reason, to
> make things easier. Laval listened to my request without
> interrupting me, then when I had finished, he said, "Martin-
> Chauffier? . . . He is, I suppose, the fellow who at the time of
> Munich wrote an article in which he demanded that I should
> be sent to the gallows?"
>
> "Yes," Mr. President, "that is he."
>
> There was a moment of silence. I looked at him firmly. Finally
> he spoke, "Tell him that his daughter will go to Switzerland
> . . . Arrange the formalities with Bousquet." "Thank you, Mr.
> President; I was sure that you would do it. And I am not sure
> that Martin-Chauffier will be grateful . . . "
>
> He motioned me back and said, "I want no thinks. I do it from
> a sense of duty to mankind."

As we have seen, Martin-Chauffier, was especially suited to
become one of the leaders of the Resistance Movement in

France. He furthermore "honored" with his (episodic) collaboration *Le Figaro, Paris-Press,* and *Paris Match.* The biographical reference work, *Pharos,* writes of him that before the war he made his political opinions clearly recognizable, and his sympathy for Communism during the Civil War in Spain confirmed them. In 1939 he traveled in the U.S.S.R. The year 1945 found him, naturally, again on the side of the Communists in the famous National Committee of Authors and among the most furious of persecutors.

Without doubt, he had to try to be forgiven for what had happened between these two dates. For today, Martin-Chauffier, like Eugen Kogon and David Rousset, holds himself aloof (or acts as if he held himself aloof) from the Communists, whose game he has played and continues to play. But, for how long? I pose this question for a very good reason.

On March 18, 1953, when I had just been sentenced by the Court of Appeals at Lyon, Jean Paulhan, since elected to the membership of the French Academy, wanted to express his sympathy; a 100,000 franc fine, together with an assessment of damages, in the sum of 800,000 francs, and a sentence of eight days in jail (which was suspended) had seemed alarming to him, and being less familiar than I was with such things, he did not know, as I did, that this judgment would surely be reversed by the Supreme Court. This is what he wrote:

> I have followed (from a distance) your trial and the iniquitous judgment that ended it. Your book was splendid, and I wish I had written it. Perhaps it is due to it, and to the obvious absurdity of the quarrels they have tried to pick with you, that I am indebted for not having been prosecuted.[4] As for Martin-Chauffier, who indeed understands grammar but poorly, he was busy in 43 getting for the Germans (specifically from Maison Beraud, metallurgy, 315 rue Grimaldi, Lyon, for Captain Schwenn) ferrous and non-ferrous ores. That is what gives him the right to speak. Yours, with all sympathy.

The witness for the prosecution at my trial, Martin-Chauffier had not dared confront me at the bar, and that is easy to understand, but he all the same sent the President of the Court a telegram in which he demanded "a merciless condemnation."

Moral: Ah! these witnesses – excuse me: Ah! these Resistants! That is all.

FOOTNOTES

1. This quotation has not been faked, in spite of the error in syntax that might make one think so, which is emphasized by the words in capital letters. In *"Le Droit de vivre"* of December 15, 1950, Martin-Chauffier claimed, in these words, that the text was correctly written: "It is useless to add that there is no error of syntax − another lie − but that a comma, inserted by M. Rassinier in place of the colon that I had put there, could deceive those not very sure of their grammar." For Martin-Chauffier is convinced that one nail drives out another. And he is too "sure of his grammar" for one to be able easily to count on him for the relations that exist between the verb and its subject or the pronoun and its antecedent. The moral: a gentleman who comes out of the *Ecole des Chartres* is evidently not obliged to know what is expected of a child of ten to get into the 6th grade. Not wanting to haggle over a penny we re-inserted the colon claimed by Mr. Martin-Chauffier which an unfortunate slip had indeed replaced with a semi-colon in the first edition: the reader who can see that this changes anything is kindly requested to write to us.

2. Emphasized in the text.

3. As far as I know this has only been cited by Jean Puissant in his book, *La Colline sans oiseaux* (Editions du Rond-Point, 1945). A generally honest and detailed monograph, one of the best testimonies on the camps.

4. On February 20, 1952, Jean Paulhan had written an "Open Letter to the Directors of the Resistance" (Gallimard-Paris) in which he had questioned the prevailing orthodoxy, and which had produced as much emotion as *Le Mensonge d'Ulysse.*

Chapter Ten

The Psychologists: David Rousset and the Universe of the Concentration Camp

Of all of the witnesses, none has matched David Rousset's ability, power of evocation, and exactness in reconstructing the general atmosphere of the camps, of which he is the acknowledged great spokesman, worldwide. Neither, has any other witness fictionalized his account more or in a better fashion.

I am afraid that history will remember his name; but mostly for his literary quality. At this level of history, properly so-called, the wrapping outdoes the contents. He was, moreover, aware of this fact and attempted to forestall objections:

> I have reported certain things as they took place at Buchenwald, and not as they are described in documents published subsequently . . .
>
> . . . Especially are there contradictions in details, not only in the testimonies, but in the documents. Most of the texts published up to the present are concerned only with aspects quite outside life in the camps, or are apologies in the form of allusions which affirm principles rather than assemble facts. Such documents are valuable, but only if one is intimately acquainted with what is being said; in that case they often

> provide another hitherto unperceived link. I have made a
> special effort to bring forth the relations between the groups
> in their actual complexity and in their dynamics. (*Les jours
> de notre Mort,* Appendix, page 764.)

This sort of reasoning allows him totally, or nearly so, to
ignore the documents, and, in view of the fact that those
pertaining to the camps in the East are both very few and very
poor, to state that, "Recourse to direct testimony is the only
proper way to proceed." He then selects from these direct
testimonies those that best illustrate his way of looking at
things at the moment. "Given these conditions," he acknowledges, "it was a bold—perhaps one should say, rash—venture
to want to present a panorama of the whole of the concentration camp world." *(Ibid.)*

One could not put it better than he does himself. But then,
why describe the camps using this method in which all is based
on categorical assertion?

L'Univers concentrationnaire (Pavois, 1946) had a deserved
success. In the midst of the minor witnesses who howled for
vengeance and death on the heels of the defeated Germans, it
tried to lay the responsibilities on Nazism and, by so doing,
marked a new direction.

By way of illustration of the atmosphere at the time, take
Frère Birin, who penned the following warning:

> The French should know and remember that the same errors
> will bring back the same horrors. They should be informed of
> the character and shortcomings of their neighbors across the
> Rhine, a race of dominators, and that is why No. 43,652 wrote
> these lines. Frenchmen, be vigilant and never forget. (*16 mois
> de bagne,* p. 117.)

And, that was the tone in all the French press, too. *"Le boche"*
was on everybody's lips, with the snarl that goes with the word
when it is pronounced correctly. In this atmosphere of hatred,
pacifist France was grateful to David Rousset for having concluded with these words:

> The existence of the camps is a warning. German society,
> both because of the strength of its economic structure, and
> the ruthlessness of the crisis which crushed it, has experienced
> a decomposition exceptional in the present situation of the
> world. But it would be easy to show that the traits most
> characteristic of S.S. mentality and the social substructures,

can be found in many other areas in world society. Less pronounced, however, and certainly not to be compared with the
developments we have seen in the Great Reich. But it is only
a question of circumstances. One would be guilty of deception
if one pretended that it is impossible for other peoples to have
the same experience because it is against their nature. Germany
has interpreted, with the originality peculiar to her history,
the crisis which led her to the universe of concentration
camps. But the existence and mechanism of this crisis derive
from the economic and social bases of capitalism and imperial-
ism. Under a new guise, analogous results could appear again
tomorrow. Consequently there is a very definite battle to be
conducted. (Page 187)

With the passage of time, what has happened in Algeria
and in Indochina and what is today taking place between
Blacks and Whites in the United States and between Jews and
Arabs in the Middle East, has demonstrated, more than could
be expected, how justified Rousset's theory was. Moreover,
what was then still going on in Russia demonstrated it no less,
but at that time David Rousset was careful not to make use of
that argument. On a more mundane level one could find still
more justifications; take this one for example:

When several hundreds of thousands of adult "displaced
persons" succeeded in getting out the the camps and in leaving
for the two Americas, thousands of children remained behind,
together with the old people, in the care of the I.R.O. . . . in
the sinister barracks of Germany, Austria and Italy. But the
International Refugee Organization is scheduled definitely
to cease its activities in a few months, and one wonders what
will be the fate of these orphans twice abandoned. Their
situation is tragic right now, because in some camps they
have not received more food in all than three to four hundred
calories a day, and no one can say if even that inadequate
ration can be kept up. The death rate under such conditions
is terrible. *(La Bataille,* May 9, 1950.)

The paper said that there were thirteen million living like that,
in a Europe that had got rid of Hitler and Mussolini. If an
investigation had been made into the treatment that they were
subjected to by their guardians, it would be interesting to see
upon whom the responsibility would be placed.

Les Jours de notre Mort (1947), which takes up the facts
as given in *L'Univers concentrationnaire* and carries them to

the limits of speculation, strays far from that profession of faith while *Le Pitre ne rit pas* (1948) ignores it entirely. From which it must be concluded that David Rousset's thinking went through such evolutions, under cover of going into details, that his books ended up on a note much more anti-German than anti-Nazi in the eyes of the public. This evolution was all the more noticeable in that being shaded with certain weaknesses for Communism at the start, it developed, in the end, into an anti-Communism, which one would not want to say could never turn into Russophobia pure and simple, if the cold war should reach such a point as to turn into a shooting war.

The originality, therefore, of *L'Univers concentrationnaire* lay in drawing a distinction between Germany and Nazism in the determination of responsibilities. But, this originality was more than matched by the sensational theory that justified the conduct of the prisoners who were in charge of running the affairs of the camps, on the basis that it was necessary to preserve, for the post-war period, the elite of the revolutionaries at the expense of all of the others. David Rousset embraced this theory by justifying the policy of saving a certain kind of prisoner, that he defined in terms of certain extra-humanitarian imperatives. As evidence of that policy, the malicious could point out that David Rousset was probably saved from death by the German Communist *Kapo,* Emile Künder, who considered that he belonged to that revolutionary elite, who showed him great friendship for that reason, and who, today, disowns him.

I. The Postulate of the Theory

> It is normal, when all the active forces of one class are the stake of the greatest totalitarian battle yet invented, that the enemies be put where they can do no harm, and, if necessary, be exterminated. (Page 107)

This statement is unassailable. His conclusion, set forth without transition, is much less so: "The purpose of the camps is indeed physical destruction." (*Ibid.*) One cannot but notice that, in the postulate itself, physical destruction is subordinate to necessity, and is envisaged only in cases where the extent of internment is not enough to prevent the individual from doing harm.

After a leap, or an off-hand deduction, of this kind, there
was no reason to stop, and he could write:

> The order bears the mark of the master. The commanding
> officer of the camp knows nothing. The *Block-Führer* (S.S.
> responsible for the livelihood of a Block) knows nothing.
> The *Lagerältester* (camp elder, prisoner selected by the S.S.)
> knows nothing. Those who carry out the order know nothing.
> *But the order prescribes death and the kind of death and how
> much time it shall take to cause death.* And in this desert
> of knowing nothing, that is enough. (Page 100, emphasis
> added.)

With this assertion he found a way both of placing the responsibility of the camps on those "high-places" of Louis
Martin-Chauffier, and of allowing him to conclude in favor
of a pre-established plan for the systematizing of terror, justified by a philosophy.

> The enemy, in the philosophy of the S.S., is the force of evil,
> intellectually and physically expressed. The Communist, the
> socialist, the German liberal, the revolutionaries, the foreign
> Resistants are the active representations of evil. But the objec-
> tive existence of certain races: the Jews, the Poles, the Rus-
> sians, is a static expression of evil. It is not necessary for a Jew,
> a Pole, or a Russian to act against National Socialism; they are
> by birth, by pre-destination un-assimilable heretics, dedicated
> to the apocalyptic fire. *Death therefore has no complete mean-
> ing. Only expiation can satisfy and appease the lords. The
> concentration camps are the astonishing and complex ma-
> chinery of expiation. Those who are to die go to their deaths
> with a slowness calculated so that their physical and moral
> downfall, by degrees, shall finally make them conscious of the
> fact that they are accursed, the expressions of evil, and not
> men. And that priest-administrator of justice feels a sort of
> secret pleasure, a deep-seated sensation of delight, in ruining
> bodies.* (Pages 108-109, emphasis added.)

From this excerpt it can be seen that, starting from concentration camps as places to put enemies where they can do no
harm, one can easily make of them institutions of extermination
and one can elaborate to infinity on the purpose of that extermination. From the moment that one reaches that stage, it
becomes no more than an intellectual exercise where one can
demonstrate his aptitude for mental constructions and his
talent for writing. But, the literary effort which produces such
a fine description of sadism is perfectly useless, and one need

not have lived through the experience to describe it like that;
one need only consult Tomás de Torquemada and copy down
the arguments of the Spanish Inquisition.

I shall not waste time with a discussion of the first part of
the explanation which ties the Russians and the Poles together
with the Jews in the minds of the Nazi leaders; it is obvious
fantasy.

II. The Labor

By labor is meant a means of punishment. Concentration
camp man-power is of secondary interest, a preoccupation
foreign to the nature of the concentration camp universe.
Psychologically, it was connected by that sadism that forced
the prisoners to strengthen the instruments of their bondage.

"It was because of the accidents of history that the camps
also became public works enterprises. On the extension of the
war to a world scale, calling for the total employment of
everybody and everything, the lame, the deaf, the blind, and
the PGs, the S.S., with lashes of the whip, enrolled the blind
mob of the concentration camps for the most destructive
tasks . . . The work of the concentration inmates did not have
as its ultimate object the carrying out of specific tasks, but
the keeping of the "protected prisoners" [1] in the strictest
most debasing confinement. (Pages 110-112.)

Since it has been decided that the purpose of the camps was
to exterminate, it is quite obvious that the work that was
performed there is hardly more than an element, negligible in
itself, in the theory of the extermination mystique. Eugen
Kogon, who will be considered in the following chapter, starting
from the same idea but with much less refinement in form,
writes regarding this issue in his L'Enfer organisé.

. . . It was decided that the camps should have a secondary
purpose, a little more realistic, a little more practical and more
immediate; thanks to them, they were going to collect and
make use of a manpower composed of slaves, belonging to the
S.S., who, for as long as they were permitted to live, should
live only to serve their masters . . . But, what were called the
secondary aims (keeping the population in fear, the use of
slave man-power, keeping the camps up as training and ex-
perimental stations for the S.S.) these aims little by little rose
to the first level, insofar as they were the true reasons for

consignment to the camps, *until the day when, the war, un-leashed by Hitler,* envisaged and prepared by him and the S.S., in an ever more systematic way, brought about the enormous expansion of the camps.
(Pages 27-28, emphasis added.)

By setting these two passages side by side it appears that for the first it was the historic accident of the war, and then only at the moment that it became world wide, which made the use of the prisoners as man-power the important purpose of the camps, while for the second, this result had been achieved *before the war,* and the war only emphasized it.

I choose the second interpretation for the following reason: the division of the camps into these categories — i.e., *Konzen-trationslager* (concentration camp), *Arbeitslager* (work camp), and *Straflager* (punishment camp, where the labor and living conditions were harder) — was an accomplished fact when the war broke out in 1939. The operation of internment, before and during the war, was accomplished in two stages: the prison-ers were concentrated in a central camp that was planned for or already was organized for labor, and which served, in addition, as a sorting station; from there the prisoners were sent on to other camps, according to the demands for manpower. There was a third stage for those who had committed offenses during the process of being interned; assignment as punishment to a camp generally still in construction, which was considered a pu-nitive camp (*Straflager*), but which, from the moment that con-struction was completed, became in its turn an ordinary camp (*Konzentrationslager*).

I shall add that, in my opinion, the use of prisoner labor had always been anticipated. This is part of the universal code of re-pression: in almost all countries of the world, the State makes those that it imprisons sweat for their livelihood by laboring for the State; there are a few exceptions — e.g., fallen government officials in the democratic nations and distinguished deportees in dictatorships. The contrary practice is inconceivable. It would be nonsense for a State to support those who break its laws and undermine its foundations. It is only the conditions of labor that vary, depending upon whether one is free or in-terned, and the margin of benefits to be earned.

For Germany, there was an added factor which needs to be noted: the camps had to be built under the imperatives of a total war. During the war, one could only think that the sole purpose of the camps was to kill people off and one was quite inclined to think so even afterwards. The erroneousness of this impression was all the less obvious since, as the war made necessary an even greater number of camps, the construction period never came to an end, and the two circumstances, superimposed in their effects, led to a generalized continuation of the *Straflager* stage, seemingly deliberate.

III. The Häftlingsführung

We know that the S.S. delegated to the prisoners the direction and administration of the camps and that this practice of self-administration was called *Häftlingsführung*. There were, for example, *Kapos* (who headed *Kommandos*), *Blockältester* (Block supervisors), *Lagerschutz* (prisoner police), *Lagerältester* (camp supervisors) along with other prisoners who composed a whole concentration camp bureaucracy which in fact wielded all of the authority in the camp. This practice also follows a pattern that is part of the code of repression all over the world. If the prisoners to whom fell all of those administrative posts had the slightest notion of solidarity with the common prison population, they would have worked everywhere to alleviate the hardships for everyone. Unhappily that is never the case. Everywhere, on taking over the post that is placed in his command, the designated prisoner (often called a "trustee") changes his outlook. It is a phenomenon too well known to dwell on and too universal to impute solely to the Germans or the Nazis. David Rousset's error was to believe that it could be any other way in a concentration camp and that, in fact, it had been otherwise – i.e., that the political prisoners were beings superior to the common mass of prisoners and that the laws they obeyed were nobler than the laws of the individual struggle for life.

This error led him to lay down as a principle that the prisoner bureaucracy of the concentration camps, not being able to save large numbers of men, deserved credit for saving the "best" of the prisoners: "With the close collaboration of a *Kapo* one could make life much easier, even in the Hell." (Page 166.) But he does not tell how one could get the close collaboration of a *Kapo*. Nor that this collaboration, except when the *Kapo* was a political prisoner, ever went beyond the kind of relationship that one would expect to exist between a patrician and his dependent. In any case, he fails to mention that only a tiny number of prisoners could hope to achieve this relationship, regardless of its precise nature.

Obviously, the positions within the *Häftlingsführung* were eagerly sought after, since to hold one improved the relative conditions that one faced in the camp. David Rousset writes: that:

> The holding of those posts was therefore a prime interest, and the life and death of many men depended on it. (Page 134)

Then trying to link everything together, Rousset asserts that those who held those posts organized, and most of those who organized were Communists: then they worked out regular political plots against the S.S.: then they drew up programs for action after the war:

> At Buchenwald the secret central committee of the Communist faction was composed of Germans, Czechs, a Russian and a Frenchman. (Page 166)

> From 1944 on they were preoccupied with the conditions that would be created by the end of the war. They were greatly afraid that the S.S. would kill them all before that. And it was not an imaginary fear. (Page 170)

> At Buchenwald, besides the Communist organization that without doubt achieved there a degree of *perfection* and efficiency unique in the annals of the camps, meetings took place more or less regularly among the political elements, from the socialists to the extreme right, which ended in setting up a program of joint activity for when they returned to France.
> (Page 81-81)

All of this activity is a possibility, but it is factually questionable that such organization ever occurred. Certainly, in all of the camps, the prisoners gathered together in numerous and unobtrusive and informal group alignments for various reasons: to better endure their common fate; to promote their self-interest; to get appointed to the *Häftlingsführung* and, once appointed, to hold that position. But, these prisoner alliances were a far cry from the picture that Rousset paints.

After the liberation, as David Rousset corroborates, the Communists were able to make people believe that the bond of their association was their doctrine, to which their acts conformed. In reality, the bond was the material advantages that were to be gained by those in the association. In the two camps which I knew, the general view was that, political or not, Communist or not, all of the so-called "Committees" were first of all associations of food thieves regardless of whatever form they took. Nothing has been uncovered to change this view. On the contrary everything has confirmed it: the small groups of Communists affronting each other over the various spoils of the system — e.g., the composition of the clique which held power; the manner in which the spoils of pillage were to be divided up; the distribution of camp assignments, etc., etc. . . . For example, during the few weeks that I spent at Buchenwald in Block 48, at the suggestion of the *Blockältester*, or with his authorization, a group of prisoners, new arrivals, had decided to bolster the group morale. Little by little they acquired a certain degree of authority. In particular, contact between the *Blockältester* and ourselves in the end could only be made through them. The group regulated life in the Block, organized discussions, assigned the duties, and divided up the food, among other things. It was pitiful to see the toadyism toward the onmipotent *Blockältester* that developed among them. One day, the principal mover in this group was caught in the act of dividing up with another the potatoes that he had stolen from the common ration . . .

Eugen Kogon relates that the French at Buchenwald, who were about the only ones to receive parcels from the Red Cross, had decided to share them equally with the whole camp:

> When our French comrades said they were going to share a large part of them with the entire camp, this act of fellowship was received with gratitude. But the distribution was organized in a scandalous manner for weeks; there was in effect only one parcel for every ten Frenchmen . . . while their compatriots in charge of the distribution, having at their head the chief of the French communist group in the camp[2], reserved for themselves piles of pracels, or used them for the benefit of their friends of the same stamp. (*L'Enfer organisé*, Page 120.)

David Rousset sees a harmful aspect in this state of things, if not a principal cause of the horror, when he writes:

The bureaucracy does not serve only in the management of the camps; it is, at the top, all involved in the deals of the S.S. Berlin sends cases of cigarettes and tobacco to pay the men. Truckloads of food arrive at the camps. Every week the men are to be paid; they get paid every two weeks or every month; the number of cigarettes is reduced and lists are made of bad workers who get nothing. The men are dying for want of a smoke. What does that matter: The cigarettes go into the black market. Meat? Butter? Sugar? Honey? Jam? A bigger portion of red cabbage, beets, rutabagas, touched up with a little carrot, that will do well enough. It is even pure kindness . . . Milk. Lots of whitened water, that will do perfectly. And all the rest: meat, butter, sugar, honey, jam, milk, potatoes, on the market for the German civilians who pay and are proper citizens. The people in Berlin will be satisfied to learn that everything arrived all right. It is enough that the records are in order and the bookkeeping verifiable . . . Flour? Of course, the bread ration will be reduced. Without even covering it up. The portions will be a little less carefully cut. The records are not concerned with such things. And the S.S. masters will be on excellent terms with the tradesmen of the area.
(Pages 145-146-147)

Here, support is given, at least as far as the food is concerned, to the legend that a plan was drawn up "in high places" to starve the prisoners. Berlin supplied everything that was needed to provide the prisoners with adequate rations, in conformity with the reports that were written to the families, but, without the knowledge of the officials, it was not distributed to the mass of prisoners. And, why not? Who does the stealing? The prisoners who were in charge of the distribution. David Rousset tells us that such theft was done under the orders of the S.S. to whom was turned over the proceeds. No, the prisoner trustees stole for themselves first, and took all that they required. Then, they paid some of it to the S.S. to purchase their complicity.

Incidentally, the same phenomenon was brought to light in May 1950 during the trial instituted against the *"Oeuvre des mères et des enfants"* at Versailles, whose ring leader was headmistress Pallu. Preliminary investigation revealed that:

The children were badly clothed, left in a repulsive state of filth, in a room crawling with vermin. The straw mattresses were foul with excrement and urine, crawling sometimes with maggots. There was but one sheet, one blanket. All the toilets were stopped up. The children relieved themselves just where they were. They were covered with impetigo and lice. That was the setting. There 13 children died of hunger. And yet they were supposed to have received, in addition to their normal rations, supplementary allocations. The children saw nothing of this: the milk was half watered.

"The children were getting too much," said a sister. "The headmistress had a liter and a half of milk delivered to her every day, chocolate, rice, meat—and of the best quality."

"The headmistress, a little brunette, sent twenty-kilo packages to her family, out of her personal reserves. All those people were well nourished, and did not wonder at that choice food during times when the daily rutabaga was the rule. And the children? Oh! that was so easy, they didn't ask for anything . . ."*(Le Populaire, May 16, 1950.)*

This account is in a class with the best accounts covering the German concentration camps. The drama took place in France, and neither the public nor even those in the administration of *"l'oeuvre des mères et des enfants"* knew anything about it. The children died there like inmates of a concentration camp, under the same conditions and for the same reasons . . . and in a democratic country, to boot!

So, to return to the subject at hand, these famous "revolutionary committees" never defended the interests of the common prisoners or prepared political plans for use after the war; the Communists were able to delude the public on these points. Rather, they existed merely to promote the well-being of their members. I shall add that those persons who succeeded in forming them, kept alive a spirit of subservience vis-à-vis the S.S., a kind of collaboration, without which the camps could not have operated.

Regarding the discussions organized in Block 48, and to which reference has been made, David Rousset has this to say:

So I organized a first discussion; a Russian *Stubendienst* twenty-two or twenty-three years old, worker in the Marty Factory at Leningrad, gave us a long exposition of the condition of labor in the U.S.S.R. The discussion which followed lasted for two afternoons. The second talk was given by a Kolkhosian on Soviet agricultural organization. I myself, gave a little later a talk on "The Soviet Union, from Revolution to War" . . . (Page 77)

I was present at that talk; it was a masterpiece of Bolshephilism, rather unexpected for one familiar with David Rousset's earlier Trotskyite activities. But Erich, our *Blockältester,* was a Communist and was in very good standing with the "cell" which exercised the preponderant influence in the *Häftlingsführung* at the moment. It was artful to get his attention and to predispose him for the day when he would have favors to dispense. "Three months later," continues Rousset, "I would certainly not have begun this endeavor again. The game was played out. But at the time we were all still very ignorant. Erich, our Block chief, grumbled, but didn't oppose the business . . ." (Page 77) To be sure. Furthermore, three months later, it was *Kapo* Emil Künder on whom siege had to be laid. The time of the talks was over, and the emphasis was on the Red Cross packages from France. If I have correctly understood *Les Jours de notre Mort,* Rousset used these packages to his advantage, and I do not reproach him for it; I myself owe my return to France to them, and I never made any secret of it.

It could be, and perhaps it will be, maintained that it was not important to establish the fact that the *Häftlingsführung* made the common prisoners suffer a treatment that was substantially more horrible than that which had been planned for them by the higher circles of Nazism and that nothing forced the *Häftlingsführung* to do it. If such a contention were made, I would then observe that it has seemed to me to be indispensable to determine exactly the causes of the concentration camp hell in all their aspects, if only to place the contentions of the *Häftlingsführung* apologists in the proper context, and to orient a little more toward the true nature of things the inquiry of the reader in whose mind this problem remains unresolved.

IV. Objectivity

Birkenau, the largest city of death. The selections on arrival; the trappings of civilization set out like caricatures to deceive and subdue. Regular selections in the camp, every Sunday. The inevitable destructions in Block 7 long drawn out. The *Sonderkommando* (special *Kommando* assigned to the Crematory) totally isolated from the world, condemned to live every second of its eternity with tortured and burned bodies. Terror breaks the nerves so decisively that the death agonies know all the humiliations, all the betrayals. And when, ineluctably, the strong odors of the gas chamber close, everyone rushes forward, crushing each other in a frenzy to keep alive, so that, when they are opened the bodies inextricably tangled fall forward in cascades onto the rails. (Page 51)

In such a fictionalized panorama as *Les Jours de notre Mort*, this passage will cause no shock. But, in *L 'Univers concentrationnaire*, which has in so many aspects the character of a true story, it would be out of place. David Rousset was not, actually, ever present at this scene of torture of which he gives so exact and so gripping a description.

In 1950, it was still too soon to pronounce a definite judgment on the existence of gas chambers in the camps; documents were wanting and those that existed were incomplete, inexact, and obviously apocryphal or falsified. But, the historian has no right to bring forth gratuitous hypotheses. Therefore, I limited myself to pointing out obvious anomalies. For example, Eugen Kogon, who in his *L 'Enfer organisé*, said that "a very small number of camps had their own gas chambers," (Page 154), was careful not to say which ones. Or again, concerning those which allegedly were installed at Auschwitz-Birkenau, Kogon told how the Germans effected the extermination by this method, according to the testimony:

. . . of a young Jew from Brno, Janda Weiss, who belonged in 1944 with the *Sonderkommando* (crematory and gas chambers) from whom come the following details, confirmed, moreover, by others. (Page 155)

To my knowledge, this Janda Weiss was the only person in the whole of the concentration camp literature who was said to have been present at such exterminations and whose exact address was given. Unfortunately, by an unhappy chance, he was in the Russian zone and only Eugen Kogon has profited by his statements. Given the historical and moral significance of the use of gas chambers as a method of repression, further steps could possibly have been taken to acquaint the public with his precise testimony, other than through a third party, and at the same time to extend its length to a little more than that of a paragraph that appeared to have been incidentally included in Kogon's comprehensive study.

There was another doubtful element in Eugen Kogon's thesis regarding the gas chambers, and it lay in this:

> In 1941, Berlin sent to the camps the first orders for the formation of special transports for gas extermination. The first ones chosen were prisoners in for breaches of the common law, prisoners sentenced for immoral behaviour, and certain political figures in bad odor with the S.S.

> These transports left for an unknown destination. In the case of Buchenwald one could see being returned the next day, clothing, including the contents of the pockets, dentures, etc . . . Through an under-officer of the escort it was learned that these transports had arrived at Pirna and at Hohenstein and that the men who made up the transports had been subjected to tests of a new gas and had perished.

> During the winter of 1942-1943, all the Jews had been examined with regard to their capacity for work. Instead of the above-mentioned transports, it was then those Jews, who, in groups of 90 men, took the same road, but ended up at Bernburg near Kothen. The doctor-in-chief of the nursing home of the district, a certain Doctor Eberl, was the docile tool of the S.S. In the files of the S.S. this operation bore the reference "14F. 13." It seems to have been carried out simultaneously with the annihilation of all the sick in the nursing homes, which little by little became the general practice in Germany under National-Socialism. (Pages 225-226)

Now, I had already studied the matter enough to know that the extermination orders to which he alludes stem from a program of euthanasia, not of extermination. The two documents that he quoted in support of his contention—and he was careful not to reproduce the orders themselves—amply proved the point. They consisted of a couple of pieces of correspondence between the camp officials at Buchenwald and the directors of a nursing home at Bernburg. In his letter dated February 2, 1942, Dr. Hoven, the camp physician states, with regard to Jewish prisoners who are unfit for work in the camp:

> Referring to our personal conversation, I send you, attached, in copy, and to be used for all purposes, a list of those Jews sick and unable to work, now in the camp at Buchenwald.

At this point, it must be noted that the list which is mentioned is not published. The second document is a letter from the nursing home at Bernburg, dated March 5, 1942, in which the writer refers to a letter of March 3, 1942. The text of this letter is as follows:

> Subject 36 prisoners, list no. 12 of February 2, 1942.
>
> In our letter of the 3rd current, we asked you to make available to us the last 36 prisoners of the last transport, March 18, 1942.
>
> Because of the absence of our physician-in-chief who is to examine medically these prisoners, we request you not to send them to us on March 18, 1942, but to add them to the March 11, 1942, transport, together with their papers which will be returned to you March 11, 1942.

One must agree that the meaning of the text has to be strangely distorted to deduce from this exchange of correspondence that extermination by means of gas chambers was involved.

These two documents, moreover, call for comment, since they apparently refer to the practice of euthanasia, and since they bear the dates of February 2 and March 5, 1942. Here is the story of operation *Gnadentod:*

On September 1, 1939, Hitler signed the *Gnadentod* order, the text of which is given as follows:

> *Reichleiter* Bouhler and Doctor Brandt are instructed, on their own responsibility, to extend the authority of physicians to designate by name, after a critical examination of their condition, those sick persons who can humanely be called incurable, so that a merciful death may be assured.

When this decree—which was not restrictive— was signed, the installation of crematoriums was begun in six sanitariums: that of Hadamar near Limbourg, that of Grafeneck in Württemberg, that of Hartheim near Linz, and the homes for the aged at Pirna, Bernberg and Brandenburg. After January, 1940, the transfer of the terminally ill to these establishments began.

During July, 1941, the rumor began to spread in German Catholic circles that some 30,000 ill persons had been subjected to euthanasia contrary to Church doctrine. The priests were aroused, and on July 6, 1941, a pastoral letter of the bishops was read aloud in all of the Catholic churches of Germany, dated June 26, 1941, of which the essential passages are the following:

Most certainly there are commands which do not call for
action on our parts if their execution would involve too
many difficulties or dangers. But there are also duties of
conscience from which no one can free us and which we must
carry out, even at the cost of our lives. Never, in any circumstances outside of war and legitimate self defense may an
innocent man be killed!

When this pastoral letter which he had energetically promoted
had no effect, and the removal of the terminally ill was renewed
in his diocese, Monseigneur von Galen, Biship of Münster,
lodged a complaint on July 28, 1941, with the public prosecutor
of the Münster Court, invoking articles 139 and 211 of the code
which put an obligation on everyone to denounce murder and
to oppose it. When this complaint had no effect, Monseigneur
von Galen ascended the pulpit on August 3, 1941, in his church
Saint-Lambert of Münster, and delivered a ringing sermon.

After recalling earlier protestations of the bishops, and also
of his own, and after denouncing a recent removal of one
thousand six hundred sick persons from the homes for the
aged at Marienthal and Warstein, the Biship of Münster stated:

Why should these poor defenseless sick people die? Simply
because according to the verdict of some doctor or commission they belong in the category of the "unfit to live." It is
stated that they can no longer be productive. They are like
an old machine that no longer works, an old paralyzed horse,
a cow that no longer gives milk! What becomes of an old
machine: it is put on the scrapheap. What is done with a
paralyzed horse? unproductive cattle? . . . But it is not a
question of old machines, horses or cows. It is a question of
men like us, our brothers and our sisters. Woe to man! Woe to
our German people if the sacred Commandment: 'Thou shalt
not kill' which our Creator engraved from the beginning in
the minds of men, is transgressed, and if this transgression is
tolerated and goes unpunished . . .

This sermon had a profound echo all over Germany and started
a movement before which Hitler retreated.

Less than a month afterwards, August 20, 1941, Hitler gave
the order to suspend operation "*Gnadentod.*" All the historians,
even the most anti-Nazi, are today agreed on this version of the
affair. Even Mr. Gerhard Jaeckel, a specialist on Nazi atrocities
and war crimes, in the illustrated Munich weekly *Quick* (June
25, 1961), has confirmed it in every detail as it is reproduced

above. And, in Paris, the newspaper *Le Monde* (May 3, 1963) has also accepted the story as it is set forth in the preceding paragraphs.

Now, the two documents that are produced by Eugen Kogon bear the dates of February 2 and of March 5, 1942, when operation *"Gnadentod"* had been terminated for more than six months. A third document that was published by Eugen Kogon in support of these two letters, which is a report from Dr. Hoven, but which has no date, has this to say, according to Kogon:

> The obligations of the contracting physicians and the negotiations with the burial services have often led to insurmountable difficulties . . . This is why I am at once getting in touch with Doctor Infried-Eberl, head physician of the nursing home of Bernburg-sur-Saale, Post Box 252, telephone 3.169. This is the same physician who carried out operation "14 F 13." Doctor Eberl has shown the greatest kindness. All the bodies of the prisoners deceased at Schoneberg-Wernigerode will be transported to Doctor Eberl at Bernburg and will be cremated, even without a death certificate. (Page 227)

The least one can say is that this report does not excuse one from the obligation of verifying the authenticity of the three documents . . . if only to find out if, in the Germany of 1942, it was possible to contravene the orders of the *Führer* to this extent.

A procedure called the *"Selektion"*, which was periodically performed in all the camps, contributed in no small measure to the dissemination of the notion that executions were common occurrences in the camps. What actually happened was this:

Periodically, the health services of the camps received the order to make up a list of all sick persons who were considered to be unfit for fairly sustained work or for any work at all, and to gather them in a special Block. Then, trucks arrived—or a line of railway cars—and they were put in, and they departed for an unknown destination. The rumor in the concentration camps had it that they were taken directly to the gas chambers; as a consequence, with a sort of cruel sense of humor, these assemblings were called *Himmelskommandos*, meaning that they were composed of persons bound for heaven. Naturally all of those who were sick tried to escape the *Himmelskommando*.

I saw two or three *"Selektions"* carried out at Dora; I even escaped being included in one of them. Dora was a small camp. Although the numbers of unfit sick were always greater than the means available to care for them, those numbers only very rarely reached proportions so large as to interfere with the operation or the administration of the camp. Auschwitz-Birkenau, which David Rousset speaks about in the quotation in question, was different. That camp was very large, a human ant-heap, so to speak. The number of unfit was considerable. The *"Selektions"*, instead of being made through the health services, often were made on the spot whenever the trucks or rail cars arrived. They took place at a rate of about one a week, and decisions as to who was to be included were made just on appearances. Between the S.S. guards and the concentration camp bureaucracy on the one hand and the mass of prisoners trying to escape selection on the other, one can imagine the confusion of what amounted to man-hunts in an atmosphere of universal panic. After each *"Selektion"*, those who were left behind felt that they had for the time being escapèd the gas chamber.

But, there is nothing to prove conclusively that any of the unfit, or those so designated as unfit, who were selected in this way, either at Dora or at Birkenau, were sent to gas chambers. In support of this statement I want to record a personal experience. In the *"Selektion"* which I escaped at Dora was included one of my comrades who did not have the same luck. I saw him depart, and I was sorry for him. In 1946 I still believed that he was dead and that he had been asphyxiated together with the entire convoy of which he was a part. In September of the same year, to my astonishment, he showed up at my house to invite me to attend some official demonstration. When I told him what my fears for him had been all this time, he told me that the convoy in question had been sent to Bergen-Belsen, a convalescent center for the sick deportees from all the camps. This story is verified by a former deportee, a fellow named Mullin who is now an employee at the Besancon railway station. After a trip that was made under appalling conditions, he arrived at Bergen-Belsen, to which had converged convoys of the unfit from all over Germany. There were so many prisoners that the camp administration didn't know where to put them or how to feed them. He spent many horrible days

there and was finally sent back to work. At Buchenwald, moreover, I had already encountered in Block 48 a Czech who had
returned to Birkenau from Bergen-Belsen in the same way.

My view on the gas chambers? Some probably did exist;
but not as many as is believed. Moreover, there probably were
exterminations by gas, but not as many as has been claimed.
The number, of course, does not in the least diminish the nature
of the horror, but the fact that the practice might have been a
measure that was decreed by a State order in the name of a
political doctrine would singularly add to the horrible nature
of it. Was that the case? The statement of Dr. Aryeh Kubovy,
Director of the *Center of Jewish Documentation* at Tel-Aviv,
which is discussed in Chapter 13, Note 8, concerning the non-
existence of orders for the extermination of the Jews has
definitely settled the question in the negative.

Nevertheless, in spite of the fact that there appears to have
been no official Nazi policy of gas exterminations, the factor
that has played the greatest role in promoting the contrary
belief, seems to have been the *"Selektion"* practice about which
there is not a deportee who cannot speak as a witness in one
way or another, and who does so, mainly, in terms of all that
he feared at the moment.

Two other documents that are quoted by David Rousset in
Le Pitre ne rit pas (1949) in support of the existence of mass
exterminations by gas do not strike me as any more convincing
than those of Eugen Kogon. The first is a deposition of a
certain Wolfgang Grosch at Nuremberg and is about the construction of gas chambers, but not their use. The second, concerning
trucks that had been fitted with asphyxiating mechanisms
which were to have been used in Russia, bears the signature
of a second-Lieutenant and is addressed to a Lieutenant. Neither one of them allows one to accuse the leaders of the Nazi
regime of having given orders for the extermination by gas.
The text of both documents will be found in Appendix C at
the end of this book.

Speaking of Auschwitz-Birkenau, Eugen Kogon had said
that toward the end of 1942 the Third Reich was contemplating
the installation of a branch of I.G. Farben Industries at the
camp, in which the use of chemical gasses would be indispensable, and I suggest that from this fact might have sprung the
accusation that the *Reich* had decided to exterminate Jews in

this way.[3] Of course, it is only a supposition. But in history as in the sciences, have not most discoveries stemmed, if not from supposition, at least from doubt?

It may be objected that there is nothing to be gained in exonerating National-Socialism in this way, whose misdeeds in other respects are definitely established. In response, I believe that there is nothing more to be gained in supporting a doctrine or an interpretation, perhaps correct, but which rests on falsities. All of the great principles of democracy die, not because of their substance, but from being too exposed in details considered as insignificant in their scope as in their substance, and dictatorships generally only triumph to the extent that insufficiently studied arguments are brandished against them. In this connection, David Rousset gives an example which in a masterly manner illustrates this way of looking at things:

> I was talking with a German physician . . . He was obviously not a Nazi. He was fed up with the war and did not know where his wife and four children were. Dresden, which had been his home, had been cruelly bombed, "Look here," he said to me, "did we go to war for Danzig?" I answered no. "All right then, Hitler's policy in the concentration camps was frightful (I bowed); but, for the rest, he was right." (Page 170)

So, by this little detail, because it was felt to be wrong to be told that they were going to war for Danzig, and that that turned out to be false, this doctor pronounced judgment on Hitler's entire policy and approved of it. I wonder in fear what he thinks of that policy now, now that he has had a chance to read David Rousset and Eugen Kogon.

V. Traduttore, Traditore

This small detail is without great significance; David Rousset sets forth his opinion as to the etymology of the word *"Kapo"* as follows:

> The expression *Kapo* is probably of Italian origin and means the head: there are two other possible explanations: *Kapo*, abbreviation of *Kaporal*, or a contraction of the phrase *Kamerad Polizei*, used during the first months of Buchenwald. (Page 131)

Eugen Kogon on the other hand is more positive:

Kapo: from the Italian *Il capo*, the head, the chief . . .
(*L'Enfer organisé*, page 59)

I suggest another explanation: the word is derived from the phrase *Konzentrationslager Arbeit Polizei*, using the initials of each word, just as *Schupo* comes from *Schutz Polizei* and *Gestapo* from *Geheim Staat Polizei.* The haste of David Rousset and Eugen Kogon to interpret, rather than analyze, prevented them from thinking of it.

FOOTNOTES

1. In German, the camps were called *Schutzhalflager,* camps for prisoners being protected (against the people's fury.)

2. He was given this title by the Ruling Clique; his name was Marcel Paul.

3. [Auschwitz and its satellite camps became, by the end of the war, a huge industrial complex where both prisoner and free labor worked in a variety of industrial enterprises, among which were extensive chemical works which manufactured from the coal of the region synthetic gasoline and "Buna" (synthetic rubber.) For a detailed discussion, see Arthur R. Butz, *The Hoax of the Twentieth Century* (Richmond, Surrey: Historical Review Press, [1976]), pages 47-52.]

Chapter Eleven

Eugen Kogon and L'Enfer Organise

I am not acquainted with Eugen Kogon. I learned all that I know about him from what he says about himself in his book and from what I have read in the book reviews. Unless I am mistaken, Kogon is an Austrian journalist of the Christian social or Christian progressive variety who was arrested following the *Anschluss* and who was deported to Buchenwald. He is known to the French public as a sociologist.

L'Enfer organisé has had more success than any other concentration camp memoir. It covers a considerable number of facts and events, most of which were experienced by the author himself. Although Kogon is to some extent naive and is somewhat prone to exaggerate, his main weakness lies in his explanations and interpretations. These weaknesses are the result, on the one hand, of Kogon's insistence at looking at things "in their political light" (Preface, page 14) and, on the other hand, of his desire to justify the conduct of the *Häftlings-führung*. His vindication of the concentration camp bureaucracy is done in an even more categorical and explicit manner than the "whitewash" that was done by David Rousset.

Otherwise, Eugen Kogon writes his report, so he says, "without any regard for the consequences . . . as a man and a Christian" (Preface, page 14), and without any intention of writing a comprehensive "history of the German concentration camps" or "a compilation of all of the horrors that were found in them; but rather a work essentially sociological in character, whose human content, both political and moral, established in its authenticity, has the value of an example." (Introduction, page 20).

The intention was good. He believed himself to be qualified for that mission, and, perhaps, he was. He describes himself as, " . . . having spent at least five years in capitivity . . ., having climbed up under the most painful circumstances, little by little reaching a position where he could see things clearly and exercise influence . . . as never having belonged to the camp police stooges . . . as never having dishonored himself in his conduct as a prisoner." (Page 20)

After having been detailed for one year to the *Effeckten-kammer Kommando* (the workshop where clothing was made), a privileged job, he became secretary to the S.S. camp physician, Doctor Ding-Schuller, an even more privileged job. In this job he was in a position to become acquainted in detail with all of the intrigues of the camp which occurred during the last two years of his internment.

After reading it, I closed the book. Then I opened it again, and under the heading of the title page I wrote, as a sub-title: *Plaidoyer pro domo* (plea in self-defense).

I. The Prisoner Eugen Kogon

At Buchenwald there was a "Section for the study of typhus and viruses." It occupied Blocks 46 and 50. In charge of this laboratory was the S.S. camp physician, Doctor Ding-Schuller. This is the way it operated:

> In Block 46 at Buchenwald camp — which was a model of cleanliness, and very well managed — experiments were not only carried out on the men, but all the typhus cases were isolated, those who had contracted it in the camp as a matter of course, and those who had been brought to the camp when they were already affected. They were cured there, insofar as they could weather this terrible sickness. The running of the Block had been put in the hands of Arthur Dietzch . . . one

of the prisoners . . . *who had gotten his medical knowledge only through this experience.* [2] Dietzch was a Communist who had been a political prisoner for nearly twenty years.[3] He was a very hardened person, naturally one of the most hated and feared at Buchenwald.[4]

Since the S.S. and the under-officers of the camp had an unconquerable fear of contagion, and since they thought typhus could be picked up simply by contact, in the air, from the cough of someone sick, etc . . . they never went into Block 46 . . . The prisoners took advantage of that, in collaboration with *Kapo* Dietzch: the illegal management of the camp made use of this, on the one hand, to get rid of those who were collaborating with the S.S. against the prisoners (or who seemed to be collaborating, or who were just plain unpopular),[5] on the other hand, to conceal in Block 46 certain important political prisoners whose lives were threatened, which was sometimes very difficult and very dangerous for Dietzch, since his servants and nurses were all "greens." (Page 162, emphasis added.)

In Block 50, a vaccine was made up for exanthematous typhus, from the lungs of mice and rabbits, in line with the procedure of Professor Giroud (of Paris). This was begun in August 1943. The camp's best specialists, doctors, bacteriologists, serum specialists, chemists, were chosen for this work, etc. . . (Page 163)

And this is how Eugen Kogon got assigned to his position.

One of the crafty political aims of the prisoners, from the beginning, was to bring into this *Kommando* comrades of every nationality, whose lives were threatened, since the S.S. had as respectful a fear of this Block as of Block 46. This fetishist fear on the part of the S.S. was sustained as much by S.S. Dr. Ding-Schuller, as by the prisoners, but for different reasons (for example, by posting bulletins on the barbed wire that isolated the Block). Candidates for death, such as the Dutch physician Van Lingen, the architect Harry Pieck and other Netherlanders, the Polish doctor, Dr. Marian Ciepielowski (production chief in this service), Professor Dr. Balachowsky, of the Pasteur Institute at Paris, the author of this work, in his capacity as an Austrian publicist, and seven Jewish comrades, found refuge in this Block, *with Dr. Ding-Schuller's approval.* (Page 163, emphasis added.)

It must be admitted that Eugen Kogon had put himself in serious pawn to the "Communist" nucleus that was preponderant in the camp—in the face of other "green" groups, politicals and even *Communists!*—in order to get assigned by them to this position of confidence. And, that assignment was made "with the approval of Doctor Ding-Schuller" it must be remembered. Now this is what he could do in this position:

> As a result of the requests which, every time, I suggested, drew up, and presented for signature, they were protected from sudden round-ups, extermination transports, etc . . . (Page 183)
>
> During the last two years which I spent as secretary to the doctor, I wrote out, with the help of the specialist of Block 50, at least half a dozen medical communications on exanthematous typhus . . . which were signed by Dr. Schuller. I will mention only in passing that I was also assigned to take care of a part of his private correspondence, including love and condolence letters. Often, he did not even read the answers; he threw me the letters after having opened them, and said to me, "Fix that up, Kogon. You know what to reply. It's some widow looking for consolation . . ." (Page 270)

And, he could state, "I had Dr. Ding-Schuller in the palm of my hand," (Page 218), and to such an extent that the fact that he was "on bad terms with the *Kapo* of Block 46" did not disturb him at all.

Clearly, on the basis of the preceding quotations, Kogon knew how to get into the graces of the influential clique in the *Häftlingsführung,* while, at the same time, staying in the graces of one of the highest S.S. authorities of the camp. All of those persons who have lived in a concentration camp will agree that such a position could not be engineered without infringing upon the rules of morality which are customarily observed outside the camps.

II. The Method

> In order to dispell certain fears, and to show that this report [that is what he calls his *Enfer organisé*] cannot be construed as an accusation against certain prisoners who held dominant positions, I read it aloud, at the beginning of the month of May 1945, as soon as it was down on paper, lacking only the last two chapters out of a total of twelve, to a group of fifteen

people, who had been members of the clandestine government of the camp,[6] or who represented certain political alignments among the prisoners. These persons approved its accuracy and its objectivity. Present at the reading were:

1. Walter Bartel, Communist from Berlin, president of the international committee in the camp.

2. Heinz Baumeister, Social-Democrat, from Dortmund, who for years had been a member of the Buchenwald Secretariat; second secretary of Block 50.

3. Ernst Busse, Communist, from Solingen, *Kapo* of the prisoners' infirmary.

4. Boria Banilenko, head of Communist youth groups in the Ukraine, member of the Russian committee.

5. Hans Eiden, Communist, from Trier, first camp elder.

6. Baptiste Feilen, Communist, from Aix-la-Chapelle, washhouse *Kapo.*

7. Franz Hackel, Left independent, from Prague. One of our friends, without position in the camp.

8. Stephan Heymann, Communist, from Mannheim, member of camp information office.

9. Werner Hilpert, Centrist, from Leipzig, member of the international committee in the camp.

10. Otto Horn, Communist, from Vienna, member of the Austrian committee.

11. A. Kaltschin, Russian prisoner of war, member of the Russian committee.

12. Otto Kipp, Communist, from Dresden, assistant *Kapo* of the prisoners' infirmary.

13. Ferdinand Romhild, Communist, from Frankfurt am Main, first secretary of the prisoners' infirmary.

14. Ernst Thappe, Social-Democrat, head of the German committee.

15. Walter Wolff, Communist, head of the camp information office. (Page 20-21)

This prefactory statement, in itself, is enough to render suspect the entire testimony: "In order to dispel certain fears, and to show that this report cannot be construed as an accusation against certain prisoners who held dominant positions in the

camp . . . " Thus has Eugen Kogon avoided reporting anything
accusatory against the *Häftlingsführung;* rather, he harbored
grievances only against the S.S. No historian could ever accept
that. On the contrary, one is justified in thinking that in this
way he has paid a debt of gratitude to those who got him his
privileged positions in the camp and that he has chosen to
defend those with whom he had common interests, as well as
himself, before the public.

And, besides, the fifteen persons listed who passed judgment on his "accuracy and objectivity" are suspect. They are
all Communists or fellow-travelers, and if, by chance, there
was an exception, he could only be under obligation to the
others. Lastly, the list is made up of the highest functionaries
of the *Häftlingsführung* of Buchenwald who, naturally, are
likely to share Kogon's point of view.

I consider such titles as "president" or "member" of this
or that "committee" with which they are tricked out to be
meaningless. They awarded such titles to themselves at the
time of the liberation of the camp by the Americans, or even
afterwards. And, I pay little attention to the notion of "committees", for reasons which I have dealt with elsewhere. As I
see it, these fifteen persons were only too happy to find in
Eugen Kogon an artful pen with which to free them from all
the responsibility for their actions in the camp in the eyes of
posterity.

III. The Häftlingsführung.

It had the following duties: to maintain order in the camp;
to maintain discipline in order to avoid the intervention of the
S.S., etc . . . this made it possible to do away with the S.S.
patrols in the camp; their task was to receive the new arrivals;
this little by little eliminated the brutal wrangling of the S.S.
It was a difficult and thankless job. The guards of Buchenwald
camp very rarely struck blows, although there were often
savage rows. The new arrivals, who came from other camps,
were terrified at first when they were met by those who were
guards at camp Buchenwald, but later they always came to
appreciate how much better their reception had been than in
other places . . . To be sure there was always this or that
member of the camp guard who, judging by his way of expressing himself, ought to have been an S.S. But that didn't matter
much. The aim alone counted: *To keep a nucleus of prisoners*

against the S.S. If the camp guard had not seen to an impeccable appearance of order in front of the S.S., what might not have become of the entire camp, and its thousands of prisoners, in the line of punitive labors and, *last but not least,* during the last days before liberation? (Page 62, emphasis added)

Looking back on my personal experience and on the reception that my convoy received at the two different camps, it is not possible for me to concede that it was any better at Buchenwald than it was at Dora. But, I must also acknowledge that conditions in general at Buchenwald and at Dora were not to be compared: the first was a sanatorium when compared to the second. But, to conclude that the relatively better conditions of Buchenwald were due to a difference in the make-up, the nature, and the political and philosophical convictions between the two *Häftlingsführung* would be an error. If they had been transposed *en bloc,* the result would have been the same. In both cases, their behavior was governed by the over-all conditions of existence in each camp, and over these factors they had no control.

At the time of which Eugen Kogon is speaking, Buchenwald was at the end of its evolution. Almost everything had been completed: the various services were installed and things were in order. The S.S. guards themselves, having to face fewer of the worries that always accompany disorder, settled into a routine that was almost without mishaps; in short, their nerves were much less on edge. At Dora, on the other hand, the camp was in full construction; everything had to be built and put into place with the limited resources of a country at war. Disorder was the natural state of things. Everything was in a jumble. The S.S. were unapproachable, and the *Häftlingsführung,* not knowing what to do to please them, often exceeded their desires. But, at Buchenwald, the exactions of a *Kapo* or a camp elder, identical in their motives and aims, were less comprehensive, because, with conditions in every way better, the consequences were not so serious for the mass of the prisoners.

As additional support for this contention, is the fact that in the fall of 1944, when Dora was, in its turn, almost completed, and with the *Häftlingsführung* having in no way modified its conduct, the material and moral conditions there could stand comparison with Buchenwald. Unfortunately, at that moment the end of the war was imminent, the bombings had interfered with the getting of supplies, and the advance of the Allies on two fronts had caused the overpopulation of Dora with prisoners who had been evacuated from camps in the East and the West. As a consequence, everything in the camp was in turmoil again.

There remains to be discussed the line of reasoning according to which it was important, in order to maintain a nucleus against the S.S., to substitute a prisoner bureaucracy for them. But, since the whole camp was naturally against the S.S., I do not understand this reasoning. It could be argued that it would have been better to keep everyone *alive* to oppose the S.S. guards, and not just a nucleus of prisoners who were under their orders, if only to create extra difficulties for them . . . Instead of that, a method was used which, while it saved that precious nucleus, it killed the mass. As Eugen Kogon recognizes, after David Rousset, urbanity was not the only thing that came into the discussion:

> In fact, the prisoners never received the scant rations which were in principle meant for them. First, the S.S. took what they pleased. Then the prisoners who worked in the food store-houses and in the kitchens worked it so they could set apart an ample share. Then the heads of the barracks diverted a good lot for themselves and for their friends. The rest went to the miserable ordinary prisoners. (Page 107)

There is room here to point out that everyone who had a shred of authority in the camp was by that very fact in a position to "set apart": the camp elder who delivered the rations in bulk; the *Kapo* and the Block chief who helped themselves copiously in the first place; the foreman and the ward keeper who cut the bread or put soup into the bowls; the police; the secretary, etc . . . It is strange that Kogon does not mention this fact. All of these people literally gorged themselves on what they stole, and walked around the camp with prosperous appearances. Not the slightest scruple stopped them:

> In the prisoners' infirmary in the camps there was special food for the sick, which was called "the diet." It was very much sought after as a supplement, and most of it was diverted to the profit of the camp personages: Block elders, *Kapos,* etc . . . In every camp could be found *communists or criminals who for years received in addition to their other advantages, the extras for the sick.* It was above all a matter of good relations with the kitchen for the sick, composed exclusively

of people belonging to that category of prisoners who dominated the camp, or of an exchange of services rendered: the
Kapos of the sewing shop, cobbler, clothing storehouse, tool
house, etc . . ., turned over, in exchange for this food, what
was asked of them. In Buchenwald, from 1939 to 1941, nearly
forty thousand eggs were made away with in this way, right
inside the camp. (Pages 110, 111, 112, emphasis added.)

Meanwhile, the sick in the infirmary were dying from the lack
of this special food which the S.S. had intended for them. In
explaining the mechanics of the thievery, Kogon just calls it
an aspect of "system D", indiscriminately used by all of the
prisoners who were involved with the distribution of the food.
Such a characterization is both inaccurate and charitable, with
regard to the *Häftlingsführung.*

The worker, in whatever *Kommando,* could not steal, because the *Kapo* and the foreman, all set to denounce him,
watched him very closely. At the most when the distribution of
rations was made, he could risk taking something from one of
his fellow sufferers. But, the *Kapo* and the foreman, working
together, could set aside something from the supply of rations,
before distribution, and this they cynically did. And this
"setting aside" was done with impunity, too, because they
could not be denounced except through the chain of command, that is, through themselves. They stole for themselves,
for their friends, for those in authority to whom they were
indebted for their positions, and, in the higher ranks of the
hierarchy, for the S.S., from whom they hoped to keep or get
protection.

As for the diet of the sick, the *Kapo* of the infirmary—the
very one who attested to the accuracy and the objectivity of
Kogon's testimony—expropriated a considerable quantity for
the benefit of his colleagues and the accredited Communists.[7]
During my stay at Buchenwald, every morning he set aside some
milk, about a liter, and some other delicacies, for Erich, chief
of Block 48. Multiply this example of plunder by the number
of persons in the whole camp, who also had the opportunity
to steal, and one can see the amount of milk which the sick in
the infirmary never received. Compared to this kind of theft,
the petty scroungings along the food distribution circuit were
insignificant.

Thus, whether it is a question of the normal rations or the "diet" for the sick, the common mass of prisoners had two reasons for dying of hunger: the food that was taken by the S.S.[8] and the food that was taken by the *Häftlingsführung*. The rank and file prisoners also had two reasons for being beaten and for being maltreated in general: the *Kapo* who stole extra, also hit harder to please the S.S. and it was rare when a simple reprimand from a S.S. guard did not bring on, in addition, a whole rain of blows from the *Kapo*. Given these conditions, there were few prisoners who did not prefer to deal directly with the S.S.

IV. The Arguments

The arguments that are used to justify the protection of a nucleus of "elite" prisoners at the expense of the common masses of prisoners are in no way more convincing than the facts. Without this prisoner elite, "what would have become of the entire camp, especially at the moment of liberation?" Kogon asks himself fearfully. From what has been said, it is already clear that the common prisoners would have had one less reason to die (*"crever"*) at the rate they were dying. It is not enough of an answer for him to add, "It was thus that the first American tanks, coming from the Northwest, found Buchenwald liberated," (Page 304) and to give the credit for that liberation to the *Häftlingsführung*. To make such an assertion does not make it true. With such an argument, one could also say that the American Army entered a liberated France, and that, too, would be ridiculous. The truth of the matter is that the S.S. withdrew before the American advance, and, trying to take with them as many prisoners as possible, they set the *Häftlingsführung* personnel, bludgeons in hand, to round up as many prisoners as possible throughout the camp.

Thanks to the willing cooperation of the *Häftlingsführung*, the manhunt took place with a minimum of disorder. And, if by some miraculous chance the American offensive had been stopped before the camp, and a vigorous German counter-offensive had reversed the outcome of the war, this reasoning would offer a sure advantage as revealed in these lines:

> The S.S. staffs of the camps were not capable of enforcing on tens of thousands of prisoners more than an outward and sporadic control. (Page 275)

In other words, with a victorious Germany each member of the *Häftlingsführung* of the camp could have pleaded his personal contribution to the maintenance of order and his loyalty, in an effort to obtain his liberation. And, the lines that we have just read could have appeared without the changing of a comma.

> Through ceaseless struggle, the system of the S.S., to mix together the various categories of prisoners, to encourage natural antagonisms and to provoke artificial ones, had to be broken and made inoperable. The reasons for that were clear to the reds. With the greens it was not at all political reasons; they wanted to be able to have a free course for their customary practices: corruption, extortion, the seeking of material advantages. Any control was insupportable to them, especially that from within the camp itself. (Page 278)

It is obvious that no matter what system the S.S. used it had to become inoperable from the moment when, used by others for the same purposes, it was applied to the same object and in the same way. Even more: it was useless. The S.S. no longer had any need to hit men, since those to whom they had delegated their power did the hitting better; nor to steal, since their minions stole better and the benefits were the same, if not more substantial; nor to kill slowly to make order respected, because others did that for them, and order in the camp was all the more perfect for it.

In spite of what Kogon says, I never observed that the intervention of the camp bureaucracy had any effect on the "natural antagonisms" between prisoners or that the various categories of prisoners were less "mixed together" than had been intended by the S.S.

Moreover, the integration of the whole prisoner population was not the objective of the *Häftlingsführung;* rather, to divide and rule, a principle that holds for any power wanting to maintain itself, was just as valid for the camp bureaucracy as for the S.S. In practice, while the latter vaguely set the mass of prisoners against those they had chosen to rule them, the former played with political nuances, with the nature of the crime, and with the selection of a nucleus of men of a certain mentality.

What is amusing — from a distance — in Kogon's thesis, is the distinction he drew between the "reds" and the "greens" concerning the manner in which each group exercised its power, accusing the latter of corruption, bribery, and self-seeking. What did the "reds" do that was not all of that? And, for the ordinary prisoner, what difference did it make to him who was in power, when it was impossible for him to see any resulting difference.

What happened in the concentration camps was that in the struggle to keep alive, appetites more or less understandable took precedence over all moral principles. At the bottom of everything was the basic desire to survive. Along with this desire, among the less scrupulous, went the need to steal food, and then the need to clan together in order to steal food better. Those who were the most skillful at organizing in order to get better nourishment — i.e., the politicals, since under the circumstances the task of organizing called more for cleverness than strength — were then the most able to obtain power, because they were better fed. And once in power, they were also better able to hold onto it, because they were intellectually more adept. But, no moral principle, in the sense that it is understood in the world outside of the concentration camps, played any part in this evolution, except by its absence. And, then to write:

> In every camp the political prisoners tried to take in hand the internal administrative machinery or, as the case might be, struggled to hold onto it. This in order to *defend itself by every means* against the S.S., not just to fight the hard battle for life, but also to further, insofar as possible, the disintegration and crushing of the system. In more than one camp, the leaders of the political prisoners, for years, worked at this end, with admirable perseverance, and complete contempt for death. (Page 275, emphasis added.)

This statement is only pap, whose laudatory tone fails to hide the fact that it puts all of the political prisoners — even those who never wanted to exercise any authority over their fellow sufferers — in a class with the least scrupulous of them. Nor, does the admission *"defend itself by every means . . . "* help either. "By every means:" this is what that could mean:

> When the S.S. asked the politicals to make a selection of
> those prisoners "unfit to live,"[9] in order to kill them, and that
> a refusal might have meant the end of the control of the reds
> and a return of the greens, then they had to be prepared to
> take the burden of that transgression. Their only choice lay be-
> tween taking an active participation in that selection, or a pos-
> sible withdrawal of their responsibilities in the camp, which,
> after all that had already been experienced, could have had
> even worse consequences. The more tender the conscience, the
> harder it was to make this decision. But since it had to be
> made, and without delay, it was better for it to lie in the hands
> of those of strong constitution, so that we would not all be
> made martyrs. (Page 327)

I have already remarked that it was not a question of selecting the unfit *to live*, but, rather, the unfit *for work*. The difference is considerable. If one wants to overlook it at any cost, I
submit that it would have been better to "risk a possible[10]
withdrawal of their responsibilities in the camp" than to have
burdened their collective conscience with this "active participation" that was always so zealously carried out. Maybe, the
"greens" would have come back to power? But, so what? In the
first place, they were not likely to have retained it. And, in the
second place, the "greens" would not have behaved any worse
than the "reds" with regard to the mass of the prisoners. They
would not have selected any greater number of prisoners as unfit; nor would they have taken any less account of the background of the designated prisoners, because, in these selections,
the "reds" were no less concerned than the "greens" over political caste. The fact was that the *Häftlingsführung*, whether
"green" or "red," used the selection procedure as a method of
getting rid of potential rivals.

Consequently, and, if it meant assuming the same moral burden, why take power away from the "greens," or seek to prevent them from holding it? It is possible that with the "greens"
in power, the selection of the unfit, with a few exceptions,
might not have been the same. But, nothing would have been
changed as far as the number of unfit was concerned, since that
figure was determined by the general work statistics and the a-
mount of provisions available in the camp for the support of

non-working prisoners. Under such circumstances, Eugen Kogon himself might perhaps not have been in a position to become, or to remain, the secretary and aide-de-camp to the S.S. camp physician Dr. Ding-Schuller, and, once returned to the mass of common prisoners, and once beaten and starved, perhaps he, too, might have been included among the number of those found to be "unfit." Probably the same thing could have happened to the fifteen others who sanctioned his testimony. Then, had this most unthinkable of catastrophes actually occurred, only this could have happened: these fifteen would have been "made martyrs," while others would have continued to live as witnesses.

As if it mattered to History whether Kogon and his associates or some others were witnesses, like Michelin de Clermont, Fernand, Francois de Tessan, Doctor Seguin, Cremieux, Desnos, among others . . . When Kogon said "so that *we* would not *all* be made martyrs," he was referring, of course, only to the privileged prisoners among the *Häftlingsführung*, and not to all of the politicals who, in spite of what has been said, made up the majority of the prison population. Not for an instant did Kogon think that by being satisfied with eating less and with beating less, the concentration camp bureaucracy could have saved almost all of the prisoners; if that had happened, today we would reap only benefits in that they too would be witnesses.

How could a man as informed as Kogon, and affecting a degree of culture, have arrived at such garbled conclusions? The reason may be seen in the fact that he tried to judge the prisoners and guards, and the events that took place in the world of the concentration camp, by the standards of the outside world. We do the same thing when we form an opinion about what is taking place in the Soviet Union or in Red China, based on the moral codes of the western world, and the Russians and the Chinese do the same to us. On both sides of the "Iron Curtain," an Order has been created, and making it function has given rise to a type of men whose conceptions of social life and of individual conduct are different and, indeed, even opposite in nature.

The same is true of the concentration camps: ten years of existence were enough to create an Order within the camps, and all must be judged on its terms. In particular, this Order gave rise to a new type of man, who can be classed somewhere between the common prisoner and the political prisoner. The characteristic feature of this new type of man resulted from the fact that the common prisoner corrupted the political prisoner, made him almost like the former, without troubling his conscience very much. It was to this level that the camp was reduced by those who had conceived of it. The camp gave direction to the reactions of all of the prisoners, "green" or "red," and not the reverse. With this fact established — and to the extent that one is willing to admit that it is not a mental fabrication — the moral code of the world outside the concentration camps can pardon what happened in the camps, but it can in no case justify what happened there.

V. The Conduct of the S.S.

I put side by side two statements:

> Those prisoners who maltreated their comrades, or even beat them to death, were certainly never punished by the S.S. but were turned over to the justice of the prisoners. (Page 98)

> One morning a prisoner was found hanged in a Block. An investigation was started and it was seen that the "hanged" man had died after having been horribly beaten and trampled on, and that the barracks man, under the direction of the Block elder Osterloh,[11] had then hanged him to make it look like a suicide. The victim had protested against a misappropriation of bread by the barracks man. The S.S. staff *succeeded*[12] in hushing the matter up and put the murderer back in his post so that nothing was changed. (Page 50)

It is true that the S.S. personnel did not usually intervene in the disputes among the prisoners and that one waited in vain for any pronouncement of justice from them. It could not be otherwise, since "they did not know what was actually happening behind the barbed wire." (Page 275) The reason for this ignorance on the part of the S.S. was that the *Häftlingsführung* made every effort to see to it that they were kept in the dark concerning the day to day happenings in the camp. By setting itself up as a veritable "court of prisoners," and by profiting from the fact that no appeal could be made against its decisions, the *Häftlingsführung* never had need for recourse to the S.S. except to strengthen its own authority if it felt that it was weakening. In any case, the camp bureaucrats did not like to see the

intervention of the S.S. for fear that the S.S. would be less severe, a situation which would have brought their authority into
question with the mass of prisoners. In addition, such intervention might have caused the S.S. to question their ability to gov-
ern, which, in turn, might have caused them to be relieved
from their duties and to be returned to the rank and file. As a
practical matter, there existed an implicit operating procedure
between the *Häftlingsführung* and the S.S.: the *Häftlingsführung* "avoided trouble" by preventing the various camp happenings from seeping through the screen of its own edifice, and the
S.S. made no attempt to know what was going on in the camp
as long as order was maintained.

In the specific case which Kogon mentions, if Block Chief Osterloh had been a "red," nothing concerning the matter would
have reached the ears of the S.S. other than the fact that the
victim had been a suicide, a fact which would not have resulted
in any difficulties. But, he was a "green," and he represented
one of the last elements of power which his category still held
in the camp. The "reds" denounced him in the hope of getting
rid of him. However, the S.S. did not settle the matter in the
way that they had hoped. This is the way of the Order: a Block
Chief, even guilty, could not be questioned or punished except
by some higher authority, and, in no case, could he be punished
from the prisoner masses. Whether a "green" or a "red," that is
the way that it was.

One can reverse the facts of the preceding example and make
Osterloh the victim, and his victim the murderer. In such a case,
the *Häftlingsführung* itself would have reacted this way: without worrying about Osterloh's color, it would have felt itself
attacked or threatened in its prerogatives and would have sent
for the S.S. – demanding an exemplary punishment unless,
which is more likely, it had first given the punishment – in
which case it would only have asked the S.S. to approve it. In
the first situation, the S.S. would forward the matter to a higher
echelon and would wait for a decision. In the meantime, blows
would rain down from everywhere on the murderer as he would
be taken to the *Bunker*[13] where he would be subjected to further corporal punishment. In the second situation, the S.S.
would endorse the action of the *Häftlingsführung,* precisely to
avoid the demands for explanations, and the sundry other difficulties, that would be forthcoming from that higher echelon. In

both cases, nothing would happen that was not compatible with the Order.

The authorities in Berlin had to intervene in the Osterloh affair, to which the "reds" had imprudently given the character of a matter of conscience in which honesty attacked the Order; this intervention stirred up so many difficulties that the S.S. staff at Buchenwald had no choice but to *succeed* in hushing the matter up. Besides, generally speaking, the S.S. staff personnel did not like to refer matters to Berlin. They feared the delays, the unaccustomed attention, indeed the scruples, which could cause troubles, the chief one being the transfer to another unit, which in war time could be most consequential. In order to hush things up, Berlin was kept in almost complete ignorance of what was happening and was informed only of what could not be concealed. The S.S. staff of Buchenwald exercised maximum control on the spot.

To the reader who might think that I have exaggerated with regard to the state of ignorance of the authorities in Berlin, permit me to point to the present situation in France. There, the Ministers of Justice and of National Education do not know what really takes place in the prisons, and the so-called houses of correction. For example, the disciplinary practices of the minor prison authorities are generally in constant and flagrant violation of the official regulations, and no one— either in the Ministries or among the general public—knows anything about it, except when there is an occasional scandal. And so it is in every country in the world that there is a "universe" of delinquents living on the fringe of the other, lifers, of whom the *chaouch* is king. Within the limits of that "universe" are also the colonial peoples; and the Colonial Ministers and the Ministers of War, to whom they are subject, are also generally ignorant of the conduct of their adjutants, unless, and until, some particularly abhorrent behavior on the part of their subordinates comes to light which, because of political considerations, cannot be ignored.

And, here is another citation from Kogon which is just as significant:

> Visits of the S.S. frequently took place in the camps. When this happened, the S.S. staff went through an astonishing procedure: on the one hand they concealed all side structures; on the other they organized regular displays. Anything that

might have led anyone to suspect that the prisoners were tortured was passed over in silence by the guides, and they were concealed. It was in this manner that the famous torture rack which was on the mustering grounds was hidden in one of the barracks until the visitors left. It seems that once they overlooked these prudent measures: when a visitor asked what the thing was, one of the camp chiefs answered that it was a carpentry model for making special forms. The gallows and the stakes on which the prisoners were hanged were also put out of sight each time. The visitors were conducted through "model · installations:" infirmary, cinema, kitchen, library, stores, laundry, and the agriculture section. If they actually went into a block, it was where the barbers and the servants of the S.S. and a few privileged prisoners lived "detached," blocks which for that reason were never over crowded and were always clean. In the kitchen garden as well as in the sculpture workshop, the S.S. visitors sometimes received presents as souvenirs. (Page 258)

This description is of Buchenwald. If one wants to know who these visitors were, we have this:

There were group visits, and visits of individuals. The latter were especially frequent during the vacations, when the S.S. showed the camp to their friends or relatives. These were also for the most part S.S. personnel or heads of the S.A., sometimes also officers of the *Wehrmacht* or the police. The group visits were of different kinds. We frequently saw batches of police or gendarme promotions from a near-by station, or batches of S.S. aspirants. After the war began, visits from officers of the *Luftwaffe.* From time to time, we also had visits from civilians. Once to Buchenwald there came youth delegations from the Fascist countries, who had come together at Weimar for some "cultural congress." Groups of the Hitler youth also came to the camp. Distinguished visitors, such as Gauleiter Sauckel, police commissioner Hennicke of Weimar, Prince Waldeck Pyrmont, Count Ciano, Italian minister of foreign affairs, commanding officers of military divisions, Doctor Conti, and other visitors in that class, more often than not stayed until the evening roll-call. (Page 257)

Thus were carefully hidden all traces of brutality not only from the general run of visitors, but also from those visitors who held the highest positions in the S.S. and in the Third Reich. I imagine that when these personages inspected Dachau and Birkenau, as well as other camps, explanations as pertinent

as that which was given for the alleged torture rack at Buchenwald would have been given them for the alleged gas chambers
at Birkenau. And, I ask this question: how can it be maintained
after all this, that all of the horrors of which the camps were the
stage were part of a plan that had been conceived "in high
places?"

When, in spite of all that was kept hidden, the authorities
in Berlin discovered something awry in the administration of
the camps, the S.S. staffs were called to account. An example
is provided by a directive coming from the Chief of Section D,
dated April 4, 1942:

> The *Reichführer* of the S.S. and Chief of the German po-
> lice, has directed that concerning his orders for the bastonade
> (this applies to men as well as to women in preventive de-
> tention) it will be proper in cases where the word "aggravated"
> is attached, to apply the punishment on the naked posterior.
> In all other cases, the method customary up to the present
> will be used in conformity with previous instructions from the
> S.S. *Reichführer.*

Eugen Kogon, who cites this circular, adds:

> In principle, before applying the bastonade, the camp staff
> had to ask approval from Berlin, and the camp physician had
> to certify to the S.S. W.V.H. that the prisoner was in good
> health. But it had been the custom for a long time in all the
> camps, right to the end in a great many of them, to send the
> prisoner first to the "rack" and to give him as many blows
> as was judged good. Then, after getting approval from Berlin,
> they began again, but this time officially. (Page 99)

It goes without saying that the bastonade was almost always
applied to the naked posterior, and that it was to combat this
abuse, and not to aggravate the punishment, that the directive
in question was sent to all of the camps.

One can certainly be astonished and find it barbarous that
the bastonade played any part in the punishment of the prisoners in the camps. But, the reason for its use is another story:
in a country like Germany where until the end of the First
World War it was prescribed as the most lenient of punishments,
under the name of "*Schlag,*" it is not so surprising that its use
was retained by the National Socialists for the punishment of
major criminals, especially when we remember that the government of the Weimar Republic was not disturbed by its use. On

the other hand, it is more astonishing—in view of the reams of French governmental circulars that have denied the use of the bastonade for almost a century—that thousands of Negroes in the French colonies continue to suffer such punishment, and in actual fact suffer it "with naked posterior," since they have the misfortune, in addition, to live in those regions of the earth where they would have no reason to clothe themselves except for protection from the bastonade.

Another directive, dated December 28, 1942, emanating from the central S.S. office concerned with economic administration and bearing the signature of General Kludre of the S.S. and the *Waffen* S.S., says:

> . . . The camp doctors should supervise the food of the prisoners more than they have up to the present, and in agreement with the administration, they should submit to the commanding officer of the camp their suggestions for improvement. The latter should not just remain on paper, but be regularly checked by the camp physicians. It is necessary that the mortality rate be appreciably lowered in each camp, since the number of the prisoners must be brought back to the level required by the *Reichführer* S.S. The head doctors of the camp shall do everything possible to achieve this. The best doctor in a concentration camp is not the one who thinks it helpful to call attention to himself through uncalled for harshness, but the one who maintains to the highest possible degree the capacity for work in every shop, by keeping an eye on the health of the workers, and in making adjustments. (Pages 111, 141)

As was mentioned in the previous chapter, David Rousset published a collection of documents relating to alleged German atrocities of all sorts under the title *Le Pitre ne rit pas;* however, Rousset does not discuss the second of the two documents that are cited above because it destroys much of his argument. He does cite the first document, but he does so in a completely twisted sense. In this respect, although there are reasons for distrusting Kogon's interpretations, we must rejoice in the fact that he was objective enough to include the second. Perhaps, there may exist more documents which support my thesis and which lie still in the German archives, or in those of the Allied victors, and which have not been brought to light yet . . . .

VI. Health Personnel

In the first years the hospital staff was incompetent. But little by little it acquired a great deal of practical experience. The head *Kapo* of the infirmary at Buchenwald was a printer by trade; his successor, Walter Kramer, was a strong and courageous person, a hard worker, and with a sense of organization. With time he became a remarkable specialist in wounds and operations. Through his position, the *Kapo of* the infirmary exercised, in all the camps, a considerable influence on over-all living conditions. *So the prisoners*[14] *never put a specialist into that position, although it might have been possible in numerous camps, but rather a person who was completely devoted to the ruling clique in the camp.* When, for example, in November 1941, the *Kapo* Kramer and his closest collaborator Peix were shot by the S.S., the post of head of the infirmary did not go to a doctor, but was given, on the contrary, to a former Communist deputy to the *Reichstag,* Ernst Busse, who, with his assistant Otto Kipp from Dresden, concerned *himself with the purely administrative side*[15] of that service, whose activity never ceased growing, and played a large part in the greater stabilization of living conditions. A specialist put at the head of that service would, without any doubt, have brought catastrophe on the camp, because he never would have been able to dominate all the complicated and far-reaching intrigues, the outcome of which was very often fatal. (Page 135, emphasis added.)

One trembles at the thought that such a line of reasoning could have been advanced by Kogon, without batting an eye, and broadcast to the public, without rousing waves of indignant protest. To understand the full horror, it is important to know that in his turn the *Kapo* chose his assistants for reasons that had nothing to do with their competence as medical practitioners. And, to think that these so-called "leaders of the prisoners," who exposed thousands of miserable men to various brutalities and who stole their food, had them treated, without being forced to do it by the S.S., by people who were absolutely incompetent.

The drama began at the entrance to the infirmary:

When the sick man finally got there, he first had to stand in line outside, no matter what the weather, and with his shoes cleaned. Since it was not possible to examine all the sick, and since there were always among them prisoners who

only had the understandable desire to escape work, a *sturdy*
doorman, a prisoner, proceeded to make the first basic selection of the sick. (Page 130, emphasis added.)

The *Kapo*, chosen because he was a Communist, picked out
a doorman, not because he was capable of telling the sick from
the malingerers, or of distinguishing those who were more sick
from those who were less, but because he was husky, and was
able to give a good thrashing to anyone who tried to get past
him without permission. It goes without saying that he was kept
in good shape with extra food rations. The reasons for the choice
of the nurses and the doctors, if not quite the same, were just
as nobly inspired. When, finally, there were prisoners who were
medical doctors in the camp infirmaries, it was because the S.S.
insisted on it. I pass over the humiliations, even the retaliatory
measures, which these doctors were made to suffer every time
that the demands of their consciences came into conflict with
the demands of politics and intrigue.

Eugen Kogon saw benefits in the procedure: *Kapo* Kramer
had become "a remarkable specialist in wounds and operations,"
and he adds:

> A good friend of mine, Willi Jellineck, was a pastry cook in
> Vienna . . . . At Buchenwald he was undertaker, a zero in the
> camp hierarchy. As a Jew, young, tall, and uncommonly
> strong, he had small chance of surviving during Koch's time.
> And yet, what did he become? Our best tuberculosis expert,
> a remarkable practitioner who helped many a comrade, and,
> in addition, was the bacteriologist of Block 50 . . . (Page 324)

I am willing to disregard the use made of, and the fate of, the
professional doctors whom the *Häftlingsführung* considered,
individually and collectively, less useful than comrades Kramer
and Jellineck. I am also willing to disregard the number of the
dead who paid for the training and the remarkable expertise of
the latter. But, if it can be conceded that these considerations
are of negligible significance, then there is no reason for not
extending this practice into the non-concentration camp world.
In pursuit of this goal, one could issue two decrees at once: the
first would disband all of the schools of medicine and replace
them with training centers for pastry cooks and machinists; the
second would dispatch to the kitchen or factory all of the
doctors who are practicing and would replace them with pastry
cooks and machinists who are Communists or fellow-travelers.

I do not doubt that the latter would emerge from such a reversal of roles in an honorable fashion; instead of blaming them for the deaths that they would cause, they would be credited for their adroitness in surviving all of the intrigues of political life. That is one way of looking at it.

VII. Devotion

> From the beginning, the prisoners attached to the dental staff tried to help their comrades as much as possible. In all the dental centers they worked clandestinely, running great risks, and in a way hard to imagine. They made dentures, artificial parts, bridges, for those prisoners whose teeth had been broken by the S.S., or who had lost them because of the general conditions of life. (Page 131)

This statement is correct. But the "comrades" who were helped were always the same: a *Kapo,* a Block chief, a camp elder, a secretary, etc . . . Those among the mass of prisoners who had lost their teeth for the reasons given above died without having recovered their loss with artificial teeth, or, if they survived, they had to wait for the liberation to be cared for. But, the clandestine nature of this work was very peculiar in view of the fact that it had the previous consent of the S.S.:

> During the war, 1939-1940, they managed to set up a clandestine operation ward, thanks to the close collaboration of a series of *Kommandos,* and with the secret consent of the S.S. Doctor Blies. . . (Page 132)

The scope and the impact of this revelation can be appreciated when one realizes that the dental and medical installations in the camps were intended for the benefit of all of the prisoners in all of the camps and, that, thanks to the complicity of certain well placed S.S. personnel, these facilities were diverted to the sole benefit of the *Häftlingsführung.* In my opinion, if those who proceeded to misuse those facilities "ran great risks," that was only very just . . . as seen from below.

Eugen Kogon himself feels the weakness of this reasoning:

> In the last year, the internal administration of Buchenwald was so closely organized that the S.S. no longer had any say over certain very important internal matters. Tired, the S.S. was now accustomed to "let things go," and on the whole the politicals had a free hand . . . . Most certainly it was always the directing clique, which identified itself more or less with

the active anti-fascist forces, that most profited from the state of affairs: the mass of prisoners benefited only at times, and indirectly, mostly in that they no longer had to fear the intervention of the S.S., since those running the prisoners had taken steps on their own authority in the interests of all. (Page 284)

Obviously, it can be explained that if the S.S. " . . . let things go, and on the whole the politicals had a free hand," it was because the S.S. were "tired" or "accustomed to doing so." This is a way of looking at things. But, I am more persuaded to believe that this delegation of authority by the S.S. was due to the fact that the politicals had proven their devotion to the maintenance of order, on numerous occasions, and thus had established a "track record" from which the S.S. deduced that they could be trusted to assume a great deal of responsibility. As for the "steps [taken] . . . in the interest of all," they might have prevented the intervention of the S.S., but it was precisely this lack of intervention by the S.S. which gave a free hand to the *Häftlingsführung* a fact which, in turn, had a catastrophic effect on the mass of prisoners. It is better to be dealt with by God than by his saints. Furthermore. if power becomes consolidated to the degree that it succeeds in neutralizing the possible opposition, reciprocally, it grows weaker from dissensions among those who share it. Looked at in this way, the S.S., by exercising a constant and meticulous control over everything that took place in the camp, would have substituted mistrust for an attitude of connivance in all of its relations with the *Häftlingsführung.* That the S.S. did not want that is easily understood. But, the *Häftlingsführung* did not want it either; this prisoner bureaucracy had deliberately crossed the Rubicon, and, although it might have shared the common lot with the mass of the prisoners of the concentration camps, it preferred, whatever the rancor of the mass, to collaborate with the S.S. and to enjoy the benefits derived from such collaboration.

VIII. Cinema, sports

Once or twice per week, sometimes after quite long intervals, the cinema offered entertaining and documentary films. Given the frightful condition of life which prevailed in the camps, more than one comrade could not make up his mind to go to the cinema. (Page 128)

A strange thing, there was in the camps something that resembled sports. Yet the conditions of life did not lend themselves very well. There were, nevertheless, young men who thought they still had energy to expend, and they managed to get the authorization of the S.S. to play soccer. And, the weak who could just barely walk, those emaciated, exhausted men, half dead on their trembling legs, the starved, went with pleasure to this spectacle! (Page 124-125)

These weak, starved, half dead men who Eugen Kogon reports watched a game of soccer with pleasure, although *standing,* are the same who he thought, given the frightful conditions of existence, did not have the heart to go to a movie where one could *sit down.*

The truth is that the common prisoners did not go to the movies because every time that there was one, all of the seats were reserved by the *Häftlingsführung* people. It was different for soccer: the field was out in the open where everyone could see, and the surrounding grounds were big. Everyone could go. And, even so, some *Kapo* might take it into his head to break up the crowd of spectators and, with bludgeon in hand, chase all of those miserable men back toward the Blocks, on the pretext that they would profit more from their Sunday afternoon by resting!

As for the "young men who thought they still had energy to expend" and who made up the soccer teams, they were men of the *Häftlingsführung* or their protégés, who were stuffed with food that had been stolen from those who were watching them play; moreover, they did not have to work and were in good shape.

IX. The Brothel

The bordello was known by the modest title, *Sonderbau* [special house] . . . . For those who did not have connections high up, the length of visiting time was set at 20 minutes . . . . The aim of the S.S. in this enterprise was to corrupt the politicals . . . . The illegal management of the camp had given the order not to go there. On the whole, the politicals obeyed the order, so much so that the intentions of the S.S. were thwarted. (Pages 170-171)

Like the movie theater, the brothel was accessible only to the members of the *Häftlingsführung,* the only ones, in any case,

who were in any state to find any use for it. No one complained about it. and there is not much point in any lengthy
discussion about it. Nevertheless, I would like to point out
that, according to Kogon "Some of the prisoners without
morals, and among them a fairly large number of politicals,
get themselves involved in frightful relations, after the arrival
of the boys." (Page 236.) My view is that the politicals would
have done better by using the brothel, since they were given
the opportunity to do so. Kogon's praise for their refusal to
use the brothel in order to avoid its "corrupting" influence
becomes hollow when it appears that—instead of normal sexual
relations—numerous politicals preferred the corruption of the
young boys in the camp. I shall add that it was precisely to
eliminate any excuse or any justification for this pederasty
that the S.S. established brothels in all of the camps in the first
place . . .

X. Informing

> The S.S. staff put spies in the camps in order to be informed
> about what was going on inside . . . . The S.S. only got results
> with spies selected within the camp itself: common criminals,
> the asocial, and sometimes the political also . . . (Page 276)

> It was very rare for the *Gestapo* to pick out prisoners in the
> camps to be spies and informers . . . . The *Gestapo* probably
> had such bad experiences with this sort of thing that fortu-
> nately it only resorted to it in very rare cases. (Page 255)

It seems quite surprising that a procedure which brought about
results when it was used by the S.S. should come to nothing
when used by the *Gestapo*. It is, nevertheless, a matter of fact
that the *Gestapo* very rarely resorted to the use of informers in
the camps; it did not need to. Everyone in the concentration
camps who occupied any position of power was more or less
an informer who reported directly, or through an intermediary,
to the S.S. When the *Gestapo* wanted some information about
someone in the camps, it only had to ask the S.S. . . .

Looked at closely, the camps were all caught in the web of
a gigantic network of informers. Among the mass of prisoners
were the little men, the professional cheats, who kept the
Häftlingsführung informed, out of congenital servility, for a
bit of soup, a piece of bread, a stick of margarine, etc . . .

or even unwittingly. Above these petty informers was the entire *Häftlingsführung* which spied on the mass for the S.S. when there was the need. Finally, the *Häftlingsführung* people informed on each other. Under these circumstances, denunciation often assumed strange aspects:

> Wolf (former S.S. officer, homosexual, camp elder in 1942) began denouncing other comrades for the benefit of his Polish friends (he was the lover of a Pole). On one occasion he was crazy enough to make threats. He knew that a German Communist from Magdeburg was to be freed. When he told him that he knew how to keep him from being freed, by telling on him for political activity in the camp, he was answered that the S.S. would be informed of his pederasty. The quarrel *grew so bitter that the illegal direction of the camp forestalled action by the Fascist Poles by turning them over to the S.S.* (Page 280, emphasis added.)

In other words, denunciation which was ignominous when it was done by the "greens," became a virtue, even a preventive measure, when it was done by the "reds." Happily, the "reds" could justify it by putting the label "Fascist" on the foreheads of their victims! And, this is a better example:

> At Buchenwald in 1941, the most famous and most sinister case of voluntary[16] denunciation was that of the white Russian émigré, Grogorij Kushnir-Kushnarev who claimed to be a former Czarist general, and who, for months, won the confidence of various groups, then proceeded to deliver into the hands of the S.S. comrades of all kinds, especially the Russian prisoners. This agent of the *Gestapo,* responsible for the death of hundreds of prisoners, also dared to denounce, in the most infamous way,[17] all those with whom he had any conflict, even for minor reasons . . . . For a long time it was not possible to catch him alone, to kill him, because the S.S. watched over him very carefully. Finally they made him the director, in fact, of the secretariat of the prisoners. Once in that position he was not satisfied just to bring about the downfall of all those who failed to please him, he clogged the wheels of the prisoners' autonomous organization. Finally, at the beginning of 1942, he felt sick and was stupid enough to go to the infirmary. Thus, he put himself in the hands of his enemies. With the authorization of *S.S. Doctor Hoven, who had long been mixed up in this affair, and was on the side of the politicals,* Kushnir was at once declared to be con-

tagious, he was isolated, and a few hours later he was killed with an injection of poison. (Page 276, emphasis added.)

This Grogorij Kushnir-Kushnarev was probably guilty of all that he was accused of, but everyone who climbed the ladder in the hierarchy of power in the concentration camps and who occupied the same position, before or after him, behaved in the same way, and their consciences are charged with the same crimes. The only difference in the case of Mr. Kushnir-Kushnarev was the fact that he did not have Eugen Kogon's approval . . . . In any case, it is difficult to believe that the S.S., in the person of the S.S. Doctor Hoven, gratuitously took so active a part in his elimination.

Eugen Kogon adds: "I still remember the sigh of *relief that went through the camp*, when like lightning the news went around that Kushnir had died in the infirmary." (Page 276, emphasis added.) The members of the clique that Kogon belonged to doubtless sighed with relief, and that fact is understandable since Kushnir's death meant the assumption of more power. But, the sigh was only one of hope in the rest of the camp, since a death by execution of no matter what influential member of the *Häftlingsführung* was always greeted with some hope of finally seeing the common lot improved. After a short time, it was evident that nothing had changed, and, until the next execution, it was a matter of indifference to everyone whether they were sacrificed on the altar of truth or of lies.

XI. Transports

It is known that in the camps the office of labor statistics, composed of prisoners, directed the use of man-power, subject to the instruction of the head of the labor force, and the labor office. As the years went on, the S.S. was overwhelmed with enormous demands. At Buchenwald, S.S. *Hauptsturmführer* Schwartz tried only once himself to make up a transport of a thousand prisoners. After having kept almost the entire camp on the grounds for half a day, to review the men, he managed to collect 600 men. But those who had been examined and selected out, slipped away in all directions, and not one remained in Schwartz's hands . . . (Page 286)

In my opinion, there was no drawback in having Schwartz's experience repeated every time that the organization of a transport to some work area was attempted; if the S.S. had never succeeded, all the better. But, unfortunately, "from that moment, the head of the labor force turned over to the prisoners in the labor statistic bureau all questions of the distribution of labor." (*Ibid.*) And, once that happened, it was no longer possible "to slip away in all directions" after the work force had been assembled on the mustering grounds, as had been the case with Schwartz. With rubber truncheons in hand, all of the *Kapos,* all of the Block Chiefs, all of the *Lagerschütz* (prisoner police), as well as others, set up a menacing barrier to any attempted flight. Compared with them, *Hauptsturmführer* Schwartz seemed innocuous. The *Häftlingsführung* people were Communists, anti-Fascist, and anti-Hitler, among other things, but, they could not bear to have anyone disturb the Hitlerian order of things or to weaken the war effort of the Third Reich by trying to escape from it. As compensation for their service to the *Führer,* they were given power to designate those prisoners who would make up a transport, and they exercised their power with a zeal beyond all praise.

XII. Tableau

One result of "power gained through corruption" was the enrichment of one or several men at the expense of the others. Sometimes this reached shameful proportions in the camps, even in those where the politicals were in power. More than one who took advantage of his position lived the life of a prince, while his comrades died by the hundreds. When the cartons of food for the camp, containing fats, sausages, jams, flour, and sugar, were smuggled outside the camp by S.S. accomplices, to be sent to the families of the prisoners in question, one can hardly say it was justified. But most exasperating was when, at a time when the local S.S. were no longer wearing high boots but only regular army shoes, the members of the small clique of "*caids*" walked proudly around in stylish clothes, custom tailored, like dandies, some of them even with a little dog on a leash! That is a chaos of misery, filth, disease, famine and death! In this case, the "instinct for self-preservation" was carried beyond all reasonable limits and ended in a phariseeism, ridiculous to be sure, but hard as rock, badly out of tune with the social and political ideals proclaimed at the same time by these persons. (Page 287)

It was like that in all of the camps. And, with certain reservations, the reason for the horror could hardly be better described, or in fewer words: the instinct for self-preservation. If one can end the commentary on this *tableau,* with the preceding observation, therein also lies the basis for pointing out that the instinct for self-preservation, an ancient conception, is quite another thing altogether from that taught by a puerile moral. From the fierce Guitton, besieged at La Rochelle by Richelieu, who had himself bled in order to feed his son on his cooked blood, to Saturn who devoured his children at birth to escape the death which the Titan threatened, self-preservation is susceptible to the most varied human reactions. In a culture which promotes the value of human life, one might think that there are more Guittons than Saturns. And, under normal conditions, the conduct of the majority of individuals would not allow one to affirm the contrary. But, this behavior is only part of the veneer of civilization, and one has only to scrape it a little—i.e., to change brutally the social conditions—in order to show what price human nature attaches to human life.

In the voices of all of the children of France, the good sense of the people cries out and echoes *Il etait un petit navire . . .* (There was a little ship . . .) and consoles itself, insofar as it believes, that it lessens the horror of the situation, by affirming that in order to find out who will be eaten, *On tira-t-à la courte paille* (we will draw straws), rather than to leave the decision to a democratic majority. But, public opinion was not less indignant when it learned that that little ship had become the airplane of the Italian General Nobile, which had crash landed on the polar ice, and that the General could be said to have survived, until the arrival of the rescue expedition, only because he had eaten one or more of his comrades. If public opinion does not react violently against the self-serving accounts of the concentration camps by former *Häftlingsführung* people, it is because the fact is not clearly made that the concentration camp bureaucracy —using every method of corruption, keeping for itself all of the straws, and having the drawing done by the S.S.—did "eat" the mass of the prisoners.

Before the 1939 war, I myself knew many people who "preferred to die on their feet than to live on their knees." Without doubt, they were sincere, but in the camps they lived prostrated in order to insure their survival. After returning to civilian life — or simply to life — they are still just as uncompromising about this precept, unaware of the defeat that they suffered. They keep making the same speeches, and now they are ready to collaborate with the Communists like they did with the Nazis.

In reality, one sees very clearly that except for the instinct for self-preservation which played a role at all levels (e.g., the ordinary prisoner in the face of the *Häftlingsführung,* the *Häftlingsführung* in the face of the S.S., and even the S.S. staff in the face of its superiors), there is no valid explanation for what went on in the concentration camp world. The instinct for self-preservation is very obvious, but one does not want to admit it. So one turns to psychoanalysis: Moliére's doctors talked to their patients in Latin, which they knew no more about than they did about their profession, and the public meekly approved.

XIII. Evaluations

> The happenings in the concentration camps were psychologically very singular, as much for the S.S. as for the inmates. In general, the reactions of the prisoners seemed more comprehensible than those of their oppressors. Actually the first were of a more human kind, while the others were markedly inhuman. (Page 305)

In my view, it would be more correct to say that the reactions of both groups were all of the human kind, in the psychological sense of the word, and that with regard to the *Häftlingsführung,* especially, and to the S.S., they were all markedly inhuman in the moral sense.

Further on, Eugen Kogon points out:

> Those who were the least affected in the camps were the a-social and the professional criminals. The reason is to be found in the parallel between their psychic and social makeup and that of the S.S. (Page 320)

Perhaps, this may be a correct analysis. But, it must also be agreed that the concentration camps were not the place to cultivate a political consciousness in the common criminals. On the other hand, the camps did provide the appropriate atmosphere for turning the political prisoners into rogues. This phenomenon is hardly unique to the concentration camps. It can be observed

constantly in all of the reformatories and in all of the prisons in
every nation of the world, where men are perverted on the pretext that they are being rehabilitated.

Dr. Sigmund Freud's theory of repression explains all of this
very well, and it would be childish to dwell on the point. In all
of the penal institutions, the mentality of the whole group, as a
result of systematic restraint, shapes itself at the lowest level,
usually typified by the guard, the link between all of the prisoners. This fact should not be surprising. The social environment in which we live, in which the idea of the concentration
camp is rejected with so much righteous indignation, but in
which, at the same time, it is carried out to various degrees, has
given the political, turned scoundrel, the right — momentarily, I
hope — to play the hero!

It is, without doubt, because he anticipated some reproach
for this kind of thinking that Eugen Kogon wrote in his Fore-
word:

> It was a world in itself, a State in itself, a lawless condition into
> which was thrown a human being, who from that moment on,
> turning to his advantage the virtues and vices — more vices
> than virtues! — ceased struggling except to save his miserable
> existence. Did he struggle against the S.S.? Certainly not! He
> had to struggle as much, if not more, against his companions
> in captivity . . . [18]
>
> Tens of thousands of survivors made to suffer more, perhaps,
> by the reign of terror of arrogant companions in captivity than
> by the infamies of the S.S., will thank me for having also shed
> light on this other aspect of the camps, for not having feared
> to unveil the role played in the various camps by certain poli-
> tical types, who, today, make a big noise over their uncompro-
> mising anti-Fascism. I know that some of my comrades have
> despaired at seeing the injustice and brutality dressed up with
> an aureole of heroism by good people who suspected nothing.
> Such profiteers of the camps will not emerge enhanced in my
> study: it provides grounds to dim these usurped glories. What
> camp were you in? What *Kommando*? What job did you do?
> What color did you wear? What party did you belong to?
> etc. . . (Page 17)

One can only say that the witness has not kept his promise:
one looks in vain, throughout the whole "report" for the condemnation of anyone who was distinctly a political. On the
other hand, from the beginning to the end, he pleads for the

Communist group, either indirectly or expressly:

> That elastic wall erected against the S.S. . . . . It was the Ger-
> man Communists who furnished the best means to realize that
> task . . . . The anti-Fascist elements, that is, first and foremost
> the Communists . . . . (Page 286)

There are almost countless other examples where he defends the
Communists or the *Häftlingsführung.* Actually by defending the
Communists, he was also defending the bureaucracy of the con-
centration camps, because only those who called themselves
Communists could claim to get into it and, once in it, stay there.
To a certain extent Kogon is making a plea for himself, and I
very much fear that, after even the least informed reader has
finished reading the book, he will feel an irresistible urge to ask
Kogon the very question that he suggests: what positions did
you hold?

The conclusion of all this? Here is what Kogon gives us: "Accounts about the concentration camps usually evoke, at the
most, astonishment or a shaking of the head; they hardly ever
touch the comprehension, and in no case, do they wring hearts."
(Page 347) Clearly, this is true, but whose fault is it? In the in-
toxication of the liberation, and in giving vent to a resentment
pent-up during the long years of the occupation, the French
public opinion believed everything. However, as social relations
became progressively more normal, it became more and more
difficult to influence it. Today, accounts of the concentration
camps seem to everyone more like justifications than testimonies. The public now wonders how it got itself caught in the
trap, and for two cents it would put everyone on the defendants' bench.

XIV. Statistics

In 1945, when Kogon's book was published in Germany,
there was still not enough data at hand to allow one to say with
accuracy how many persons of all nationalities had been imprisoned by the Germans in the concentration camps. Eugen Kogon
acknowledges this and warns that the figures he was able to get
are only approximate:

> Without the slightest doubt, thousands of persons went
> through the camps during the twelve years of the National-

Socialist regime. If we take as a basis for an estimate the
number of dead at Auschwitz, which alone seems to come to
between three and a half million, as well as the number of
dead in the other camps of that kind, it is easy to see that
the total number of interned came to at least eight or ten
million. (Page 34)

Then, going into detail (Page 147), he produces precise statistics
for this period; the total for all the camps and for the sum of
the deportees, racial or not, is the following:

Total number of prisoners:	8,000,000
Survivors:	500,000
Total number of dead:	7,500,000

This figure of 7,500,000 means that about 94 percent of the
total number of prisoners died in the camps. But, if the rest of
his statistics are studied carefully, we see: (1) that the number
of non-racial deportees comes to 606,000, up to 1939 (Germans
only), and to 3,538,000 from 1939 to 1945, for a total of
4,144,000; and (2) that Kogon does not give the total number
of racial deportees, but only that of those deportees who died,
or the sum of 5,620,000. These two sums add up to 9,764,000
deportees. The margin of approximation is therefore quite
broad: about 2,000,000. But, Kogon warned us of that fact.
(Page 34)

On the other hand, if we take into considerations the non-
racial deportees, the figures show that out of a total of 4,144,000
deportees, about 1,827,000 are estimated to have died, leaving
2,317,000 survivors, about 56 percent of the over-all total.
Conversely, the number of dead amounted to about 44 percent.
Naturally, in the press, it was the manifestly false figure of 94
percent that served to illustrate the horror, or some very similar
percentage that had been pulled out of thin air; in France, it
was usually 82 percent, and I have never learned just how the
statisticians arrived at that figure.

What puzzled me most of all at the time was the total number
of deportees: 9,764,000—or even only 8,000,000. For the
Germans to have deported that number of persons during a
twenty-seven month period (March 1942 to August 1944[19]),
it would have called for transportation facilities which, from
the facts, the Germans in the midst of war did not have at their
disposal. The magnitude of such an operation can be seen upon

reflection: three to four hundred thousand persons per month, or ten to thirteen thousand per day, needed to be transported without fail. To do this would have required a minimum of six to nine trains a day, assuming that each train could transport about fifteen hundred persons (plus the accompanying guards and their equipment), as was the case for those trains that left from France. If Kogon is correct, that was quite a lot of rolling stock to divert from the German war effort. Although I am not a railway expert, I made some calculations that were based upon the duration of these trips by train. The deportees from the West, like those from the East, all said that their trips had lasted from four to six days, which would mean, taking five days as the average, that for the entire period of the deportation, there were between sixty to ninety trains, constantly, day and night, going back and forth at this job. When spare equipment is added into the picture, the amount of necessary rolling stock would include between eighty to a hundred locomotives and between three to four thousand railway cars. And, I did not estimate the huge number of personnel, both railway workers and guards, that would have been required.

After the appearance of Kogon's book, other means of estimating the number of deportees appeared. For example, at Nuremberg, the Attorney General Charles DuBost, representing France, stated on January 29, 1946:

> The census taking which we have carried out in France allows it to be affirmed that there were more than 250,000 deportees from France: only 35,000 have returned. Document F. 497, filed under the number R.F. 339, indicates that, out of the 600,000 arrests made by the Germans in France, 350,000 were made with internment in France or in Germany in mind. Total number of deportees: 250,000. Number of deportees returned: 35,000. (IMT, VI, p. 338)

The percentage of survivors was, therefore, 14 percent and the percentage of the dead was 86 percent. But, to a question put to him by the Minister for Veterans and War Victims of the French government, DuBost answered, through the official journal, *Débats parlementaires*, on February 24, 1962, in this way:

> According to statistical information released on the first of December 1961 in the multi-copy card file of the deportees and internees of the 1939-1945 war, kept by the National

Institute of Statistics and Economic Studies, the number of cards given out to deportees and internees, or to their beneficiaries, is as follows:

	Living	Deceased
Deportees (Resistants)	16,702	9,783
Deportees (Politicals)	13,415	9,235
Internees (Resistants)	9,911	5,759
Internees (Politicals)	10,117	2,130
TOTALS	50,145	26,907

From DuBost's figures, it can be seen that the total number of deportees was 49,135 and that the total number of dead was 19,018. This means that about 38 percent of the deportees died while 62 percent (or 30,117) survived. Obviously, it is difficult to determine from these figures the exact number of survivors and of dead that existed during the month of May 1945. Returning from the camps, even after having spent only short periods of time there, the survivors were a very frail lot whose annual mortality rate was understandably way above normal. Consequently, I would not be surprised to be told that out of the 19,108 who were dead on February 24, 1962, 35 to 45 percent died after their return to France. In that case, one would have to concede that on May 8, 1945, the proportions of living to dead were the following: 75 to 80 percent were survivors and 20 to 25 percent were dead. While tragic enough, this latter estimate is quite a different thing from 86 percent dead and 14 percent living as deduced from the figures that were brought forth at Nuremberg by the Attorney General DuBost; in fact, this estimate is so different that it almost represents inverse proportions!

What supports my opinion that these proportions, which I have noted for France, are valid for all of the camps, is my detailed study of the statistics of the Buchenwald camp, where I was deported myself. As a result of my study, I came to the following conclusions: to Buchenwald and its satellite camps there seem to have been deported, from 1939 to 1945, a total of 238,980 persons, of whom statistics show that 56,545 died or 23 percent. But, I cannot vouch for this rate of 23 percent, for the following reasons: the incoming prisoners were registered just once, while the outgoing, being dead, were often subject to double registration, the first time in the satellite camp in which they died (Dora, for example) and a second time at Buchenwald, where, until the time that each of the satellite camps was equipped with a crematorium, they were cremated. In the statistics that were produced, those who died in the camps like Halberstadt, Ellrich, Beuchow, and Dora, among others, were, in fact, added to the number of persons who were cremated at Buchenwald. The mortality rate might, then, have been a little less, but not much; even 20 percent for example, would still be enormous. The Assistant Bishop of Munich, Mgr. Neuhäussler, did the same sort of research that I did, but concerning the Dachau camp where he was interned. For Dachau he came to the same conclusions as I did for Buchenwald: there were between 199,519 and 206,206 internees (the uncertainty arises from the fact that there were two numbering systems on the camp register) of whom 67,665 died, or 28 percent. The same observation applies for Dachau as for Buchenwald with regard to the adding of the dead in the satellite camps to those of the central camp. Still, it must be noted here that the card index of the S.S. camp staff showed only about 26,000 dead, according to Mgr. Neuhäussler, in his book *So war es in Dachau.* But, Pastor Niemöller claimed, in a speech given on July 3, 1946, and published with the title *Der Weg ins Freie* by Franz M. Helbach at Stuttgart, that "238,756 were cremated at Dachau," or a greater number than there were internees. On a visit to Dachau in 1945, I was able to take a photograph of a sign that had been put up between two trees at the entrance of the camp; the inscription on the sign read as follows: "This area is being retained as a shrine to the 238,000 individuals who were cremated here." Without a doubt, this sign which had been prepared for the benefit of the tourists was based on the conclusions of Pastor Niemöller who was interned in that camp, and who then became its authority.

I must add that since he published *So war es in Dachau* in 1969, Mgr. Neuhäussler has made new discoveries which have caused him to modify his first conclusions and that he had the honesty to make them public, on March 16, 1962, in a speech that he gave at Dachau to the representatives of some 15 nations that had gathered there to commemorate the liberation of the camp. *Le Figaro* of March 17, 1962, reported the statistical data that was contained in that talk as follows:

> This afternoon in bitter cold and in spite of a snow storm,
> pilgrims gathered together at Dachau camp where thirty
> thousand men were exterminated, out of the two hundred
> thousand from thirty-eight countries who were interned there
> from 1933 to 1945.

Moreover, all of the other newspapers of the day printed the
same figures. So it was 30,000 deportees who were cremated
at Dachau (or 13 percent, which is still enough), and not
67,665, which was the number that Mgr. Neuhäussler had
calculated initially. In other words, the card index that had
been maintained by the S.S. staff reflected the truth, but very
good care has been taken not to take it into consideration. It
is possible that some day similar figures will be determined
for Buchenwald.

Such is the extent of the exaggerations which no one doubted
in 1950, which Mr. Eugen Kogon did not hesitate to authenticate
and to disseminate, and which the world press still echoes on
a daily basis in spite of all of the new information that has come
to light. Moreover, in France, no commemoration of war events
takes place that does not loudly re-affirm that 250,000 French
nationals were deported to Germany, that only 35,000 came
back, and that six million Jews were exterminated in the gas
chambers.

Concerning the Jews, Kogon gives the number of dead as
5,620,000, as we have seen. In the camps where the Jews were
interned, the mortality rate—while far from the percentages
that have been published by the press for propaganda purposes
—was certainly as high as that suffered by other prisoners. Although we do not yet have reliable documents concerning these
camps, we shall see in the following chapters what one may
think, both of the means that were used allegedly to exterminate
the Jews and the number of alleged Jewish victims.

XV. Nota bene . . .

There are a number of the most unlikely tales, as well as
certain examples of journalistic sensationalism, that I must
point out before I finish with Mr. Kogon.

Among the unlikely tales must be included most of Kogon's
statements concerning the listening to foreign broadcasts. I

sincerely doubt that it was possible for anyone to set up and to use a secret radio receiver inside any of the concentration camps. If the Voice of America, the B.B.C. or Radio Free France were occasionally heard in the camp, it was with the consent of the S.S.; moreover, only a very small number of privileged prisoners could have been among the listeners, and, then, mainly by chance. Thus it happened to me personally at Dora during the short period that I served as the *Schwung* (orderly) for the *Oberscharführer* who commanded the *Hundesstafel* (the company of guard dogs).

My work consisted in cleaning a whole barrack which housed the more or less ranking members of the S.S. staff; among other things, I waxed their boots, made their beds, cleaned their mess kits, etc . . . all things that I did most humbly and conscientiously. In everyone of the rooms in this barrack was a radio. For all of the gold in the world, I would not have taken the risk of listening to one, even when I was absolutely certain of being alone. However, at about eight o'clock in the morning, when all of his subordinates had left for work, it happened two or three times that the *Oberscharführer* called me into his room, where he had tuned to the B.B.C. that was broadcasting in French, and asked me to translate for him, which I did under my breath.

In the evening, back in my Block, I passed on the news in a whisper to my friends Delarbre (from Belfort) and Gourguet (from the Creusot) urging them either to keep it to themselves or to repeat it only to comrades of whom they were very sure, and even then to do so in such a way so that it could not be traced to its source.

We did not constitute a "committee," and not one of us claimed that we were in touch with the Allies. Moreover, nothing happened to us. But during that same time, there was a stir that centered around the listening to foreign broadcasts in which, I believe, Debeaumarché was mixed up. I never knew exactly what it was all about. One of the members of that group approached me one day saying that there was a secret listening post in the camp, that a political movement was getting orders from the English, etc . . . He backed up what he was saying by telling me the news that I had listened to that very morning, or the evening before, with the *Oberscharführer.* I expressed my skepticism in such terms that thereafter he considered me someone to be avoided. It was just as well for me. A few days later, there were massive arrests in the camp, and among those arrested were the fellow who I just mentioned and Debeaumarché himself. The to-do ended with a few hangings. In all likelihood, it began with a prisoner in my situation who had talked too much, and what he had said was imprudently bruited about, until it reached the *Sicherheitsdienst* (S.S. secret police) through an informer in the *Häftlingsführung*.

When Eugen Kogon writes:

> I spent many a night, with a very few who were in on it, before a 5-tube receiver which I had taken from the S.S. Doctor Ding-Schuller to have it repaired in the camp. I listened to the Voice of America in Europe as well as to the *Soldatsender*, and I copied down the important news. (Page 283)

I am willing to believe that he may have listened to foreign broadcasts; but I am inclined to think that he listened to the broadcasts in question in the company of Doctor Ding-Schuller. As for all of the rest, it is only an embellishment which is intended both to make believable the revolutionary activity on the part of those in the *Häftlingsführung*, and to better excuse their monstrous exactions.

I believe that Kogon listened to these broadcasts in the company of his S.S. patron Doctor Ding-Schuller, or at least with his connivance and consent, because Dr. Francois Bayle reports in his *Croix Gammée contre Caducée* this curious testimony that was given by Kogon at Nuremberg: Doctor Ding-Schuller asked him to take care of his wife and children in case Germany was defeated! From this testimony, I gather that their relations were surely more cordial than Kogon has admitted. And, I shall add that if this request implies a *quid pro quo* which Kogon would not admit in any case!—the privileged position of this singular prisoner would be explained by a mutual collaborative understanding whose inspiration and aims would appear to be much less noble than it has so far been convenient to concede

Further speculation along these lines is not likely to be productive; nevertheless, the record may reflect that the collaboration between Kogon and the S.S. was, by his own admission, profitable, friendly, and often intimate. There was also the collaboration between Kogon and the Communists, as has been mentioned in earlier sections of this chapter.

As for Kogon's journalistic sensationalism, I quote the following example which should provide the reader with an idea of what I mean:

> Let us recall the taking of oath of those aspiring to the S.S., at midnight, in the cathedral at Braunschweig. There, before the bones of Henry the First, the only German emperor on whom he set any value, Himmler was fond of expatiating on the mystique of the "*Communauté de conjurés*." Then, after that, *in the gay sunshine he would go to some concentration camp in order to watch the political prisoners being whipped*[20] one after the other. (Page 24, emphasis added.)

> Mme Koch who previously had been stenographer in a cigarette factory sometimes *took baths* in a tub filled with madeira. (Page 266, emphasis added.)

Statements of this sort abound concerning all of the important personages of the Nazi regime, and they produce pleasant sadistic reactions. They also exhibit some of that same state of mind that made *Le Rire* publish, in September 1914, a photograph of the child with his hands cut off or *Le Matin* describe, on the 15th of April 1916, the Emperor William II as being a paranoiac with cancer, with at the most just a few more months to live, when, in fact, he had neither of those afflictions. Furthermore, the state of mind seems to have caused Henri Desgranges in *L'Auto,* in September 1939, to "thumb his nose" at a Goering and say that the *Reichsmarschall* was without soft soap with which to wash himself. The banality of the method is equalled only by the credulity of the public and by the imperturbability of those who make use of it and keep repeating it about all enemies in all wars.

FOOTNOTES

1 *La Jeune Parque,* November 1947. It was published in Germany in 1945 under the title: *Der S.S. Staat.*

2 During this time, for example, a Doctor Seguin never succeeded in getting himself recognized in his professional capacity by the *Häftlingsführung.* Having never been acknowledged as a medical doctor by the Communists, they sent him to work in the quarry where he died.

3 It seems that the National Socialists took him over from the Weimar Republic. This fact is not without its humor because it shows that the jailing of Communist troublemakers was a policy which was common to both regimes.

4 He does not seem to have encountered a Martin-Chauffier.

5 The "disposal" of "troublesome" prisoners by the *Häftlingsführung* was often done for reasons much more base than those that are mentioned by Kogon. For example, those prisoners who got in the way of the ruling clique or those who might possibly get in the way by being placed in influential positions by the S.S were often marked for death. The argument of collaboration is, moreover, worthless; this "illegal management"—i.e., the *Häftlingsführung*—collaborated openly with the S.S., as is shown elsewhere in this book.

6 Eugen Kogon sometimes uses the word "illegal" and sometimes the word "clandestine" to describe the operation of the *Häftlingsführung.* Actually, there was nothing the least illegal or clandestine about it inasmuch as it had been set up by the S.S.

7 There were many Communists who were not "accredited", and they were, above all, decent people. They were lost in the mass and shared the common lot.

8 It is well to note that the S.S. generally did not steal from the prisoners. First of all, they enjoyed better rations to begin with and, thus, had no pressing need to obtain more. Secondly, when they did desire to supplement their rations, they let other prisoners do the stealing for them and were thus better served.

9 These quotation marks appear in the original text.

10 I want to emphasize the word "possible."

11 Osterloh was a "green," and that is why the incident is described as having been a "good example."

12 Emphasis added.

[13]The *Bunker* was the prison within the camp. If Kogon is to be believed, "it was not the S.S. but the first elder of the camp, Richter, who invented it," (p. 174) when the S.S. had not even thought of it.

[14]This is an improper generalization. It was a question only of those who had made themselves their leaders, thanks to the authority that they derived from the S.S.

[15]All of the Buchenwald prisoners can testify that his main concern was for the actual delivery of health and medical services to the prisoners.

[16]Since this way of thinking doubtless admits a denunciation . . . involuntary! As we see, ways to get out of things are not lacking!

[17] It seems that there are other ways of denouncing which are less infamous or which are not infamous at all, evidently!

[18]This statement is an improper generalization. As a common prisoner, one had to struggle against those who exercised power on behalf of the S.S., while distrusting his fellow prisoners among the common lot.

[19]This twenty-seven month period is generally recognized as being the time period during which the vast majority of the foreign internees who were incarcerated in the German concentration camp system were deported by the Germans from whatever locale in which they had been arrested.

[20]If the rack at Buchenwald (if, indeed, there was one) was hidden from the Chief of Police of Weimar during his inspection of the camp, it is hardly likely that it would be shown to his superior *Reichführer-S.S.* Himmler.

PART III
The Drama of the European Jews

Chapter Twelve

Raul Hilberg: His Doctrine and His Methods

Between the *Commentaries on the Holy Scriptures* of Saint Thomas Aquinas (1225-1274) and *The Destruction of the European Jews,* (Chicago, Quadrangle, 1961) an exhaustive commentary on the Nuremberg documents by Mr. Raul Hilberg, there is plainly no common measure. Indeed, one can feel assured that in seven centuries the latter will not be spoken of at all, or, if it is still mentioned, it will only be mentioned in reference to something unworthy of notice except as an example of the most scandalous aberrations of our times. Now, after seven centuries, when Saint Thomas Aquinas is spoken of it is to point him out as having been the originator of a philosophy also aberrant, which from the 17th century on was called *ancilla theologiae,* by the Humanists and the Free-thinkers. Nevertheless, this philosophy was that of centuries of faith. It was substantial; it opened windows onto a world which was the dream of the epoch; and, thus, it deserved to become that Thomism to which reference must be made today, if the broad currents of contemporary philosophy are to be correctly explained. To construct his system, the man had, of course, to mutilate Aristotle; but in the 13th century printing had not yet been discovered, manuscripts were scarce, and the means of research at the disposal of intellectuals were so rudimentary that he was the only one who knew it. Then, three centuries later, having discovered the trickery, the Humanists and the Free-thinkers spoke of *ancilla theologiae.* But there was no scandal. The fraud was attributed to an imperfect acquaintance with the writings of Aristotle. Today, more light has been shed on the matter, and Thomism has a place. But, there will never be any *Hilbergism.* And if the 790 large size pages, based on almost 1,400 documentary references, of *The Destruction of the European Jews,* some day are found to be the *ancilla* of something, it will only be of a not very nobly inspired purpose. Therein lies the difference, and it is not a small one.

Having admitted that neither in their persons nor in the value and influence of their respective works are the two men comparable, if thought of Saint Thomas Aquinas nevertheless came to mind after having read Mr. Raul Hilberg, there were good reasons. The most important reason of all is this one, which is the central theme of this chapter: the Nuremberg documents that Mr. Raul Hilberg used to prove to us that 5,100,000 (p. 767) or 5, 407,500 (p. 670) Jews were exterminated by the Germans during the Second World War – 1,000,000 in the gas chambers at Auschwitz, 950,000 in five other camps much less well equipped, 1,400,000 (if I have understood correctly his complicated and often contradictory calculations) by *Einsatzgruppen,* and the rest, either 1,750,000 on page 767, or 2,069,500 on page 670, in camps and in ways which could be called pottering compared to the others – are of the same kind and the same worth as those in which Saint Thomas Aquinas, like all the Church Fathers before him, found the proof that the first act in the creation of the world, the separation of light from darkness, took place exactly 4,001 years before the birth of Christ, that Joshua had stopped the sun in its course, that Jonas sojourned in the belly of a whale, etc.

And, then there is the problem of misuse. Mr. Raul Hilberg in making the documents say what they do not say, except after having been removed from their context and rewritten, is an example on a small scale of what Saint Thomas Aquinas did on a large scale in giving to the writings of Aristotle that interpretation which oriented the entire intellectual work of the Middle Ages in Europe to the celebrated formula, *Aristoteles dixit,* when Aristotle had, in fact, not said it. In this respect, they both, each at about the same distance in time, illustrate that moral which was quite well defined by Saint Ignatius Loyola, according to which, since the end justifies the means, all means are good to justify the end. But here again, to permit a fair appreciation of both, the coordinates of the point which they have in common must be given. Saint Thomas Aquinas found himself in the presence of the writings of Aristotle, which at that time were spread about Europe with so much success by Jewish rabbis and Arab clerks that they were threatening to unsettle Christian thought, and for him it was a purely philo-sophic problem. But, in the case of Mr. Raul Hilberg, it is a question of justifying by a proportional number of cadavers the enormous subsidies which Germany has paid annually since the end of the war, and which she continues to pay, to the State of Israel as reparations for a wrong which she did not do to Israel, either morally or legally, since at the time these wrongs for which she is charged were taking place, the State of Israel did not exist. In short, it is only, purely and very basely, a material problem.

Here I would like to point out — in order to underline the extent of this swindle, which has no other name in any language — that the State of Israel was not founded until May 1948 and that the Jewish victims of the Nazis were the nationals of various states but not of Israel. Nevertheless, Germany pays to Israel sums calculated on the basis of about 6,000,000 dead. In addi-tion, since at least four-fifths of these 6,000,000 were very much alive at the end of the war and countable, she pays to those still living in the other countries of the world, aside from Israel, and to the beneficiaries of those who have since died, substantial reparations as victims of Nazism. This means that for the enor-mous majority, she is paying twice.

All of these indemnities that are so generously granted to the Jews seem, moreover, to have made the gypsies desire to cash in on this "bonanza" in a manner similar to that of the State of Israel and Zionism. If Le Monde of December 29, 1961, is to be believed, the gypsies have now given themselves a king with the name of H. M. Vaida Voievod III, who claims to be the "Supreme and spiritual head of the gypsy people" and who expects to obtain from the United Nations a corner in the world, where the great wandering of their caravans will come to an end, just as, theoretically, the State of Israel was to end the Diaspora.

When he is asked what corner of the world he lays claim to and where it is, he answers that it is Romanestan, and he places it, now on a Pacific Island, now in a country near Israel. Furthermore, he specified that the number of his subjects strolling along all the roads of Europe add up to 12 million, and that the reason there are not more is that between 1939 and 1945 the Nazis exterminated three and a half million. Unfortunately, for him, in this case, there are statistics to put the number of gypsy victims of Nazism between 300 and 350,000 only, which is, of course, quite atrocious enough. Things have not come to a point where one can be accused of anti-Romanestanism as easily as one can be accused of anti-Semitism, every time the fantastic statistics of the *Center of Contemporary Jewish Documentation* are mentioned, and one does not run the risk of being accused of the same low intent if one speaks of the 3,500,000 Nazi victims of H. M. Vaida Voievod III in a humorous tone. If, then, the U. N., let us say, should grant the gypsies the right to regroup in this Romanestan, which only needs to have its geographical location determined, Germany will have no choice but to subsidize them. Having granted the State of Israel an appreciable and substantial indemnity for the victims of Nazism among the Jewish people, it would be difficult to refuse the same to Romanestan, whose claims the U. N. could not fail to support as they did those of the State of Israel. Then the 3,500,000 gypsies exterminated by the Nazis would dispute the 6,000,000 Jews for the limelight in the world press. But, the Reverend Father Fleury, Chaplain of the gypsies of France, already warns that H.M. Vaida Voievod III is only an impostor, and many agree with him. It must be acknowledged that the number of people is much smaller who have the same opinion of the leaders of the State of Israel and their supporters, whose policy, while in every point similar, and just as poorly grounded, has nevertheless succeeded. To the extent that it has shown post-war Zionism to be very closely related to what can be called Romanestanism, the burlesque story of the hero of this adventure deserved to be cited here, if only to give the reader as exact an idea as possible of the worth of the work to which Mr. Raul Hilberg has devoted himself.

But I would like to return to the problem of misuse, and on this subject to be well understood. Having spent an appreciable number of months in the horrible physical and moral conditions of a concentration camp, I know what I am talking about. What I am discussing is only the degree of the horror, since the truth — without further exaggeration — is quite enough. The fact that some poor uneducated devil of a fellow like the curé and the other witness to whom I have referred elsewhere tell us that they have seen, the one, thousands enter the gas chambers in the camp where we were interned together and where there were none, and the other, the heads of human beings buried up to their necks, crushed by the wheels of barrows pushed by the prisoners on order of the SS, is understandable. They are victims who are fired by a resentment in proportion to what they suffered, and the guilty one is the judge who believed them. That a general of an *Einsatzgruppe,* testifying under threat of death, tells what he thinks will be most likely to save his life, and that Hoess, a former commandant of Auschwitz, does the same, like many others, is easily understood and calls for no explanation. The fact that in order to get into the good graces of his captors, some poor SS private, attached to an *Einsatzgruppe,* reports that his unit exterminated "thousands" or "tens of thousands of Jews," as is seen in the documents cited by Mr. Raul Hilberg, is not at all astonishing. Nor, is it strange that a Martin-Chauffier, guilty of many things, tries to have them forgiven by howling with the wolves and that a David Rousset, whose main concern in the camp was to obtain the protection of the communists, and a Eugen Kogon, who had no other concern than to establish as comfortable a balance as possible between the SS and the communists, have recounted what they did. The background and motivation of the witness is an important factor when considering the amount of weight that should be given to his testimony. And, it is the business of the judge and of the specialists in the human sciences to establish this credibility as a step toward distinguishing whether the testimony is likely to be true or false. If I am struck by the fact that the judges at Nuremberg did not pay much attention to the credibility of the prosecution witnesses — especially since they had already decided upon a verdict prior to the trials and only required the testimony to support it — I am much less impressed when a journalist believes all of these people right from the start. It is well known that journalists are generally supposed to be more skeptical and questioning than most people.

I shall go even further. A man like Dr. Francois Bayle, the author of *Croix Gammée contre Caducée,* to whom I have referred, when faced with the documents and testimonies of Nuremberg, is only half responsible for the conclusions he drew from them.

Dr. Francois Bayle is a doctor in the Navy and is, therefore, a military man. On reading his work one perceives that he has a passionate interest in psycho-somatology and psychoanalysis. The defendants at Nuremberg strike him, above all, as being sick men, or at least, tainted, which amounts to the same thing. How he would have liked to have had the chance to write up their cases! He is a brilliant fellow, and circumstances assisted him. On October 19, 1946, he was appointed to the scientific commission on war crimes, and soon he was at work with the original documents and transcripts of the Nuremberg Trial, at which he was present, and where he had free behind-the-scenes access. As a military man, he did not question the authenticity of the documents that were made accessible to him by the authorities on whom he depended. In the military more than anywhere else the fundamental principle on which the system of hierarchy rests is that "every subordinate owes complete obedience to his superior and submission at all time," and he himself relies on the postulate that a superior may not misuse his subordinate. In this state of mind, Dr. Francois Bayle could not ask questions. And if any questions had occurred to him, not having been prepared for the work in which he was left to orient himself, he would not have been able to answer them correctly. Anyway, he can, therefore, be excused. Those who cannot be excused are his superiors, the ones who allowed him and encouraged him to direct his efforts along the line that is mentioned above. In the main, everything happened as it does in the *Figaro* of Beaumarchais, where the role of mathematician was assigned to a dancer. A historian was needed for the job, and it was given to a medical doctor. Was a doctor also needed because it was a matter of medical analysis? Perhaps, but what I maintain is that the doctor, if he had not been present during the medical experiments and if he was not at the same time a historian, absolutely could not study the documents correctly unless assisted by a historian who would have, previously, verified all of the testimonies and documents which attested to the facts and which described, not the scientific environment — since for this a historian would not have been qualified — but the social environment, the historic moment in which they had been performed, particularly, in times as emotional as those in question, and the criminal nature—if any—which could be imputed fairly to such conduct. Who was responsible for all this? No one, unless it is whoever is responsible for the distribution of knowledge and the forming of the elites of our times and whoever—while pushing specialization greatly to the detriment of culture in general on the pretext that an industrial civilization needs more than anything good technicians in well defined and narrowly limited fields — lets it be believed and, when necessary, sees to it that it is believed that any specialist at all is qualified to speak *ex-cathedra* on all specialties.

Mr. Raul Hilberg's case is quite different from that of all these people. He was not deported, he was not a victim of Nazism, and he has no apparent reasons for having a guilty conscience such as Martin-Chauffier, David Rousset, and Eugen Kogon. In addition, he is neither uncultivated, as was that poor curé — mentioned above — who invented gas chambers at Buchenwald and Dora, nor a stumbler of hit or miss education like adventurers in the search for subsistence, rather ill-defined before the war, as were David Rousset and Eugen Kogon, who, besides their need to clear their conscience, probably recounted all that they did in order to assure themselves of the best and most lasting post-war livelihood, a goal which they both achieved remarkably well. He is not even like Dr. Francois Bayle, a medical doctor led astray in the study of historical documents. He is a "political scientist," who is properly sheep-skinned, as his biographical note says, who specialized in international relations, and who worked in the "War Documentation Project" of the American government. It is unfortunate that his education in the field of "public law and government," which prepared him to work in a profession in which the science of statistics plays such an important part, did not better equip him for the study of documents and testimonies on which his profession is based and for the study of history in which the social phenomena, which are the subject matter of statistics, have their roots. If, therefore, Mr. Raul Hilberg acts as though he had no idea as to whether a witness and his testimony can be regarded as creditable, or under what conditions a document should be admitted as evidence, he has only one excuse, and that excuse is dishonesty. I say "excuse" because, as I continue to read his biographical note, I find that he is a collaborator in the *Jewish Encyclopedia Handbooks* and, in my judgment, that fact explains everything. And, this particular interest, of course, applies not only to Mr. Raul Hilberg, but to many others. It applies to Mme. Hannah Arendt, for example, who has the same intellectual outlook, who often refers to Mr. Hilberg in her reports of the Eichmann Trial which the *New Yorker* published in five issues (February-March 1963), who was – or still is – *Forschungsleiterin* (Research directoress) of the Conference on Jewish Relations, *Verwaltungsleiterin* (Directoress of administration) of the Jewish Cultural Reconstruction, *Stipendiatin* (Fellow) of the Guggenheim Foundation, and who coolly informs us (*New Yorker*, February 23, 1963) that "3 million Polish Jews were massacred during the first day of the war," the one explaining the other. Mme. Hanna Arendt would do well, in my opinion, to ask Mr. Raul Hilberg where he found the "about 2,000,000 *Polish* Jews, who were transported to their deaths in 1942 and 1943" of whom he speaks on page 311 of his book. (Emphasis added.) It would be a good thing to come to an understanding: were there in Poland 3 to 3.3 million Jews before the war, as all statisticians unanimously claim, including those who are Jewish, or were there 5,700,000 as Mme. Hannah Arendt is obliged to claim, since here are 5,000,000 exterminated, and, since Mr. Shalom Baron, brandishing his title of Professor of Jewish History at Columbia University, claimed on April 4, 1961, before the Jerusalem Tribunal, that 700,000 of them were still living in 1945 when the country was liberated by Russian troops? Really, one would like to invite all of these people – these three and the multitude of others in the same boat – to please get together and agree on their figures, before undertaking to explain us to ourselves. But, particularly to Mr. Raul Hilberg, one could advise him to agree with himself. On page 670 of his book, he in fact points out to us that of the 9,190,000 Jews, who he says were living in territories occupied by German armies during the war, only 3,782,500 survived, which makes 5,407,500 dead; but on page 767, by some mathematical mystery, these 5,407,500 dead become 5,100,00; It must also be pointed out that for Poland, which together with Russia and the Danubian countries is the crux of the problem, he finds only 50,000 survivors, where his colleague Mr. Shalom Baron found 700,000. However, a journal,

in French, published in Switzerland *(Europe Réelle,* Lausanne,
No. 44, December 1961) claims that the Israeli periodical *Jedoth
Hazem,* issued in Tel Aviv (No. 143 of 1961) states, without
turning a hair, that "the number of Polish Jews at present living
outside of Poland approaches 2 million." By way of compensation, for that part of Russia occuped by German troops, the
Paris and Tel Aviv Centers of Jewish Documentation both agree
in placing the number of Jews exterminated at 1,500,000
(Figaro Littéraire, June 4, 1960), while the Institute of Jewish
Affairs and the World Jewish Congress *(Eichmann's Confederates
and the Third Reich Hierarchy,* already cited) give the figure of
1,000,000; Mr. Raul Hilberg finds only 420,000. This inconsistency is all a little irresponsible, and it is embarrassing that the
supporting documents, which are the same for all, speak so
different a language to each of these specialists.

Having said this, let us render unto Caesar what is Caesar's.
As far as I know, of all of this kind of writing, (which has
been published until now) in which the Nuremberg documents
and the appended testimonies have been endlessly hashed and
rehashed and in which they have been perverted more and more
in order to support the contention that about 6,000,000 Jews
were exterminated by the Germans in the Second World War,
The Destruction of the European Jews is without any doubt the
most precise and the most complete in the number of references
it contains. For that very reason, without being more convincing
than all that has been published in this line, it is the more vulnerable. Moreover, an analysis of Mr. Hilberg's book has one
advantage: in displaying all of its weaknesses, those of all the
others show up, too. I have, therefore, decided to take *The
Destruction of the European Jews* as the point of reference for
much of the following discussion. It will, of course, be understood that I will not examine each of the 790 pages one by one,
although there is hardly a page that could not be used for illustration. To put each one to the test in detail would require as
many pages as Mr. Raul Hilberg needed to present his thesis,
and it would be tedious. I have already said that Mr. Raul
Hilberg has succeeded in making his documents reveal what he
wants them to reveal simply because he accepted them just as
they were—that is, rewritten, picked over, and taken out of
their context. It is this context that I shall try to reconstruct
by comparing the documents with others and by dwelling only

incidentally on the grossest manipulations.

To make myself clearly understood I must make a brief digression, the theme of which is the following: History is a sequence of historical moments. Self-evident? In form, yes. But in implications, quite something else. Some historians think that each moment in history posits to man only those problems which allow a single solution, a Hobson's choice. It then follows that since the beginning of time, all the moments of history, each an exact prolongation of the other, are arranged in a sort of straight line, which is the meaning of history, and that by correctly analyzing each one of them, one arrives at historical determinism. Pursuant to the concept of historical determination, the only question man can possibly ask is, not where he wants to go nor what he should do to get there, but simply, where he is going. For an answer to that question he has only to look behind him and to project the historical line, and then turning forward he sees before him Socialism. At the most, he might hesitate (as before the picture of the turn which Socialism has taken in Russia, for example) and slow his step. In no case can he stop or change directions. The ground burns under his feet, and on each side of his road are deadly precipices. And, so he goes toward Socialism, but not very fast. Such historians are Marxists, and they were in favor in the nineteenth century. But, by reducing to nothing or almost nothing the role of the individual in history, this theory was so over simplified that it has lost favor in the twentieth century: consequently, Marxian historiography is disappearing today.

On the whole, most historians believe, in fact, that each moment of history presents man with an infinity of problems; that for man each moment holds an infinity of solutions—even though, without any doubt, only one is rational and good: and that between the good solution and the more or less bad ones, man's choice depends upon a more or less correct conscientious appraisal of the aspects of the problem. Modern historians also think that in this infinity of problems there are some that man can skirt all his life without even suspecting their existence; that among those which he perceives there are some that are more or less important, more or less momentous, and more or less urgent; that, not being able to resolve them all at once, man is obliged to take them one by one in fixed order; and that the very determination of this order already presupposes a correct and conscientious appraisal of the choices among the possible solutions. Depending on the quality of his appraisals – and, here, we must note that it is a question of collective problems and that the mental age of the group is in inverse proportion to the number of individuals who compose it – the man in each historic moment sees a more or less large number of problems presented to him. Those that he does not see, however, are not necessarily the most negligible ones.

Returning to Mr. Raul Hilberg, he begins his study several historical moments behind and announces *Luther dixit*, in 1963 no less! I am inventing nothing. In the introduction to *The Destruction of the European Jews*, he seriously explains to us, in substance, that National Socialism descends in a straight line from the anti-Semitism of the Germans in the Middle Ages, from their Catholicism, and from Martin Luther. This assertion calls for a few remarks:

1. Luther was not anti-Semitic, but was anti-Jewish, which is quite a different thing. Historians are of the opinion that there have been eight Semitic peoples (Assyrians, Chaldeans, Phoenicians, Hebrews, Samaritans, Syrians, Arabs, and Ethiopians) of which three are in existence today (Arabs, Hebrews or Jews, and Ethiopians). Catholicism in the Middle Ages and Luther were only against the Jews.

2. This anti-Judaism was of a religious nature only. Equally universalist, both the Roman church of the time and Luther thought that all of the people of the earth except the Jews were pervious to the seductions of their system of propagating the Faith. It went no further.

3. During the Middle Ages all of Europe was religiously anti-Jewish, and to the same degree everywhere. In countries like Holland, where Lutheranism has remained the same as it was in Luther's time, and in other countries like Spain and Hungary, where the Roman church has remained what it was in the Middle Ages, anti-Jewish feeling has been considerably attenuated during the past six centuries. Nevertheless, neither Holland, Spain, nor Hungary was the theater of a phenomenon similar to that of National Socialism. Indeed, in our days it is in Germany that the Church, Lutheran as well as Roman, is the most open to the problems of science!

4. National Socialism itself was anti-Semitic, but only because it was racist. It maintained, for example, the best relations with the Arabs. It would also have maintained good relations with the Jews if they had not claimed to be a distinct people – chosen

DEBUNKING THE GENOCIDE MYTH   223

besides! — in Germany itself. (Its relations with the Arabs would
not have been much better had they made the same claim.) The
attitude of the Nazis on this point was clearly defined, doctrin-
ally, on the one hand, through its conception of the idea of a
people (in one specific area, one race protected against cross-
breeding), and, on the other hand, through the international
Zionist movement, to which National Socialism attributed
a determinant role in the unleashing of the First World War
(to get Palestine, it claimed) and in the formulation of the
Versailles Treaty (which would permit, it claimed again, the
Jewish people, after having gotten Palestine, to take over the
Middle East with the help of Bolshevism).

Thus, it was from its very beginning that National Socialism
held the Jews responsible for all of Germany's troubles after the
Treaty of Versailles. Once in power, the Nazis unceasingly
accused them of wanting to provoke a Second World War, in
permanent collusion with Bolshevism, in the hope of destroying
Germany and, at the same time, of gaining the help of Bolshevism
in the Middle East.

These were the two main, fundamental reasons for the policy
of National Socialism with regard to the Jews. Anti-Semitism?
That is saying both too much and too little; racism is the right
word. These reasons, in any case, bear no relation, either by
association or affiliation, to the anti-Judaism of the Roman
Church in the Middle Ages or to that of Martin Luther, and it
is a little embarrassing to have to recall this, if not to teach this,
to an American professor of political science, with his university
degrees and his apparently solid credentials. But, since 1933
(when Mr. Raul Hilberg was a youngster) and, especially, since
1945 (when he was just leaving adolescence) so many papers
and journals have explained, for the benefit of public opinion,
that National Socialism traced its roots to Roman Catholicism
in the Middle Ages and to Martin Luther, and that, therefore,
anti-Semitism and racism were a fundamentally German tradition, that Mr. Raul Hilberg, preeminently a man of preconceived
ideas and dogmas, accepted the idea without feeling the need to
verify it. In Hilberg's case, it is not even *Luther dixit*, but rather
Vox populi dixit. To have been correctly informed on this issue,
it would have sufficed for him to have read *Das Weltbild des
Judentums: Grundlagen des Antisemitismus* by the Austrian
Bruno Amman (Vienna, 1939) or *Warum-Woher-Aber Wohin*

by the German Hans Grimm (Lippoldsberg, 1954). Although
the first was written by a partisan of National Socialism and the
second by an independent, they are two of the most serious
studies on the origins of National Socialist racism and the answer
it expected to find for the Jewish problem because they are the
best documented. But, Mr. Raul Hilberg does not seem to find
it necessary to read anything more than what comes from the
prophets and the political friends.

Once having been caught in this mesh, the only thing that has
to be done is to prove that the prophets and the political friends
are right. However, since the position of these prophets and
political friends is grounded upon various historical inaccuracies,
an attempt to justify it historically results in error upon error,
because everything is linked together. For example, having a
false idea of the origins of National Socialist racism, Mr. Raul
Hilberg could not possibly have a correct idea of its historical
form. Thus, he states theoretically that Hitler had decided to
exterminate the Jews; Chaim Weizmann and Ben Gurion *dixit*.
To support this contention he cites (p. 257) a passage from a
famous speech that Hitler made before the *Reichstag* on January
30, 1939:

> Today I want to be a prophet once more: if international
> finance Jewry inside and outside of Europe should succeed
> once more in plunging nations into another world war, the con-
> sequence will not be the Bolshevisation of the earth and thereby
> the victory of Jewry, but the annihilation of the Jewry race in
> Europe.

I have already had occasion to remark (with regard to the
Hossbach document) that threatening observations of this kind
abound in the writings of statesmen the whole world over.
Historians usually consider them as representing the kind of
defiance that was hurled by the ancient heroes and, as a consequence, attribute little significance to them. Between the two
wars Russian statesmen addressed such threats in profusion
toward capitalism, and, at the United Nations General Assembly
of 1960, Mr. Khrushchev once more bellowed, word for word,
the same threat to the Americans while hitting his desk with his
shoe. At Nuremberg only once was this passage from the speech
cited (T. III, p. 527), but without attaching importance to it. It
does not figure in the prosecutor's charge. Mr. Raul Hilberg,
doubtless, thinks that was by mistake and heavily insists on

citing (p. 266), by way of confirmation of the decision for extermination, another passage from another speech, given in the Sport Palace on September 30, 1942:

> At one time, the Jews of Germany laughed about my prophecies. I do not know whether they are still laughing or whether they have already lost all desire to laugh. But right now I can only repeat: they will stop laughing everywhere, and I shall be right also in that prophecy.

But, not only was this passage not sustained at Nuremberg, it was not even cited: in short, it was not serious evidence. On January 30, 1939, the concentration of Jews in camps had not yet begun (according to the Jewish historian Til Jarman, there were only six concentration camps in Germany at the beginning of the Second World War, and they contained, all together, 21,300 internees, of which 3,000 were Jews; *The Rise and Fall of Nazi Germany*, New York, 1956), and, on September 30, 1942, the concentration of Jews which until then had taken place only in Poland (1940-41) was just beginning (March 1942), on a scale similar to that of Poland in other parts of Europe that were occupied by German troops.

Without doubt, Mr. Raul Hilberg had foreseen this objection, since, in nearly 700 pages, he sets before us a methodical plan in four stages: *Definition of the Jew; Expropriation; Concentration;* and, finally, *Extermination.* Mr. Raul Hilberg could then reply that to carry out an enterprise of such a scope took time, and that in 1942 they could not have gotten very far with the work, but that that does not mean it was not planned. What the basis for that conviction is we do not know. Mr. Raul Hilberg does not offer a single document corroborating this plan, which allows us to presume, in any case, that during peacetime much more time was necessary (1933-1939) to define and expropriate the nearly 600,000 Jews (the total for Germany in 1933, Austria from 1938 on, and Czechoslovakia in 1939) on hand in Germany during that period, than to transport and exterminate 6,000,000 during total wartime conditions (1941-1944). Not less surprising is this contradiction: after having told us (p. 177) that the intentions of National Socialism were to exterminate the Jews along this methodical plan, Mr. Raul Hilberg then tells us (pp. 257-258) that "Hitler hesitated in his policy of extermination, until he was convinced that there was no other alternative. From 1938 to 1940 he made the most extraordinary efforts to work out a vast plan of emigration." In another place in his book (p. 256) he wants to prove to us that 1.4 million Jews were exterminated by the *Einsatzgruppen,* but after having used all means to prove it (reports of unit leaders, testimonies of victims who survived, etc.) he is still lacking 500,000 bodies, to come up to his total, so, coolly he adds, on his own authority, 250,000 for "omissions" and 250,000 more for "gaps in our sources." I do not think a better example of this kind of hare-brained thinking could be found.

Moreover, light has today been shed on these extermination orders which were allegedly given by Hitler, which show up every fifty or hundred pages in *The Destruction of the European Jews* and which bear all sorts of dates. As I have already stated, in *La Terre Retrouvée* (Paris) of December 15, 1960, Dr. Kubovy, Director of the *World Center of Contemporary Jewish Documentation* at Tel Aviv, has agreed that no extermination order by Hitler, Himmler, Heydrich, Goering, or any other member of the ruling circle of the Third Reich, exists.

If we were to go into further detail, we would find that there is no end to the factual distortions of which Mr. Raul Hilberg is guilty. The following list is a sample of some of them: his presentation of the so-called "Crystal Night" (November 9 and 10, 1938) as having been planned by the high authorities of the Third Reich through the citation of telegrams (all dated November 10, 1938) from minor officials within the ranks of the police and the N.S.D.A.P. (pp 19 and 655); the *Einsatzgruppen* which he shows as having been in action in Poland in 1939 when such units were not created until May 1941 (see, the testimony of Ohlendorf, N.M.T. IV, p. 322); his interpretation of the German expression *"Judenfrei"* to mean to be "free of Jews" by means of "extermination" when, in reality, the term was applied to a given territory to mean that it was to be "free of Jews" by their transfer into concentration camps or other areas; his distortions of such documents as the "Wannsee Protocol" in which he translates the expression *"weitere Lösungsmöglichkeit"* (meaning, "new solution possibility") as *further* solution possibility (p. 264); his statistical errors where he has some Jews die twice, like the ones at Simferopol, where the city was "freed of the 10,000 Jews who were living there in December 1941, so that the army could have a quiet Christmas" (p. 192) and who then were "exterminated in February 1942"

(p. 245); his failure to deduct from the total of the exterminated all of those Jews of whom he says (p. 192) that "on the road from Smolensk to Moscow [and] . . . in many towns, the Soviets had evacuated the entire Jewish population" (to behind the Urals from which on their own they proceeded on their way to Hong-Kong, or southward to Turkey and the Middle East); the 10,000 Jews of Chernigov who numbered only 300 when the Germans arrived (*ibid.*), the 100,000 of Dniepropetrovsk who were only 30,000 *(ibid.)*, those of Mariupol and Taganrog who were evacuated to a man by the Soviets *(ibid.)*; there appear to be 1,500,000 Jews in all (p. 190) who seem not to have been deducted from the general statistics of total Jewish losses, because otherwise it would not be possible to arrive at a total of 5,407,500 (p. 670) or even of 5,100,000 (p. 767); his crude errors in figuring such as: 3,350,000 Jews given as living in Poland in 1939 (p. 670), 3,000,000 dead in 1945 (p. 767) but only 50,000 survivors (p. 670), etc.

Of what use is it to continue? I think that I have given a good enough idea of the doctrine and of the method of Mr. Raul Hilberg to convince the reader that he cannot regard *The Destruction of the European Jews* to be an objective piece of scholarship. Now, the time has come to examine Mr. Hilberg's source materials: his witnesses, his testimonies, and his documents.

Chapter Thirteen

Witnesses, Testimonies, and Documents

I. Generalities

Unfolding my usual newspaper on May 17, 1963, my eye was caught by the following: "Legal error uncovered in Austria: innocent persons have been in prison for fifteen years." Then followed the explanation, in the form of a press dispatch from Vienna, dated the day before:

> Sentenced sixteen years ago to hard labor for life, two Austrians, Hubert Ranneth, 43, and Joseph Auer, 30, were yesterday set free.
>
> Following a new investigation ordered last November by the Austrian Minister of Justice, light was thrown on one of the worst legal errors of the century.
>
> In 1947 Ranneth and Auer were sentenced for having murdered with iron bars three workmen in a steel works. But it was only last November that an important fact became known. The "complete confession" of Auer, on which the accusation had been based, had been extorted by means of a shot of scopolamine, a euphoric medicine, paralyzing in big doses. Finally the medical experts have established that the iron bar, at the time, the item that led to conviction, could not have been used to murder the victims.

Many good people think that this information offers an explanation for the sensational confessions in the celebrated Moscow trials. It does not seem that this method of Austrian justice was used at Nuremberg, at least not during the thirteen big trials. That drugs might have been used in the multitude of minor trials which have taken place since, against former S.S. or petty bureaucrats of the Third Reich, is quite possible. Most of these cases never came to a hearing except after a long period of imprisonment of the defendants, after having been many times postponed, and that fact raises all sorts of suspicions. The drugging of the defendants seems to have been the case, for example, in the trial of the "Death busses," March 1963, where the accused gave technical details of the operation which experts cannot accept. This could be the case again in the trial of the second commandant of the camp at Auschwitz, where the matter has been under preliminary investigation for three years and where the trial has been postponed four times already. As of the date of this writing, the Prosecutor has still not succeeded in proving that 437,000 Hungarian Jews were gassed at Auschwitz between the 16th of May and the middle of October 1944. Perhaps, that is why the defendant, instead of committing suicide like Gerstein (whose case will be discussed farther on), decided to die of a "heart attack"; in 1963 it has become very difficult to have suicides. This could be the case with Eichmann. Once the first injection is admitted, one is permitted to think that others may have come later, a fact which would explain a lot of things.

Additional means at the disposal of justice include compulsion through bad treatment and physical torture (Streicher, Pohl, Ohlendorf), intimidation (Sauckel, whose wife and nine children in the hands of the Russians were, according to his statement at the Trial of the Major War Criminals, used to exert pressure on him, by the Soviet examiners), psychological torture or "brainwashing," and, finally, the situation that the defendant found himself in with regard to the charges (Hoess, Kurt Becher, Hoettl, Wisliceny, von dem Bach-Zelewski).

Next followed the witnesses who were not brought to the bar by any charges and who gave evidence without any pressure being exerted on them: the partisans of guilty conscience. One easily understands why the Czech communist, Doctor Blaha, saw a gas chamber in action at Dachau where none existed. It was communist doctrine to say so. Furthermore, as a prisoner belonging to the *Häftlingsführung* of the Dachau camp, this individual could not have had a clear conscience. One can just as easily understood an analogous declaration of the S.S. Hoellriegel concerning other imaginary gas chambers at Mauthausen. It is an example of a guilty conscience in its pure form on the part of a man who had to get himself pardoned for his participation in the drama, and who, furthermore, might have to jump, from one day to the next, from the role of witness to that of defendant. I have explained this factor in connection with the cases of Louis Martin-Chauffier, David Rousset and Eugen Kogon. I could have added to their names the names of others such as the Reverend Father Riquet of the Society of Jesus, Professor Pierre Bertaux and many others who, having given during the German occupation certificates of good conduct to collaborators or *Gestapo* agents, later became fierce upholders of the Resistance orthodoxy in order to excuse their former actions.

The most typical case of this kind of guilty conscience seems to me to be that of the German Pastor Martin Niemöller.

In short, he is a man who could have been at the defendants' bench at Nuremberg under the charge of "Crimes against peace," for having participated in the Nazi "Plot," which the indictment included, from 1920 until 1936. Such a conclusion is inescapable when one reads his own book, *Vom U-Boot zur Kanzel* which came out in Germany in 1935, when Hitler had been in power for two years, and which was written on the theme *"Damals versank mir eine Welt."* It is the harshest of any indictment of Bolshevism that I have yet read; it is also a narrow and chauvinistic profession of faith in nationalism, and it shows the most complete adherence to the general policies of the N.S.D.A.P.

To get pardoned for all that, Pastor Niemöller, President of the Council of the German Protestant Church, in a speech which he gave on July 3, 1946, and which was published under the title *Der Weg ins Freie* (F.M. Hellbach, Stuttgart, 1946), testified that 238,756 persons had been exterminated at Dachau, although we know today that in reality there were only about

30,000 deaths there; he confirmed the existence of a gas chamber, and we know today there was not one there; and since 1945, every time he has opened his mouth to speak, he has preached the unilateral responsibility of Germany, and the collective responsibility of the German people, in the war of 1939-1945. He is today at the head of a pacifist movement, and he defends without exception all of the contentions which are the basis of Soviet Russia's foreign policy. There is no doubt that if he had not conducted himself in the way that he has, he would have been one of the chief objects of the accusations that the Soviets incessantly make against the Germans. Pastor Niemöller, in short, has the same attitude as all of those people of the Parisian gentry, or of the world of arts and letters, who led a *Dolce Vità* in the company of the highest German personages of occupied Paris, rejoicing in the champagne of Hitler's victories, and who, as soon as the wind turned, gave their allegiance to the communist party and became the most severe denouncers of the collaborators, in post-war France, solely with an eye to escaping the defendants' bench.

It was people like that who gave the prosecutors and the judges at Nuremberg their most striking evidence and who continue to enrich the archives of Rehovot (Israel) and of Warsaw with all those documents, as fanciful as they are new, which are discovered from time to time and which are published to the sound of trumpets in order to keep alive in the world those anti-German feelings on which the world policy of Bolshevism and Zionism depend.

At Nuremberg, the Prosecution and the Judges got sensational results by this method. Notice this curious document P.S. 3319 (N.M.T. XXXII, pp. 159-92) which Mr. Raul Hilberg cites and comments upon (pp. 502-709). In question is the organization, by the Ministry of Foreign Affairs of the Third Reich, of an anti-Jewish congress at Krummhübel on April 3 and 4, 1944, with all the representatives at foreign posts participating. In 27 pages a certain Ludwig Kohlhammer, *Landesgruppenleiter,* reports very exactly on the number of participants — 31 persons — and their names and what each one said.

Now, this congress never took place. This is how the matter was presented to the Nuremberg Tribunal:

> March 27, 1946, von Steengracht (Secretary of State, Foreign Affairs, Third Reich) is interrogated by Colonel Philimore, deputy prosecutor-general for the English, who asks him:

"I would now like to bring up the question of the Jews. You told us yesterday that you yourself and Mr. Ribbentrop had prevented the anti-Jewish Congress of 1944 from taking place. Is that true?

"Yes," answered von Steengracht. (T.X., p. 137.)

And this is what he stated the day before in reply to a question put by Dr. Horn, von Ribbentrop's counsel:

"Our liaison with Hitler informed us that the latter, informed by Bormann, had ordered Rosenberg's office to organize an anti-Semitic congress. Ribbentrop did not want to believe it, but after having had a conversation with the liaison agent, he had to believe it. Since this decision made it impossible for us to prevent the congress through official channels, we tried to prevent it with a policy of hesitation, delay and obstruction. And, although the order had been issued in the spring of 1944, and the war was still not over in April 1945, the congress never took place." (T.X., p. 125.)

On April 2, 1946, von Ribbentrop is interrogated by Mr. Edgar Faure, who at the time was deputy prosecutor-general for France, and who later was to become President of Council in France:

Mr. Edgar Faure (to Ribbentrop): "During the examination of your witness Steengracht, the English prosecutor brought forth document P.S. 3319, which has the English No. G.B. 287. I would like to refer to this document just for one question: In this document appear the minutes of a congress, of a gathering at which were present all the reporters on Jewish matters in the various diplomatic missions in Europe. This congress was held at Krummhübel on April 3 and 4, 1944. It had been organized by Schleier. That was read the other day. You knew about this congress, I suppose?"

von Ribbentrop: "No, I am hearing about it for the first time. What was that congress? I have not even heard that such a congress took place. What sort of a congress was it?"

Mr. Faure: "The document has been filed with the Tribunal, and I simply want to ask you one question. You have testified that you did not know about this gathering at which were present thirty one persons, almost all of them diplomatic personnel. I point out to you that during this reunion Counsellor of Embassy von Thadden made a declaration which was reported in the following terms:

> 'The orator is showing why the Zionist solution of
> Palestine and other similar solutions should be re-
> jected, and why there are grounds for the deporta-
> tion of the Jews to the eastern territories.'
>
> I suggest that this declaration made by a Counsellor of Embas-
> sy before thirty one persons in your department represented
> your own thesis on the subject."
>
> *von Ribbentrop:* "Yes, but I do not know at all what you are
> trying to say. Will you please put the document at my disposal
> so that I may answer?"
>
> *Mr. Faure:* "I have no intention of showing you this document
> .... (T.X., p. 420)."

That was the proof of forgery. It was also a typical breach of
the Rule of Procedure No. 2 of the Tribunal itself which provided that "all the documents appended to the Indictment shall
be put at the disposition of the defendants not less than 30 days
before the trials" (T.I., p. 21). This matter was never spoken of
again. If one looks in the Index of Names (T., 24) for information on *Landesgruppenleiter* Ludwig Kohlhammer, he is not
listed. But, Document P.S. 3319 was admitted into evidence.
One can hardly understand why. If Mr. Edgar Faure wanted to
prove that the Zionist and other similar solutions, according to
the thesis of the Reich Minister for Foreign Affairs, were rejected in April, 1944, there was no need to invent a document. It
was common knowledge that the main obstacles to these solutions derived from the strategic operational situation, and that,
as the affair of Joël Brand proved the following month, the
Allies turned them down, through neutrals. One understands
even less how it is that seventeen years later, Mr. Raul Hilberg
still does not know that this document was a common forgery.

Shall I speak to Mr. Raul Hilberg about his principal witness
on the missions of the *Einsatsgruppen, Gruppenführer* Ohlendorf? On January 3, 1946, in the morning session, he said, "On
the subject of Jews and communist commissars, the heads of the
Einsatzgruppen received *verbal* [sic] orders before each mission," and that "on Russian territory [we admire the precision]
that meant that they were to be assassinated" (T. IV, p. 322),
and in the afternoon session, to the question as to whether this
had been arranged in the agreement between the O.K.W. and
the R.S.H.A., he replied that "he did not remember, but that in

any case that job of liquidation was not mentioned" (T. IV, p. 319). Every two hours he was asked if "most of the heads of the *Einsatzgruppen* came from the R.S.H.A.," to which he replied that "they came from all over the *Reich*," (*op. cit.* p. 325); then, again to the same questions, he stated that "they were furnished by the State police, the *Kripo*, and to a lesser extent by the S.D." (*op. cit.* p. 332). The poor fellow, with the threat of a death sentence hanging over him, had completely lost his head and did not know what Saint to turn to for help to escape his destiny. He was hanged in 1951 in spite of his willingness to please, and after having suffered such treatment! At his trial in 1948, when all that he had said at Nuremberg was brought up against him, he said that all previous declarations had been extorted from him under pressure and were worthless.

The preceding paragraphs are concerned only with the witnesses, testimonies and earlier documents on which Mr. Raul Hilberg bases his work. At Rehovot (Israel) and Warsaw (Poland) the Zionists and Communists have for fifteen years been concentrating on a search for new documents to back up the earlier ones so as not to halt the wave of hatred against Germany, which is playing both Zionism's and Bolshevism's game. The most famous of all these testimonies which have their place on the shelves of the libraries of these two centers is surely the *Diary of Anne Frank* (Paris, Ger. tr. 1958, Calmann Levy). This document did not capture the attention of Mr. Raul Hilberg, but some day he might be drawn to consider it. Far from me to claim that it is a forgery. A teacher who lives near Hamburg did this, and he received a heavy sentence. Furthermore, I must admit that this matter did not engross me very much, although I followed it closely enough. What immediately struck me as being most peculiar was the handwriting itself of the unfortunate child. Aside from the fact that if the text is read in the different languages in which it has been printed in none of them are the same things found, the two specimens of the child's handwriting, one is presented by her father in the German edition and the other as shown by *Life* (September 15, 1958), appear to be quite different – i.e., written by different persons.

I want to be clearly understood. I do not say that the *Diary of Anne Frank* is a forgery[1]. I do not want to make any trouble! I only ask if these two writings are by the same person

of the same age, since I am not a graphology expert. After that, I
shall decide about the authenticity of the document. Perhaps,
Mr. Raul Hilberg will take this problem up . . . .
And now, moving from the general to the particular, let us
speak a little about the late Messrs. Rudolf Hoess, Kurt Gerstein,
and Miklos Nyiszli, who, in varying degrees are the stock witnesses of Mr. Raul Hilberg.

II. The Witness Rudolf Hoess
Der Lagerkommandant von Auschwitz spricht

Born in Baden-Baden on November 15, 1900, Rudolf Hoess
was a soldier in the First World War. As a member of the
N.S.D.A.P. from 1922 on, in May 1923, he and two accomplices killed Walter Kadow who had turned over to French
occupation troops in the Ruhr Leo Schlageter, a sabotage
organizer in the occupation area. Hoess was sentenced to ten
years but was paroled after serving six.

Hoess was a member of the S.S. from 1934 on; while in the
S.S., he became a block chief (*Blockführer*) at Dachau at the
end of 1934; later he was promoted to manager of the prisoners' belongings and, then, deputy to the commandant of the
Sachsenhausen Camp. He served as Commandant at the Auschwitz camp from May 1940 (the camp was not ready for prisoners until June 14) until the end of November 1943. He was
arrested for the first time at Heide (Schleswig) in May 1945 by
the English, who released him almost immediately, and was
arrested again in May 1946 at Flensburg (Holstein), where he
was interrogated with "whip and alcohol," as he says in his
book, *Le Commandant d'Auschwitz parle*, (p. 211, French ed.).
He was then transferred after a few days "to Minden on the
Weser, an interrogation center in the British zone," where he
suffered "the most brutal treatment from the military prosecutor, an English commander." (*ibid.*) He came to Nuremberg at
the beginning of April as a defense witness for Kaltenbrunner.
He testified at Nuremberg on May 15, under threat of being
turned over to the Soviets. Knowing what treatment they had in
store for him, it was quite natural that he said what he thought
was best calculated to keep the Americans from doing that.
Professor Gustav Gilbert, a psychologist attached to the prosecution staff, was at the Trial and, encouraging this hope, adroit-
ly suggested what he should say. He did not complain about his

treatment at Nuremberg: on the contrary, he said it was a "health cure" (p. 211) when compared with what he had undergone at Heide and Minden. Unfortunately for him, he was claimed as a war criminal by Poland, and was transferred there on May 25 where, on July 30, he was incarcerated in the Krakow prison. At Krakow he experienced a change of scene that was much worse than Heide and Minden, and "without the intervention of the Prosecutor they would have finished me off," he said (p. 214). His case was heard from the 11th to the 29th of March, 1947. He was condemned to death on April 2 by the Warsaw Supreme Court and was hanged on the 4th at Auschwitz.

In prison, while waiting his trial, he wrote his memoirs. For this purpose, he was given not a pen and ink but "a pencil." The advantage, for those who wish to exploit it, is that facsimiles — and surely the originals, too — from pencil writings are almost illegible. It follows that authenticity can only be attested by experienced specialists, the kind who work on Egyptian palimpsests, and so far the original manuscript has not been submitted to one, if my information is correct. The original document is in the Auschwitz Museum where the International Committee of the camp has custody of it, and where its inspection by scholars has been carefully restricted. Just try to examine it there! To my knowledge, one part of it has been published in German entitled *Autobiography* (1951), but it does not seem to have been translated into any other language except Polish. As far as I know only a few fragments, cited by authors more fortunate than I (for example, Michel Borwicz, *Revue d'histoire de la seconde guerre mondiale*, October 1956, pp. 56-87) have appeared until now. Another part was published with the title, *Le Commandant d'Auschwitz parle* (1959) in French, English, German and Polish. It seems that the whole manuscript has not yet been published and that, at the present time, specialists are studying and preparing the rest for publication, doubtless in "pencil" too. It looks like there are many fine days ahead for the historians. In short, together with the testimony of the author at Nuremberg, on the same subject, we have at hand three texts from the same person. What do these texts say?

The judgment of the Supreme Court at Warsaw which sentenced Hoess to death and which served as the introduction to *Le Commandant d'Auschwitz parle* (pp. 9-13, French ed.) charges him with taking part in the killing of:

about 300,000 persons confined in the camp as prisoners, and listed in the camp register.

a number of people, whose exact number is difficult to determine, but at least 2,500,000 mostly Jews brought to the camp by wagons from all over Europe for immediate extermination, and not in the camp register for that reason.

at least 12,000 Soviet prisoners of war held in the concentration camp contrary to the law of nations with regard to the treatment of prisoners.

Therefore, the Polish court claimed that 2,912,000 persons in all for the period from May 1940 to the end of November 1943 died at Auschwitz. By assuming that this figure was correct, and by adding those who were exterminated from the end of November 1943 to January 1945, witnesses at Nuremberg spoke of 4,500,000 dead. In October 1956, Mr. Henri Michel, a former French deportee and the editor-in-chief of the *Revue d' histoire de la seconde guerre mondiale,* put the total number of dead at Auschwitz at 4,000,000, in this way: "This camp was the most international and the most western of the death factories, and its soil is enriched with the ashes of four million corpses." (p. 3.)

In reply to the question put by Dr. Kaufmann, Kaltenbrunner's legal counsel at Nuremberg, "Did Eichmann tell you in fact that more than 2,000,000 Jews were destroyed at Auschwitz camp?", Hoess answered, "Yes, that is right." (T. XI, p. 409.) Behind the scenes he is supposed to have told the American psychologist, Gustave Gilbert that "Every day two trains brought in 3,000 persons, for 27 months" (therefore, for the whole length of the period of deportation, from March 1942 to July 1944). "So that makes a total of about 2,500,000 people." (Statement of Professor Gilbert before the Jerusalem Tribunal in judgment on Eichmann, May 30, 1961.) But, when it came to giving details about these 2,500,000 people he wrote in the *Le Commandant d'Auschwitz parle* (p. 239, French ed.):

As for me, I never knew the total number, and had no way of determining it. I can only remember the number in the most important cases, often pointed out to me by Eichmann or one of his deputies:

From Upper Silesia, or Poland in general:	250,000
From Germany, or Theresienstadt:	100,000

Holland:	95,000
Belgium:	20,000
France[2]:	110,000
Greece:	65,000
Hungary:	400,000
Slovakia:	90,000
TOTAL:	1,130,000

The figures concerning cases of less importance are not graven in my memory, but they were insignificant compared with the above. I think the figure 2,500,000 much too high.

These figures, too, have to do with the whole period of deportation and Hoess got them from Eichmann. And, Eichmann definitely did have things to say about the matter, but when Hoess' statement at Nuremberg is compared with his book, we see that these things do not always agree.

It is my opinion that very few Jewish deportees came to Auschwitz from countries other than those which appear on Hoess' list. It is possible that this total corresponds to the reality, although it is still very high. Apparently, this realization was admitted by the Institute of Jewish Affairs in *Eichmann's Confederates and the Third Reich Hierarchy* when it concluded that "at Auschwitz, [together with its satellite camps, best known of which was Birkenau, located to the south not far from Krakow] . . . about 90,000 Jews perished." Probably, Mr. Raul Hilberg referred to this estimate, too, in order to figure at a million (p. 572) the number of Jews who died there. What is the basis for the estimation of the number of survivors, one of 230,000, and the other of 130,000? Neither in *Eichmann's Confederates and the Third Reich Hierarchy* nor in *The Destruction of the European Jews* is there an explanation of how these figures were determined. Therefore, they are probably conjectural. In Mr. Raul Hilberg's case, it is a little troublesome because (p. 670) he finds only 50,000 survivors for the whole of Poland, which is astonishing considering that there were already 130,000 at Auschwitz.

But, we shall not anticipate the discussion of the general statistics which will follow in another chapter; we are concerned here with the witness Hoess, not the general statistics. And, about those two trains that for 27 months brought 3,000 people to Auschwitz every day, witness Hoess does not seem very certain. On this subject I invite the reader to think about these three propositions:

1. "As far as I can remember the convoys arriving at Auschwitz never carried more than 1,000 prisoners." (p. 220.)

2. "Following some delays in communications, five convoys a day, instead of the expected three, arrived." (p. 236.)

3. "In the extermination of Hungarian Jews, convoys were arriving at the rate of 15,000 persons a day." (p. 239.)

From which it appears that under certain circumstances five trains per day of 1,000 persons each delivered a total of 15,000 persons.

To the Tribunal on April 15, 1946, Hoess had stated that these trains carried 2,000 persons each (T. XI, p. 412). To Professor Gustave Gilbert he said that they contained 1,500 each, and in his book, he comes down to 1.000. What is certain is that for the period given none of these estimates on the capacity of the trains corresponds to a total of 1,130,000. The last one is the closest to the truth with an exaggeration of only 300,000. Since Mr. Raul Hilberg takes under consideration six "killing centers," an exaggeration of 300,000 for each one would yield a total exaggeration of nearly 2,000,000 persons and, out of six million a total exaggeration of that magnitude is quite important.

The same observation holds for the soundness of this testimony: "In the middle of spring, 1942, *hundreds* of human beings perished in the gas chambers." (p. 178.) But, as we have seen, Document No. 4401 establishes beyond any doubt that the so-called "gas chambers" were not ordered for Auschwitz until August 8, 1942, and Document No. 4463 establishes that they were not actually installed until February 20, 1943. At Nuremberg, Hoess had already stated in his deposition that "in 1942, Himmler came to visit the camp and was present at an execution from beginning to end," (T.XI, p. 413); no one called his attention to the fact that even if it were possible that Himmler had gone to Auschwitz in 1942, it was not possible for him to have been present at an execution, since the gas chambers had not been constructed yet. And, furthermore, we know that it would have been unlikely for Himmler to have been present at an execution because as we learned after the war from his physician, Dr. Kersten, he could not bear the sight of an execution.

Hoess' comments concerning the capacity of the gas chambers and the crematories also are grossly contradictory. For example, he says on one page that:

> The maximum figure for the number of people gassed or incinerated every 24 hours was a little more than 9,000 for *all* the installations. (p. 236, emphasis added.)

But, then, he says a few pages later:

> As I have already said, Crematories I and II could incinerate about 2,000 *bodies* in 24 hours; it was not possible to exceed this if one wanted to avoid damage. Installations III and IV were supposed to incinerate 1,500 *corpses* in 24 hours. But, as far as I know, these figures were never reached. (p. 245, emphasis added.)

How can one fail to deduce from these flagrant contradictions that here is a document which was fabricated hastily after the event by illiterates?

Moreover, this fabrication, after the event, can be detected just from the kind of book it is, written in pencil and carefully preserved in the archives of the Auschwitz Museum, where, unless one is a well-known communist, one cannot examine it. Although it bears the date of February-March 1947, it became known and published only in 1958; this fact further clouds the reliability of the document. In addition, it is attributed to a dead man who, in any case, cannot protest what is said over his signature; this fact, in itself, tells all too much.

Finally, a careful analysis of the following language reveals a pearl:

> Toward the end of 1942, all the mass graves were cleaned [crematory ovens had not been built yet, and incineration was done in mass graves]. The number of cadavers buried there exceeded 107,000. This figure [as Rudolph Hoess explains farther on] includes not only convoys of Jews gassed from the beginning, until the moment when they went on to incineration, but also the cadavers of all the prisoners who died in Auschwitz-Birkenau camp. (p. 231)

From this statement one infers that in nearly three years 107,000 persons died. I say "in nearly three years" because the two phrases, "toward the end of 1942" and "until the moment when they went on to incineration," are paradoxical, since the cremations could not have been begun, according to the official thesis, before February 20, 1943. Therefore, for the two to be concomitant, which is called for here, it is absolutely necessary that both should have occurred on this last date. Since the camp was opened on June 14, 1940, one has to speak of almost three years. Hence: the cremation of 107,000 cadavers before February 1943 must mean that all of the rest were cremated at a later date. Taking into account that between February 1943 and October 1944 (the official end of the extermination) there are 17 months and that, as the *Kasztner Report* tells us, for 8 or 9 months (the autumn of 1943 to May 1944) the gas chambers at Auschwitz were out of order and not working, it remains to be established how many persons more than 107,000 could have been "incinerated," from February 1943 to October 1944, when the camp was equipped with four crematory ovens of 15 burners each. I would be very astonished if a cremation expert, given these facts, should reply that it was possible to cremate the million bodies that are claimed by Mr. Raul Hilberg, or even the 900,000 of the Institute of Jewish Affairs. And, here we must also remember that Eichmann gave May 15, 1944, as the date when Himmler ordered that cremation be stopped and that, therefore, the period during which the killings and the cremations took place — if they took place — could not have been longer than 5 or 6 months (March-Fall 1943).

But, there it is a question of how much credence can be given to Hoess' different versions, and after what we have seen I should imagine that his credibility is very limited.

What follows is, unhappily for Mr. Hilberg, not much more convincing. Witness what Hoess says about the development of the final solution in the direction of extermination.

We have seen that when he visited the camp in March 1941, Himmler told Hoess about his intention to transform the camp into "a great armament plant, which would keep 100,000 war prisoners occupied." Therefore, at that date, Auschwitz was not destined for the extermination of Jews, and so Mr. Raul Hilberg's contention — based upon a speech of Hitler's on January 30, 1939, that after such extermination was decided upon, it was carried out according to a mathematically progressive plan that already had been worked out — is destroyed.

On the contrary, there seems to have been no planned extermination. In fact, it seems that gas was used for the first time to kill prisoners without any order whatsoever, with gassing appartus that was makeshift, and without anyone in a responsible position in the camp, from top to bottom, expecting it:

> During one of my business trips (1942) my substitute, *Schutzhaftlager* Fritsch, made use of gasses with a group of political officers of the Red Army. For this he used cyanide (Zyklon B) which he had at hand, because it was used all the time as an insecticide. He informed me as soon as I returned. (Page 172)

Thus, from the fortuitous initiative of a subaltern is supposed to have arisen the method which was supposed to have been used on a massive scale against the Jews.

Many times, in his work, Rudolf Hoess says (or he is made to say) that verbal orders from the highest government offices, particularly that of Himmler, told him to exterminate the Jews with gas, but, he then adds, "We never got a clear-cut decision on this matter from Himmler" (p. 233). Moreover, when Hoess was all for gassing on a large scale, he states that, "I often brought this up in reports, but I could do nothing against pressure from Himmler who always wanted more prisoners for armaments factories" (p. 189). So now, Himmler was against the gassings? In any case, it is not clear how Himmler could have had more and more prisoners for munitions work if he was exterminating more and more with gas.

In addition, we must note that when Himmler verbally asked Hoess to construct gas chambers at Auschwitz (in the summer of 1941), Hoess "submitted a detailed plan of the proposed installations." About these plans, he stated, "I never had an answer or a decision on this matter" (p. 227). Nevertheless, gas chambers were constructed, because, says Hoess, ". . . later Eichmann casually told me [−verbally, therefore; everything is verbal in this business! −] that the *Reichsführer* approved" (p. 227). Himmler, then, could never have given the order to construct the gas chambers − the admission is tremendous! It seems that Himmler wanted at one and the same time to destroy as many and as few as possible of the same people. Hoess adds that:

> The Jewish prisoners under his [Himmler's] jurisdiction were to be treated with every consideration . . . . They could not do without the great supply of manpower, especially in the armament industries. (Page 191)

You figure it out!

It does not clarify matters to look into the method used for extermination. We have seen above that the gas used was an insecticide, Zyklon B, which was used, Hoess tells us, for all asphyxiations after the gassing of the political officers of the Red Army. It is strange, to say the least, that to carry out such an order, even given verbally, that some gas other than an insecticide was not provided.[3]

Be that as it may, this is what Zyklon B is: "Zyklon B exists in the form of blue pellets, delivered in boxes, out of which gas is formed under jets of water vapor." (p. 228.) But, as we shall see further on, Dr. Miklos Nyiszli claimed that the gas was formed on contact with air. It was so dangerous to handle that after it had been used in a room, the room "had to be aired for two days" before it was safe to go in that room again (p. 229), but the gassing of the Jews "lasted on an average of half an hour" (p. 173), after which "the doors were opened and the *Sonderkommando immediately* began the work of clearing out the cadavers" (p. 230, emphasis added). In fact, sometimes they dragged ". . . the corpses out while eating and smoking" (p. 180) and without incurring the least harm. Equally incredible is the account of the first extermination which took place in a morgue. In order to get the gas in there, "while they were unloading [the future victims from] the trucks, several holes were rapidly made in the stone and concrete walls of the morgue" (p. 172). We are not told how the necessary water vapor was let in, nor how the holes were stopped up after the blue pellets were put in; no doubt, that was done rapidly too, with old rags.

I would like to add that in addition to the contradictions that can be uncovered from one page to another in *Le Commandant d'Auschwitz parle* and in addition to those which appear when it is compared with what its author said at Nuremberg, the testimony on Auschwitz-Birkenau is written in a style that is strangely similar to the public confessions of the defendants in the famous Moscow trials, which no one in Western Europe took seriously. Perhaps, this strange style is further corroboration of my contention that Hoess' memoir is a fraud. Arthur Koestler told the whole story in his *Le Zero et l'Infini* — I must not fail to refer to that!

III. The Witness Miklos Nyiszli
Doctor at Auchwitz

In March 1951, in *Les Temps Modernes*, a monthly review
run by Jean-Paul Sartre, a certain Tibère Kremer presented,
with the title *S.S. Obersturmführer Docteur Mengele*, and sub-
title, *Journal d'un médecin déporté au crematorium d'Auschwitz*, a piece of false evidence concerning that camp which will
remain one of the most abominable pieces of trickery of all
time. The author was, he said, a Hungarian Jew named Miklos
Nyiszli, a medical doctor by profession, as is indicated in the
sub-title. The article contained 27 pages of selected extracts
from the doctor's memoir (pp. 1655-1672). The April issue of
the review devoted 31 more pages (pp. 1655-1886). This false
evidence had just been presented to American public opinion
by Mr. Richard Seaver, with a preface by Professor Bruno
Bettelheim. It was only in 1961 that it was published as a
whole, in German, by the Munich illustrated weekly *Quick* in
five issues (January to February) under the title *Auschwitz*,
and, in French, by Julliard Publishers in a volume of 256 pages
with the title *Médecin à Auschwitz*, and the sub-title *Souvenirs
d'un médecin déporté*.

It made a sensation in France in 1951. The trial over *Mensonge d'Ulysse* was in full swing, and in the eyes of the public I
had the blackest of souls. In 1961 it made a sensation again,
but the world over this time — the Eichmann trial was in full
swing.

The things he had to say, this Doctor Miklos Nyiszli! And, in
addition, he gave the first detailed account of all the horrors
that took place at Auschwitz, including the exterminations in
the gas chambers in particular. Among other things, he claimed
that in this camp was a gas chamber, 200 meters long (width
was not given), together with three others of similar dimensions.
They were used to asphyxiate 20,000 persons a day, and four
crematory ovens, each with 15 burners, incinerated the victims
as the operation proceeded. He added, in another connection,
that 5,000 other persons were, every day, done away with by
less modern means in two immense open air hearths. And, he
added again that for eight months he had been personally present at these systematic massacres. Finally (this is on page 50
of the Julliard edition), he stated specifically that when he
arrived at the camp (about the end of May 1944 at the earliest)

the exterminations by gas, at the rate cited above had been "going on for four years."

From the aforementioned trestimony, the following contradictions can be gleaned. First, this fellow did not know that if there were gas chambers at Auschwitz they had not been installed or made ready to work until February 20, 1943 (Document No. 4463, already cited).

Second: He did not know that the area of the gas chambers, officially and respectively, was 210 square meters for the first (the very one he mentioned), 400 square meters for the second, and 580 square meters for the last two. In other words, the gas chambers which he saw, and whose operation he describes so minutely, must have been only 1.05 meters wide. In fact, it must have resembled a long hall. Since he states precisely that down the middle of the chamber there was a row of columns with holes from which the gas came out (these columns came up through the roof, and into these openings hospital attendants wearing Red Cross arm bands threw the tablets of Zyklon B), that there were along the walls on both sides benches for sitting (surely not very wide, those benches!) and that 3,000 persons (they were gassing batches of 3,000!) could move about easily in the room, I claim that one of two things is true: either this Dr. Miklos Nyiszli never existed, or, if he did exist, he never set foot in the places that he describes.

Third: If the gas chambers at Auschwitz, together with the open hearths, exterminated 25,000 people a day for four and a half years (since according to this "witness" they continued to exterminate for six months after his arrival) that makes a total of 1,642 days. And at the rate of 25,000 persons per day for 1,642 days, there would have been 41 million cadavers, a little more than 32 million in gas chambers and a little less than 9 million in the open hearths.

I shall add that even if it had been possible for the four gas chambers to asphyxiate 20,000 persons a day (at the rate of 3,000 per batch, as the witness says), it was absolutely not possible to cremate that many at the same time, even if there were 15 burners and even if the job took only 20 minutes, as Dr. Miklos Nyiszli also falsely claims. Taking these figures for a basis, the capacity of the ovens, all working together, could not have consumed more than 540 corpses per hour, or 12,960 for the 24-hour day. At this rate the ovens could not have been put out until several years after the liberation. And only then on the condition that not a minute was lost for nearly ten years. Now, from information from Père-Lachaise on how long it takes to incinerate three bodies where there is one burner, we see that the ovens at Auschwitz are still burning, and that they are not anywhere near ready to be put out!

Since, I have made my point regarding the ovens, I shall pass over the two open air hearths (which were, our witness says, 50 meters long, 6 wide, and 3 deep and in which were burned 9 million cadavers during their four and a half years of operation) without further comment.

Fourth: There is another impossibility, at least as far as extermination by gas is concerned, since, if there were gas chambers at Auschwitz, they were not officially operating except from February 20, 1943 to November 17, 1944, or for 17 or 18 months. The number of deaths by this means, based on Dr. Miklos Nyiszli's facts, would then be about 11 million, and with the 9 million of the open hearts, about 20 million, which – by some unknown mathematical process – are reduced to 6 million by Tibère Kremer in his presentation of this "testimony."

Fifth: That is not all. This Dr. Miklos Nyiszli is as much in contradiction with himself as he is with all those who testified before or after him about Auschwitz. The following is a comparison of his testimony with that of the others: it is he who says (p. 56) that the gas was produced from pellets of Zyklon B "on contact with air!" Hoess told us that it was "in contact with water vapor." It is he who tells us (p. 56) that "in five minutes" everyone was dead; according to Hoess the Zyklon B took "half an hour." Again, it is Dr. Nyiszli who tells us (p. 36) that the Hungarian Jews were transported to Auschwitz at the rate of "four or five trains a day," each of which contained forty cars, which, in turn, contained 80 persons (p. 15), or 3,200 persons altogether, but a few pages later, he says that they each carried "about five thousand people . . ." (p. 18).

This last statement must cause surprise, since we know that the deportation of Hungarian Jews lasted for 52 days (May 16 to July 7, 1944) according to the *Kasztner Report*, and that the *"Histoire de Joël Brand"* agrees on this point; Hoess said at Nuremberg that the deportation took "a period of four to six weeks." (T.XI, p. 412.) Let us make some calculations concerning the four possibilities:

1st: 4 trains of 3,600 persons equal 14,000 persons
        per day, and for 52 days yield 748,000 persons

2nd: 4 trains of 5,000 persons equal 20,000 persons
        per day, and for 52 days yield 1,040,000 persons

3rd: 5 trains of 3,600 persons equal 18,000 persons
        per day, and for 52 days yield 936,000 persons

4th: 5 trains of 5,000 persons equal 25,000 persons
        per day, and for 52 days yield 1,300,000 persons

But, in statistics from Jewish sources, the highest figure given for Hungarian Jews is 437,000[4]. I leave it up to the reader to figure out this odd item. I shall add that the *Kasztner Report* tells us that on March 19, 1944, Eichmann arrived in Budapest with a company of 150 men and that 1,000 rail cars were at his disposal to carry out the transportation of the Jews. If, as Dr. Miklos Nyiszli, says, the trip lasted four days — which is plausible; it took that long to go from Compiègne to Buchenwald in the convoy I was in — then after six days there were no more cars in the railway station at Budapest! Consequently, the work of deportation was halted until the 9th day when empty cars began returning. And, this estimation is made without taking into consideration the number of railway carriages that were necessary to bring to the assembly points all of the Jews who had been rounded up all over Hungary. The court of the Jerusalem Tribunal that condemned Eichmann to death moreover completely destroyed this testimony in stating (in Exhibit No. 12) that "in less than two months 434,351 persons were deported in 147 sealed freight trains, with 3,000 persons in each train, men, women and children, two or three trains a day on the average," and so, as we shall see farther on, this new version is not any better.

The passages in the testimony of Dr. Miklos Nyiszli where he contradicts himself are numberless: the crematory in action, his nose and throat assailed "by the smell of flesh burning and *hair scorching*," (p. 19); "the hair of the dead is clipped off" (p. 60), *after* removal from the gas chamber and *before* incineration; then, "coarse hands cut off the tresses of their well-kept hair" (p. 168), *before* they were sent to the bathing place and then to the gas chamber. And, so it goes.

But, what is more significant than the contradictions in the texts themselves is what one finds by comparing the French ver-

sion of this so-called testimony with the German version which
appeared in the Munich illustrated weekly *Quick* in successive
issues after January 15, 1961. In the latter version, the crematories all together are not incinerating more than 10,000 persons a day instead of 20,000. A pistol shot which hits the target
at 40 to 50 meters in French, does so only at 20 to 30 meters in
German. An institute which was "the most celebrated in the
Third Reich" in the one case becomes "the most celebrated in
the world" in the second. "Pretty rugs" become "Persian carpets." Auschwitz camp which could hold "up to 500,000 persons" in the French version is no more than "gigantic" in the
German version, all precision having disappeared, without
doubt, because between 1951 and 1961 the author – long since
dead, as we shall see – discovered through an intermediary that
at Nuremberg Hoess had stated that "it held up to 140,000
persons." (T. XI, p. 416.) A distance of three kilometers is reduced to 500 meters, or vise versa, etc.

One of two things can be concluded from the preceding discussion: either it is an authentic document, in which case it
should be the same in 1951 as in 1961, in its French and in its
German versions, or, if it is not the same, then it is apocryphal.
The fact that the two versions do not agree with each other in
almost any respect and that neither one agrees with the descriptions, for example, that were derived from the documents produced at Nuremberg permits one to maintain, at least, that this
Dr. Miklos Nyiszli never set foot in Auschwitz. That fact I
suspected after having read the very first page of his testimony.
Did he not say of the convoy of which he was a part that after
"leaving behind us the Tatra mountains, we went past the stations of Lublin and Krakow" (in order to get to Auschwitz from
the Hungaro-Rumanian frontier). This statement proves that in
addition to not knowing the camp at Auschwitz he did not
know the route to get to it either. And, to think that a publishing house was found in Paris that would place such utter nonsense as this testimony before the public!

In April, 1951, when the extracts from his testimony were
published by *Les Temps Modernes,* I wrote to him. In October
of the same year he answered, through the agency of Mr. Tibère
Kremer, that actually "2,500,000 persons had been exterminated in the gas chambers at Auschwitz . . . . " In February 1961,
after having read the entire text in *Quick,* I decided to write to

Mr. Tibère Kremer. The letter was returned to me with the notation "no longer at this address" stamped on it. I next wrote to Dr. Nyiszli in care of *Quick*, and I was told that my letter could not be forwarded to Dr. Nyiszli because he was dead.

In November 1961, after having read the entire text in the French version, I wrote to Julliard Publishers, asking them kindly to forward the enclosed observations to Mr. Tibère Kremer, whose address they surely must have since they had just published his translation. I added:

> Historic documents are rightly respected and versions of them should not be published unless their authenticity is guaranteed. It happens that for ten years, in connection with my research, I have been seeking the original of this one, and no one has ever been able to tell me where it can be consulted. The best qualified historians in the world know nothing about it. The versions which have been published are divergent and contradict each other on every page. The author speaks of places which he has obviously not been to, etc. Therefore, if you could give me sufficient assurance to allow me to state "authentic document" in the case of Dr. Nyiszli, in the references in my work, I would be very much obliged.

On the 8th of December, in the name of Julliard Publishers, of which he is one of the literary directors, Mr. Pierre Javet answered:

> Thank you very much for having sent me a typewritten copy of your letter of November 16th.
>
> I am forwarding it today to Mr. Tibère Kremer, translator of Dr. Miklos Nyiszli's "*Médicin à Auschwitz*," so that he may reply to you.
>
> Meanwhile, I may tell you that it is true that Doctor Nyiszli is dead, but his wife is still alive. Moreover, I have showed his book to several deportees who have confirmed its authenticity.

I am still waiting for an answer from Mr. Tibère Kremer. However, it is quite probable that I shall never receive it. First, as we have said, on October 24, 1951, Mr. Tibère Kremer sent on to me a reply from Dr. Nyiszli to my letter of April, 1951. Then as a result of my continued research concerning this singular witness, I learned from New York, where the book was published in 1951, that Dr. Nyiszli *had died long before his testimony was first published.* If this fact is true, this dead witness — another one — was thoughtful enough to write to me after his death. And, so Mr. Tibère Kremer's silence is understandable. No further comment is necessary.

IV. The Witness Kurt Gerstein

June 6, 1961: The Jerusalem Tribunal in judgment on Eichmann is overwhelmed with testimonies on the subject of the extermination of Jews that was said to have taken place at the camp at Belzec. All of the journalists reporting the hearings say just about what this one from *Le Figaro* (Paris, June 7, 1961) says:

> The third extermination camp in question [at the hearing of June 6 during the Eichmann trial], that of Belzec located between Lublin and Lemberg, had only one survivor at the war's end, and he has since died.
>
> The prosecutor bases his case on a series of depositions made before Allied officers by Kurt Gerstein, lieutenant in the Health Service of the *Waffen* S.S., who afterwards hanged himself in a military prison in Paris. Gerstein had been ordered by Eichmann to look into quicker poisons.

And, here again in the limelight is Kurt Gerstein, as he was in January 1946 at the Nuremberg trial and as he was recently in Germany in the drama *Der Stellvertreter* (Hamburg, 1963) by a certain Rolf Hochhuth. It is a story as gruesomely phantasmagorical as that of Dr. Miklos Nyiszli.

In the very first days of May 1945 (the 5th, it seems) French troops on going into Rottweil (Württemberg) found and took prisoner in a hotel a certain Kurt Gerstein. He was wearing the uniform of the S.S. with the epaulettes of a *Obersturmführer.* He was taken to Paris where he was interned in a military prison, according to some, in the Cherche-Midi, according to others, or in the prison at Fresnes, still others said, where he is said to have committed suicide. In short, no one knows exactly where he was imprisoned. As for when he died, a morning in July – the 25th almost all the annotators say, in particular, Professor H. Rothfels (*Vierteljahrsheft für Zeitgeschichte*, No. 2, April 1953, p. 185) – is given, but nothing could be less certain. On March 10, 1949, the widow Gerstein is said to have announced that she received from the *Ecumenical Commission for the Spiritual Aid of War Prisoners*, headquartered at Geneva, only the following terse communication on the death of her husband:

> Unfortunately, in spite of repeated attempts, it has not been possible to learn more about the death of your husband, nor can the whereabouts of the grave be determined.

At the present moment neither the arrest, nor the death of the man, seem to have been made public. At least, there has been no publication to my knowledge. In any case, it was only on January 30, 1946, that this fact became sensational news through the attention drawn to it by some first class blunderers.

Without doubt, the first and best known of these blunderers was Mr. DuBost, the French prosecutor at the trial of the Major War Criminals at Nuremberg. In the archives of the American delegation he had found a number of invoices for Zyklon B that had been furnished to the Auschwitz and Oranienburg concentration camps by DEGESCH Gesellschaft, of Frankfurt/M; they were dated April 30, 1944, and were appended to an account in French, signed by Kurt Gerstein, *Obersturmführer* of the S.S., which pertained to the extermination of Jews in the gas chambers at Belzec, Chelmno, Sobibor, Maïdanek and Treblinka; the account does not give the date of these exterminations. (T. VI, pp. 345-347.) Subsequently, Mr. Hans Rothfels tells us (*Vierteljahrshefte f.Z., op. cit.* p. 177) that this document was made use of by the prosecution in the German language, in its principal passages, as evidence at the so-called "trial of the doctors," which was conducted at Nuremberg on January 16, 1947. And, then, the part about Zyklon B and the appended invoices were used at the trial of the DEGESCH Gesellschaft at Frankfurt in January 1949.

The date of this document, April 26, 1945, was made public for the first time at the "trial of the doctors." And, until the article of Mr. Hans Rothfels, mentioned above, only the French version was used, which for various legal purposes was translated into German. In *Le Bréviaire de la Haine* (Paris, 1951, pp. 220 ff.), Mr. Poliakov gives this French version, but without the date. In 1959, Heydecker and Leeb in *Le Procès de Nuremberg* do the same. In *Der Gelbe Stern* (Hamburg, 1961) Mr. Schoenberner gives the date as May 4, 1945. But in 1961, Exhibit No. 124 of the Jerusalem Tribunal which condemned Eichmann gives no date, and, furthermore, the French version therein is in no way similar to the version that was published by Mr. Poliakov in 1951. What is remarkable is the fact that it is thanks to Mr. Poliakov that we know about this second version (*Le Procès de*

Jerusalem, Paris, 1962, p. 224 ff.) and that he gives it, apparently without remembering that it was he who gave us the first.

We had to wait for the "trial of the doctors," in January 1947, for that of the DEGESCH Gesellschaft, in January 1949, and – above all – for the article, cited above, by Mr. Rothfels, in order to learn how this document got into the archives of the American delegation, where Prosecutor DuBost had found it, together with not only the two invoices from DEGESCH Gesellschaft that are mentioned above, but 12 of them, bearing dates between Feburary 14 and May 31, 1944. At the same time, we learned that the French version, composed of six typewritten pages ending with a handwritten statement attesting to the authenticity of the contents, followed by the signature of the author (*Vierteljahrshefte f.Z., op. cit.* p. 178), had two more attached pages, also handwritten and signed, but in English, bearing the same date, in which Gerstein said that not more than four or five people had been able to see what he had seen. There was one more page in which he asked that his statement not be made public before finding out whether Pastor Niemöller had died at Dachau or had survived, plus 24 typewritten pages in German with a handwritten note, dated May 4, 1945, but not signed (*Vierteljahrshefte f.Z., op. cit.* p. 179). It seems – at least that is what Mr. Rothfels tells us – that this German version in 24 pages, and the French version, are "on the whole identical on all points." Since there are two different French versions, the one published by Mr. Poliakov and the one that was Exhibit No. 124 at Jerusalem, nothing is lost in asking him which of the two he takes as his basis for comparison.

Now, let us return to these two French versions. In January 1946 the Americans had not yet realized the importance of this document – which existed in two versions, even three versions if one believes Mr. Rothfels – and they did not think it was worth being produced in evidence against the defendants at the Tribunal. Fortunately, Mr. DuBost was there. On January 30, 1946, he brought it out of his brief case, and submitted it as reference P.S. 1553-RF. However, before we discuss what happened, we should first learn a little more about its author Kurt Gerstein.

Who was Kurt Gerstein? To this question, no answer is to be found anywhere in the forty-two volume report of the proceedings of the Nuremberg Trial. For reasons which the reader will not fail to understand, the Tribunal, in fact, did not want to hear anything about either Kurt Gerstein or his testament; out of the bundle of documents that were produced by Mr. DuBost, it accepted only two invoices of April 30, 1944, each for 555 kilos of Zyklon B, one for Auschwitz and the other for Oranienburg.

The next day, January 31, 1946, in such a form that no one could doubt its authenticity and its admission into evidence by the Tribunal, newspapers all over the world reproduced this document which was not allowed to be read at the hearing the day before. It was this "press offensive" that started the exploitation of this document, which has continued for fifteen years by those eminent historians from the *Ecole Normale Supérieure, de la Rue de la Libération* (sic). founded by Father Loriquet, such as Mr. Poliakov (*Le Bréviaire de la Haine* — what a nice title!) and a few others like the Germans H. Krausnick (*Documentation sur l'extermination par les gaz*), J.J. Heydecker and J. Leeb (*Les Procès de Nuremberg*), and Gerhardt Schoenberner (*L'Etoile Jaune*), among others.

As much as one can gather from the writings of these brilliant historians, Kurt Gerstein was a chemical engineer. In 1938 he was arrested by the *Gestapo* and was interned in the concentration camp at Welzheim. How he managed to get out we do not know. In any case, we find him again in 1941 in the political S.S. and in 1942 in the *Waffen* S.S., with the rank of *Obersturmführer* in the "hygiene division" (*Abt. der Entwesung und der Entseuchung*) of the Central Sanitation Service (*Hauptamt des Sanitaetsdienst*). In this capacity it was his business to receive the orders for Zyklon B, a chemical that was used as an insecticide by the *Reichswehr*, since 1924, and then by the *Wehrmacht*, which was not fortunate enough to know about DDT. These purchase orders he passed on along with a request for delivery, to the chemical works of DEGESCH Gesellschaft of Frankfurt/M. or to its subsidiary, Testa of Hamburg. And, naturally, when he received the disinfectant he got invoices.

The facts that he tells about — or to be more correct — which are found in the account that is attributed to him — belong in 1942. So, on the 8th of June he met in his office with S.S. *Sturmführer* Günther who said he urgently needed 100 kilos of Zyklon B to be delivered to a place which was known only to the driver of the truck.

A few weeks later, the driver of the truck in question presented himself; he was accompanied by Günther. They loaded the 100 kilos of Zyklon B in the truck, Gerstein got in, and they drove off for Prague and then for Lublin where they arrived on the 17th of August. On the same day, they met *Gruppenführer* Globocnik, who is charged with the extermination of Jews in Warthegau and who has not found any better way to carry out his task than by using the exhaust gas from Diesel motors, which he has arranged to have piped into rooms especially fixed up for the purpose.

Naturally, the *Gruppenführer*, who has a sense of logic, starts by talking to Gerstein and detailing the scope of his entire operation. In his region there are three installations for exterminating Jews with diesel fumes: Belzec (on the route from Lublin to Lwow) with a capacity of 15,000 persons a day; Sobibor (he is not sure just where that is!), with a capacity of 20,000 per day; Treblinka (120 kilometers NNE of Warsaw), with no indication as to capacity according to Mr. Poliakov, but Heydecker and Leeb are more precise and give the figure of 20,000 per day. (This remarkable document does not speak the same language to one and the other!) A fourth installation, Maïdanek, is in preparation, but nothing is said by anyone about where it is or what its capacity was anticipated to be. To be thorough about this, we must add that in *L'Etoile Jaune* (German ed.), by Mr. Gerhardt Schoenberner, this part of the document is not given; doubtless, it is an example of another sort of historical method. In citing the four locations, nevertheless, Mr. Gerhardt Schoenberner attributes to Gerstein's pen a total capacity of 9,000 persons per day for the four installations.

From *Le Bréviaire de la Haine* of Mr. Poliakov and the *Documentation sur l'extermination par les gaz* by Mr. Krausnick, we deduce in addition that the *Führer* was at Lublin two days before (apparently, they do not shrink at anything in these factories where historical forgeries are fabricated!) with Himmler, and that they gave the order to "speed everything up." But this part of the document is not reproduced in either *L'Etoile Jaune* by Schoenberner, or the *Procès de Nuremberg* by Heydecker and Leeb.

Finally, Globocnik — but only according to these two authors — informs Kurt Gerstein of his mission to improve the gas chambers, particularly with the use of a more poisonous gas and less complicated mechanisms. Then, the men part company, after deciding to go to Belzec the next day.

And, after having repeated all that he was told, Gerstein recounts what he saw. Upon arriving at Belzec on August 18th, Mr. Kurt Gerstein began by visiting the camp under the guidance of a person that Globocnik put at his disposal. Mr. Poliakov was not able to read the name of this person. But after working at it, he thought he could make out "Wirth." More fortunate than he, Mr. Schoenberner was able to read clearly "*S.S.-Hauptsturmführer* Obermeyer von Pirmasens." Unfortunately, when the latter speaks of S.S. Wirth, who is quite another person than the one mentioned by Mr. Poliakov, he gives him the rank of "*Hauptmann*," a grade that never existed in the S.S!

In any case, during this visit Gerstein saw gas chambers in action using Diesel exhaust, and he measured the places: 5x5 or 25 square meters in area; 1.90 meters in height or 45 cubic meters, he calculated. We will say nothing about his 2.5 cubic meter error. Messrs. Krausnick, Heydecker, Leeb, and Schoenberner did not say anything about it either. More concerned about what was probable, Mr. Poliakov corrected the document (as we have had the honor to tell you!). He calculated that the chambers were 93 square meters in area (*Bréviaire de la Haine,* p. 223, 2nd ed.), without any further details, and that figure was more prudent. But, in the *Procès de Jerusalem* (Paris, 1962) when the Tribunal admits into evidence the 25 square meter version, Mr. Poliakov is not at all put out, and agrees with that figure, too. How right he was to correct the document! Later on, Kurt Gerstein recounts, as factual, that the next day, August 19th, he saw the gas chambers — four according to some; ten, protest the others — in action.

At the crack of dawn, a trainload of Jews arrived from Lemberg at the Belzec station, on the very edge of the camp, composed of 6,700 — Mr. Poliakov gives 6,000 — men, women and children, who were crammed into 45 cars (therefore, between 148–150 people per car, and, for those who know the size of Polish freight cars, quite a figure). It is certain that with its 6,000 to 6,700 people, this train of 45 cars was the most nightmarish of all deportee trains. Please recall that Dr. Miklos Nyiszli did not dare to give more than "about 5,000 persons per train." This Kurt Gerstein certainly has no eye for estimating or measuring, and for an engineer that is not very good.

Two hundred Ukrainians, with whips in hand, hurl themselves at the train doors, tear them open (i.e., actually rip them off of the cars!) and make everyone get out, under the surveillance of other Ukrainians, with loaded guns in hand. "Captain of the S.S. " Wirth directs the operation, assisted by a few of his fellow S.S.: the prisoners are forced to undress completely, to turn in their valuables, to have their hair cut off; then, they are taken to the gas chambers.

"The rooms are filling. Everyone squeeze closer, ordered Captain Wirth. Many people were standing on the tips of their toes, 700 to 800 in an area 25 meters square, and 45 cubic meters. The S.S. pack the room as full as they can. The doors are closed." relates Mr. Schoenberner in *L'Etoile Jaune*, and, except in style, the others say the same thing, except for **Poliakov**, who sticks to his 93 square meter area.

The point on which everyone agrees, on the other hand, is the duration of the operation, measured by Gerstein, chronometer in hand. First the 700 to 800 persons who are jammed into the gas chambers had to wait two hours and forty-nine minutes before the diesel motor would run; then, it took thirty-two minutes for everyone to die. These times come from Gerstein who clocked them with his chronometer in hand, I repeat.

It was this fantastically gruesome account that Mr. DuBost — not just anyone, but a prosecutor, and, doubtless, a well known one too, since he was chosen from among his peers to represent France at Nuremberg — wanted to have accepted by the International Tribunal on Janaury 30, 1946. The Tribunal did not go along. But, one must say that for the Tribunal not to go along it had to be really a little thick, because in other circumstances it swallowed, apparently without the flick of an eyelash, lots of other tricky things of this kind. This refusal of the Tribunal to consider the evidence did not keep the world press from issuing, the next day, January 31, 1946, *ad nauseam* and to cry yourself to sleep, the Kurt Gerstein story as an unquestionably authentic document. And, even today — fifteen years later — men who lay claim to the title of historian still dare to present it as unquestionably authentic in their books. Nor, by doing so, do they lose prestige or the favor of the world press. This reality was demonstrated at the Eichmann Trial. And, as we have mentioned above, the story has recently been staged in

Germany by an actor of sorts, on a text written by Rolf Hochhuth, who obviously is seeking literary publicity by the presentation of a shocking subject matter.

In the Eichmann Trial, the Kurt Gerstein account was presented by the public prosecutor as being one of a "series of
depositions given by Gerstein before various Allied officers."
The judgment at Jerusalem did not refer to that series of depositions, and they were never made public. It seems that we do not
know all that there is to know about the Gerstein dossier. Why?
I am afraid that the answer to that question lies in this one little
fact: in the article by Hans Rothfels (*op. cit.*) we find him writing that "*So fehlt insbesondere die im französischen Text ein-
gefügte verallgemeinernde und sehr übertreibende Schätzung
der Gesamtzahl an Opfern*" (p. 179), and in a note (p. 180)
"*G. schätzt hier auf 25 millionen (Nicht nur Jeden, sondern
vorzugsweise Polen und Tschechen).*" The preceding sentences
translate as follows: "Thus is lacking in particular the generalized and very exaggerated estimation of the total number of victims inserted in the French text. G. estimates here 25 million
(not only Jews, but especially Poles and Czechs)." It really was
a little unbelievable. What is astonishing is the fact that those
who made use of this singular document did not discover that
gas chambers 25 meters square with a capacity of 700 to 800
persons was an even more shocking exaggeration. This oversight
reveals quite a lot about their intellectual faculties as distinguished "Professors." Only those statements of Kurt Gerstein
that were considered "objective" (*Sachlich*, Mr. Rothfels says,
p. 179) and, therefore, true, were made public and used at the
tribunals. Another case of testimony that has been tampered
with.

In the case of the Hochhuth play, we have only to point out
the sources which he leans on for the authenticity of all the
assertions in the Gerstein document as it was made known to
the public, especially the assertion that "700 to 800 persons
[were] asphyxiated" in gas chambers whose "floor area [was]
25 square meters." Among these sources there figures, naturally,
Pastor Martin Niemöller (and, we have seen what his testimony
concerning Dachau was worth), a certain Professor Golo Mann
(who attests to gas chamber exterminations at Mauthausen from
1942 on), and various other persons of about the same
including even Bishop Otto Dibelius, who I held in esteem until

then as having much greater discernment; various newpaper articles by unqualified people and numerous rumors round out
Hochhuth's source material.

All this passes understanding. It is true that one should be astonished at nothing: at that Eichmann trial the judges accepted
as truth, for days on end, the statements of people who saw —
with their own eyes — the gas chambers at Bergen-Belsen working, which even the *Institut für Zeitgeschichte* at Munich, that
model of world resistantialism, admitted as having never existed.

Without doubt as a worthy counterpart to the *Stellvertreter*
of the aforesaid Rolf Hochhuth there has just been brought out
in France the *Tragédie de la déportation* in which, endorsed by
Mrs. Olga Wurmser and Mr. Henri Michel, even people like
Mademoiselle Geneviève de Gaulle and the gentle Germain Til-
lon come forward to reaffirm the existence of gas chambers and
the systematic extermination by that means in one or the other
of those camps where the *Institut für Zeitgeschichte* says that
they did not exist.

Every day, with pen quivering with indignation, the press
wonders at the resurgence of naziism, racism, and anti-Semitism
— among which, however, they draw no distinctions. What
makes me wonder is why the text tamperings of Mr. Poliakov
and the others have so far not injected even more poison into
the racism and the anti-Semitism which are aimed against the
Jews. Nothing has been overlooked that would lead to that
effect.

We know that Kurt Gerstein was an engineer, and, as such, he
probably had a logical mind and probably was trained to make
careful and accurate observations. Consequently, if it is true
that he made the statement of which we have just read the résu-
mé,[4] this man was obviously not, or was no longer, in possession of all his faculties when he did so. It is of interest to find
out why. On this point, the clues we have about the circumstances of his death are to me very revealing. If we are to believe
Hans Rothfels (*op. cit.* p. 185, note 25), the widow Gerstein
was informed that he had hanged himself, with the following
notice: " . . . Death was due to hanging. This manner of killing
oneself can absolutely not be prevented in a prison." That may
by true, but it is no reason for not telling her when the event
took place or what was done with the body; and, the fact that
the authorities professed ignorance on both scores seems to me

to explain a lot of things.

Suppose, for instance, that the two military inquisitors – a Major D.C. Evans and a J.W. Haught – who were said to have started the interrogation of Kurt Gerstein, found themselves in the presence of a man who, at the time they confronted him, had not yet written anything, or, between the date of his arrest and his first interrogation, had written only what he had actually seen, which would have been horrible enough, knowing the savage character of the war in the East on both sides. To read the memoirs of all those who were arrested in Germany at this time, and under these conditions, that is generally what happened to them. They were invited by those who had arrested them to write their confessions; so, this is not an entirely gratuitous supposition. Whether Kurt Gerstein wrote his confession in French or in German is not important. It is possible that he wrote them in both languages – at least, so they say. Let us suppose again, and this is not entirely gratuitous, either, given the ways of the military and the police, that after the French version was written they attempted to force him to say what is in the document which bears his name, but which represented their view at the moment of the events in question; on the Allies' side, concentration camps, gas chambers and "genocide" were in general the central theme of the anti-German propaganda, and being familiar with the intellectual level of the military and the police in all countries of the world, it would not be astonishing if that view represented their profession of faith. They might, themselves, have gone on to the editing of the French text, which was then presented to Kurt Gerstein for his signature; at the same time they could have asked him to write a few lines at the end of the last page to make its authenticity positive. One can imagine the scene – Kurt Gerstein – an engineer, and a man who was a precise thinker refusing to countersign and to authenticate all of those technical impossibilities which do not stand examination, and the two inquisitors giving him the beating that was usual in such cases. They were pretty brutal with him, no doubt, since Kurt Gerstein was usually described as a man who could not be pushed without resisting into saying what he did not want to say. Later, we can imagine the same scene for the German text, which lasts much longer but takes place in the same manner. The German text was written on a typewriter with a handwritten endorsement, but was not

signed. Another detail must be noted: the handwritten endorsement is shorter, and the formula of certification under oath
which occurs in the French text is missing. So, my conclusion is
that Kurt Gerstein was beaten unconscious, and then he died
before getting to the oath and the signature . . . .

Everything now becomes very clear. Since he died during the
interrogation at Rottweil (in Germany) as a result of the torture
inflicted on him to obtain his confession, Kurt Gerstein could
never have been transferred to Paris to be put at the disposal of
the *Sécurité Militaire*. This imaginary transfer would not have
been thought up in the first place, unless a simple examination
would have shown to the naked eye the real causes of his death.
By spiriting away his corpse, an autopsy was avoided and, thus,
the inevitable subsequent scandal was also avoided. This hypothesis would explain, furthermore, how the Americans came
to let the document that bears his signature lie undisturbed in
the archives of their delegation at Nuremberg where Prosecutor
DuBost found it. It is easy to understand, under such circumstances, why they had no desire to bring this body up to the
surface by producing his so-called confession before the Nuremberg court. By rejecting it as not probative and by preventing
Mr. DuBost from even reading it, the President of the hearing of
January 30, 1946, knew very well what he was doing. But,
Mr. DuBost, who had come so close to making a blunder, had
given it out to the press. From then on, it could not be re-
tracted, and its authenticity had to be sustained in order not to
lose face before public opinion, which was thus already alerted.

There are only three other possible hypotheses:

First, at Rottweil, interrogated as Kurt Gerstein must have
been to get a confession from him so manifestly out of line with
the technical truths, he could have thought that the Americans
would have him confirm the confession at the bar of some tribunal, at which time he could retract it and tell how it had been
forced from him; however, foreseeing how he would be handled
most likely by the ones thus exposed, in a moment of depres-
sion, he wanted to end his life quicker, suffer less, and, thus,
committed suicide. Then, the body had to disappear so as not
to reveal the marks it carried;

Second, he was actually transferred to Paris, where, to make
him confess more, he was tortured again as he had been at Rottweil, and, for the same reason, he committed suicide; and, again,

for the same reason the body had to disappear;

Third, either at Rottweil or at Paris, thinking that they could not get any more out of him than what he had said, or to avoid having him retract it in court, those who interrogated him murdered him in cold blood so that his supposed testimony could be presented by the prosecution without any risk of being contradicted by its author; in this latter case, it was still necessary to get rid of the body in view of the state that it was in, a condition which would have controverted the contention of suicide.

I maintain that the most plausible of these four hypotheses is the first. And, I maintain this opinion for the following reason: In July 1945, all of the French administrative services were in operation again, if not yet perfectly at least normally, and in all of the military or civil prisons, the prison registers were kept up to date. Therefore, one of two things must have happened: either the name of Kurt Gerstein occurs on the register of one of the prisons in the column "entered on . . . ;" the column "released on . . ." is blank, and the "observations" column records his death, the person or group to which his body was turned over, and the place where he was buried. Or else, which is the case, there is no notation for Kurt Gerstein, which means that he was never imprisoned in any military or civil prison in Paris. That fact would indicate that, if he left Rottweil for Paris, he never arrived. Was he assassinated en route? It is possible. In any case, the most precise of all those who have told us where he committed suicide is the always incredible Rothfels who writes:

> Gerstein was then [after his arrest] put on his honor for the time being by the French occupation forces, with permission to go back and forth between Tübingen [where his family lived] and Rottweil. Then he was brought to a prison in Paris [at what date he does not tell us]. There on July 25, 1945, in the "military prison of Paris" he committed suicide. (*op. cit.* p. 185)

Aside from the freedom of movement that was allowed this prisoner while he was still at Rottweil, and which in itself should not cause the slightest surprise, the most curious thing in this statement is that he killed himself in "the military prison of Paris." In Paris there is not *one,* but *several* military prisons, each one being administratively designated by its own name, the most famous of which is the *"Prison militaire du Cherche Midi."*

In 1945, given the extraordinary number of people, both military and civil, who were incarcerated, there were "military divisions," in addition, at la Santé, Fresnes, and other places. The official paper which mentions the death of Gerstein could only have as its letterhead: "Military Subdivision of Paris – Military Prison of Cherche-Midi," or of Fort Montrouge, or of Caserne Neuilly, etc., or "Penitentiary Administration – Prison la Santé, (or Fresnes) Military Division." Depending on the administration which issued the communication, it could also, of course, have had other headings. For instance, the heading could have been "Sécurité militaire" or "Sureté Générale;" but in no case could it have been "military prison of Paris." And if, in spite of this, it has this heading and if an official statement with another stamp gave notice of the death of Gerstein only in these terms and in quotation marks, then it is just a forgery that was prepared for the occasion by someone who knew nothing about the French police services, or about the French safety, intelligence, military and civil administrations. In short, it is a clumsy forgery—another one!

Finally, the preceding discussion which has led us to the discovery of a forgery until now unnoticed, explains why the statements that are imputed to Kurt Gerstein seem to be those of a man who was not in possession of all his faculties: at the moment when they were given to him for his signature he was already on the point of death because of the methods that had been used to extract them from him, and he only had time to sign the French version before dying. The very form of the French version, as reproduced in Exhibit No. 124 at the Jerusalem trial, militates in favor of this contention. To my French eyes, which claim to know the maternal language fairly well, it looks much more like French written by an American (or an Englishman) rather than French written by a German. I would not be surprised if, when the day comes when this document can be examined, specialists discover that it was typed on an English or American machine, since, judging by its tenor, the intellectual level of those who wanted to make Kurt Gerstein endorse it seems to have been so low that they probably did not think it indispensable to type it out on a German or French machine. As it is, it would not be very bold to ask oneself if the handwritten notes on the French version are really in Kurt Gerstein's writing.

The value that can be placed on the Gerstein document having been assessed, what now must be done is to consider the value that Mr. Raul Hilberg placed on the document. I shall say right now that for once Mr. Raul Hilberg is very prudent. He devotes only three pages to the subject (pp. 570-572), and those pages mention, in passing, that Gerstein was present at "a gassing which took an especially long time" and that "to Wirth's great embarrassment and mortification [he] timed the operation with a stop watch." However, nothing is said about the size of the gas chambers or about the figures concerning the extent of the exterminations by gas. The invoices for Zyklon B, which are appended to the document, are mentioned too. Here, I must point out that, basing himself on these invoices (12 of them according to Rothfels *op. cit.* p. 179; two, claimed by Prosecutor DuBost at the Trial of the Major War Criminals, with one for Oranienburg and the other for Auschwitz) and those invoices which were produced in the court of the Tribunal which in 1949 judged the DEGESCH Gesellschaft, producer of Zyklon B, Mr. Raul Hilberg calculates (p. 570) that the amounts of this product which were delivered in 1943 and 1944 by this company to the German Army, were 160 tons, and to the sanitation services of the SS were 125 tons (12 for Auschwitz in 1943, none in 1944, but 7.5 tons in 1942). In the aggregate these figures seem plausible to me; in any case, they seem proportionate—but in the aggregate only. If from 1942 to the end of the war, the German Army ordered and had delivered 160 tons of Zyklon B, it is quite possible, judging by their needs in the face of the exigencies of the first Russian campaign during 1941, that the sanitary services of the SS would later have required 125 tons. But, in detail I am much more cautious, and the shipments to Auschwitz particularly distress me. In the 12 invoices that were appended to the Gerstein document, bearing dates between the 14th of February and the 31st of May 1944, there were indeed some that pertained to Auschwitz, as Messrs. DuBost and Rothfels have told us. However, of these dates none are given in Mr. Raul Hilberg's calculation. And, the absence of dates make the exactness of his calculations awkward to follow.

Since I am not a specialist in the use of Zyklon B for hygienic purposes, I am not in a position to give a definitive analysis of the significance of an all-inclusive delivery to Auschwitz of 19.5

tons of Zyklon B, allowing for the fact that a greater amount was delivered, since Mr. Raul Hilberg forgot to include the deliveries of 1944 in his calculations. However, even if I were such an expert, quite a number of factors that would be needed to shape an estimate would be lacking. Therefore, this is all that I can say:

1. Just the fact that the Zyklon B was delivered to a concentration camp does not permit one to conclude that it was used to asphyxiate the prisoners; otherwise, one must conclude that it was similarly used in other camps where it was delivered but where no extermination of that kind has been shown;

2. Auschwitz was a *Stammlager* (central camp) which means that there were more *Kommandos* stationed around there than, I suspect but cannot however confirm, were located, at Chelmno, Belzec, Maïdanek, Sobibor and Treblinka. This figure for total delivery is then not just for the Auschwitz camp, but all those *Kommandos* around the camp, a list of which, as far as I know, has never been made known.

3. In order to estimate the consumption of Zyklon B correctly, we would have to know how many tons of this overall total were used and how many were not, how many persons went through the camp, and how many kilos of Zyklon B were required to disinfect their clothing on their arrival at the rate of 1,500 to 2,000 persons per convoy. Then, we would have to know how much Zyklon B was used for the minimum disinfection of underclothing necessary for the total population of the camp, and for the *Kommandos,* every fifteen days. Even if we find out someday about how many persons were involved and about how many tons of Zyklon B were required, we still shall not know how many tons were effectively used, because we shall never know, there having been no inventory, how many were not used. And, so we shall never be able to make a comparison which would allow us to say whether much more Zyklon B was used than was required for disinfection—in which case one might speak of exterminations using this material. And, this means that we have to keep searching until we find other methods of assessment;

4. Was all of the Zyklon B that was delivered to Auschwitz used? If so, then we would have proof that more was used than was reasonable, and we would have to concede the point, but that possibility is excluded. All the camps were abundantly

supplied with this product, and I shall give but one example of it: the train in which I was evacuated from Dora, which left the camp at the last minute, and which I left and then got on again under circumstances which I have described in an earlier chapter, included a car three-quarters full of iron bound boxes with labels all over them: some of the labels bore *"Blausäure"* (Prussic acid) on a red background while the others h' d *"Vorsicht"* (danger) on a white background. Below the *"Vorsicht"* there were some lines which I did not read. I had more things to worry about than stuff that was labeled dangerous. I was looking for a bag and shoes which obviously were not to be found there, and I was not interested. Moreover, I was far from being able to surmise what the *Blausäure* was to be used for. It was much, much later, after I read Kogon, that I put two and two together. But, I only wanted to say that there is no reason for not thinking that the other camps, and especially Auschwitz, were just as abundantly supplied as Dora and that the total amount of Zyklon B delivered to Auschwitz was no more used up than was that which had been delivered to Dora. And here we are once again faced with the unanswerable question: how much of it was used?

If this question cannot be answered, one might as well say that no significance can be attributed to the deliveries of Zyklon B that were made to Auschwitz which are laid out so complacently — and, alas, so incompletely — by Mr. Raul Hilberg, except that this product was, by definition, not a man-killer, but an insecticide and a disinfectant and was used as such since 1924 by all the German military and civil health services.[5] The invoices produced, in any case, are not grounds for going beyond this statement itself without foundering in suppositions and conjectures, all of which are absolutely, indisputably, and shockingly gratuitous. What we have just seen on this point provides it only too well.

Mr. Raul Hilberg was well inspired not to retain either the description of extermination by gas, as the Gerstein document says its author witnessed (Remember: 700 to 800 persons in a room 25 meters square in area!), or the statistics concerning the Belzec, Treblinka and Sobibor camps. At least he avoided the misadventure of that poor Mr. Rothfels.

Let us recall, too, the statistics as they occur in the German text (in the French text given by Mr. Poliakov in the *Bréviare de la Haine* they are not the same, and, doubtless, for the same reasons that Mr. Raul Hilberg, and the Jerusalem court, did not use them) which were made public following the article by Mr. Rothfels (*op. cit.* pp. 187-194), and according to which the extermination capacity of the camps was the following:

Belzec:	15,000 persons a day;
Treblinka:	25,000 persons a day;
Sobibor:	20,000 persons a day.

About that, Mr. Rothfels wrote (*op. cit.* p. 181) that "600,000 having perished at Belzec, Gerstein's estimate of 15,000 per day is not plausible" (*von 15,000 pro Tag nichts unwahrschein-liches*). This camp officially began exterminating in March 1942, and stopped in December of the same year (Poliakov, *op. cit.* p. 224), which makes the duration of its operation some nine months or 270 days; 15,000 times 270 equals 4,050,000 persons and not 600,000.

Let us continue with this kind of reasoning: Treblinka and Sobibor were officially exterminating from March 1942 to "the autumn of 1943," about 18 months or 540 days. At the daily rate which is given in the preceding paragraph, we get an extermination total for the first of 13,500,000 persons and for the second of 10,800,000 persons. In all, for these three camps alone there must have been 28,350,000 persons exterminated. And, if we are to believe Mr. Gerstein, they were all Jews! Incidentally, this total does not count those extermi-nated by the same process at Chelmno, which the Gerstein document does not cite, and at Maïdanek, which it cites as being "in preparation" at the time of his visit in August 1942, so he could not estimate its capacity.

And that is the sort of testimony that they have the audacity to present to us as being "reliable!" To complete the picture let us point out that, when they come to summing up and to giving the totals of Jewish losses in each of these camps, those who seriously offer this nonsense arrive at figures like the one Rothfels found for Belzec. Below is a table giving these losses as estimated by the Polish Commission on War Crimes (from Poliakov, *op cit.* p. 224), and Mr. Raul Hilberg (*op. cit.* p. 572):

Camps	Estimate of Losses	
	Polish Commission	Raul Hilberg
Chelmno	300,000	"over a hundred thousand"
Belzec	600,000	"hundreds of thousands"
Sobibor	250,000	"hundreds of thousands"
Treblinka	700,000	"hundreds of thousands"
Maïdenek	200,000	"tens of thousands"
Total	2,050,000	950,000[6]

One wonders just how the Warsaw Commission and Mr. Raul Hilberg came to these conclusions; there is no evidence that they referred to the Gerstein document, and neither one cites any other documentary references worthy of the name.

For Auschwitz, in the same table, Mr. Raul Hilberg gives one million dead, whereas to my knowledge no one else ever gave less than two million,[7] with most of the witnesses mentioning four. I do not think that I go too far in saying that if people who examine the same occurrence and who claim to be as qualified as the Polish Commission on War Crimes and as Mr. Raul Hilberg, Professor at the University of Vermont, can arrive at such disparate results as we have seen, it must be that their units of measure, or their bases of reference, are purely conjectural, do not rest on anything positive, and derive from different and extremely doubtful sources. The proof which supports my observation is furnished by the Polish Commission and Mr. Raul Hilberg themselves. I have before me at least one hundred of the references which the Polish Commission turned to in order to arrive at figures for which it is responsible in the preceding table. Among these references, one finds such things as: *German Crimes in Poland* (Warsaw, 1948), which is a pack of contradictions by people of whom it cannot even be said that they existed and who are given as "survivors;" or, "Testimony of Dr. Rothbalsam (dead!), gathered by Mme. Novitch;" or *Belzec,* (Cracow, 1946) which is a book of recollections on the camp, by someone named Reder, given as "sole survivor," about whom it was said at the Jerusalem trial (hearing of June 6, 1961) that he had been "dead since . . ."

As for Mr. Raul Hilberg, on almost every page of his book, one finds references, in footnotes, such as these: "Affidavit by Rudolf Schonberg, survivor" (p. 311, nt. 14), or "Borkomorowski, *The Secret Army*" (p. 315, nt. 32), or the testimony of an unnamed survivor taken by Cohen in "*Human Behaviour in the Concentration Camp*" (p. 625, nt. 22), or, again, another testimony, of another survivor, named this time but just as hypothetical, taken by a certain Friedman in his book, *Osviecim* (p. 622, nt. 8), etc . . . etc. And, in addition to personal testimony, there abound extracts from papers and documents which were written during the war or since its end. In the first case, they are papers published under German control. Bits of statistics are found in them that are not always in agreement; often these documents are annotated or evaluated by journalists who are not specialists; these documents and papers may discuss the steps that were taken to plunder, to ghettoize, or to concentrate; they may outline the bad treatment of which the Jews were victims, but *never* do they say anything whatsoever that could justify an interpretation in the sense of murder or extermination by gas or otherwise. The word "*Judenfrei*" often recurs, applied to a territory, a country or a region, but it means "freed of Jews," not their extermination as Mr. Raul Hilberg insinuates. In the second case, they are papers that were published after the war ended. One finds that these documents and papers, annotated by non-witnesses, contain accounts which were given by witnesses, who, for the most part are not named. If they are named, they generally are given as "dead since," thereby precluding the possibility of being cross-examined, in a controlled manner, by qualified persons.

How, indeed, could one possibly think that these witnesses are objective observers, people who, if they are still alive, will admit that since their release from the concentration camps, every move that they have made, and still make, in their lives is dictated by the hatred that they have forever sworn for the Germans? Quite a number of witnesses of this kind appeared before the Jerusalem court to testify that they had *seen* gas chambers in camps where, as is acknowledged by everyone—including Jewish sources, none existed.

The basic shortcoming of this kind of testimony—if one wants to obtain the truth—is found in the fact that it was given by people who were not witnesses, in the sense of relating honestly what they actually saw, but who were demanding reparations—as well as retribution—for what they have suffered. Consequently, they had an interest in saying those things which were calculated by them to support their objective. In all of this extermination business there are mostly accusers, who back each other up, and forgeries, crudely fabricated, whose authenticity is verified only by false witnesses. And, like Mr. Rothfels when faced with the Gerstein document, Mr. Raul Hilberg, with a frightening lack of conscience and an unimaginable contempt for the most elementary rules of his profession, pretends not to have seen the existence of bias and interest which undermines the credibility of his source material. And, here we are again back to the fundamental problem of our times: the extraordinary intellectual and moral prostration of the elites.

This latter observation is not addressed to the Commission for War Crimes of Warsaw, or, for example, to Madame Hannah Arendt; these two, from all evidence, do not belong to the elites. The first was created on the other side of the Iron Curtain, not to verify historical facts, but to produce evidence that can be used for certain kinds of propaganda. To take part in the Warsaw Commission it is not at all necessary to be a historian, but just a communist.

As for the second, Mme. Arendt is obviously a Zionist propagandist. Much of the data which she uses in her report of the Eichmann Trial (*The New Yorker, op. cit.*) derive from what she has read in the book by Mr. Raul Hilberg, which she assimilated badly, which she dishes back to us even more clumsily than the manner in which it was given in the first place, and which she cites with the clearest and most positive avowals. Mr. Robert Kempner, that former Prussian Police commissioner who is a much higher ranking agent of Zionism, is, moveover, not at all pleased with the manner in which she carried out her task. In *Aufbau* (Vol. XXIX, No. 15, April 12, 1963) he administered one of those blistering attacks which I recommend the reader to read. *Asinus asinam castiget,* the Romans of today would say of this shabby controversy.

To return to the Gerstein document and to finish with it, I now ask the following question: If it is not true that the gas chambers at Belzec, Treblinka, and Sobibor could asphyxiate between 15,000 and 25,000 persons a day; if it is not true that a gas chamber 25 meters square could hold 700 to 800 persons; if it is not true that a train with 45 cars could transport 6,700 persons; and if it is not true that Hitler was at Belzec on August 15, 1942, I ask what does it contain that is true since it contains nothing else? Are the Zyklon B invoices that are appended to the document genuine? Perhaps, but they prove nothing.

Of all those who have endorsed the authenticity of this document, only one grieves me, Otto Dibelius, Bishop of Berlin, whose fine independent spirit and sureness of judgment I have drawn attention to, particularly with regard to the Nuremberg Trial. According to Mr. Rothfels, (*op. cit.* pp. 181-182) he wrote a letter to the *Institut für Zeitgeschichte* at Munich, dated November 22, 1949, in which, after a series of praises addressed to Gerstein, we find the following sentence: "Through it I was in a position to establish that Gerstein's communication to me, insofar as his Swedish acquaintance came into the question, had been absolutely according to the truth. So had also been his original report." Of Eugen Kogon, David Rousset, Golo Mann, Hans Rothfels, Hannah Arendt, Raul Hilberg, among others, I have made a special and individual study of each of them, and it does not seem that anything else could have been expected of them.

V. Conclusion

With regard to gas chambers, the almost endless procession of false witnesses and of falsified documents to which I have invited the reader's attention during this long study, proves, nevertheless, only one thing: never at any moment did the responsible authorities of the Third Reich intend to order — or in fact, order — the extermination of the Jews in this or any other manner.[8] Did such exterminations take place without orders? This question has haunted me for fifteen years, and it is the Gerstein document, the worst and most immoral forgery of all, that indirectly put me in a position finally to answer it in a positive way.

It was June 1963. The first and the second part of my *Le véritable procès Eichmann ou Les Vainqueurs incorrigibles* had just come out in German with the title *Zum Fall Eichmann* and the sub-title *Was ist Wahrheit? . . . oder die unbelehrbaron Sieger.* For fifteen years, everytime that I heard of a witness anywhere, no matter where in the portion of Europe that was not occupied by the Soviets, who claimed to have himself been present at gas exterminations, I immediately went to him to get his testimony. And, each time the experience ended in the same way. With documentation in hand, I would ask him so many precise and detailed questions that soon it became apparent that he could not answer except by lying. Often his lies became so transparent, even to himself, that he ended his testimony by declaring that he had not seen it himself, but that one of his good friends, who had died in the camps and whose good faith he could not doubt, had told him about it. I covered thousands and thousands of kilometers throughout Europe in this way.

One day in the month of June 1963, I had a strange visitor, a German, who was large and of good carriage, who looked about sixty (but during our conversation I learned that he was actually much older) who had a little something military in his bearing, who was very distinguished in appearance, and who was exquisitely polite. In his hands was my first book on the subject, the German edition of *Mensonge d'Ulysse,* in which a book marker was sticking out.

He introduced himself and told me about the purpose of his visit, which he wanted kept absolutely confidential. I promised to preserve that confidentiality, and that is why I have presented what was said in our conversation in such a way that he cannot be identified; the account of what he told me alone being authentic.

He did not want to have his name given because during the war he had been a high ranking civilian in an important government service. He had not been a military man, but was a professional within the civil service. He did not conceal from me, that, although he had not been an active National Socialist, he had, nevertheless, given his support to the Party in 1933. When the war was over, he had narrowly escaped being a defendant at Nuremberg. Although he had been "deNazified" like everyone else, he had lost his former governmental position. He had suffered a great many difficulties, and he had had enough. He did not want to begin all that again. The story that he had been carrying around inside him for twenty years burdened him, but he was to be excused for the cowardice which had made him keep it to himself until the present. When

the war ended, he had four children, all very young, and, at
more than fifty, a whole new career to carve out.

I willingly and very sincerely conceded this. I understood
the moral—and often physical—misery that millions and millions
of Germans have lived through and still live with, and which
reduced them to a silence that they only break when they vote
periodically for Chancellor Adenauer, although his politics do
not please them, but whom they consider the only German
capable of protecting them a little against the punitive measures
of the German counterparts of Tomás de Torquemadá, like
Prosecutor-General Bauer.

These things said, and his conditions having been accepted by
me, my interlocutor opened his copy of *Le Mensonge d'Ulysse* to
the marked page, set it down in front of him, and without
further preamble started right in.

"You say, and I believe you," he said in substance, "that
not one of the witnesses who have claimed to have been present
at exterminations by gas have, until now, been able to prove it
to you. I have just read your last writings on the matter, and
I feel that you are on the point of concluding that there were
none. Seeing the interest that your works have aroused, I
thought that it would be very dangerous, both for you and for
Germany, if you do, since you could not fail to be discredited,
a fate which you do not deserve. Moreover, if you were discredited, Germany, at the same time, would have lost her only
defender who has some hearing. And, so I have come to tell
you myself that I have been present at an extermination by
gas . . ."

"Then I do not understand you," I answered. "It does not
seem to me that if you told your story publicly that you would
risk, as you claim, being imprisoned again. Witnesses of this
kind are being sought by Prosecutor Bauer, who has so far not
found anyone who is trustworthy, and if you are sure of yourself, go to him; he will lay down the red carpet . . ."

"Be patient," he interrupted, "In Germany in order not to
be thrown into prison, it is not enough to state that one has
witnessed an extermination by gas. It has to be told exactly
as it was described in a document or by a witness officially
recognized as reliable, and that is not my case. You will see.
I was on an official trip to Lublin, and I had just gone in to see
Globocnik when Gerstein was announced. Chance had it that I

found myself again with him the next day at Belzec. And, if I say that I also was present at the extermination that is referred to in the document which is attributed to him, I must also add that everything said in it concerning the gassing operation, as well as the circumstances under which he was present and his conversation with Globocnik, is, from one end to the other, utterly false. Without any doubt, such testimony on my part would be enough to have me thrown automatically and immediately into prison."

I understood less and less. "If everything is false from beginning to end," I ventured, "there was, therefore, no extermination . . ." "There was one all right," he said. "But let us begin at the beginning." And, then, he told the story . . . From his long recital, which I have abridged in order to stick to the essentials, it turned out that:

1. In the conversation that he had at Lublin with Gerstein, in the presence of my visitor and two or three military men whose names my visitor only remembered because they are given in the Gerstein document, Globocnik had spoken only of Belzec and absolutely had not mentioned any other camps. Concerning the number of persons that could be exterminated at the Belzec installation, not one figure was given. Furthermore, he did not begin the conversation by talking of extermination; he talked only of the disinfecting of clothing. It was only further into the conversation that, while deploring the limited means for disinfection available at Belzec, he said, in passing that he had found a very efficient method which would permanently resolve the Jewish question. When inquiry was made by my visitor as to what he meant, he described his Diesel engine at Belzec . . . "But," declared Globocnik, "it is only a make-shift installation; what I need is a more deadly gas, which is easier to use. That is why I have sent Günther to get from Gerstein those things that are better adapted to do this job."

"I was horrified," my visitor said to me. "Because of my civilian position, I was the only one listening to Globocnik who could say anything. 'But after all,' I said to him, 'it is a crime, and are you sure that that is the solution that the *Führer* has in mind for the Jewish problem?' 'Certainly I am sure,' was all that Globocnik answered, shrugging his shoulders. And, with a knowing look, but without saying it precisely, he suggested that the authority for his project came from the *Führer* himself.

Moreover, he insisted that it must be kept secret. Unlike what is said in the Gerstein document, he did not state that Himmler and Hitler had been to Lublin two days before—that is pure invention."

2. During the conversation, my visitor remarked that Globocnik had said that he had sent Günther to Gerstein to get a more poisonous gas and less complicated apparatus. My visitor had noted that this was not the normal operating procedure, and he had wondered why Globocnik had not addressed himself directly to the supply office by letter. This fact made my visitor suspicious about the entire operation. My visitor said that Globocnik's assignment at Warthegau was a punitive measure that had been imposed for a number of misdeeds which he had committed during his tenure as *Gauleiter* in the Vienna area. At Berlin he also had a very bad reputation, at least, so my visitor claimed. Thus, with the intention of speaking about this business as soon as he got back to Berlin, my visitor decided to go to Belzec — even though his business did not require him to go — so as to be in a position to speak about the matter with some first hand knowledge.

At Belzec he saw a very small camp, with enough barracks to have housed four or five hundred people. He saw the inmates walking around the camp and they appeared to be well fed and in good shape. Moreover, upon inquiry he learned that they were all Jews. He was told by a Jewish inmate that there was a small railway station with a single track that served the camp. From time to time, a short train would arrive full of his co-religionists. The people in the camp were to greet the arrivals and were to assist in their extermination by herding them into a little house, which was shown him, where they were asphyxiated. On the house was a sign which read *"Fondation Heckenholt,"* the name of the Jew who was in charge of starting and keeping the motor running. The inmate told all this while eating a jam tart, which clouds of flies tried to settle on and which he kept brushing away. A disgusting smell similar to that of a freshly opened grave pervaded the camp. The flies and the stench came from the massive pits where the victims were buried after each gassing. *Hauptsturmführer* Wirth, formerly an officer with the Stuttgart criminal police and commandant of this camp, received my interlocutor on his arrival. He and another S.S. officer, his deputy, who accompanied them during his visit, both complained incessantly about the *Kommando* to which they had been assigned. They begged him to use his influence to get them transferred to another unit as soon as he returned to Berlin. Neither one of them could understand how they could be required to do such work, and they were sure that at Berlin nothing was known about what was going on here. "Why do you not ask for a transfer yourselves?" asked my visitor. "Then, after getting it you could expose this disgraceful business . . . . " "This is just what Globocnik is afraid of," he was told. "And another thing, we could not apply for a transfer without going through channels, and that means going through him, and for fear of being exposed, either he would not grant it, or he would have us shot at once on some pretext or other. We know of cases . . . . Fortunately you have come here and you can, at the same time that you get us out of here through your connections in Berlin, stop this shameful business . . . . Fortunately, too, it is only a small train with few cars that arrives from time to time, two or three up to now.[9] Otherwise, with the limited means we have at hand for burying the bodies, we would be living in a regular center of infection, breeding every imaginable disease . . . . Tomorrow a train is scheduled to arrive at about seven in the morning . . . . "

3. My interlocutor told me that, upon being informed of the expected train, he decided to stay. Accompanied by Wirth and his S.S. aide, he again visited the little house that had been fixed up for exterminations, and he described it to me. It had a raised ground floor, and a hallway with three small rooms on each side, which he did not measure, but which he thought had an area of surely less than 5 x 5 meters, perhaps 4 x 5 maximum, and all of them were rectangular, not square. At the end of the hall was the room where the Diesel motor was located in the center on a cement base and a little below floor level. I asked about this motor and how it was connected up to exhaust outlets in each of the six rooms. It was a truck motor, about 1.50 meters long, a little less than 1 meter wide, and a good meter in height, including the concrete base. Its power he did not know; perhaps it had 200 horsepower, he said. I pointed out to him that it was said to have been a marine engine, and, therefore, it must have been much bigger if it had been built for a ship. "Surely not," he said. "It was a truck motor, at least its dimensions led me to visualize it on a truck." He remembered the

number of cylinders, six in one row. As for the connection with the exhaust pipes, in order to proceed faster, he made a drawing for me, which showed that the motor exhaust was introduced into each room by means of a pipe that was connected to an outlet in the floor. "I do not wonder," I said, "that Globocnik wanted to find a more efficient method. It must have been horribly long . . . . " "A quarter of an hour," he interrupted.

If until now this account had seemed plausible to me, after this remark, this "quarter of an hour" weighed heavily on the rest of our conversation. We talked about it at length, and we kept returning to it, with me maintaining that it was absolutely impossible and with him insisting that it was nevertheless true. I had already studied the Gerstein document together with automotive engineers and toxicologists and I knew what I was talking about. In response to my technical objections, he said that he had seen it and that "nevertheless it was true." In vain I tried to explain to him that, with 200 horsepower or even more, a Diesel engine could not produce, in a quarter of an hour, the necessary toxic concentration in 250 to 300 cubic meters of air to cause death. That faced with the impossibility of getting 700 to 800 persons — 40 to 50 at a maximum, my interlocutor corrected — into rooms of 40 to 45 cubic meters, and knowing the limitations of a Diesel engine, the writer of the document had to reduce to almost nothing the quantity of air to be made toxic. I added that the atmosphere in the house in question would not be sufficiently toxic to kill everyone until after 32 minutes and that if the day before Globocnik had said himself that the method was not very efficient, it was just another proof that the operation must have lasted a long time. Finally, I pointed out that after twenty years his memory could not be so exact, etc. Nothing budged him. He would not change his mind about the quarter of an hour, except to say that he had not timed it with his watch and that without doubt his estimate was within a minute or two of being exact. Moreover, his demeanor reflected only good faith. Since then I have, with his sketch in hand, questioned many experts on combustion engines, fluid combustion, and toxicology; no one has been willing to give less than one and a half to two hours . . . .

During the rest of the conversation, nothing else came up that I took exception to, but this objection is an important one and is very disturbing. There was one other thing that was strange about the asphyxiating apparatus. I did not understand why the designer had divided the space into six rooms instead of leaving it in one, which would have been less costly and less complicated; but, I did not press the point.

4. Meanwhile, Gerstein arrived with three or four people; my visitor was no longer quite sure how many. Globocnik, who had come with them, turned right around and went back. During his conversation the day before with Globocnik, my visitor reported that Gerstein had related that his trip from Berlin to Lublin had not been uneventful. What he had with him was not Zyklon B in crystals, as one might think, but liquid prussic acid in bottles, and with the incessant jolting on a road in bad repair, one or two of these bottles had broken in the truck. He and his driver had been very frightened. My visitor then asked him how his trip from Lublin to Belzec had been. "Very good," he replied. "We left the goods at Lublin . . . . "

They inspected the camp together, and in the evening, still together, they were served at dinner by a couple of Jewish prisoners. The atmosphere was heavy; the most talkative one was Gerstein. He seemed keyed up, and everything he said seemed to be aimed at belittling Globocnik. He inspired confidence in no one, at least my interlocutor had that impression. And, when he heard several years later, from one of his friends who had had Gerstein as a student, that the latter was a psychopath, he was not surprised.

The next morning, between 7 and 8 o'clock, the expected transport of Jews arrived; it was a train of four or five cars, with some 250 to 300 men, women, and children, and not with 6,000 or 6,700 persons, piled into 45 cars, as the Gerstein Document claims. Likewise, the 200 Ukrainians that are mentioned in the Document were in reality about two dozen Jewish inmates from the camp. There was no brutality; no doors were wrenched from the cars; no one was struck with rubber truncheons. Rather, there was a brotherly reception from their co-religionists, plainly intent on creating a feeling of confidence in the arrivals.

In preparing the victims for the gassing, they were required to deposit their valuables and jewels at the *Effecktenkammer* in return for a receipt; then they proceeded to the barber. Finally, they were made to undress. The undressing was the longest process and took almost all morning. These unfortunates asked

their coreligionists, who had received them under the armed
guard of a few listless and inattentive S.S., what was to become
of them. They were told that they were to be disinfected and
that, after that, they would be assigned to labor *Kommandos*
according to their abilities. They were told to take a deep
breath during the disinfection process – a hideous spectacle for
those who knew.

Then, they were herded into the building where the gassing
was to take place. Haphazardly they were divided up among the
six rooms – 40 to 50 per room, my visitor repeated. The doors
were closed, and the lights were put out. At this moment, the
only things to be heard were the prayers of these unfortunates,
and the cries of fright from the women and the children. The
engine was started and, a quarter of an hour later, the bodies
were removed by the *Totenkommando*, which was composed of
Jewish prisoners. The corpses were carried to a waiting grave.

"But that grave," I interrupted, "they must have seen it,
since, really, for 250 to 300 people it must have been quite
sizeable." My visitor replied, "No. It had been dug some distance behind the gassing house, and they could not see it. The
bodies were taken out through side doors in each room, directly
to the outside, sort of garage doors. The dimensions of the
grave? I have an idea that it must have been about 20 meters
long, 5 wide, and barely 2 deep . . . ."

And, he explained the dangers of that kind of burial. Wirth
had told him that into that huge grave lots of gasoline had been
poured over the heap of corpses. But, the attempt to cremate
the corpses in that manner had been only partially successful.
Earth was thrown on top of the corpses, but after two or three
days this earth raised up from the pressure of gas rising from below. And, it infected the air. Also, the rotting flesh attracted
the clouds of those flies which one saw everywhere. Deciding
that he now had seen enough, my visitor left the camp without
delay and returned to Lublin.

I tried to return the conversation to a discussion of the
"quarter of an hour" that the gassing was supposed to have
lasted, by expressing the opinion that the length of the breakdown of the diesel engine, which lasted two hours and forty-
nine minutes, according to the Gerstein Document, could actually have been not a breakdown, but the added time that this
engine required to poison the air sufficiently to cause death. I

had no success with this suggestion. My visitor was sure that there had been not the least engine trouble and that the gassing took only a quarter of an hour.

My visitor's business in the region around Lublin took longer than he had anticipated. He was detained in Lodz for a good two weeks, and he could not get back to Berlin until about September 15. Immediately upon his return he went straight to Dr. Grawitz who was a friend of his and a close associate of *Reichsführer-S.S.* Heinrich Himmler. After hearing his tale, Dr. Grawitz jumped up, horrified, and rushed without delay to Himmler.

"I cannot now be specific about the dates," he added, "but about ten days later, Dr. Grawitz came himself to tell me, while at the same time congratulating me for my intervention, that an inquiry was underway about what I had reported, and, a few weeks later — I remember that it was just a few days after All Saints Day — that the camp had been closed and Globocnik once again had been transferred.[10] That is all I know."

I told my visitor about Dr. Konrad Morgen's testimony at Nuremberg on the 7th and 8th of August 1945 (I.M.T., Volume XX, pp. 520-553). He knew about it and gave it no credit. The portrait that Morgen drew of Wirth, making him an unscrupulous criminal, corresponded in no way with what was the actual fact. Morgen had described him as being the commandant of four camps and the *Deus ex-machina* of the whole business (*op. cit.* pp. 528-29), while, in reality, he was the despairing commandant of the Belzec camp only, and, furthermore, he was bullied and terrorized by Globocnik. Then again, Morgen had testified that he had met Wirth, and if he had met Wirth, it could only have been at Belzec. But, he gave the date of this meeting as "the end of 1943" (*op. cit.* p. 527), when the camp had been closed at the latest in December 1942. This Dr. Konrad Morgen was a man who had held the rank of *Obersturmbannführer* in the S.S., who had headed the criminal police office of the *Reich*, with special powers that had been conferred by Himmler himself, and who probably had many things on his conscience, my visitor concluded.

I had no difficulty sharing that view with him. Morgen had said that the had met Hoess, as Commandant of the Auschwitz camp, " . . . towards the end of 1943, beginning of 1944" (*op. . cit..* p. 540), when Hoess had not been in that post after the end of November 1943; Morgen placed all of the exterminations by gas at Monowitz (*op. cit.* p. 540), when all witnesses have subsequently placed them at Birkenau; Morgen claimed that Wirth received his orders directly from Hitler's Chancellery (*op. cit.* p. 531), when, etc. . . .

5. It was at this moment in our conversation that the eyes of my interlocutor fell on *Le Mensonge d'Ulysse* open before him, and to which until then he had not made any reference. "I have read your books," he continued; "In my opinion your critique of the testimonies and documents produced at Nuremberg is impeccable and will one day bear fruit. Thanks are due you. But what interests me (he took the open book in both hands) is the problem of gas exterminations, the only issue that truly touches upon the honor of Germany. So this is what I have come to tell you. Here (he showed me the book) you have given, in 1950, a most correct interpretation, when, in formulating your judgment, you came to the conclusion that there had been very few such exterminations and those few were the work of, I quote, 'only one or two insane persons in the S.S.' I would have said 'one or two criminal sadists.' Believe me, I knew this crowd well. As a whole it was a decent group, but it was not free – like all social groups – of a few sadists who were capable of the most unimaginable crimes. Globocnik was surely one of them. I know Hoess only from what I had heard of him in Berlin from the people in my branch of service who knew him. He did not have a good reputation either. And, it is possible that at Auschwitz he behaved the way Globocnik did around Lublin. I do not know that for certain; I only say that it is possible. And, judging from what you yourself have written about that camp, it would have been easy for him since everything which was needed to make such activity possible was obtainable at Auschwitz."

I agreed, although I had not directed my supposition to any one particular camp – for the very reason that one could give so little credit to that mass of false testimony and false documents on the subject that had been gathered by the various military tribunals. It was one of the hypotheses that I had advanced for the camps in general with the old adage, "where there is smoke, there is fire," in mind. Actually, all of my efforts tended to show that if there had been exterminations by gas they could only have been conducted on a very limited. basis since there was no positive evidence to support the existence of the widespread practice.

"There were exterminations by gas," he concluded. "I have brought you an example." Then he added: "However, they were neither massive nor deliberately ordered by the hierarchy of the Third Reich, in spite of what the evidence that was created out of thin air at Nuremberg, and that was verified by unscrupulous people, seemed to indicate; rather, such activities were the deeds of a few isolated criminals. What is certain is that each time that the authorities of the Third Reich were informed about things of this kind, they put an end to it, and I brought you proof of that. At Nuremberg, the prosecution simply made use of these isolated instances of criminal activity in order to establish the existence of an officially sanctioned practice for the purpose of dishonoring Germany. It is a little like claiming that the French systematically killed all of the German prisoners that they took during the war, basing the claim on the one case at Annecy on August 19, 1944. There are potential criminals among all peoples, and war — which unleashes their instincts — nurtures their depravity to incredible dimensions. Take the example of the French Resistance in whose name and protection those criminals, of which unhappily France has the same kind and as many as Germany or any other country, committed their crimes.[11] Consider the behavior of your troops during their occupation of Germany after May 1945 . . . . "[12]

He paused for a moment and then said, "Let it go at that, Sir. The honor of Germany will only be saved when it is definitely established that the exterminations by gas were the exception, and then only the act of a few criminals who were disowned as soon as they were uncovered. As for the rest, Heavens, it was war, and we are no better than Germany's enemies."[13]

I reassured him by telling him that if I stubbornly questioned every line of every document and deposition upon which was based this monstrous indictment of which Germany was the victim and that if my examination of this evidence caused me to conclude that it was nothing but the crudest of fabrications, it would not allow me to claim that there never had been an extermination by gas. Moreover, I had never claimed that, but only had stated that I had never found any reliable evidence to support that contention. "I am happy that I was fearful over nothing," he said. "Excuse me. Germany's honor owes much to you, and you richly deserve it."

And, that was the end. The discussion lost itself in generalities, but later we returned to the subject of Globocnik. I maintained that if he had only been transferred, which did not seem to me to have actually happened, the punishment had indeed been very light. "That," answered by interlocutor, "is characteristic of totalitarian systems. Those people sent so far from Berlin had been sent with the power given to Roman proconsuls. Moreover, the Nazi state was racist, and it did not consider crimes against the Jews in the same light as it viewed crimes against others; it was more indulgent towards those guilty of the former. The case of Koch, commandant at Buchenwald, who was shot for lesser crimes that had been committed against prisoners considered Aryan, is the proof. But, see what the State of Israel does. If they are gentiles, it demands the death sentence for all the *Kapos* guilty of crimes in the exercise of their duties as guards of gangs of prisoners in the concentration camps, and if they are Jewish, it finds many excuses for them and dismisses the charges or, at the most, imposes jail sentences of a few months, which are then suspended."

I shall spare the reader the details of the other subjects that we touched upon during the balance of our rambling conversation: the Versailles Treaty and its responsibility for the rise of German National Socialism, and, consequently, the outbreak of the Second World War; the war; wars, etc.

If I have made a point of ending this chapter with this testimony, it is because, on the one hand, a historian worthy of the name should not suppress anything that he knows which is relevant to the subject under discussion, and on the other, because I was not seriously able to impeach it except on one point. Moreover, whether right or wrong, the good faith of its author and his sincerity seemed obvious. It is one of the canons of historiography that a testimony cannot be impugned if it seems inconsistent on one point only. After all, history does not, so to speak, offer examples of testimonies that are perfectly consistent. This one, in fact, summed up the opinion which I had formed after a study of all of the documents and the testimony that was produced at Nuremberg on the subject of the extermination of the Jews by gas.

All this, however, does not at all mean that I endorse this testimony. *Testis unus, testis nullus,* that is also one of the laws of history, and I know only too well the ancient truth that nothing resembles perfect good faith more than perfect bad faith. Without going so far as to claim that this aphorism applied to my interlocutor, and I am far from wanting to conceal the pleasure and interest that I took in his conversation, I still must say that in spite of all that argues in his favor, and although his entry on the scene, regrettably late, can be excused by circumstances, his testimony can only be accepted with the most distinct reservations. All that one can say is that it is more acceptable than what we have so far been accustomed to, and in which we have been completely submerged. We shall not know what it is really worth unless those, who so zealously suppress impartial inquiry into the subject in an attempt to throttle the historical truth that they know, renounce the drastic measures that are resorted to to keep it from coming to light, and, instead, assist it to return to an atmosphere of free discussion. Then, all of those persons who know or who think that they know something about any event whatsoever concerning the war can come forward and can publicize it, without fear of being thrown into prison. Incidentally, I can add that if some day I could be sure that my interlocutor could be questioned without running this risk, I am authorized to make known his name. He will not run away, he told me, and this is another good point for him and his testimony, and for everyone it might be the beginning of a return to free discussion. Check! Your turn to play, Mister Inquisitors.

FOOTNOTES

[1] [The fact that the "Diary of Anne Frank" is a fabrication has been established pretty well since 1962 when Professor Rassinier was writing this book. It seems that the American Jewish writer Meyer Levin was hired by Otto Frank, the father of Anne, to write the *Anne Frank Diary*. The existence of this "literary collaboration" came to light when Mr. Levin sued Mr. Frank in the New York State courts for breach of contract. The dispute seems to have been settled out of court with Mr. Levin receiving the sum of $50,000. For a further discussion of this matter, see the following: Richard Harwood, *Did Six Million Really Die?* (Richmond, Surrey: Historical Review Press, n.d.), pp. 19-20; Teressa Hendry, "Was Anne Frank's Diary a Hoax?" *The American Mercury,* Summer, 1967, pp. 26-28.]

2   Exhibit No. 100 of the Jerusalem judgment (Eichmann Trial) mentions
    that for France only 52,000, mostly non-French, had been deported
    by July 21, 1943, and that no deportation after that date was noted.

3   [It is strange, indeed, that the Germans—who were far more advanced
    than the Allies in the development of chemical weapons—should relay
    upon Zyklon B, an insecticide and disinfectant, as their primary killing
    agent in these alleged exterminations by gas when they had much more
    efficient gases, which had been designed specifically as "man-killing"
    agents, to choose from. For example, as early as 1936, I.G. Farben-
    industrie was producing *Tabun,* the first of a family of nerve gases
    which the Germans were to develop by the end of the Second World
    War. (By contrast, the best gas in the Allies' arsenal was an improved
    version of the World War I "mustard gas.") *Tabun*—which was re-
    garded as a "quick kill" agent of tremendous potency—was followed
    by the development of *Sarin* (1938) and *Soman* (1944). Only about
    140 mg/meter^3/minute of *Tabun* is needed to induce severe convulsions
    which are almost immediately followed by collapse, paralysis, and
    death. *Sarin* is twice as deadly as *Tabun* and *Soman* is many times
    more potent than *Sarin.* (See, Steven Rose, ed., *CBW: Chemical &
    Biological Warfare,* Boston: Beacon Press, 1968 pp. 23-24) By the end
    of the war, the Germans had stockpiled nearly twelve tons of *Tabun*
    and more than 250,000 tons of the more conventional chemical war-
    fare agents like phosgene gas. (See, Seymour M. Hersch, *Chemical and
    Biological Warfare: America's Hidden Arsenal,* Indianapolis: Bobbs-
    Merrill, 1968, pp. 7-12)]

4   Not taking into account the fantastic figures of Mme. Hannah Arendt,
    who does not seem to be very certain of herself in this area. Does she
    not in fact say (*New Yorker,* February 2, 1963) that "in less than two
    months 147 trains transported 434,351 Hungarian Jews to Auschwitz,"
    and, (*New Yorker,* February 16, 1963) that among the Hungarian
    Jews there were 476,000 victims; *"Que souvent femme varie,"* as the
    French song says, *"Comme la plume au vent,"* from one page to an-
    other with this one!

5   ["The most typical use of the Zyklon was in disinfecting rooms and
    barracks. Everything was sealed and then the necessary amount of
    Zyklon which came in green cans . . . was emptied in. After the proper
    time interval it was assumed that all the lice and other insects and
    pests were dead and then the enclosure was aired out. The Zyklon
    could be used for disinfecting clothing by employing an 'extermination
    chamber' . . ." Arthur R. Butz, *The Hoax of the Twentieth Century*
    (Richmond, Surrey: Historical Review Press, [1976]), p. 105. How-
    ever, Zyklon B also was lethal to human beings in as much as its crystals,

"when exposed to air, sublimated into "Prussic Acid' (hydrogen cyanide gas)." (*op. cit.* p. 104.)]

6 To reach that total I took the general total of Jewish losses given by Mr. Raul Hilberg (p. 767) for the five camps and for Auschwitz, that is 1,950,000, and I deducted his estimate of Jewish losses at Auschwitz (p. 670), that is 1,000,000, which leaves 950,000. So as not to overlook anything, we must state that in his own table (p. 570) Maïdanek is listed under "Lublin district."

7 Except the Institute of Jewish Affairs of the World Jewish Congress, in *Eichmann's Confederates and the Third Reich Hierarchy,* which gives 900,000 (p. 18).

8 We have seen that Dr. Aryeh L. Kubovy, Director of the *Center of Contemporary Jewish Documentation* at Tel-Aviv, admitted in 1960 that "there exists no document signed by Hitler, Himmler, or Heydrich speaking of exterminating of the Jews and . . . the word 'extermination' does not appear in the letter from Goering to Heydrich concerning the final solution to the Jewish question." In regard to this issue, Mme. Hannah Arendt, who makes the Führer's order to exterminate the Jews the central theme of her report on the Eichmann Trial at Jerusalem, labors in vain. This divergence of opinion is a problem which needs to be worked out between herself and Dr. Kubovy, and we can only advise her to come to an understanding with him, who for once—by chance, mischance, or good faith—is himself in agreement with the historical truth.

9 This incident took place on August 18, 1942. The construction of this camp—which had been authorized at the Wannsee conference—had been begun at the end of March of that year, and it had taken a very long time to build, mainly because of the fact that a single track rail line had to be constructed as a branch line in order to connect the camp to the nearest existing mainline tracks. That mainline track had to be either the one that went from Budapest to Warsaw, via Przmysl and Lublin, or the one from Budapest to Wilna, via Lvov. My interlocutor could not tell me whether the branch line had been attached near Przmysl or Lvov. In either case, it would have required the building of at least 50 km. of track, and this track was not ready for use until the end of July.

10 According to Jewish sources, which are unanimous in agreement, this camp was not closed until the beginning of December 1942. It does not appear that Globocnik was demoted or punished. In any case, if he was, the punishment was light, especially when that punishment is compared with the punishment that was given to Karl Koch, the celebrated commandant of Buchenwald, who was executed for doing much less.

[11] [For a good account of that bloody period which followed the so-called "Liberation of France," see *France: The Tragic Years 1939–1947* (New York: Devin-Adair, 1955) by Sisley Huddleston, especially Chapter Twenty-three. Contrary to the impression that has been created by the scores of Hollywood war movies which have dealt with the period, French "resistance" to the German occupation of France during World War II was not a "mass movement" by any means. Rather, the number of Frenchmen who collaborated with the Germans — to one extent or another — far exceeded the number of "resistants" who, it seems (based upon the number of membership cards that were issued by the French government after the war to veterans of the resistance) totaled somewhat more than 250,000. In any case, the combined number of "resistants" and collaborators was small when compared to the vast majority of the French population which remained apathetic and outwardly indifferent to the German occupation. After all, it made little practical difference to the average "man on the street" whether it was the Germans or his own countrymen who were actually guiding governmental policy once the French civil service had resumed operation and once life had returned to its normal pace following the signing of the Armistice with Germany on June 22, 1940. This uncomfortable reality was the subject of the four and one-half hour television film "*Le Chagrin et la Pitie*" which was produced by Marcel Ophuls in 1969 and which, incidentally, was not aired over the state-controlled French television network until after the death of Charles de Gaulle. A portion of the filmscript has been published in an English translation under the title *The Sorrow and the Pity* (New York: Outerbridge and Lazard, 1972).

The French make a distinction when they speak of "resistants": there are those few persons — like Paul Rassinier — who engaged in organized resistance against the Germans almost immediately following the defeat of the French army in the spring of 1940; and, then, there are those numerous individuals who joined the "resistance" after the German fortunes of war began to wane — i.e., generally after June, 1944. Many of these so-called "late" resistants joined the "underground" in an eleventh hour attempt to redeem themselves for their earlier collaboration with the Germans. Many others were Communists. In fact, the cadres of the resistance movement at that late date were almost exclusively made-up of Communists who were financed by the Americans, who were armed by the British, and who followed the Stalinist line.

It was the Communists who were primarily responsible for escalating the ineffectual guerilla war against the Germans and who, indirectly, caused so much suffering among the innocent French populace in the form of German reprisals. The Communists, moreover, did not confine themselves to the assassination of Germans. They took advantage of the general disorder following the "Liberation" to murder as many of their domestic political opponents — whom they prudently had branded as "fascists" and "collaborators" — as they could get their hands on. The precise number of victims has never been determined. However, a former French minister of the interior has estimated that about

105,000 "summary executions" occurred between August 1944 and March 1945. (Huddleston, *op. cit.*, pages 299-300.) Others have placed the number at about 50,000. (See, e.g., Donald B. Robinson, "Blood Bath in France," *The American Mercury,* April 1946.) Regardless of what the true figure may be, there can be little doubt that, as Huddleston put it, "there has never been, in the history of France, a bloodier period than that which followed the Liberation of 1944-1945. The massacres of 1944 were no less savage than the massacres of the Jacquerie, of St. Bartholomew, of the Revolutionary Terror, of the Commune; and they were certainly more numerous and on a wider scale." (Huddleston, *op. cit.*, page 296.)]

12 [The behavior of the Allies during their occupation of Germany was so generally atrocious that it has been a subject that most liberal apologists for the American participation in World War II would like to forget, especially when moralizing about the crimes and the shortcomings of the Germans. For a more objective view of the military occupation of Germany, the following titles offer an adequate, but by no means an exhaustive, treatment of the subject: Andy Rooney & Bud Hutton, *Conqueror's Peace* (Garden City: Doubleday & Co., 1947); Victor Gollancz, *Our Threatened Values* (Chicago: Henry Regenry, 1946) and *In Darkest Germany* (Chicago: Henry Regenry, 1947); Marshall Knappen, *And Call It Peace* (Chicago: University of Chicago Press, 1949); Freda Utley, *The High Cost of Vengeance* (Chicago: Henry Regnery, 1949); W.K. Turnwald, ed., *Documents on the Expulsion of the Sudeten Germans* (Munich: University Press, 1953); Ernst von Salomon, *Fragebogen* (Garden City: Doubleday & Co., 1955); Juergen Thorwald, *Flight in Winter* (New York: Pantheon Books, 1953); Nicholas Balabkins, *Germany Under Direct Controls* (New Brunswick, N.J.: Rutgers University Press, 1961); Harold Zink, *American Military Government in Germany* (New York: Macmillan, 1947).]

13 [For the reader who desires to obtain a better understanding of the "atrocities" that were committed by the Allies during World War Two, the following titles provide a good introduction to the subject: Hans Grimm, *Answer of a German: An Open Letter to the Archbishop of Canterbury* (London: Euphenon Books, 1952); F.J.P. Veale, *Advance to Barbarism* (Appleton, Wis.: C.C. Nelson, 1953) and *War Crimes Discreetly Veiled* (New York: Devin-Adair, 1959); Hans Rumpf, *The Bombing of Germany* (New York: Holt, Rinehart & Winston, 1963); Louis Fitzgibbon, *Katyn, A Crime Without Parallel* (New York: Scribners & Sons, 1971); Julius Epstein, *Operation Keelhaul* (Old Greenwich, Conn.: Devin-Adair, 1973); Peter H. Nicoll, *Britain's Blunder* (East Orange, N.J.: Communications Archives, 1973), especially pages 117-125.]

Chapter Fourteen

Statistics: Six Million or ...

After some fifteen years of historical research, I have come to the following conclusion: it was in 1943 that National Socialist Germany was accused for the first time of the systematic mass extermination of the Jews in the gas chambers. The author of this first, horrible and infamous accusation was a Polish Jew, a refugee in England and a jurist by profession, by the name of Rafael Lemkin. And, he made that accusation in a book published in London, and in English, in that year, entitled *Axis Rule in Occupied Europe* (Am.ed., New York: Columbia Univ. Press, 1944). At the time the book did not receive much attention; in October, 1943, when I was arrested by the *Gestapo*, it was still completely unknown in the best informed circles of the French Resistance, and I only heard of gas chambers for the first time at Dora, toward the middle of 1944. But in 1945-1946, *Axis Rule in Occupied Europe* was the topic of all conversation behind the scenes at the Trial of the Major War Criminals at Nuremberg, where it was cited by the prosecution in the case of Seyss-Inquart (T. XIX, pp. 70 and 92). And, the view maintained in the book was supported by the *Kasztner Report* on the tragedy of the Hungarian Jews, a report which was also talked about in the corridors during the trial. But, we must be precise and say that it was only after January 30, 1946, the date when French Prosecutor DuBost made public his discovery of the Gerstein document, that these two pieces of writing took on importance. In fact, it was on that day that, in the world press, the gas chambers mythology began its dance to every tune and diabolical rhythm; that unrestrained saraband full of missteps has not stopped since.

Let us try to reconstruct the facts. Until January 30, 1946, aside from the *Axis Rule in Occupied Europe* and the *Kasztner Report*, which were only secondhand testimonies, the prosecution and the judges at Nuremberg had only direct testimonies which, juridically, were not much more authentic, given the way in which they were adduced by their authors. All of these witnesses had been interned at Auschwitz, and, as for gas chambers, either they knew nothing about them, or they only knew about them through their prison comrades who were "trustworthy" and who they generally did not name, or who were already dead, if they did name them. Second hand testimony again. An example of this kind of testimony is provided by Dr. Benedikt Kautski who did not appear at court, but, as we have seen, who wrote a book and had his short hour of fame. Another is that of Madame Vaillant-Couturier who arrived at the Auschwitz camp in January 1943, who was a communist, who, for that reason, was hidden away in the hospital where she was an important personage in the *Häftlingsführung*, and who, in answer to the question as to whether the hospital had been open to Jews when they were sick, coldly replied to French Prosecutor DuBost, "No, when we got there the Jews did not have the right to go there; they were taken directly to the gas chamber if they were sick." (T. VI, p. 219.) Now, never was a false witness brought before the bar of a Tribunal with such calm assurance, since in January 1943 there existed—if indeed, there ever existed—no gas chamber at Auschwitz, the official word being that they were not installed until the end of February 1943. There is no end to the number of false witnesses of this kind that could be cited. But, for the first time, with the Gerstein document, the prosecution had a first-hand witness. But wasn't Gerstein dead? Yes, but he had written, or, at least, he had signed, a statement—at least that is what was claimed. Was not this statement about Auschwitz? No, not in so far as it concerned what he had seen; but invoices for Zyklon B that was delivered to that camp were appended. His description of extermination by gas in other camps portrayed the operation in such a degree of horror that the journalists assigned to the trial decided that their emphasis of that theme would be sure to sell newspapers at home. The judges themselves accorded much less importance to the Gerstein allegations, but they allowed the journalists a free hand; even though they did not actually encourage them, they never gave them their true impressions of the Gerstein document, which was presented to public opinion as though it had been admitted into evidence when actually it had been rejected (as was discussed in the preceding chapter).

Dr. Benedikt Kautski's book did not come out until the end of 1946. Therefore, it did not play a part in the trial of the Major War Criminals. As a secondhand testimony on gas chambers it would not have been any great help. To have a description of the gas exterminations at Auschwitz as precise as that of the Gerstein document on Belzec, the prosecution had to wait until 1951 and *Médecin à Auschwitz* by Miklos Nyiszli, about whom we have also learned what to think in the preceding chapters. Since then, nothing. No other *de visu* witnesses. The literature of the concentration camps—the historians like Hans Rothfels, Golo Mann, or Raul Hilberg, the *War Crimes Commission* of Warsaw, and the *Centers of Contemporary Jewish Documentation*, their propagandists like Leon Poliakov or Hannah Arendt, the *Institut für Zeitgeschichte* at Munich, or showmen and film directors like Piscator (producer of *Der Stellvertreter* by Hochhuth)—has never been able to bring forth, as far as I know, any more than those two testimonies, both of which I believe I have proved were obviously apocryphal. I shall not belabor the point.

Not having been able to establish the existence of gas extermination any better than that, those championing the genocide indictment did not have much better luck when they wanted to number the losses in human lives. In 1945-1946, during the trial of the Major War Criminals, they found themselves in the following situation: Mr. Rafael Lemkin said simply, "millions;" Dr. Rudolf Kasztner spoke only of Hungarian Jews whose number he estimated to be about 800,000 (page 1 of his *Report*), and he calculated (page 8) that "500,000 had been deported on the

Karchau-Odenberg route between May 15, 1944, and the beginning of July," that is, the 7th, as he makes clear a little
farther on; the figures given in the Gerstein document led to
results so astronomical that they were useless (it is, perhaps, not
useless to recall that all the rest of the material in the document
was, at the time, used only by the press because the President of
the Tribunal refused even to have it read by the French Prosecutor DuBost); Hoettl and Wisliceny, who, under the circumstances we already know about, spoke in terms of six and
five million respectively, estimates that both said came from
Eichmann. Finally, Mr. Justice Jackson, as we have seen, added
to this confusing state of affairs when he stated in his speech of
November 21, 1945, that:

> Of the 9,600,000 Jews who were living in Nazi dominated
> Europe, it is estimated, with full knowledge of the facts, that
> sixty per cent perished; 5,700,000 Jews are missing from
> countries where they lived before, and more than 4,000,000
> cannot be accounted for, either by a natural death rate, or
> immigration into other lands. (I.M.T. II, p. 128).

The figure of 4,500,000 exterminated was the claim of the
prosecution, and it was just the beginning. But, it is not easy
to see how, between May 8, 1945, and the 21st of November,
Mr. Justice Jackson was able to obtain full knowledge of the
facts. Since no official census took place during that period of
time—in any case, how could it have taken place in such a
chaos of populations displaced and moving about in every
direction?—it is plainly only a purely conjectural estimate.
Be that as it may, it was not sustained in the judgment against
the Major War Criminals, and the press sustained Hoettl's estimate. Since then, except for Mr. Gerald Reitlinger, who alone
came to a conclusion more or less in accord with Mr. Justice
Jackson—i.e., of 4,200,000 to 4,600,000 exterminated, everything has happened as if, once having laid down the principle
that Hoettl's estimate was well founded, all of the other statisticians who have worked on the figures in the same spirit
as the *Warsaw Commission,* the Centers of Contemporary Jewish
Documentation, or the *Institute für Zeitgeschichte* of Munich
had never had any other purpose except to prove that the
estimates of Hoettl and Wisliceny corresponded with reality.
What is noticeable from the very first is that while they have all
come to an overall result in the neighborhood of six million,

they do not come to it by the same routes, since the allocation
in detail by countries of these six million presents considerable
disparities. The clearest example of these differences, it seems
to me, is Poland, where Mr. Shalom Baron, holder of the chair
of Jewish History at Columbia University, found that on the
arrival of Russian troops in the country 700,000 Jews were still
there (according to his statement of April 24, 1961, at the
Eichmann Trial); the *World Center of Jewish Documentation* at
Paris gave the figure of 500,000 (communiqué to the *Figaro
littéraire* of June 4, 1960); the *Institute of Jewish Affairs* claimed some 400,000 (*Eichmann's Confederates and the Third
Reich Hierarchy*, p. 59); and Mr. Raul Hilberg found only
50,000 (*The Destruction of the European Jews*, p. 670). The
distribution by camp, or sector of destruction, is not the same
either, and offers disparities just as glaring, depending upon
which one of these statisticians is referred to. For example:
about 4,000,000 Jews met their fate at Auschwitz, the rest
in other extermination camps, or in the open at the hands of
the *Einsatzgruppen*, we are told by Leon Poliakov, Olga
Wurmser, and Henri Michel, among others. This distribution
manifestly takes into account the Warsaw judgment that condemned Hoess to be hanged on the charge of having caused the
death at Auschwitz of 2,812,000 persons, 2,500,000 of them
Jews, from May 1940 to December 1943; therefore, it is argued
that this figure is not so far from the four million figure that is
claimed for the whole term of the camp; to round things out,
1,950,000 is claimed for all the other camps, another million
at Auschwitz (900,000 as corrected by the *Institute of Jewish
Affairs*), 1,400,000 by the *Einsatzgruppen*, and the remainder
in "Mobile operations" as Mr. Raul Hilberg tells us. We must
also point out that the latter does not seem to be very sure of
the figures himself since he comes to a total of 5,100,000 on
page 767 of *The Destruction of the European Jews*, while he
gets 5,407,500 on page 670. For all extermination camps other
than Auschwitz Mr. Raul Hilberg gives us 950,000, but the
Warsaw Commission and the Judgment of the Jerusalem Tribunal found "850,000 for only four out of five of them"
(Chelmno, Belzec, Sobibor and Treblinka, *cp.* chap. XXIII,
p. 80).

All this shows how serious they are and how much to credit
their documentary sources, which, although the same for all the

statisticians, speak to each of them in so different a language that the only point of agreement is the total number of Jewish losses between 5 and 6 million human lives, when they all make their additions—except for the more modest Reitlinger and for Poliakov who says "between 5 and 7 million" *(Le Troisième Reich et les Juifs).* However, with regard to Reitlinger and Poliakov, they settle on 6 million, which is the mathematical mean.

The reader will readily understand that, faced with this jumble of contradictory calculations, rather than to take up each of the references one by one and to go over each of the additions, I have preferred, by using statistics all from Jewish sources, to try to reconstitute in detail, country by country, the world Jewish population of 1946, and compare it with what it was when National Socialism came to power in Germany in 1933. Rightly or wrongly, this procedure seems to me to be the best method, as we go along, to show up the shameless falsifications of the *Warsaw Commission,* the *World Center of Contemporary Jewish Documentation,* the *Institut für Zeitgeschichte* of Munich, and all of their supporters, authors, propagandists, journalists, historians, and others. I imagine that the reader will also readily understand that the statistics which follow cannot be considered correct down to a unit. In the matter of population statistics it is never possible to arrive at more than approximate conclusions, since the figures are based purely on interrogations of interested persons whose answers, when they can be gotten, are always unreliable, or they are not to be had at all because of the faultiness, or even the lack, of a civil service in a very great number of countries.

In the matter of the Jewish population, the vague sort of aversion which all Jews, since the days of Herod, have shown toward census taking is another source of errors. It is these two constant reservations which make approximations of all statistics. Nevertheless, as all statisticians concede, the errors will be so slight as to be negligible in the conclusions drawn from a comparison of two or more sets of figures, if they are of the same origin. With that granted, where do we stand in this month of July 1963?

II. Post-war Statistics

In 1951 the *World Almanac* published statistics from which
it was concluded that there were then only 11,303,350 Jews in
the world as against 16,643,120 in 1939. This conclusion was
given as the result of research on the part of the *American Jewish
Committee Year Book* and the Jewish Statistic Bureau of the
Synagogue Council which had spent the years 1949 and 1950
at it.

Presented as they were, there are many reasons for thinking
that the *World Almanac* statistics of 1951 were primarily an
answer to a study which appeared on February 22, 1948, in the
New York Times on the statistical data given by Hanson W.
Baldwin, the *Times* expert on Jewish population matters. He
claimed that in 1947, based on a secret census undertaken by
the Jews themselves, there were living in the world between a
minimum of 15,000,000 and a maximum of 18,000,000 Jews.
He also claimed that between 650,000 and 750,000 of these
Jews were living in Palestine and that 500,000 were living in the
other countries of the Middle East. In October 1959, the *American Mercury* (pp. 14 to 17) reviewed all of these figures and
brought the controversy up to date. In reply to the *American
Mercury,* the 1960 edition of the *World Almanac* gave, for the
year 1959, a world Jewish population of 12,299,780. Then,
another bit of information from a Jewish source, which was
widely circulated by the world press, appeared in 1963. The
Hamburg daily, *Die Welt,* of April 1, 1963, for example, reported that:

> There are only about 13 million Jews still in the world. In
> 1939 there were 16,673,000. This information was given
> out over the weekend by the London Institute of Jewish
> Affairs. Most of the Jews, about 5,500,000, are today living
> in the U.S.A. In Israel there are 2,045,000 in the Soviet
> Union 2,300,000, and in Great Britain 450,000 Jews. [1]

But, in the *Israel Almanach* (5719 in the Jewish calendar;
1958-1959 in the common calendar, p. 282) a Mr. Eric Peretz
tells us that "the Jewish population of the state of Israel represents one eighth of the world Jewish population," and he
fixed it at "one million eight hundred thousand." Meanwhile,
a Mr. Marc Cohen puts that eighth at "two million." So, in that
year, the thirteen million Jews of whom a world census was
taken again in 1962 by the Institute of Jewish Affairs of London

was either 14,00,000, if one prefers the first estimate, or 16 million, if one chooses the second. Incidentally, the *Israel Almanach* is published in Jerusalem by the "Youth and Hehabouts Department" of the world Zionist movement.

Only out of concern for accuracy and completeness do I give the puerile statement which Mr. Shalom Baron, waving his title of Professor of Jewish History at Columbia University, made before the bar of the Jerusalem Tribunal on April 24, 1961; it is herewith summarized from a report that appeared in the *Figaro* of the next day:

1. "Since 1945 the world Jewish population has increased at the rate of 20%."
2. "In 1939, there were about 16 million of us in the world. We should, therefore, be about 19,000,000 today, and we are only 12 million."

He makes up for his lack of historical knowledge with a very good knowledge of mathematics: 16 million minus 6 million equals 10 million, which, in turn, plus twenty per cent equals 12 million. His conclusion is mathematically indisputable! Now, it only remains for the Professor to establish, first, that the rate of increase of the world Jewish population was indeed 20% in 16 years and, second, that 6 million Jews were indeed exterminated. Well, let us proceed . . .

Let us proceed with the consideration of one particular element of world Jewry: the Jewish population in the United States. In 1959, the *American Jewish Committee Year Book* and the Jewish Statistical Bureau of the Synagogue Council estimated the American Jewish population at 5,185,000 for the year of 1949, and in 1959, at 5,260,000 for the year of 1958. From which we can conclude that if the world Jewish population increased by twenty per cent from 1945 to 1961, or 1.25% per year, as Mr. Shalom Baron proclaimed at the Jerusalem Tribunal, America, at least, was an exception to the rule where the population was decreasing. And, for Russia, the information from the Institute of Jewish Affairs, which puts the population at 2,300,000 in 1962, hardly seems any more serious, if Mr. Nahum Goldmann is to be believed, who, in a report to the World Jewish Congress on September 12, 1963, said: "From 1948 to 1963 Jews in the USSR increased to about *three million,* according to five writers since dead, and one almanac and two periodicals." *(Le Figaro,* Paris, September 13, 1963). In 1961 Mr. Nahum Goldmann had already produced these figures before the World Jewish Congress. Just the same, there is a difference of 700,000 between 2,300,000 and 3 million . . .

During the whole of 1959, the Jewish population of the United States was the object, in the United States itself, of very strained discussion, after the publication in 1951 of *The Iron Curtain Over America,* (Dallas: Wilkinson, 1951) in which the author, Mr. John Beaty, complained that the 1924 immigration law was constantly broken and that "since the end of the Second World War the problem of illegal entry has increased tremendously." (p. 45). And, he cited the Jewish immigration from eastern Europe as an example of such illegal immigration. (pp. 36-43). Here again it is the *American Mercury* which gave emphasis to the discussion. It underlined two things in particular concerning the Jewish immigration:

1. "The principal world Zionist organizations proudly proclaim that two-thirds of the Jews of the world are now living in the United States." And it concluded that if the figures which Hanson W. Baldwin published in the *New York Times* of February 22, 1948, correspond to reality, it was not of 5,185,000 or 5,260,000 that one should speak, as the statistics from Jewish sources claimed, but of 10,766,666 or 12,800,000 (in 1947!). In any case, Jewish statistics for 1959 claimed that the *world* Jewish population had risen that year to 12,299,780 persons. If it is true that two-thirds of them were living in the United States, that makes, after all, 8,200,000, or, according to the information of *Die Welt* (also from a Jewish source) 8,667,000 for the year 1962, and not 5,500,000 as that information claims.

2. The other aspect of the problem was that during the year 1959 the Census Bureau of the United States government decided to conduct a census in 1960 to determine the extent of illegal immigration into the United States. All of the world Zionist organizations immediately protested—and successfully, the *American Mercury* pointed out—when the Census Bureau turned to the churches and to the synagogues with the object of finding out the number of persons who claimed membership within their congregations. The Zionist leaders stated, still according to the *American Mercury,* that it was "a violation of

the principle of the separation of Church and State"—as set forth in the Constitution of the United States—for such a census to be taken and even that the proposed action of the census officials ". . . would draw down the wrath of God." The true reasons for this opposition can be seen easily; such a census, conducted in that manner, would have brought to light the vast extent of the Jewish immigration into the United States since 1933 and would have forever destroyed the myth of the six million Jewish victims of Nazi "genocide." That none of them at once calculated the Jewish population of the United States at 12 million is not astonishing, particularly if they had read the *New York Times* article!

Since then, the figure of 12 million has become accepted, more or less, by American public opinion makers, as shown by this excerpt from the *National Observer* of July 2, 1962:

> The nation's major religious groups, representing more than 40 Protestant, Eastern Orthodox, Roman Catholic, and Jewish denominations have joined forces to tackle one of the country's thorniest domestic problems: race relations.
>
> They have called the first National Conference on Religion and Race to be held next January in Chicago. About 600 clerical and lay leaders, representing nearly 100,000,000 Americans, are expected to participate. One stated objective of the conference is to demonstrate the concern of religious leaders over racial segregation by a "statement of conscience."
>
> Participating will be the National Council of Churches, an organization of 33 Protestant and Eastern Orthodox denominations with nearly 40,000,000 members; the National Catholic Welfare Conference, the administrative agency of Catholic Bishops (there are 43,000,000 Catholics in the nation); and the Synagogue Council of America, which is representative of Jewish bodies at the national level. (Rabbinic bodies of Orthodox, Conservative, and Reform Judaism are represented. There are about 12,000,000 Jews in the United States.)

Such are the points of view that confront each other concerning the Jewish population of the United States. We shall see farther on that for Poland, Russia, and, in a general way, for all of Central and Balkan Europe, statistics of Jewish origin pose in no less a brutal fashion the problem of their obvious falsification.

III. Pre-war Statistics

In 1932, a Jewish journal that was published in New York, the *Menorah Journal,* (No. 2, February) printed an analysis of the world Jewish population, the facts for which had been taken from the most noted Jewish statistician of the times, Mr. Arthur Ruppin.[2] The latter, said the *Menorah Journal,* had classified the Jews of the whole world, by occupation and by country. By occupation, it gave the conclusions just as they had been formulated by the statistician. By countries, it gave, in diminishing order, only those where there were more than 100,000 Jews, being content, for the others, to classify them in three categories, between 50,000 and 100,000, between 10,000 and 50,000, and less than 10,000. The following is how the figures appeared:

A. By occupations

Commerce	6,100,000	or 38.6%
Crafts and industries	5,730,000	or 36.4%
Rentiers	2,000,000	or 2.7%
Professions	1,000,000	or 6.3%
Agriculture	625,000	or 4%
In service, laborers	325,000	or 2%
Totals	15,780,000	100%

B. By countries

United States	4,500,000
Poland	3,100,000
Russia	3,000,000
Rumania	900,000
Germany	500,000
England	330,000
France	250,000
Palestine	250,000
Argentina	240,000
Austria	230,000
Canada	170,000
Lithuania	160,000
Low countries	120,000
French Morocco	120,000

Iraq 100,000
Other. 1,810,000
                                                    _____

                    Total   15,780,000

The other countries showed up this way:

1. Countries with between 50,000 and 100,000 Jews: Latvia, Greece, Yugoslavia, Belgium, Italy, Turkey, Bulgaria, Algeria, South Africa, Tunisia, Egypt.
2. Countries with between 10,000 and 50,000 Jews: Switzerland, Brazil, Mexico, Uruguay, Persia, Syria, Yemen, India, Afghanistan, China, Spanish Morocco, Tripoli, Australia.
3. Countries with fewer than 10,000 Jews: Danzig, Sweden, Denmark, Esthonia, Ireland, Spain, Rhodes, Memel, Portugal, Norway, Finland, Cuba, Chile, Japan, Singapore, New Zealand.

All of the preceding figures are dated from 1926 to 1928 and represent 0.8% of the population of the world, then calculated at two billion inhabitants.

In 1932, population movements only interested me professionally, that is, in their major lines of force, and, as far as the Jewish population was concerned, at that time these statistics seemed to me to give a good enough picture so that I felt informed on the matter. I remember having noted that from 1877 to 1932 the Jewish population of the United States had risen from 230,000 to 4,500,000, while that of France had increased from 150,000 to 250,000 between 1850 and the same date, and I concluded that the migration of European Jews was in the direction of the United States via Western Europe. From the lands of pogroms to the land of liberty. For me that was the main point. So, in 1934, when Arthur Ruppin's *Les Juifs dans le Monde moderne* came out in France, I did not read it. But, that was a mistake. Had I read Ruppin's original work, I would surely have noticed that the *Menorah Journal* had, for instance, failed to mention Hungary and Czechoslavakia. I was wrong again in not foreseeing that later on I would need figures more exact than those that that publication gave for Belgium, Yugoslavia, Greece, and the like. After the war, when I needed all that information, I was not able to put my hands on a copy of Arthur Ruppin's work, which had so mysteriously disappeared from circulation, except after exercising the wiles of a Sioux Indian. In 1960, when I published *Ulysse trahi par les siens,* I had not yet succeeded, and for Hungary and Czechoslovakia I had to be satisfied with working out, as a note to the figures quoted, the figures of the *World Center of Contemporary Jewish Documentation,* leaving it up to the reader to add them to the total which I found for the population of European Jews in countries occupied by Germany, and which came to 8,700,000, but at the same time cautioning the reader that the figures were clearly exaggerated by some 404,000 for Hungary and some 315,000 for Czechoslovakia.

Here now are Mr. Arthur Ruppin's statistics for those countries of Europe occupied by the Germans during World War Two:

Poland	3,100,000
Russia	3,000,000
Rumania	900,000
Germany	500,000
Hungary	320,000
Czechoslovakia	260,000
France	250,000
Austria	230,000
Lithuania	160,000
Low countries	120,000
Latvia	80,000
Greece	75,000
Yugoslavia	70,000
Belgium	60,000
Italy	50,000
Bulgaria	50,000
Denmark	7,000
Esthonia	5,000
Norway	2,000
Finland	2,000
Luxemburg	2,000
Total	9,243,000

From 1932 to 1939, philo-Semites or anti-Semites, everyone who talked about the European or the world Jewish pop-

ulation referred to Arthur Ruppin. In Europe, the first drew
attention to the fact that about 9 million European Jews were
menaced by National Socialism; the second made use of his
classification by occupations to conclude that according to the
Jews themselves, few among them really worked, and, in Germany, that was one of the grounds of National Socialism for
the accusation of Jewish social parasitism.

I should say that in his study Arthur Ruppin warned that
because of the difficulties inherent in all population studies, in
particular that of Jewish populations, the figures he gave did
not have an indisputable and absolute value. With that consideration in mind, I shall concede that the 9,243,000 Jews
in Europe occupied by the Germans could just as well be 9
million. In addition, I shall concede that in figuring 9.6 million,
Mr. Justice Jackson had not exaggerated so badly; at least, his
overestimation was very much less than the post-war statisticians of the *World Almanac* (*cp.* on p. 103, the estimate of
the Jewish population in 1938, as published in the 1948 edition). In fact, one can hardly say that he exaggerated at all. He
had not left anyone out, that's all. His great mistake was in not
having thought that in 1939 the Jewish population of those
countries was not the same as in 1931; in other words, he erred
by not taking into account Jewish emigration during the period
when they were directly threatened by National Socialism. He
should be censured, therefore, for having stated positively,
without any proof—not having and not being able to have "full
knowledge of the facts," as he boldly claimed—that sixty per
cent of that population, certainly overestimated by him, were
absent from the roll call at the time he pronounced his indictment.

Finally, in parallel columns, on page 302, are the estimates of
Jewish losses published by the *World Center of Contemporary
Jewish Documentation* at Paris (*Figaro Littéraire,* June 4, 1960)
and by Mr. Raul Hilberg in 1961 (*The Destruction of the
European Jews,* p. 670).

My first idea had been to put into parallel columns three
sets of statistics, the third being those published also in 1961
by the Institute of Jewish Affairs in *Eichmann's Confederates
and the Third Reich Hierarchy.* But that compilation was limited to a list of Jewish losses by country without further reference to their numbers in 1939 other than by percentages.

Country	World Center, Jewish Documentation[3]			Raul Hilberg[4]		
	1939	1946	Losses	1939	1946	Losses
France	300,000	180,000	120,000	270,000	200,000	70,000
Belgium	90,000	50,000	40,000	90,000	40,000	50,000
Holland	150,000	60,000	90,000	140,000	20,000	120,000
Denmark	7,000	6,500	500	6,500	5,500	1,000
Norway	1,500	600	900	2,000	1,000	1,000
Esthonia	5,000	1,000	4,000	4,500	---	4,500
Latvia	95,000	10,000	85,000	95,000	---	95,000
Lithuania	150,000	15,000	135,000	145,000	---	145,000
Poland	3,300,000	500,000	2,800,000	3,350,000	50,000	3,300,000
Germany	210,000	40,000	170,000	240,000	80,000	160,000
Czechoslovakia	315,000	55,000	260,000	315,000	44,000	271,000
Austria	60,000	20,000	40,000	60,000	7,000	53,000
Hungary	404,000	204,000	200,000	400,000	200,000	200,000
Yugoslavia	75,000	20,000	55,000	75,000	12,000	63,000
Rumania	850,000	425,000	425,000	800,000	430,000	370,000
Italy	57,000	42,000	15,000	50,000	33,000	17,000
USSR	2,100,000	600,000	1,500,000	3,020,000	2,600,000	420,000
Bulgaria	50,000	43,000	7,000	50,000	47,000	3,000
Greece	75,000	15,000	60,000	74,000	12,000	62,000
Luxemburg	3,000	1,000	2,000	3,000	1,000	2,000
TOTALS	8,297,500	2,288,100	6,009,400	9,190,000	3,782,500	5,407,500

By stretching Mr. Raul Hilberg's figures for Poland, Czechoslovakia and Russia a little, the *Institute of Jewish Affairs* gives a total of 5,717,000 exterminated, representing, it points out, 68 percent of the Jewish population of those countries in 1939. From which one can conclude that the pre-war Jewish population of those countries came to 8,400,000. The discrepancy is significant only with regard to Poland, for which the Institute gives 400,000 survivors, where Mr. Raul Hilberg came up with only 50,000; Mr. Shalom Baron got 700,000; and the *World Center of Contemporary Jewish Documentation* of Paris, found 500,000. Where it found two million survivors in Russia, Mr. Raul Hilberg found 2,600,000. 360,000 Jews are claimed by the Institute to have been living in Czechoslovakia in 1939, while Mr. Raul Hilberg is content with 315,000, and Mr. Arthur Ruppin with 260,000. In addition, there are a few other misuses. Upon reflection, the dose of phantasy which is provided by the statistics which are set forth on page 302 struck me as quiet enough for the time being, and I finally decided to refrain from citing the third set of figures in addition.

Now, let us have a look at our two sets of statistics. They have the following in common:

1. In comparison with the statistics of Mr. Arthur Ruppin they both take into account the Jewish migration between 1933 and 1939, but for Germany and Austria only. With regard to this emigration everyone, including the statistics of Richard Korherr, head of the Population Bureau of the Third Reich, dated April 17, 1943, is in agreement, a most rare occurrence, in estimating the Jewish emigration at 300,000 from Germany, and 180,000 from Austria. The exaggeration of Mr. Raul Hilberg is unimportant because, being of the same magnitude and kind in the two columns, it does not involve the number of exterminated obtained by comparison. It calls for only one comment: one piece of the record with which he was not acquainted.

2. The victims are largely accounted for by overestimating the pre-war Jewish population and minimizing the post-war Jewish population, a little everywhere, but mainly in Poland, Hungary, and Czechoslovakia. We notice that these pre-war overestimations lie between 50,000 and 100,000 per country, sometimes more (200,000 for Poland!). If they have minimized proportionately the number of survivors, and on the supposition

that ten out of the twenty countries concerned in these statistics are affected by an exaggeration of this kind (it was obviously not possible everywhere, in Norway or Denmark, for instance), an exaggeration of at least 50,000 per country would account for a million of the total number of those who claimed to have been exterminated, obtained by the difference, and an exaggeration of 100,000 per country, would yield a total of 2 million. But, that is only a gratuitous supposition, and I only make it here to show how a little stream can easily become a great river. Later on we shall see what the actual worth of these two statistics is. Each thing in its own time.

Next, let us examine the divergencies that are presented by comparing the aforementioned statistics:

1. The total number of survivors varies by about 1.5 million from one to the other, and of those exterminated by a little more than 600,000. In both cases such a variation is a significant margin;

2. Looking at it closely, this divergence derives from the evaluations, respectively, for Russia and Poland. For the first, the figure of 2,100,000 given by the *World Center of Contemporary Jewish Documentation* at Paris does not include the whole of Russia, but only that part which was occupied by German troops. The only persons who know this are those who have read *Le Troisième Reich et les Juifs* by Leon Poliakov, from which these statistics are extracted and in which this particular detail is mentioned. If one reintegrates into the two columns the million Jews that Mr. Poliakov very arbitrarily subtracted, the estimate of survivors differs by exactly *one million* from one to the other for that country, the total number of the exterminated for all countries still differs by a little less than 600,000. Who can say how Mr. Poliakov managed to get the figure, 2,100,000 for the number of Jews living in that part of Russia occupied by German troops; he does not tell us. But, we can be sure that there is no question here of a census evaluation; such a procedure is absolutely impossible on the local level unless that level corresponds to the existing civil administrative districts. Thus, no census could have been made in Russia, because the O.K.W. decided to conquer Russia in accordance with the geographical imperatives of strategy instead of by one administrative district after another. Mr. Poliakov's figure is a purely conjectural evaluation, therefore, and one which seems to

assume that the Jews of this region, instead of fleeing before an invasion which they knew was fatal for them, waited nicely in place for the coming of their executioners. Nor can it be said how Mr. Poliakov managed to estimate at 600,000 the number of survivors in 1946, when we can be sure that, with the war over for only a year, order had not been sufficiently reestablished to permit census-taking; obviously, that figure is still another rough estimate! That it showed a loss of 1.5 million was doubtless all that mattered to Mr. Poliakov, and, without doubt, he also worked out ahead of time the result that he was to come to, so that it would harmonize with the legend of the six million. He did not realize that Mr. Raul Hilberg was right behind him!

3. On reading Mr. Raul Hilberg's monograph, we see that he has taken into account the flight of the Jews before the advance of the German armies in Russia. But to what extent does his estimate correspond with reality? That is what we shall see farther on. One must concede, in any case, that when he gives 3,020,000 as the number of Jews living in Russia in 1939, he is in agreement with Mr. Arthur Ruppin; and, when he calculates at 2,600,000 those among them who survived, which gives 420,000 lost, he is also in agreement with the Jewish journalist, David Bergelson, who wrote in *Die Einheit,* on December 5, 1942, that "Thanks to the evacuation, the majority (80%) of the Jews of the Ukraine, White Russian, and Lithuania and Latvia, were saved" (cited from *Der Weg,* Buenos Aires, January 1953). Where Mr. Raul Hilberg is no longer in agreement is with himself. If, as he says, 2,600,000 Russian Jews were saved, how can he maintain (p. 190) that for Latvia, Lithuania, and Russia only 1.5 million "escaped behind the Russian lines" at the time of the advance of the German troops? And, how can he also maintain, as he does in his own statistics, that not one Latvian Jew survived?

4. Poland: Here the statistics are more or less in agreement on the Jewish population in 1939, but not at all on the number of survivors; 500,000 for one, 50,000 for the other, a ratio of 1 to 10—compared to the 1 to 14 of Mr. Shalom Baron. We do not know how the *World Center for Contemporary Jewish Documentation* came to this conclusion; there is no reference. As for Mr. Raul Hilberg, he is irretrievably lost in the fog of figures that he builds up around himself. Indeed, we have seen that on page 767 of his book he gives 3,000,000 Polish Jews

exterminated, and on page 670, he gives just 50,000 survivors out of 3,350,000; any explanation is superfluous. From what we have seen thus far, we can detect the playing of a little game. These statistics are indiscriminately, and even sometimes simultaneously, supported by the *World Center of Contemporary Jewish Documentation* and various other Zionist organizations and spokesmen. The reader is free to choose between the two and to put himself in the place of one who might find the Jewish population of 1939 as given by the World Center at Paris and the number of Jewish survivors in 1945 as given by Mr. Raul Hilberg closer to reality. Or the other way around. In this saraband of figures, anything goes. In the first case we get: 8,297,500 minus 3,782,500 or 4,515,000 victims; and in the second case 9,190,000 minus 2,288,100 or 6,901,900 victims. The result yields quite an impressive difference. By pursuing further this comparison of the two statistics we could doubtless find even more striking anomalies, but to what purpose?

I think that the moment has come to talk of more serious matters, namely, of that migration of the European Jews between 1933 and 1945, to which I have only alluded so far. Because this movement has not been studied in any detail by any of the authors who we have been discussing, it is full of question marks and is suspectible to all kinds of manipulation. If it is true, as the *American Mercury* claims, that the Zionists will not permit a census of world Jewry — what an admission! — and that that refusal makes an accurate head count impossible, then they have little ground for complaint if any of my conclusions, which are based upon their own statistics, are wrong; after all, the following study would not have been necessary if there were such a census, since the entire truth would be revealed by it.

IV. The Jewish Migration, or "The Wandering Jew"

In order really to understand the movements of the European Jews from 1933 to 1945, it seems to me that a brief historical survey of Jewish migration is indispensable; in short, a history of the "wandering Jew."

Successively or simultaneously popularized as Cartaphilus, Ahasverus, or Laquedem, depending upon the place and the time, the "wandering Jew" seems to have come into the European tradition in about the thirteenth century. Image and song had characterized him definitely in the eighteenth century in a naive ballad in twenty-four couplets, a "Portrait drawn from nature by the citizens of Brussels, at the time of the last appearance of the Jew, the 22nd of April, 1774," which in its own way gives an account of one of the oldest and earliest of historical realities: the Jewish migration. One of the oldest, the peregrinations of that branch, considered legitimate, of the descendants of Noah by Sem and Abraham,[5] it is, in its legendary and mythical form, the substance of the Old Testament, which dates their first steps back to the no less legendary and mythical Flood. The earliest: coming into history at a very uncertain date but very probably contemporary with the invasion of Egypt by the Hyksos (18th c. B.C.), in any case, between the 20th and the 12th centuries before Christ, when all the other human migrations had long since come to an end. Not only is the Jewish migration not ended, but twenty centuries after Christ it is still being described in the same legendary terms, and still has the same motive power. "The commercial bent of the Jewish people," Otto Heller said (*La Fin du Judaïsme*. Paris: Guilde, 1933), "is of long tradition." In fact, from Sumer, which, if one is to believe the Old Testament, was its first objective, to New York, which seems to be its present objective, the Jewish migration has followed, as have all human migrations, the great natural arteries, but not in the same haphazard way. Rather, the Jews have constantly turned toward those points or regions on the globe which have achieved the highest economic development. That is why, instead of going directly from the East toward the West, like all the other human migrations, this one went in a zig-zag fashion in all directions. That it encountered various misadventures, particularly the hostility it attracted in certain areas it had chosen for expansion, is certain. But these accidents scarely modified the movement with regard to the ever constant aims. Incidentally, this hostility was never, historically speaking, either systematic or permanent, doubtless because, unlike all the other human migrations, it was itself never massive or aggressive; instead, it was characterized by the suppleness of the professional tradesman. However, there are two exceptions to this historical generalization. In its Biblical phase, during the time when first Saul, then David, and then Solomon tried to settle permanently and by force at the place where the two great commercial arterial routes of their times intersected—routes that connected Europe and Asia to Africa, that is to say in Palestine—

with the hope of living there by extracting a tithe of all the trade obliged to make use of this passage. And today, still in Palestine where international Zionism plans to reconstitute, in the form of a State Bank, the Kingdom of Solomon, since Israel finds itself once again on the most important commercial arterial of the modern world, the one going from New York to New York, around the world via London, Paris, Tel-Aviv, Calcutta, Singapore, Hong-Kong, Shanghai, and Tokyo. In any case, that is what one gets out of a small book, by a certain Kadmi Cohen, a spokesman for international Zionism, which had some fame between the two world wars: *L'Etat d'Israel* (Paris: Kra, 1930). The theme of this book seems to be, although presented in vague terminology so as not to reveal the cloven hoof, that the international Zionist movement should not aim at assembling all of the Jews of the world in a country the size of the Kingdom of Solomon and at organizing them into a modern nation, but only its outer flank, whose task it would be to make it a home-port for a Diaspora which would rationally apportion the riches of the world at the point where they converge, after, naturally, siphoning off a portion for themselves. But, on the scale of the modern world, that would in a way be a repetition of the operation which was realized in the first century B.C., on the scale of the Roman world, which was described by Cicero in his celebrated speech *Pro Flacco*, and which was seen in the periodic shipment, on galleys headed for Judea, of all the gold of that world, which had until then, converged on Rome. If, twice, Rome commissioned Titus (70 A.D.) and then Hadrian (135 A.D.) to destroy the Kingdom of Judea and to disperse its people throughout the Empire, among other reasons, it had this one: to get back what she considered to be her gold. Until Titus she had been very benevolent toward the Jews, as shown by the Bernice story.

Today, speaking metaphorically, the aim is the gold of Fort Knox. If the plan should succeed—and all that is needed is for the American branch of international Zionism to get its hand on Wall Street—the Israeli home-port of the Diaspora would become not only the commercial home of the Atlantic world, but, since oil is the primary source of energy for its development, and control of that would be totally assured from the Middle East to Texas, it would also become the command post of all of the world's industry. "You will earn your bread by the

sweat of your brow," the Eternal One said to Adam; and to
Eve, "You will give birth in pain,"as he chased the couple from
the earthly Paradise he had created for them and for their
descendants. The women of Israel would, to be sure, continue
to bear their children in pain, but their men would earn their
bread and that of their children by the sweat of other's brows.
Then, at the very least, it could be said that the designation
"Chosen People," which the Jews claim for themselves, would
assume it full significance.

The chances for this to succeed? In 1932, Mr. Arthur Ruppin
(Les Juifs dans le Monde Moderne, op. cit.) told us that in 1927
in the United States, the 4,500,000 Jews controlled a substantial
number of periodical publications; they can be broken down in
this way: 9 dailies, 68 weeklies, 18 monthlies, 16 others. Furthermore, he specified that 65 of these publications came out in
English, 41 in Yiddish, 3 in Hebrew, 2 in German, and that the
most widely read of the dailies, the *New York Vorwaerts*, had a
circulation of 250,000. Here it is a question only of the internal
press of Judaism, whose aim was solely to maintain homogeneity.
No account was taken of Jewish financial participation in the
press at large, which Mr. Arthur Ruppin describes as being very
significant. And what of this Jewish control of the "mass
media" today? We shall see its effect farther on when we take
up the significance of the Jewish population in the United
States. As for the importance of the internal press of the
Zionist movement, I have not one fact which would allow me
to estimate it. But it cannot be less than it was in 1927. And,
as for the significance of Jewish financial participation in the
public press—as well as in cinema, radio, television, and book
publishing—it will suffice for me to remark that that press
publicizes, with remarkable consistency, and assumes responsibility for all the theses of the American Jewish Committee.
That these theses are not always in accord with those of the
World Center of Contemporary Jewish Documentation, and of
its subsidiaries, whose propaganda is inspired by Mr. Ben
Gurion, is to be accounted for in the political dissension between
him and Mr. Nahum Goldmann, who is the inspiration for the
American Jewish Committee. The discord between these two
men and the two organizations lies only in details and is only
barely perceptible in shades of meaning. When it comes to
essentials they are always in agreement on the general theme.

And their respective adherents follow their example; Mr. Raul
Hilberg and Madame Hannah Arendt offer us the best illustration. At the service of Mr. Nahum Goldmann, they credit
Auschwitz with *one* million Jews exterminated (nearly *three*
million less than Leon Poliakov, or Olga Wurmser, or Henri
Michel of the *World Center of Contemporary Jewish Documentation* and its subsidiaries!) and give 950,000 for the five
other alleged gas extermination centers (more than *one* million
less than the figure given by the World Center group; in all,
a margin of error of nearly *four* million out of a total of *six*!)
But, when they come to make their additions for the balance
sheet of Jewish losses, they still manage to come to a figure
near, or at least on the same sort of scale (this is the shade of
meaning in the general theme) as the *six* million of the *World
Center of Contemporary Jewish Documentation* and its subsidiaries at the service of Mr. Ben Gurion. The same holds
true for the analysis of the Jewish losses by countries, where,
depending upon whether you follow the contentions of the
American Jewish Committee, as expressed by Mr. Raul Hilberg
or by Mr. Shalom Baron, or those of the *World Center of
Contemporary Jewish Documentation,* as expressed by the
Poliakov group, you get a total for survivors which varies
from 50,000 to 700,000 for Poland, from 500,000 to 2,600,000
for Russia, from zero to 85,000 for Latvia, and from zero to
several millions for each one of a dozen other countries, without the overall figure for losses for all the countries being
noticeably affected. All this means that in the general contention, shared by both, that six million Jews more or less were
exterminated, these two theses nullify each other when it comes
to the details.

But, let us return to our examination of Jewish migration.

Of the accidental historical circumstances which had an
influence on the general direction which the Jewish migration
took, the most important seem to have been the Babylonian
Captivity (588-536 B.C.), the intervention of Titus (70 A.D.)
and of Hadrian (135 A.D.), the reactions of Christianity in the
Middle Ages (especially from the 13th to the 16th century),
the policy of the Russian Czars in the second half of the 19th
century, Bolshevism, the, so to speak, atavistic hostility of the
Polish people since the end of the First World War, and finally
Hitler from 1933 to 1945. However, there were other significant

circumstances which were not hostile: since 1850, the progressive assumption of industrial and commercial world leadership by the United States has been a positive factor which has been decisive in orienting the actual migration of the Jews, and in accelerating the orientation. The figures are revealing: 230,000 Jews in the United States in 1877; 475,000 in 1890; 1,775,000 in 1906; 3,300,000 in 1916; 4,081,000 in 1926; 4,461,184 in 1936, according to Mr. John Beaty (*The Iron Curtain over America,* p. 41), who claims to be citing from various official censuses of the American population.[6] And, that means that during these sixty years the Jewish population of the United States has multiplied more than twenty-fold, a veritable invasion. However, it is true that during these sixty years, it is not only Jews who have been drawn to the United States. In 1936, the date of the last official statistics which are referred to by Mr. John Beaty, out of a total population of 128 million, there were about 115 million whites. Among these 115 million, approximately 33 million were either foreign-born or of the first generation of foreign-born. These sixty years corresponded to what we in Europe call the *Gold Rush,* which was first set in motion in 1848 by the discovery of gold in California and which laid the foundation for the extraordinary development of San Francisco. It was really an "Industrial Rush" in the United States after 1877.

In 1926 the Germans, or descendants of Germans, made up the largest ethnic or national group in the United States with 7,250,000; the English were next with 5 million; then came the Irish with 4 million; and the Italians with 3,500,000. However, with its 4,081,000 individuals, the Jewish group was the one which was, with regard to its world-wide importance, by far the strongest contingent. It must also be noted that while the other groups settled in the United States between 1850 and 1900, the Jews only began to arrive in large numbers about 1900, particularly after 1906, and, as the statistics show, they were mostly Russian and Polish in origin; those who were not were almost all German. It seems that one can associate the beginnings of the massive migration of the Jews to the United States with two events, contemporary with it: (1) the setback of Theodore Herzl (who died in 1904) in his attempt to found a Jewish state in Palestine, which was especially of concern to the Russian and Polish Jews who were victims of periodic pogroms, and (2)

the first steps taken by the United States to establish immigration quotas (1917-1924) which, according to the figures
cited above, make it clear that the immigration of the Jews
was largely clandestine after 1917. One quickly gets an idea
of what it has been since that date. No error is risked in saying
that the Russian, Polish, and German Jews have lost no ground
since the beginning of the century, and that, especially between
1933 and 1945, their immigration was not any the less clandestine in spite of the existence of the National Origins Law of
1924 which, observing how Jews in Europe were being persecuted, was never brought—to the honor of America—into
effect against them during this period, although in theory
this law was never officially repealed.

If every time the Jewish problem has arisen in the world it
has been stirred up by Russian, Polish, and German Jews—at
least—it is due to the shattering intervention of Titus and Hadrian
in Palestine, an intervention which displaced what one might
call the center of gravity, or nutrient reservoir, of the Jewish
migration in the European triangle lying between the mouths of
the Volga, the Danube, and the Vistula. Mistreated as they were
by Rome, the refugees from the massacres were scarely drawn
to Egypt, also Roman, as their fathers had been in the time
of Herod; they preferred to work their way beyond the *limes,*
most of them by way of the Caucasus, with the rest going to
settle in Babylon, which had earlier been assigned to their
ancestors by Nebuchadnezzar during the time of the Captivity (6th c. B.C.). In the tolerant reign of the Arsacides,
the latter formed a sort of vassal state which, from the third
to the fifth century, intellectually illuminated the entire Jewish
world through its theological academies of Sora, Poumbadita
and Hahardea. There, and during that epoch, the so-called
Babylonian Talmud was codified. But that branch progressively
joined with the larger migration and was incorporated within it.

Had their Palestine experience taught them a lesson? Very
likely. The fact remains that all the writers who have described
or commented upon these events are agreed on this point:
the Jews were very well received on the other side of the
Caucasus by the autochthonous peoples among whom they
appeared as the bearers of a new religion to whose proselytism
they yielded. As they made converts among these people so
did they mingle with them, and they rapidly swarmed into the

area between the mouth of the Danube and that of the Volga; then, clever merchants as they had remained, they were drawn to the Baltic Sea, and they soon occupied a triangle formed with the mouth of the Vistula, through which necessarily passed all the land routes, highways and rivers, which contributed to the trade between continental Europe and Asia, via the Black Sea and the Caspian.

Caracalla did away with the measures taken against them by Titus and Hadrian. Consequently, during the whole of the third century and until Constantine, who persecuted them again (beginning of the fourth century), their commercial progress was favored by the normalization of their relations with their co-religionists who were still in the Empire, and they too appeared as the bearers of a standard of living, until then unknown to the barbarian peoples of those regions, which attracted the native population as much as, if not more then, their religion did. With conversion and intermarriage contributing, the two or three tens of thousands of Jews, who fleeing before the soldiers of Titus and Hadrian had crossed the Caucasus, had become by the Middle Ages hundreds of thousands, living in trading communities closed to the uninitiated, whose synagogues were at the same time the cement and the keystone, but whose ethnic formation was quite different from the original group. On the eve of the war of 1939, there were several million of the Askenazim in world Jewry, as compared to the Sephardim, descendants of those who had gone into western Europe along the shores of the Mediterranean, without mingling with the autochthonous populations of the countries they went through and who had kept their original ethnic type.

I shall take advantage of the opportunity here presented to say that from the Askenazim to the Sephardim, world Jewry of the twentieth century is composed of men and women of an infinity of types, very clearly distinguishable in their somatic characteristics—there are even yellow and black Jews!—who are united only by a religion, customs, a way of life, or, to sum it up, a tradition which is the binding element made up of a singleness of viewpoint and a solidarity that survives all strains, but which is not of the kind that defines a race in the biological sense that we give to the word. By giving a racial character to their struggles, both Hitler and Ben Gurion committed the same error: that of the latter in wanting, in the creation of the State of Israel, not only to save men, but to save a type of man who no longer exists, if he ever did; that of the former in wanting to protect from intermarriage by that imaginary man a German society which he labelled the Germanic type, but which racially was no more that than the Israeli society is Jewish. With regard to its population, this is what Mr. Ben Gurion's State of Israel is: a conglomeration of human types from the Yemenite Jew influenced by the Arab, to the German Jew mixed with the German type, and the Russian, Rumanian or Hungarian Jew infiltrated by the Slav; in short, Israel is populated with all of these types which have few or no somatic characteristics in common. The only things that the Zionist movement can hope for from so anomalous a group are, ethnically or racially speaking, the evolution of a new type of Jewish human being, issuing from a long series of mixtures of all these types, insofar as they consent to be mixed, and, politically speaking, the development of a theological state, a community in its most archaic form, which would correspond with the intellectual level of that community, perhaps very high in religious or mystic qualities but certainly very low, or backward, from the philosophical point of view. So, we see that for peoples as primitive as the Yemen Jews—together with whom it is proposed to merge into one single people all the Jews of the world in the land of their ancestors, a land much less common to them all than they claim—international Zionism is not held with the same insurmountable aversion which, ever since Theodore Herzl held it over the baptismal fountain, it has experienced among the peoples of the highest European civilizations. It is commonly known with what stubborn indignation international Zionism has constantly rejected the ideas of the greatest Jewish philosopher of all times, Moses Mendelsohn (1729-1786), who, wanting to put an end to Jewish apartheidism, preached the assimilation of the Jews with the peoples among whom they lived. The reason why his ideas are opposed is that in trying to raise Judaism above the level of religion and racial myths to the level of philosophy, the ideas of Moses Mendelsohn would have meant, if they had been seriously considered, the end of the Rabbinat, a convenient screen behind which was created, and has prospered ever since, the most vast and ambitious commercial enterprise of all time. Threatened with extinction, or, at the least, with a diminution of its profits, by a society greatly enlarged by the assimilation of the Jews with the civilized Europeans, this commercial enterprise runs no risk at all by merging with the Yemenite Jews on Israeli territory. But, one shudders to think what this future Jewish type would be, with Judaism now proliferating among the blacks and yellows as it has proliferated in Europe.

As seen from the same angle, Hitler's Germany was quite similar: a society of people of an infinity of types, in which the German type, characterized by a blend, in one person, of considerable height, dolicocephalic head, and deficient pigmentation (pale skin, blond hair), represented only a very small minority. "Between 1874 and 1877," Pierre Gaxotte (*Histoire de l'Allemagne,* Paris, 1963, Vol. I, p. 21) says, " a study made in German schools involving about six million children, showed only 31% were blond. Other studies show that the north Germans, whom tradition calls as the best preserved type, are only 18% dolicocephalic." Let the Germans not be disturbed. A comparable study to determine, for example, the Celtic type in the French population would give the same sort of results. In western Europe, where the population is a millenary brew of all the migrations meeting there and of the killing of each other off, there is no homogeneous people, anthropologically speaking, not even a type of any one of the migrations which could be called representative of any majority, or perfectly preserved. Even granting that it is possible to define the original Jewish type with as much accuracy as the German or Celtic type, it is very probable that if the same sort of studies were made in world-wide Jewish societies, roughly the same results would be obtained. The Sephardim Jews, who are surely the closest to that original type, do not, in any case, represent more than a tiny minority. And, this shows how far both Hitler and Ben Gurion went astray in the battle with a myth, at the racial level, at least. There is no doubt but that twentieth century humanity is faced with a racial problem: the relations that can or should exist between the white race and the colored races. It is a problem that exists both on a physical level and on an intellectual level and that is a little bit more in harmony with the facts of modern anthropological science. But, concerning the Jews especially, it is not a race that today they represent, but a way of life and its aspirations. And, it is not a racial problem that they pose, as the State of Israel proves so well, but an economic and social problem, of such dimensions that, under the wing of a tradition that is essentially religious, it envisages the setting up of a mercantile feudal system, which, as we have said, would take in the whole world.

To return to the Jewish migration at its beginning, we must first say that the greatest impact on Western Europe was made by the Askenazim Jews, by far the most numerous, and that is the case today in the United States. From Constanza via the Danubian artery, which was about their only access to the West until about the eleventh century, and from Warsaw via countries touched by Hanseatic trade (which could not fail to attract them!), which later became a secondary route, they gradually worked their way to the major Rhone-Rhine artery, uniting the North Sea and the Mediterranean. Certainly England interested them at the time of the Hanseatic League, but more especially after the discovery of America. Mention must be made of Spain and the French Midi, regions that attracted their co-religionists who had remained within the Roman Empire after the loss of its western provinces (fourth century) and after the discriminatory measures against them were reintroduced by Constantine, which measures were not imposed in the eastern regions except progressively as those areas were detached from the Empire and, then, definitively upon their fall and conquest by the Turks (fifteenth century). This was the branch of the migration that worked its way to western Europe along the shores of the Mediterranean. At the moment when America was discovered, this spearhead of Judaism—or rather, what was left of it, since in the meantime the Inquisition had made inroads into it— found itself on the Madrid-London line where the new commercial centers were relocated, since commerce that was once Euro-Asian now had become global in scope.

In that part of western Europe that was free of the Roman Emperors, it seems that the first violent reactions against the Jews can be dated from the tenth century.[7] But it was also in the tenth century that the influence of the Christian church, which was sanctioned by Charlemagne and which the Crusades established as the most important spiritual force, began to be felt a little everywhere. Struck by this coincidence, most historians have perceived these violent reactions as being attributable to Christianity, the word being used in the sense of Christianism. The Inquisition—and, there is a tendency to forget that it was aimed not only at Jews, but at all heresies, and so it absolutely cannot be said to have been inspired with anti-Semitic or racist feelings—which was rampant in the twelfth and thirteenth centuries in Spain and the south of France confirmed them in this view. It is true that the Church did not like Jews: against them was held, not their race (because in spite of everything it must be recognized that one of the historic invariables of its doctrine is that even in its most obscurantist undertakings, it was always universalist and never looked at the heresies of men except in relation to dogma), but what it considered the greatest of all crimes, the crucifixion of the Christ. The hostility of the western European peoples toward the Jews was manifested much earlier than the period when the Christian Church exerted its influence on them, and it seems that it had its origins in the nature of the communities that the Jews formed as they worked their way toward the west and in the manner in which, through trade and usury, they drained toward themselves all of the cash wealth of the regions where they settled. Also, for fear of falling into Jewish hands and finding themselves dispossessed, the burgeoning system of Feudalism forbade them, whom they accused of exploiting the people, to become owners of landed wealth. Even before Christianism was talked about, the Roman Patriciate had shown the same defensive reaction against them. Thus, it seems legitimate to me to think that the Christian Church only added religious reasons to those that were essentially economic of Feudalism or of the Roman Patriciate, and not the other way around. If this way of looking at the problem were justified, what I call a confusion on the part of the historians would not be important except insofar as it determines the original cause of anti-Jewish reactions among Europeans in the Middle Ages. Indeed, it would very well explain things: on the one hand, just when the first of these reactions was noted, the European consciousness was that of being, not European, a politically unknown idea at that time, but Christian, and Christendom stood against paganism, which was synonymous with barbarity; on the other hand, it was the Church, Catholic or Reformed, which led the struggle against the Jews and either claimed this honor in its fight against heretics, or endowed those who imputed "heresy" as a crime with the responsibility of carrying on the struggle. But, that is a problem for Mandarins: whatever the hypothesis, the tangible reality for the Jews, from the tenth to the sixteenth century, was that in all Christendom they were, in one place or another, periodically stripped of their wealth, which they were reputed to have acquired in a wrongful way, by the princes, the kings, or the emperors, all with the blessing or at the instigation of the Church, which was in on the division of the spoils. The procedure was simple: confiscation of goods together with prison or exile. And, the excuse was always the same: usury, or the profaning of a place or object of piety, or both. One can even cite numerous cases of the bourgeoisie—since they were very dangerous competitors for them—accusing the Jews of some profanation or other before the ecclesiastical authorities in order to get them imprisoned, and thus to escape their debts to them.

Doubtless, the worst period for the Jews was during the twelfth, fourteenth, and fifteenth centuries,[8] during which time they surged back to eastern Europe, which remained fairly liberal toward them, since conversions to Judaism were constantly being registered. Indeed, it was only later, as the Orthodox religion gained ground in these regions and as the idea of the Empire of all the Russias was born, that the hostility toward the Jews was born which was to manifest itself in far more terrible forms than in the West—the word *pogrom* is from the Russian vocabulary. In the West it was the advent of Humanism that brought the first alleviations in the condition of the Jews, and it was the Encyclopedists who dealt the decisive blow to the hostility against them. The French Revolution made them citizens like everyone else (1791), and this practice spread in Europe: Prussia (1812), the Germanic Confederation (1848), England (1858), Italy (1870). But, the era of *"pogroms"* had begun in "all the Russias". Migration toward the west swelled again, until in the second half of the nineteenth century it brought about the appearance of the word *anti-Semitism* in all the dictionaries, and anti-Semitism itself—however, wrongly, as has been said—in all national policies.

It was in the second half of the nineteenth century that the first significant numbers of Jews crossed the Atlantic, attracted by the Gold Rush and by the dynamic industrialization of the American economy — where, deriving mainly from "all the Russias" including Poland, and from Germany, the Jews who had spent more than twenty centuries, according to their own statistics, growing to a little more than ten million in the rest of the world, needed only sixty years to approach five million in the United States.

In the twentieth century, the Russian Revolution, the general policy of Poland, especially from the time in 1932 when Colonel Beck began to play a role in it, and finally Hitler hastened the movement of Jews toward the United States, and only those who lacked the means to get there remained behind in Holland, Belgium, England and France. Some of them tried to reach the "Jewish national hearth," created in Palestine by the Balfour Commission (on November 2, 1917), and succeeded in doing so, in spite of the hostility of England, which had fixed entry quotas. But the United States was the attraction *par excellence*. In 1928, the policy of Stalinist Russia, while hardly benevolent towards the Jews, still wanted to keep them within the frontiers. These borders, the gates to the exit to the west, were closed to them, as they were closed to all Russians. The area of Birobidjan, located on the borders of Manchuria, was set up and placed at their disposal as an autonomous territory in the heart of the USSR. Stalin very quickly saw that although the number of Jews in the Ukraine and White Russia was diminishing, it was not increasing in Birobidjan, where they were nevertheless making their way, but only to reach a frontier close to China, where with the connivance of the Chinese, who at that time were hostile to the USSR, they were able to flee the Soviet regime. From there, via Hong Kong and Shanghai, they went to the United States, which, with the connivance of those who had gone there before them and who had become politically quite powerful, they were entering clandestinely. Just before the Second World War began no one in Russia, nor in the rest of the world, was talking any more about the Jewish autonomous territory of Birobidjan. During the war the matter was almost brought up again, in circumstances which will be described. For the moment, it is enough to say that in making the Jews take the Siberian route again — "Central Asia" as it was called by those fresh from Russia — a significant consistency was given to their migration toward the United States by way of the East.

V. The Movement of the European Jewish Population from 1933 to 1945

In 1933, the staging area for the Jewish migration, or, if you prefer, its supply area, was no longer the triangle marked by the mouths of the Vistula, Danube and Volga. There had been successively added to those Danubian countries in which political instability and trouble following the First World War had stirred them to leave the nations of Germany, Austria, and Czechoslovakia. And, since 1917 (Balfour Convention) besides the United States, there was a second destination point: Palestine.

In spite of the confusion that has been systematically created by various leaders of the Zionist movement around the period of this migration, a certain number of facts are positively known and irrefutably established which mark the routes that were made use of by the Jews and which definitely destroy the thesis of the extermination of six million Jews. Furthermore, it is international Zionism itself — which by its policy with regard to Germany and with regard especially to the numerous trials, that have become almost incalculable,which it unceasingly demands against the Germans to prove again and again that these six million were really exterminated — that has revealed most of these facts to us (if we did not already know them) or has confirmed their actuality (if we only had suspected their existence). An incalculable number of trials calls for an even more incalculable number of witnesses to give weight to the accusations and of journalists to report the hearings; and, it was fatal that among them should be found blunderers like Mr. Shalom Baron (a professor at Columbia University and a witness at the Eichmann trial who, on top of everything else, had actually seen nothing!) or like Hannah Arendt (a journalist assigned to cover the same trial by the *New Yorker* who will be discussed elsewhere) to give the game away. It was no less fatal that there arrived at the bar of the Tribunal of History, Mr. Raul Hilberg and that he should make use of all of these in such a way that not only was everything that had been said earlier reduced to contradictions, but even that which he said himself. "He who tries too hard to prove . . ." as the proverb says.

All of these facts which have set us on the path to historical truth, have been made positively known and have been irrefutably established, unfortunately, only by specialists, most of whom, out of indifference or political interest, have suppressed them or have tried — as we have seen, and as we shall see again, with' regard to the facts concerning the international Zionist movement — to keep them out of sight. I am among those who, out of respect for my profession and submission to the moral imperatives proper to it, attach great importance to their becoming known to the public at large. I am also concerned that this very lack of information might tend to lead societies in their evolution toward impasses and catastrophes. It is because governmental policies are based generally on conjectures, more often than not elaborated in the personal interests of the politicians who proclaim them and not with regard to established truths, that societies are periodically thrown into these impasses and precipitated into these catastrophes. Consequently, there lies the necessity for finding out and for establishing, for the benefit of the mass of honest people, those truths which will permit them to defend themselves against the interested undertakings of the politicians.

Historians tell us that history is learned by tracing its course through time and, then, is verified by tracing it back again. The police, in their jargon, express this idea by saying that it is by "tracing every clue to its source," not by following every clue, that the truth is discovered. Since it is a question of verifying a statistic, therefore an addition, let us borrow the language of the mathematicians who in accounting teach that in order to verify an addition, it must be done from bottom to top, or inversely to the way that it was done in the first place. The top, in this case, is the area where the Jewish migration started. And, Europe, where it took place, is a forest of testimonies giving only partial views of events which are all overlapped and, which in addition, are falsified by the constituent elements of the psychology of the witnesses. It was from the top that the Zionist historians and statisticians began to total their deaths, pretending, because that is the way they wanted it to be, not to see that the sum which they obtained could only be infinitely reduced, just as a landscape would be enlarged to infinity by placing end to end all of the partial photographs taken of it, without first having removed from each all of the overlapping elements figuring in others. The views of the witnesses overlap just as do the photographs, and a landscape in nature is no more the sum of the latter, retouched by topographers, than a historical landscape is the sum of the former uncounted by historians. Until a gereral accounting is made, everything will remain confused, uncertain, and conjectural, in the very places where the events took place. However, it does not seem as though such an accounting is likely to be done in the near future given the absurd "fifty years' rule," or whatever else suits the politicians. Until that period is passed, if historians are nevertheless tempted to clarify the circumstances of that drama — and the urgent need for an assault against the historic myth presses them every day — they will be forced to proceed by successive stages from the established facts. And, it is in that context that this study is enscribed.

At the bottom of the addition are the two destination points of the migration, the United States and Israel, where, on the other hand, almost everything is known, although obscured by what one might call after the title of a recent film, the *Night and Fog* of Zionist propaganda. To take the advice of the historians and trace history back, or that of the policemen and trace every clue to its source, or that of the mathematician and go over the addition means to take an inventory of the Jewish population of the world, starting with what it is today in the United States and Israel. The method offers the signal advantage of obeying the basic rule of all scientific investigations: to proceed from the known to the unknown and, thereby, to shed light on the unknown by means of the known. I shall begin with a census of **Israel** first.

In 1926, Mr. Arthur Ruppin tells us that there were 250,000 Jews in Palestine. But the official statistics of the State of Israel as reproduced by Mr. Andre Chouraqui (*L'Etat d'Israel*, p. 62) tell us that there were only 150,000 in 1927, and 174,610 in 1931, the eve of the coming to power of Beck in Poland and of Hitler in Germany. Since this study attempts to show that, aside from the fact that they do not agree with each other, all statistics of Jewish origin published after the war do not agree with those published by Mr. Arthur Ruppin before the war, and, taken as a base of reference, one must, if one is to make useful comparisons with the latter, first know exactly what the former have to say about the evolution of the Jewish population in

Israel. And for the period after 1931 this is what Mr. Andre Chouraqui has to tell them: 1947 — 629,000; 1952 — 1,450,000; 1957 — 1,763,000.

On the level reached in 1962 we have, on the other hand, two bits of information, perhaps contestable but at least in agreement, of which the first is already known to the reader: the communiqué of March 31, 1963, of the *Institute for Jewish Affairs* of London, published on April 1 by *Die Welt* of Hamburg in which it is said that that population had reached 2.045 million;9 and a speech given on July 17, 1963, before the *Knesseth* (the Israeli Parliament) by Mr. Levi Eshkol (successor of Mr. Ben Gurion) in which it is said that out of a total of 2.27 million inhabitants in the State of Israel, 2.05 million were Jews. We shall assume that Mr. Levi Eshkol, President of the Council of the State of Israel, is very probably better informed than the *Institute for Jewish Affairs* of London, and we shall retain his figure. In any case with a difference of only 5,000 it is without importance.

Here we are presented with four significant dates in the evolution of the Israeli population: 1931 (just before the rise to power of Beck in Poland and Hitler in Germany); 1947 and 1952 (the eve and the day after the creation of the State of Israel); and finally 1962 (the year in which this study was written).

In order to determine the importance of Jewish immigration into Israel from 1931 to 1962, a third factor is missing, the normal rate of increase of the world Jewish population. Now, Mr. Shalom Baron supplied us with one when on April 23, 1961, he came before the bar of the Jerusalem Tribunal to state that in relation to what it had been in 1945 this population had increased by twenty per cent.

However, "one swallow does not make a summer." I categorically refuse to accept such an estimate as being well founded. A normal rate of increase of twenty per cent over sixteen years amounts in fact to an annual increase of about 1.25 per cent, that is, of the world population, which demographers estimate will double every 80 years at its present rate of proliferation. But, this rate is reached only in the eightieth year. What it is in the 16th year does not seem to have been calculated, or if it has, I do not know about it. What is certain is that it is much less. The population of France, which, it seems, proliferates at the world rate, has, for example, gone from a little less than 42 million to a little more than 46 million during these sixteen years, or at a global rate of increase of 10 per cent, or annually about .62 per cent. During the same period, the Italian population, which proliferates at a faster rate than the world rate, still has not gone from more than a little more than 43 million to a little less than 50 million, or a global rate of 14 per cent, annually about .89 per cent. The United States seem similarly to have gone from 141 million to 186 million, that is a global rate of about 12 per cent, annually about .75 per cent, but there we must reckon with a significant immigration which the legislative measures of 1901 to 1924 failed to block.

And, what about the world Jewish population? First of all, using the demographers' scale of eighty years, and of the century, this is what Professor Shalom Baron's estimate produces, facts which most surely cannot be admitted:

```
16th year  10     million plus 20% equal 12     million (+1.25% per year)
32nd year  12     million plus 20% equal 14.4   million (+1.37% per year)
48th year  14.4   million plus 20% equal 17.28  million (+1.51% per year)
64th year  17.28  million plus 20% equal 20.76  million (+1.68% per year)
80th year  20.76  million plus 20% equal 24.83  million (+1.86% per year)
96th year  24.83  million plus 20% equal 29.86  million (+2.06% per year)
```

Baron's figures show that, more than doubled after the 64th year, the world Jewish population would be more than tripled after the 96th year. This projection is like saying that the Jews are, if not *more*, at least *as* prolific as the Chinese, a fact which is not attested to by all their other information on the subject.

In the absence of any verified information concerning the Jews, I examined the normal annual rate of increase, which would be applicable to them, and I arrived at the following conclusions:

    a.   The world Jewish population is always in a state of migration.

    b.   Migrating populations increase proportionately less than sedentary populations.

    c.   A sedentary population which doubles every 80 years reaches an annual rate of about 1 per cent after the 64th year.

    d.   But we are concerned with the periods between 1931 and 1962, and the calculations cannot include more than 31 years, and should be 16, or 10 or 5 or 4, which means that the 1 per cent annual rate of increase, if used in the calculations, would give the Jews, migrating, a higher rate than sedentary Italians, all things being normal. However, let us retain the 1 per cent, on the principle of the benefit of the doubt.

The method of calculation: the natural growth of a population is the difference between the number of births and the number of deaths. If we are able to determine the natural increase in each of the great waves of the four important dates of Jewish immigration into Israel, it should suffice to subtract that from the Jewish population of the State of Israel in 1962, to add the number of deaths there to the result obtained, and to arrive at the actual number of immigrants for the period 1931-1962. In this particular case account must be taken of those who, disappointed in the venture, left again, and their number should be added. An analysis of these factors — natural growth, immigration, mortality among immigrants, and emigration — follows:

1. *Natural growth*:10
   a. from 1931 to 1962, the 174,610 counted in Palestine in 1931, have grown by 31% or *54,129* persons.
   b. from 1947 to 1962, the 629,000 counted in 1947 have grown by 15% or *94,350* persons.
   c. from 1952 to 1962, the 1,450,000 counted in 1952 have grown by 10% or *145,000* persons.
   To this must be added the natural increase of:
   a. those 629,000 Jews counted in 1947 who arrived in Israel between 1931 and 1947;
   b. those 1,450,000 counted in 1952, who arrived between 1947 and 1952;
   c. those 2,050,000 counted in 1962 who arrived between 1952 and 1962.

Here are the results obtained from the second series of calculations, organized along the elementary rules of arithmetic:
   a. from 1931 to 1947, the 174,610 Jews counted in 1931 have increased by 16% and have become: $\dfrac{174,610 \times 116}{100}$

= 202,547. It follows that, with their natural increase included, the new arrivals in this period represent 629,000 minus 202,547 or 426,453, and, their natural increase itself; $\frac{426,453 \times 16}{116} = 58,821.$

b. from 1947 to 1952, the 629,000 Jews counted in 1947, grew by 5% and were: $\frac{629,000 \times 105}{100} = 660,450.$ It follows that, with their natural increase included, the new arrivals during that period represent 1,450,000 minus 660,450 or 789,550, and their natural growth itself $\frac{789,550 \times 5}{105} = 37,598.$

c. from 1952 to 1962, the 1,450,000 Jews counted in 1952 increased by 10%, thus: $\frac{1,450,000 \times 110}{100} = 1,595,000.$ It follows that, including their natural increase, the new arrivals during this period represent 2,050,000 minus 1,595,000 or 455,000, and their natural growth itself $\frac{455,000 \times 10}{110} = 41,364.$

The preceding figures in italics give a total natural increase of 431,262.

2. *Actual number of immigrants during this period* (not adjusted for on the spot mortality). To obtain this number one must not only subtract this figure from the Jewish population of the State of Israel in 1962, but also the 174,610 persons counted in 1931, who are included, which gives 2,050,000 minus (431,262 plus 174,610) equal 1,444,128.[11]

3. *On the spot mortality among the immigrants.* Jewish sources are not very exhaustive on the death rate, and not on the birth rate either, at least to my knowledge. Concerning the latter one finds from time to time data of this sort: "The average number of children per family is 3.8" (*L'Etat d'Israel,* Andre Chouraqui, p. 77) which is meaningless. As for the death rate, also from time to time, some journalists now and then will give a figure: 13, 14 and sometimes as low as 10 per 1000. Specialists of Shalom Baron's caliber are fascinated by the natural rate of increase only, and they establish it on the level of the world Jewish population, not in terms of the number of births

and deaths, but in terms of the representation that they wish to present to the world for the two dates, 1946 and 1962 , after having first subtracted the six million exterminated. It is a rate subject to political pressures, and fluctuations, as we have seen. The Israeli Jewish population is a young population; in all migrations, it is the young who leave, and the old who remain. For example, in Buchenwald, where Jews were interned, I do not remember having encountered one who was less than 50 years old. Among the peoples of Western Europe the death rate is about 17 per 1000. That it lies between 13 and 14 in Israel is probable. But, in 1946, 1947, and 1948, there were consequences of the war which raised it a little for the whole period. So, let us say about 14 per thousand, or about 20,504. In any case, if I miscalculate it cannot be by more than a few thousand at most, and I am prepared to make corrections. Thus, with mortality included, the immigration between 1931 and 1962 totaled 1,464,632 persons.

4. *Emigration*. There were those Jews who were disappointed with the "promised land" and there were also those who thought of Palestine, afterward Israel, as a way station imposed by circumstances, from which to proceed elsewhere. Until 1939, for example, a certain number of Polish, Russian, or German Jews, as well as others, did not have the financial means to proceed further. Some, for that reason, even could not go beyond North Africa, in view of the limitation that England put on immigration to Palestine. Between 1939 and 1945 Palestine became, for those who continued to escape secretly either via Istanbul or Constanza, the only accessible refuge. For those who were pushed across the Urals and the Volga by the German armies, a considerable number who even in 1962 have not all succeeded in getting out of Soviet territory, Israel is still the most accessible refuge, unless they are nearer to China; those nearer to China go through Hong Kong and Shanghai to reach the United States. Well, Mr. Andre Chouraqui tells us that "95 out of every hundred immigrants manage to overcome the difficulties of adapting to the country and found families there, while 5 give up." (*op. cit.*, p. 75). Very few, but we will not argue the point. Therefore, the total immigration between 1931 and 1962 is determined by the following calculation:

$$\frac{1,464,632 \times 100}{95} = 1,541,718$$

And now, a last step before finishing with Israel: to take into consideration those among these 1,541,718 immigrants who came from Europe. Here we are furnished with an estimate by Mr. Andre Chouraqui:

> Asia, since 1948, furnished Israel with 258,181 immigrants, representing 28.8% of the total immigration. These 258,181 persons came from Turkey (34,797), Iraq (122,987), Iran (31,274), Yemen (45,887); Syria, Lebanon, Aden, even India and China furnished a contingent of 14,092 souls. Africa is third in line (24.8%) after Europe (43.4%), and Asia (28.8%), and supplied a contingent of 222,806 immigrants representing 24.8% of the recent immigration. North Africa, leading the African contingent, supplied more than 150,000 immigrants originating mainly from Morocco and Tunisia. (*op. cit.* p. 65.)

The data given in the preceding quotation are dated December 31, 1957. From this excerpt the following conclusions can be drawn:

First, the nonsensical style in which this information is written throws doubt on the authenticity of the percentage of the immigrants of African origin, presented in one sentence as a proportion of the total immigration, and in the next as a proportion of the "recent immigration." And, so it can be assumed that other percentages are no more authentic or more significant.

Second, the three per cent of the immigrants who are not accounted for in this enumeration, and we don't know whether they are a portion of the total immigration or of the "recent immigration," concern the American and Australian continents. It is, however, exact enough to show that very few Jews came from those two continents.

Third, except for those Jews from Yemen, whose well-known odyssey could be the subject of a novel of dark humor,[13] all the other immigrants taken into account by Mr. Andre Chouraqui could be either Jews who left Europe after 1931, or their descendants born in Africa or in Asia. Please note that I say "could be" and not "were." Palestine, for example, is in Asia, and all those who arrived in Israel from the non-Israeli parts after 1948 could be considered as having originated from Asia, in Mr. Andre Chouraqui's data. Such an interpretation is all right for those born there, but what about their parents? Turkey, Iraq, Iran, Syria, Lebanon, are also in Asia, and it is precisely those countries which were before and during the war most accessible to the European Jews. Often, those countries were the only ones. Some got to Africa via France, particularly until 1939, and the same argument could be made about them. Put yourself in the place of the Polish Jew who left his country in 1932 or 1939: he could not get to Israel before 1948 since a country by that name did not exist, and in most cases he got there only after 1948, often very long after, with the children he had meanwhile had, that is, after having spent fifteᵉ n or sixteen years or more in Palestine, Iraq, Syria, Algeria, Tunisia or Morocco, and, if asked whence he came, there is nothing astonishing if he named the country he last lived in, since cosmopolitanism is one of the characteristics of the Jewish soul. It is a long time since he was Polish, if he even remembers it. For him, Poland where he was born was never a native land, but only a "land of welcome," an expression used by Jews the world over to designate the country in which they live, even if they were born there, when they speak among themselves. To his mind, Poland has become the country which treated him badly, and his true "land of welcome" is where he took refuge when he was obliged to leave Poland. And, the same holds for all those who, between the years 1939 and 1945, succeeded in leaving clandestinely not only Poland but also Czechoslovakia, Hungary, Bulgaria, Rumania, and Russia, and who have only arrived in Israel in the last few years. Mr. André Chouraqui takes up only immigration into Israel; that factor is all that interests him, and that is his right. That is the subject he treats and he cannot be reproached for limiting himself to his subject. But, it is a very convenient limitation: he can reduce at will the number of European Jews who have immigrated to Israel by having them come from their last residence before 1948 − pardon, from their last "land of welcome" − which was Africa or Asia. And, at the same time, he can increase the number of those who were allegedly exterminated. To what extent has that subterfuge been used? The principal element of the answer to that question is given in the following paragraphs.

Finally, Mr. Andre Chouraqui's book is dated 1959, and the things described therein date from 1957, as I said. Now, he tells us, in 1957 "Asia, since 1948, furnished Israel with 258,181 immigrants representing 28.8 of the total immigration" up to December 31, 1957. Hence, a simple calculation yields the following: $\dfrac{258{,}181 \times 100}{28.8}$ = 896,462. This figure of 896,462, then, represents the total immigration through the end of 1957 – according to Mr. Andre Chouraqui.

But again, the Israeli Jewish population went from 1,763,000 on December 31, 1957 (Andre Chouraqui *op. cit.* p. 74, and the official statistics for that year) to 2,050,000 on December 31, 1962, which indicates an increase of 257,000, which, after deducting the natural increase, represents 159,381 new immigrants[14] during that period of five years. Since there was a total of 1,541,718 immigrants on December 31, 1962, there were 1,382,337 (1,541,718 - 159,381) already there. And, based on his own figures, Mr. Andre Chouraqui's error, I mean the coefficient of minimization, is about 1.54.

Another example of Chouraqui's erroneous analysis is provided by the immigration of Moroccan and Tunisian Jews who, he tells us, rallied to Israel to the number of 150,000. But, let us have a look. In Morocco, Mr. Arthur Ruppin told us, they numbered 120,000 in 1926, and in Tunisia 60,000. Total for both countries is 180,000. In 1948 there must have been 219,600, adjusting for a natural increase in population. If 150,000 of them went over to Israel, there remained at that date 69,600. And, these in 1962 had become 79,344. However, the study by the *Jewish Communities of the World* instructs us that in 1962 there remained 125,000 Jews in Morocco and 35,000 in Tunisia, which gives a total of 160,000. *The Jewish Post Weekly* of April 19, 1963, confirms this. Consequently, it appears that 80,656, of the Jews listed as Moroccan and Tunisian by Mr. Andre Chouraqui were not such; rather, they were the ones who had come from Europe earlier and had not been able to proceed farther for personal or other reasons. Therefore, the actual number of Moroccans or Tunisians (which is achieved by subtracting 80,656 from 150,000) was 69,344. Here it is a question of a coefficient of exaggeration (it is the same thing, this manipulation of figures in both ways having no other object than to augment the number of those exterminated in Europe and to diminish the number of those who succeeded in leaving), and it is from 1 to 2.16 exactly.

Another example, as is seen from Chouraqui's treatment of the German Jews. "The German Jews," says Mr. Andre Chouraqui (*op. cit.* p. 66), "were *almost totally exterminated* by the Nazis." Now however, we know, and all the Jewish historians and statisticians agree, including Mr. Andre Chouraqui himself, that out of the 500,000 given by Mr. Arthur Ruppin as living in Germany in 1926, or the 540,000 given by post-war Jewish statistics for the number living there in 1933, about 300,000 left the country between 1933 and 1939, and that 40,000, according to Mr. Poliakov and the *Center of Contemporary Jewish Documentation*, or 80,000 according to Mr. Raul Hilberg were still alive in 1945. Hence, the total number of survivors is 340,000 or 380,000 depending on whose figures are used. With some 340,000 survivors out of a population of 500,000 or 540,000 a conclusion that German Jewry was "almost totally exterminated" is hardly an example of intellectual honesty. By which it is seen that the nonsensical style that allows one to sow confusion also allows one to develop a sensational effect. As the figure for the total immigration for December 31, 1957, he gives the figure of 896,462, according to his data, on page 65, and the figure of 896,085, according to the data of others, on page 66. Finally, when he gives it straight from the statistics themselves, it becomes 905,655. The same is true for the total population of the State of Israel which on December 31, 1957, is 1,954,954 at page 64, and which becomes 1,763,000 Jews and 213,000 Christians and Moslems, yielding a total of 1,976,000 at page 74. If it were a question of orders of magnitude one would understand it and overlook it, but in every case these are estimates down to the unit. So it is a test. Mme. Hannah Arendt and Mr. Raul Hilberg, I confess, have not done much better.

There is no end to the examples that could be cited. In short, what I want to say here is that if these coefficients of exaggeration are of the same order — and why not, since there is no question of error here but of deliberate calculation? — as far as the percentages are concerned of those European, African, or Asian Jews, who, according to him have immigrated into Israel, it is enough to apply the median coefficient of exaggeration to re-establish them approximately in their actual relationships. The average coefficient is figured as follows: $\dfrac{1.55 + 2.16}{2} = 1.85$.

For the Jews of Africa and Asia: $\dfrac{24.8\% + 28.8\%}{1.85} = 29\%$. And, for the European Jews: 43.4% + (53.6% - 29%) = 68%. Still missing is the "three per cent" which I discussed above in my first conclusion concerning Mr. Andre Chouraqui's data.

Converted into figures, the number of immigrants of European origin then becomes, based on the total immigration (mortality and emigration included), $\frac{1,541,718 \times 68}{100} = 1,048,368$ and, based on the number who survived and remained, $\frac{1,444,128 \times 68}{100} = 982,007$. So, there it is in mathematical terms, at least the way I learned mathematics. Furthermore, it is reasonable, and for this reason: these figures correspond almost perfectly with those published by the *New York Times* on February 22, 1948, based on data supplied by its expert, Hanson W. Baldwin. And, to avoid any misunderstanding I cite from the text itself:

> There are 650,000 to 700,000 Jews in Palestine. Another 500,000 inhabit other countries in the Middle East .... In these countries the Jews are tied by bonds of religion to the rest of the fifteen to eighteen million Jews of the world.

Among these 1,150,000 to 1,200,000 Jews in Palestine and the other countries of the Middle East in 1947, a deduction drawn from the number a Jewish source said were living there in 1931, there were a few more or a few less than 750,000 immigrants, depending upon whether one bases one's opinion on pre-war or post-war Jewish statistics. And, almost all of these immigrants came from Europe for the good and simple reason, almost without exception, that there was no reason for those from other areas to move there *en masse*. The former had been the first to rejoin Israel, since they were more or less already there. Then they were joined later by 200,000 to 250,000 more European Jews, and to determine the immigration from that origin we get into figures of the kind that result from my calculations.

If I involve Mr. Hanson W. Baldwin in support of my thesis, it is not only because his estimates are credible but for a more solid reason: insofar as the figures for the Palestinian Jewish population are concerned, they have been confirmed by the official Israeli statistics published at the beginning of 1949, for the year 1947, which gave the number as 629,000. They were also given for Palestine by Mr. Ben Gurion himself, who in May 1948 estimated the Jewish population to be 650,000 (*Le Peuple et L'Etat d'Israel*, Paris 1959, p. 102). Therefore, there is nothing conjectural about them: on this point at least it is a verified estimate. And, it verifies mine.

I shall go further: if Mr. Hanson W. Baldwin was so well informed about the Jewish population in Palestine in 1947, there is no reason to think he was less informed on the world Jewish population, and therefore close to the truth in estimating it between 15 and 18 million on the same date. The *New York Times* said that the data came from the Jews themselves (in its own words: "from the secret census made by them in every country in the world"), and that explains everything: in one way or another Mr. Hanson W. Baldwin was informed about this "secret census." But it makes no difference. If this "secret census" really took place, and if the leaders of the Zionist movement know so exactly the actual number of Jewish losses, then we have a case of extortion (the payment of indemnity to Israel by West Germany) built up with premeditation — and much better done than the robbery of the Glasgow-London train by gangsters that everyone is talking about at the moment. I used the words "so exactly," and I wish to call attention to the nuance, because I do not believe in that "secret census."

But, to return to the European Jews who immigrated to Israel between 1931 and 1962, their number is estimated to be 1,048,368, mortality and re-emigration included. Jewish sources admit to 388,901 for the December 31, 1957 date, and in 1963 this figure is still publicized by the world press. And, we already have 659,467 European Jews who were not exterminated by the Nazis, but who all the same figure in the list of exterminated in statistics of Jewish sources. Or, if you prefer, subtract 1,048,368 from the 9,243,000 given by Mr. Arthur Ruppin as living in the European areas which were controlled by the Nazis, in numbers and for various lengths of time between 1933 and 1945, or from the 9,600,000 given at Nuremberg by Justice Jackson. Take your choice.

My estimates are given down to units, too, but that is because if one is making mathematical calculations one cannot escape that servitude, mathematicians not having yet invented any other way of making calculations. I trust that the reader understands that it was a question of rounding off orders of magnitude. All of the elements that have entered into these calculations have been kept at the lowest possible figure so that I may not be accused of error greater than that which fits the contentions of the *World Center of Contemporary Jewish Documentation* and all the rest. It is my opinion that in orders of magnitude, these estimates show that 1,100,000 European Jews are to be subtracted from the figure that is given for the European Jewish population prior to the accession to power in Germany of Hitler, and that 700,000 be subtracted from the announced six million, depending on the method preferred. If new data are brought forth to make a revision necessary, there is no doubt in my mind that a raising, and not a lowering of the number to be subtracted will result. And, precisely because, in keeping the figure down to the lowest level within my system, more than once I have found that the level was too low.

For the benefit of those who want to see the picture at a glance, in round numbers, but almost to the unit here is a recapitulation table of the preceding study, which shows at the same time the structure of the Israeli Jewish population in 1962 and that of the immigration from 1931 to 1962:

Jewish Immigration 1931–1962			Jewish Population 1931 – 1962		
Origin:	European	Non European	Total	In 1931	Natural Increases	In 1962
Over-all:	1,048,368	493,350	1,541,718			
Settled:	982,007	462,121	1,444,128	+ 174,610	+ 431,262[b] = 2,050,000	
Mortality:	13,943	6,561	20,504			
Emigration:	52,418	24,668	77,086			
Verification:	1,048,368	493,350	1,541,718	Levi Eskhol's population estimate: 2,050,000[a]		

[a] cf. p. 323.

[b] I warn the reader who is unfamiliar with demographic studies that if he is tempted to think that the natural increase should correspond to the number of Jews actually living in Israel, less than 31 years of age, he will be committing a grave error; those, for example, who left Germany in 1938 in the arms of their parents are today only 24, and figure among the 1,444,128 immigrants. The same for all European children born in North Africa or elsewhere. Among them there are those who arrived in their parents' arms in 1957 or 1958, only 4 or 5 years old in 1962 and still could not be included in the natural increase column. They are immigrants just as much as their parents.

Now let us proceed to a study of the Jewish population of
the **United States.** The study of the Jewish Israeli population
has so far led us only to the European Jews who succeeded in
reaching Palestine, later the State of Israel, and who got there
either from the west or by the Danube route via Constanza or
Constantinople or both. There is another aspect of the migration of the European Jews between 1933 and 1945, the movement toward the East.

This other aspect is disclosed to us in at least two Jewish
sources: Dr. Rudolf Kasztner (*Bericht des Komittees zur Rettung
der ungarischen Juden*) and Alex Weisberg in collaboration with
Joël Brand (*l'Histoire de Joël Brand, un echange de 10,000 camions contre un million de Juifs*). (And, incidentally, it is confirmed by both Mr. Raul Hilberg and Mme. Hannah Arendt,
also.) This is what the former says:

> Up to March 19, 1944, our chief work concerned the rescue
> and care of Polish, Slovakian, Yugoslavian refugees. With the
> German occupation of Hungary our efforts were extended to
> the defense of the Hungarian Jews . . . . The occupation
> brought the death sentence to Hungarian Jews, numbering
> almost 800,000 souls, (*op. cit.* p. 1, *Einleitung*)

Hungary, where the Jews were not persecuted by Admiral
Horthy's government (a Jew, the banker Stern, was in fact a
member of the Council and numerous others were deputies),
was actually an asylum for Polish, Czechoslovakian and Yugoslavian Jews. This text sets the facts down and shows their
significance: 800,000 minus 320,000 (Arthur Ruppin *dixit*)
equal 480,000 Polish, Czechoslovakian and Yugoslavian Jews in
Hungary on March 19, 1944.

Dr. Kasztner also tells us how the *Committee for the Safety
of the Jews of Budapest* went about their work, but the Alex
Weisberg-Joël Brand team is more precise: it was through emigration via Constanza after supplying them with genuine or
false passports. Once at Constanza they were saved because
Rumania did not persecute the Jews, except during a very brief
period, between 1939 and 1945. To cut the discussion short, let
us cite from the two associated authors:

> In their haste to get rid of the Jews the Germans cared very
> little whether they disappeared over the border or into the
> crematory ovens . . . . Foreign passports were the surest pro-
> tection . . . . Within a few weeks (after March 19, 1944) there

were more nationals of the Republic of San Salvador (in Hungary) than of all the other countries combined . . . . After a protect from the Pope and President Roosevelt, the Swedish and Swiss governments issued thousands of passports, and we added thirty to forty thousand. Possessors of this viaticum were immunized against deportation. (*op. cit.* pp. 55-56.)

To get "thirty to forty" thousand Swedish and Swiss passports circulated with impunity in a country as well watched over by the German and Hungarian police as Hungary was, Sweden and Switzerland would have had to issue, if not many more, at least that number. And since there were in circulation "more from the Republic of San Salvador than all the other countries combined" there must have been about 200,000 "immunized" against deportation.

But for all that, these "immunized" persons did not have absolute peace of mind about their fate just because of their passports, whether genuine or forged. Most of them got the passports only in order to leave Hungary more easily. There were some who left without a passport. And, that emigration occurred almost with Eichmann's complicity, since, as our authors tell us, Eichmann, "who had before the war worked on the mass deportation of Jews . . . interrupted when Germany went to war with Russia . . . had taken the idea up again, as soon as he arrived in Budapest." (*op. cit.* p. 93.) Further on, they tell us in substance that with or without passports many Jews made it to Constanza, and from there they tried to find ships to take them to Haifa, a thing that was not always easy to do. If they failed in this, they tried at least to get to Constantinople. Nor was it always easy to disembark at Haifa. Those who succeeded could not all remain in Palestine because of the limitation imposed on immigration by England, and, in order to avoid arrest, many were obliged to scatter into the other countries of the Middle East, from whence they tried to get to Hong Kong, and from there to the United States or some other country on the American continent (Argentina, Brazil, Canada, etc.). Similarly, it was difficult for them to disembark at Constantinople.

But, it is Mr. Raul Hilberg, with the information that he unwittingly supplied so well and that he interpreted so poorly – precisely because he is not aware of it, who makes it possible for us to reconstruct in its breadth and in its entirety the movement of the European Jews toward the American continent via Hong Kong. Really, it would be more accurate to say that his information only confirms the authenticity of the data, because we already have the facts and already had used and published most of them. I speak here of the Polish and Russian Jews who between 1939 and 1945, during the war operations, never found themselves on the German side of the battle line. There was a considerable number of them, and the study of the horrors of the Second World War to which I have devoted myself for a good fifteen years has convinced me that many of them found their way to the American continents, where they are best represented in the United States. The few detours that we shall be led to make in Europe during the course of this study will enable us to settle on the number who were able to get there via the West.

As far as the United States is concerned, our peripheral point of departure, here the obvious lie leaps to the eye right away: it is not true, as the *Institute of Jewish Affairs* of London claims, that 5.5 million Jews were living there in 1962. In 1926, Mr. Arthur Ruppin gave us a figure of 4,500,000 Jews, and the official U.S. census figure for that year was 4,081,242 (a total which census officials seem to have regarded as being "incomplete"). Curiously, for once almost all of the historians – and the Jewish statisticians as well – are in agreement that the best estimates lie close to the Ruppin figure. Nevertheless, we shall give the *Institute of Jewish Affairs* the benefit of the doubt and shall use the official 1926 census figure, keeping in mind that it is probably too low and that a figure which is closer to that of Mr. Arthur Ruppin is doubtless closer to the truth. Applying the coefficient of natural growth, one per cent annually, to the 1926 census figure, we get an American Jewish population of 5,550,489 persons in 1962 – i.e., 36 years later. And if we had used the coefficient of Mr. Shalom Baron of twenty per cent every sixteen years, we would have gotten 4,897,490 in 1942; 5,876,988 in 1958; and 6,170,837 in 1962. I could not have asked for a better opportunity than this one to be able to accuse the *Institute of Jewish Affairs* of London of underestimating the American Jewish population by 670,837 persons instead of by only some 50,489. But, that is not my way of doing things, and I am content to show to what extent the two Jewish authorities are in disagreement between themselves. So, the American Jewish population in 1963 is 5,550,489 persons –

without taking into account the Jewish immigration since 1926, an important consideration.[15] And, also without taking into account the Jewish emigration, but that factor is negligible. In fact, Mr. Andre Chouraqui tells us (*op. cit.* p. 67) that only 7,232 immigrants came to Israel from the Americas and Oceania between 1933 and 1957. And, it is not easy to imagine what reasons would urge them to go elsewhere.

In any case we are concerned with an examination of the Jewish immigration to the United States. We have already seen how since 1848, but particularly since 1880, immigration to the United States was part of the general movement of European peoples, known, in part, as the "Gold Rush." Between the two wars, in France, which was the best place to observe it since France was an almost obligatory passageway toward the West, the stream was fairly slow until the 1930s. From 1932 on, when Colonel Beck took over the post of Minister of Foreign Affairs in Poland, we began to see Polish Jews arriving in great numbers. And, after 1933, we began seeing the German Jews. The first Polish Jews who arrived in France went into business using methods so at variance with local custom and so unorthodox that they often aroused indignant protests. Then, one fine day they vanished, but it was soon seen that the heads of their businesses had been replaced by other Polish Jews. The German Jews, on the other hand, usually went straight through. At the end of 1937 the Austrian Jews appeared, and this stream was reinforced in 1938 after the *Anschluss*. And, at the end of 1938 and the beginning of 1939, came the Czechoslovakian Jews. From the end of World War I until 1932, we were aware mainly of the passage or settlement of Russian, Rumanian or Bulgarian Jews, among whom only a few Polish Jews had mixed, all chased from their respective countries by the Bolshevist storm and the instability that followed it. They came in small numbers, I repeat. For the over-all picture, from Jewish as well as government sources, shows that it was not a matter of moving whole populations of them. The Jewish population increased only from 250,000 to 300,000 from 1926 to 1939[16] (to 270,000, according to Mr. Raul Hilberg) or exactly the natural increase rate, barely more.

How many then went through France, and where did they go? It is easy enough to give the number of German Jews. In 1939 there remained in Germany not more than 210,000, according to the *World Center for Contemporary Jewish Documentation,* and 240,000 according to Mr. Raul Hilberg. Official German statistics, in particular those of Mr. Richard Korherr, head of Hitler's population bureau, give a figure within the same range: 220,000. So if it were said that about 300,000 Jews had left Germany before 1939 everyone would agree. But, Mr. Andre Chouraqui (*op. cit.* p. 66) says, that "120,000 immigrated to Israel between 1933 and 1939," which seems to indicate that at least 180,000 went somewhere else. Here, may I be permitted to bring forth my personal testimony? At Belfort, a city near the Franco-German frontier, and right on the itinerary of the largest number of Jewish refugees, because it is also near the Franco-Swiss border, I was, between 1933 and 1939, the leader of the Socialist Party. Because of that capacity, those German Jews who were Social Democrats and who had managed to cross the frontier, generally knew my address, and, in order to continue on their way, they preferred to turn to me for help rather than to the Jewish community. Most of them told me that their aim was to get to the United States where they had relatives who would make it easy for them to enter the country and to remain there in spite of the quota laws on immigration, which they knew were, under the circumstances, rarely enforced against them. A few of them spoke of Canada for the same reasons. Very few mentioned Brazil or Argentina; in these two countries it was only after the war that Jewish immigration assumed considerable proportions. During the occupation, still at Belfort, but where I then had the greatest responsibility in the most important and judicious Resistance movement (*Liberation-Nord*), which was the only effective channel for them, the same situation existed except that they first had to go over the border into Switzerland, where, with the help of the *Joint Distribution*, whose representative was Sally Mayer, they hoped to get a regular passport for the American continent, preferably for the United States or Canada. Not one of them ever, either before or during the war, mentioned England, for which they nourished a staunch hatred.

In 1937-1938, the same phenomenon occurred with the Austria Jews, and in 1938-1939 with the Czechoslovak Jews. We saw no more of the Jews from these countries in France during the war; they went by way of the Danube, the first after the *Anschluss*, the latter after the settling of the Sudeten affair.

For Austria, the statistics of the *World Center of Contemporary Jewish Documentation* and of Mr. Raul Hilberg agree with German sources: before 1939, 180,000 out of 240,000 had succeeded in leaving Austria. And, Mr. Andre Chouraqui finds that the number of Austrian Jews who immigrated into Israel is so insignificant that he doesn't see any need to mention it. Where, then did they go? I can only keep repeating: all those who turned to me, before, as well as during the war, gave the United States as their preference, or, in any case, a country on the American continent.

So, we have a total of 480,000 German and Austrian Jews who managed to leave Europe between 1933 and 1939. In this case, both the *World Center for Contemporary Jewish Documentation* and Mr. Raul Hilberg had the honesty not to include the latter among the number of Jews who they claimed were exterminated. We shall see, in the recapitulation table of the actual number of European emigrants, if they have been included in the number of those who augmented the Jewish population of countries other than Israel, where they must have gone, since they are no longer in France.

On the number of Polish Jews, or those from the Danubian countries, who reached the American continent or Africa via the West, I had no accurate information which would permit me to establish it as other than "appreciable." Happily, my excellent collaborator, Mme. Hannah Arendt, came forth most usefully to complete my documentation. Mr. Raul Hilberg, too, from whom she had taken nearly everything she had said, proved to be quite useful. If I prefer to cite from Madame Hannah Arendt, it is because she expresses herself much more clearly than Mr. Hilberg; she borrows nearly everything from him, but her talent for clarity must be recognized. It is with regard to the French, Luxemburg, Belgian and Dutch Jews that she has so usefully completed my documentation of the Jews of Poland and the Danubian countries who left Europe via the West.

In France, she writes in the *New Yorker*, March 9, 1963, there were about 300,000 Jews in 1939 (that I knew), and, in February-March 1940, before the events which brought about the occupation of the country, 170,000 foreign Jews had joined them; that figure is what I was not sure about. At the time, all the French papers, as I remember, spoke of some 200,000 foreign Jews who had fled their countries in the face of Nazism, and that it was our duty to help them. But, I had kept no clippings. I was much more occupied in aiding the Jews than in counting them. Among them, were 40,000 Belgians and as many Dutch. What about the others? I have no precise facts. In any case, the total number probably was 170,000; one can be sure that Mme. Hannah Arendt, however, did not overestimate it. Since the government of Marshal Petain refused to turn over the French Jews to the German authorities, and since he made so much trouble for them about the foreign Jews, she goes on, that of this mass of 470,000 Jews, only 52,000, among them 6,000 of French nationality, had been deported at the end of the summer of 1943, that is, in 18 months (massive deportation operations did not begin until March 1942). In April 1944, two months before the Allied landing, there were still 250,000 Jews in France, she says, and no further measures were taken against them. Therefore, they were saved. This fact does not keep Mr. Raul Hilberg from putting only 200,000 in the survivor column in his statistics. And, one must not think that the difference − 470,000 minus 250,000 equals 220,000 − were deported. On this difference, outside of her indication that there were "52,000, among them 6,000 of French nationality," at the end of the summer of 1943, Mme. Hannah Arendt gives us no information at all. But, the *World Center of Contemporary Jewish Documentation* tells us that 120,000 Jews in all were deported from France, without specifying the number of those of French nationality, which does not prevent it, when it comes to tallying the survivors, from stating peremptorily that there were only some 180,000, as we shall see on the chart for France, Belgium, Holland and Luxemburg. The *World Center* simply did not figure in this difference except among the number of those living in France in 1939, without taking the immigration factor into account.

And, here is Mme. Arendt's conclusion for Belgium: the 40,000 Belgium Jews who fled to France before the German invasion, together with 25,000 who were foreign to that country, were, she says, nearly all deported and exterminated. With the 50,000 which the *World Center of Contemporary Jewish Documentation* said were living there in 1945, we get a figure of 115,000. But, official Jewish statistics give only 90,000 Jews in Belgium in 1939. And, there is another important detail: no

Belgian Jew was deported, because – as Mme. Arendt explains – in Belgium there was no Jewish Council (*Judenrat*) to register them and to designate them for deportation. But the foreign Jews, on the other hand, were all deported: they were nearly all Poles or Russians, and their very appearance called them to the attention of the German authorities, as she says.

And, for Holland: the 40,000 Jews who fled to France, plus the 118,000 who were deported (and exterminated naturally), plus the 60,000 that the *World Center of Contemporary Jewish Documentation* found still living in 1945 yield 218,000. But, according to official Jewish sources, there were only 150,000 Jews living in Holland in 1939.

Finally, for Luxemburg: 3,000 Jews lived there in 1939, minus the 2,000 who were deported gives 1,000 survivors in 1945.

Therefore, if we draw up a recapitulative table for these four countries in 1945, this is what it looks like:

Deportation of Western European Jews			Survivors in 1945				
Country	1939	1940[a]	Deported	Actual	More or (less) than in 1939	Official	Officially counted as exterminated
France	300,000	470,000	120,000[b]	350,000	50,000	180,000	120,000
Belgium	90,000	115,000	25,000	90,000		50,000	40,000
Holland	150,000	218,000	118,000	100,000	(50,000)	60,000	90,000
Luxemburg	3,000	3,000	2,000	1,000	(2,000)	1,000	2,000
Totals	543,000	806,000	265,000	541,000	(2,000)	291,000	252,000

a Actually for the year 1940 there should be two columns in this table; one with the data for before the invasion of Holland and Belgium (spring), which is this one, and one with the data for after the invasion, which would take into account the 40,000 Belgian Jews and the 40,000 Dutch Jews who fled to France. It would look like this: 75,000 in Belgium, 178,000 in Holland, and 550,000 in France in July 1940. The general total for the four countries would not have changed, nor the other data, nor the circumstances, so it was not thought useful to tangle up the calculations with figures that ended in the same results.

b I repeat that Exhibit No. 100 of the Jerusalem court claimed only 52,000 deportees from France, as of July 21, 1943.

Thus, of the Jews who are claimed to have been arrested in France, in Belgium, in Holland and in Luxemburg during the war, some 265,000 among them are said to have been exterminated in the concentration camps to which they were deported. But, when the war was over there were still in the four aforementioned countries, taken as a whole, 541,000 Jews or 2,000 less than there were living in them in 1939. This conclusion comes from the very figures that Mr. Raul Hilberg, his protégé, Mme. Hannah Arendt, and the *World Center of Contemporary Jewish Documentation* have given us. But, without knowing how, or why, the latter, when it comes to drawing official conclusions from these figures, concludes that there were only 291,000 survivors, and, for the number of exterminated, it finds a figure in the same range: 252,000.

Doubtless to distinguish himself and to demonstrate originality, again without knowing how or why, Mr. Raul Hilberg comes up with 261,000 survivors, and 242,000 exterminated, drawn from the same figures. And, naturally, Mme. Hannah Arendt follows in his footsteps. In *Eichmann's Confederates and the Third Reich Hierarchy,* the *Institute of Jewish Affairs* of the World Jewish Congress finds 261,000 survivors and 292,000 exterminated (p. 59). So, with only shades of difference, the Jewish sources seem to be in agreement.

The mechanism of this operation, which is so crude that it stares you in the face and which is found in all of the figuring of all of these people, is quite simple: in 1945, during the post-war turmoil, the Jewish communities of every country were supposedly invited to state very quickly what their losses had been so that Justice Jackson could take them into account in his speech for the prosecution at the Nuremberg Trial where such figures were prefaced with the expression: "it is estimated in full cognizance . . . ."[17] As unscrupulous as we know Justice Jackson to have been, it is certain that, although he does not say what, he must have based his opinion on something. And, that something could only have been information of this sort. This information was assessed, not in the terms of *all* Jews who were survivors in a given country, but in terms of those who were nationals of that country and who were, then, subtracted from the number of their members who had lived there in 1939. The difference between these two figures was claimed to be the number of Jews who met their deaths in Nazi gas chambers. It

was up to the Jewish communities in each country to account
for Jews of other nationalities among them. But this was not
done. In each of the European countries the same practice was
followed, and, in the present instance, it developed that some
250,000 Jews were not counted as survivors anywhere, and
that this missing 250,000 always turned up in the column of
those exterminated in the statistics. It is by this process, multiplied by the number of countries, that the figure of six million
exterminated European Jews was arrived at.

Considering only these four countries, the "non-nationals"
were not the only ones involved. There were also those who
possessed the nationality, but who had not yet returned —
many never returned — and, therefore, were not present at the
time when that fabricated inventory was drawn up. Since they
were absent, they were included among the exterminated. However, most of them had emigrated. Although that emigration
could not be proven in 1945, it can be today. We know, for
example — even if only through the Arendt-Hilberg team —
that at the moment of the arrival of the German troops in
Belgium, no more than 5,000 Jews remained who had Belgian
nationality, and that since no Jewish Council denounced them
to the Germans, not one of them was arrested (Hannah Arendt,
op. cit.). From this fact, the following can be concluded:

a. Since there were 60,000 Jews in the country in 1926
   (Arthur Ruppin *dixit*), and therefore not many less than
   70,000 in 1939, including the natural rate of increase, it
   was not 40,000 who fled to France as Mme. Arendt says,
   but between 60,000 and 65,000.

b. When the *World Center of Contemporary Jewish Documentation* puts 40,000 Belgian Jews in the exterminated
   column, this is a wretched fraud.

And, the same conclusion holds for France where we know
that at the end of the summer of 1943 only 6,000 Jews of
French nationality had been deported. Here again, the Arendt-
Hilberg tandem is in agreement. For the period from the end of
summer 1943, to the end of the war, no exact information has
been made public, as far as I know. But, Mr. Leon Poliakov
(*Le Troisième Reich et les Juifs*), Mr. Michel Borwicz ("*Les
solutions finals àla lumière d'Auschwitz-Birkenau*" in the *Revue
d'Histoire de la seconde guerre mondiale,* October 1956), and

Mr. Joseph Billig (*Le Dossier Eichmann*), all say that it was during the course of 1942 that the greatest number of French Jews was arrested and deported, in order to arrive at the admirably Jesuitical formula that "in all about 120,000 Jews were deported from France." But, if the greatest number of French Jews to be deported was 6,000, there is very little chance, mathematically speaking, that the number could have exceeded 11,999. Since the largest number was 6,000, arithmetically, the smallest number could not be larger than 5,999. The question remains: what became of the other 110,000 (or, at the least, the other 108,000) who are among the 120,000 French exterminated, when it has been established that they were not even arrested and deported? If I answer that question by saying that they had left France, I do not think that I can be accused of conjecturing. Because if they were not deported, if they were not exterminated, and if they were no longer there, then they must have gone somewhere else.

It was from Holland that the greatest number of national Jews was deported. How many? The contradictory data in the recapitulation table permit two equally contradictory replies, one of which is necessarily without value:

On the one hand, if 40,000 Dutch Jews fled to France, where they were not deported and where they were found again in 1945, and if in 1945, 60,000 were found still surviving in Holland, then, by referring to the statistics for 1939, we subtract 40,000 plus 60,000 from 150,000 and get 50,000 national Jews actually deported who did not return – at least they had not returned by 1945;

On the other hand, if out of the 543,000 from the statistics for the countries of France, Belgium, Holland and Luxemburg considered as a block, who were living there in 1939, only 291,000, who had one or the other of the four nationalities, were found again in 1945, then 252,000 (figured by subtracting 291,000 from 543,000) of the former did not have one or the other nationalities, were strangers there, and had replaced, number for number, 252,000 French, Belgian, Dutch or Luxemburg Jews who were not arrested there, were not deported, and yet were no longer there. Among them, it is known from an assured source, that there were a minimum of 108,000 French and 60,000 Belgians. There were 1,000 Luxemburgers who also were officially there. Therefore, by subtracting 169,000 from

252,000 we have a maximum of 83,000 Dutch Jews. In the column of deportees, who had not returned in 1945 there were 67,000, which is determined by taking 83,000 from 105,000. And, that is the only true fact that can be given as being verified by Jewish sources themselves, with regard to the details that they give. What it might be in reality, is another story. And whether these 67,000 Dutch deportees were exterminated is also another story. In any case, it is far from being established as fact, since to do that it would require that no one came back after being deported, and such a contention is untenable. This conclusion holds true not only for Holland but for France and Luxemburg, too. There is no problem with regard to Belgium, since not one Belgian Jew was deported, or at least very nearly so.

Considering France, Belgium, Holland and Luxemburg, *en bloc*, the obvious conclusion is the following: a maximum of 12,000 French Jews, 67,000 Dutch Jews, and 2,000 Luxemburg Jews yields a total of 81,000 Jews who were deported according to the data provided from Jewish sources, and not 252,000 as they claim. (As has been pointed out in the preceding paragraphs, no Jews were deported from Belgium.) Even if not one came back, which is improbable, it would still result in an exaggeration of 171,000 Jews, to be subtracted from the column of exterminated. And, that figure is just for these four countries.

But there are other conclusions to be drawn: With regard to the 252,000 Jews of these four countries who were not exterminated since they had not been deported, and yet were not in one or the other country in 1945, one or two things can be said: either they returned after 1945, in which case they must be included again in the European Jewish population, or else they did not return and they must be included in the population of the country to which they went and in which they remained. It is the second case that must be looked into since no Jewish source lists them as having returned to Europe. The question remains: where are they then? Are they in the United States, in Canada, in Argentina, in South Africa? These questions cannot be answered until we determine the total number of Jews who succeeded in leaving Europe. One way of making this determination is by conducting an investigation into the Jewish population in all the countries where they increased the population, and there is only one for which there is no Jewish source: the United States. In any case, not having officially returned to Europe, these 252,000—who could not have left Europe until after 1940—must be added to the 300,000 German Jews and the 180,000 Austrian Jews who had left before 1940. In other words, we have a total of 732,000 European Jewish emigrants.

With regard to the 252,000 Jews who did not have the nationality of any of the four countries in question, who replaced number for number the 252,000 Jews who are discussed in the preceding paragraph, and who were found still living in 1945, the following is clear: in the statistics of the countries from which the latter came they are listed in the exterminated column, and, in order to take mathematical count of the living and the dead of those countries, which is the first task to be done, they must be reintegrated among the living. But "to reintegrate them among the living" in the statistics does not mean that they returned to those countries. Officially not one returned, since not one was officially reintegrated into the statistics, nor in actuality either, since, with the exception of western Germany, these countries are on the other side of the Iron Curtain. For the same reason, the same is true for France, Belgium, Holland and Luxemburg. The second task to be done will be to reintegrate them into the population statistics of the countries to which they went after their number has been determined. In any case, it is already possible to say that here we have again 252,000 more European Jews who have emigrated, and that figure, when added to the 732,000 figure that is mentioned above, makes a total of **984,000**.

Finally, with regard to the 265,000 Jews who were arrested in France, Belgium, Holland and Luxemburg, we find that among them, as we have seen, 81,000 were nationals of one or the other of these countries. So it follows that 184,000 were without the nationality of any of these countries. The same logic as above applies here, with the exception that those 184,000 Jews should be reintegrated into the exterminated (it would be more exact to say, people missing in 1945) columns of the countries from which they come.

To correctly reintegrate those 252,000 survivors, who are listed as dead, and those 184,000 who are listed as exterminated, for a total of 436,000 Jews, into the statistics of the countries from which they came, we must know which countries. But, can we determine these exactly? Mme. Hannah

Arendt – via Mr. Raul Hilberg – says that they were "Poles,
Russians, Germans, etc. . . . ." However, it is not very clear who
that "etc." covers. It is not likely that it covers the Yugoslavs
who left Europe by way of Italy, Greece, or Hungary; the
Austrians who took the Danube route or went via Switzerland
after the *Anschluss*; or the Czechoslovakians who took the
Danube way through Hungary, as Dr. Kasztner specifies. Moreover, the Russians could only leave via Constantinople and the
shores of the Caspian or the Birobidjan after the war began.
Following the outbreak of hostilities, only the Germans continued to emigrate secretly through Holland and Belgium or
Luxemburg for the reason that the Rhine had to be crossed, and
it was easier for them to cross it on German territory than
where it forms the frontier. Therefore, there were Germans in
appreciable numbers, doubtless, but surely not in significant
numbers because they were only those who had remained in
Germany after 1939. The others, as Mr. Chouraqui has told us,
had already left Europe, and 120,000 among them were in
Israel. There remain the Poles for whom the truly mass emigration began in the spring of 1939, when the situation between
England and Germany was disintegrating, and for whom Belgium, Holland, and France were their escape routes, too. Until
the end of August 1939, they could even cross Germany with
Polish passports. They constituted almost the whole of those
436,000 Jews who were neither French, Belgian, Dutch, nor
Luxemburger, and who were to be found in one or the other
of those countries in May 1940 when their emigration route
was cut by the German armies during the "Battle of France."
    I have no precise information available that would allow me
to divide up these 436,000 Jews among the nationalities cited,
as should be done, because they can no longer be counted, and
to deduct them separately from the statistics of Jewish sources,
given for each of them for 1939, or to reintegrate them into the
1945 statistics taking the dead and the living into consideration.
Aside from that, any of them who were not Polish or German
were the exception; that is, they were a negligible number. The
Germans, themselves, were only a small contingent, amounting
to 20,000, 30,000 or 40,000 perhaps, but no one knows for
certain. It is about that, in any case.
    After that time, two methods are possible: First, one can
study the Jewish population in the aggregate, for all the above-
named countries, by deducting as a whole from the start those

436,000 persons from the 1939 statistics, and, in accordance with the calculations, by adding for 1945 the 184,000 who were arrested to the corresponding column. Since we are looking at the European Jews, not Jews by nationality, mathematically and on that level, no error would have been made. But there are two things against it: the division of the Polish Jews between the Russian and the German zones after the German-Russian invasion, and their migration toward Hungary, which, by leaving out so significant a number as 350,000 to 400,000 Polish Jews, could only lead to results whose aberrant character as far as Poland is concerned, would inevitably have had repercussions multiplied on a European scale.

Second, since those 436,000 Jews were in the great majority Polish, they can be considered — mathematically — as being all Polish, and they can be integrated into Polish statistics only. In terms of such a calculation, the results were off by no more than 20,000, 30,000 or 40,000 of them who were not Polish, but the error did not exceed, on the whole, one or two tens of thousands of persons on the nationality level. And, on the other hand, mathematically, it could be automatically and exactly corrected on the level of the Jewish population of Europe, by an error exactly corresponding, inversely, if I decided not to take into account those 20,000, 30,000 or 40,000 in the study of the German Jewish population. It is the second method that I adopted: the solution of a problem by the well-known process of false supposition. Having given this explanation, which is indispensable for an understanding of what follows, we take **Poland** first.

In Poland, Mr. Arthur Ruppin tells us, there were 3,100,000 Jews in 1926. In 1939 there were 3,300,000, as the *World Center for Contemporary Jewish Documentation* and the *Institute of Jewish Affairs* of New York tell us. Mr. Raul Hilberg goes even further, with a figure of 3,350,000. But it is nonsense to think that this could be right, since they were constantly, and in numbers, migrating since 1932. Let us say that there were 3,100,000 in the spring of 1939, when mass migration began. We have decided that arithmetically 436,000 were on their way through Holland, Belgium and France, when the invasion of those countries by German troops took place. So, there should have remained in Poland at the moment of invasion 2,664,000. In reality there were less, because the Polish Jews had also tried to leave by the Danube route: the *Kasztner Report*, as we have seen, tells us that a certain number of the latter were still in Hungary on March 19, 1944, mixed with Czechs and Hungarians. And since the Nazi invasion of Hungary took place on March 19, 1944, how many Polish Jews fell into German hands?

First, we must determine how many there were in the aggregate for the three nationalities? There had been, as Dr. Kasztner specifies, 800,000 Jews in Hungary, more or less permanently since the beginning of the war. In 1926, Mr. Arthur Ruppin had counted 320,000. With the natural rate of increase these 320,000 had become 361,600 in 1939, and not 404,000 as claimed by the *World Center of Contemporary Jewish Documentation.* Taken together, the Poles, Czechoslovakians and Yugoslavs, who were living in Hungary, added up to 438,400 persons. And by taking each of these three nationalities separately in detail, we get the following:

1. **Czechoslovakians:** the statistics drawn up by Mr. Richard Korherr (already cited) for the Wannsee Conference, which was to have taken place on December 9, 1940, but which did not take place until January 20, 1942 (*Protocole de Wannsee* in *Eichmann und Komplizen*, Robert Kempner, *op. cit.*) — that is, before deportation of the Jews was undertaken — tell us that in Bohemia-Moravia there were still 74,200 of them, the rest having fled to Slovakia, when Czechoslovakia was dismembered (1938-39), and 88,000 in Slovakia. Mr. Arthur Ruppin's statistics for 1926 give 260,000. With the natural increase rate of 1%, which we have used throughout this study, that makes the Jewish population 293,800 in 1939 and not 315,000. And, that means that in Hungary, continuing along the route by which they were fleeing, there could have been 131,600 Czechoslovakian Jews, this figure being determined by subtracting 74,200 plus 88,000 from 293,800.

2. **Yugoslavs:** Mme. Hannah Arendt takes from Mr. Raul Hilberg the fact that when Hermann Krumey arrived in Zagreb at the end of 1943 he found a certain number of Jews in the country and deported 30,000. On this point all Jewish sources are in agreement. The Wannsee Protocol mentions 40,000 at the end of 1941. The rest had fled to Italy and Hungary. In all there were 75,000 Jews in Yugoslavia in 1926, as Mr. Arthur

Ruppin says, and this figure is accepted by the *World Center of Contemporary Jewish Documentation*. It could be that the Yugoslavian Jewish emigration matched the natural increase since that is a country where not only Jews, but all the ethnic groups, and in all periods, were numerically very fluctuating. The·difference, or 35,000 could be equally divided between Italy and Hungary, or 17,500, a little more or less for each. The *World Center of Contemporary Jewish Documentation* found 20,000 Jews there in 1945, and that would indicate that out of Krumey's 40,000 deportees, 20,000 returned from the concentration camps where they had been sent, and the rest died in the camps.

3. **Poles:** Without counting those who, with or without genuine or forged passports which were given to them by the Committee for Jewish Safety of Budapest (Joël Brand *dixit*), had succeeded in leaving Poland for Hungary after 1939, there were approximately 289,300 Poles. This figure is determined by subtracting the 149,100 Czechoslovakian and Yugoslavian Jews from 438,400.

On the basis of the preceding discussion, we can conclude that there remained in Poland under German-Russian occupation 2,374,700 Jews, figured by subtracting 289,300 from 2,664,000 and not 3,100,000, 3,300,000 or 3,350,000. Moreover, that number was divided up between the German and the Russian zones.

Now, another question arises: in what proportion were these 2,374,700 Jews divided between the two zones? With the fine want of realization which seems to keep him from making the simplest of accurate calculations, Mr. Raul Hilberg, who found 3,350,000 Polish Jews in 1939, puts 2,100,000 in the German zone and 1,200,000 in the Russian zone. At least, that is the idea one gets. But, it is a worthless estimate; in terms of what has been said, which is as historically as demographically irrefutable, it does not bear examining.

Then, how many were there on each side? In order to answer this question as exactly as possible, two elements must be taken into account: the flight of the Jews before German troops pushing into Poland, and the steps taken against them from July 1940 on.

Like the Dutch and Belgian Jews, the Polish Jews fled before German troops, either toward Hungary, or into that part of

Poland destined to be occupied by the Russians. The proportion of the latter cannot be determined, it seems, unless the number of those who did not go in that direction can be determined. A very large number, without doubt, fell into Russian hands, because there was actually for a certain time a German policy of turning over to the Russians Jews encountered in the German area. This is attested to by Zwi Patcher and Yacov Goldfine, two witnesses for the Prosecution at the Nuremberg Trial, who later testified on May 1, 1961. The first stated:

> All our money and our jewelry were taken from us. Then, in the columns of four, we were conducted toward the East. It was in December. It was cold, rainy and we were shivering. When one of us dropped with fatigue, he was taken aside and a pistol shot put him out of his sufferings. But it was forbidden to turn one's head, or one was shot, too. At the end of three days our group had been greatly decimated. We arrived at the frontier of the Soviet occupation zone in Poland. Our executioners had ordered us to put our hands on our heads and to shout "Vive Stalin." But just the same the Russian sentinels pushed us back into a German area, where we were left to ourselves. During the night, we crossed the frontier to reach a small Jewish village in the Russian zone, where our co-religionists gave us shelter. (*Le Figaro*, May 2, 1961.)

The second made an analogous statement. Helped, even though so brutally, by the Germans to get into the Russian zone, quite a number of Polish Jews must have made it.

The story of the steps taken against them is more specific. Mme. Mary Berg tells us (*Le Ghetto de Varsovie*, Paris, 1947), and Mr. Leon Poliakov, who seems to have taken his information from her, confirms it (*Le Bréviaire de la Haine*), that in Poland the Germans were not seriously concerned with the Jews until war operations in the West were over, that is, during July 1940. Until then, the Jews were under surveillance, suffered innumerable persecutions and vexations, but they were not confined to their houses; and, they took advantage of that fact to make a run for Hungary via Slovakia. After the construction of the ghetto in Warsaw was completed (October 16, 1940), escape was possible, but only at great risk. They were all under house-arrest, and the Jew hunt began that was to round them all up there. But, in July 1941, the Jewish population in Warsaw, counted in 1939, had increased from 359,827 to only half a million, all within the ghetto.

Therefore, in all of the German zone, the German police authorities had been able to find only 140,000 to 150,000. To escape the measures to concentrate them, the Jews began to flee toward every remote spot, in the mountains and the forests. When they were found they often were considered to be partisans; consequently there were struggles during which many of them perished. But, even if the Germans who were tracking them all over had succeeded in capturing a quarter or a fifth of them during that period (and, in view of the efficiency of their police at that time, this is a plausible estimation because in France it was about the same when they went after those subject to forced labor), that fact still does not put the Jewish population of the German zone, the Warsaw ghetto included, at more than about 1,100,000. Thus, out of 2,374,700 who made up the total Jewish population of the two zones, 1,274,700, were in the Russian zone. And, even if Mr. Raul Hilberg did not know how to subtract, this figure is not very far from his. Let us congratulate him all the same. We regret at the same time that he did not find so approximate a result for the German zone. We know about the Jews who went behind the Russian lines; the Jewish journalist, David Bergelson, told us (*Die Einheit*, December 5, 1942, *op. cit.*) that thanks to evacuation measures 80 per cent of them were saved and were transported to Central Asia by the Soviet authorities. So, the following calculations show the fate of the Polish Jews:

$$\frac{1{,}274{,}700 \times 20}{100} = 254{,}940 \text{ who fell into German hands and}$$

$$\frac{1{,}274{,}700 \times 80}{100} = 1{,}019{,}760 \text{ who did not.}$$

And in the German zone? It seems that only by comparisons of the difference can we find out. On the one hand, here are 1,019,760 survivors found in the Russian zone. On the other, in 1945 Mr. Shalom Baron found 700,000 for both zones (according to his testimony at the Jerusalem Tribunal). The total of those not found in 1945 can be figured as follows: 2,374,700 - (1,019,760 + 700,000) = 654,940. And to this 654,940 for the whole of Poland may be added the 182,000 arrested in Holland, Belgium, France and Luxemburg, or 836,940. All of the preceding data, it must be remembered, comes from Jewish sources. We shall not dispute whether or not they were all arrested; but that they were all exterminated we may, just the same, doubt.

So, now we can begin to determine the total number of survivors: first, we must reintegrate into the statistics, the 252,000 who in 1945 were found still alive in Holland, Belgium, Luxemburg, and France. We can do this by adding the 1,019,760 survivors from the Russian zone together with the 700,000 that had been found by Professor Shalom Baron and these 252,000. We get a total of 1,971,760, based solely on the total number of Jews remaining in Poland after 1939. Second, we must add in those Jews who had tried to flee westward. Here we shall add 2,374,700 plus 252,000 plus 182,000 to get 2,812,700. The number of Jews who, having fled to Hungary (289,300) were either deported from there or found alive there in 1945, can only be included in the totals made for Hungary itself.

But, we have not finished with Poland yet. Mr. Raul Hilberg found 50,000 survivors there; the *Institute for Jewish Affairs* of New York found 400,000; the *World Center of Contemporary Jewish Documentation* found 500,000; and, from the calculations based on Mr. Shalom Baron's data, put into its historical context, there were actually a minimum of 1,971,760 survivors out of a population of 2,812,700 Jews (excluding those who succeeded in leaving Europe via Hungary and whose number is unknown because, as we have seen, it has been possible to count in Hungary only those who remained there). After 1945 it was possible for the *World Center of Contemporary Jewish Documentation* to make its calculations easily by asking all the Jewish communities for a report of their numbers by nationality, and it is the latter which should have figured in the statistics. It could also have included the Polish Jews deported and then found as survivors in Hungary, which would have saved us all this figuring, if it had honestly given the results of its investigations. Instead of that, for Poland, it gives 500,000 survivors only, or 1,472,760, who are listed as dead in the European statistics, but who are alive and who are not listed as such in any statistics of any country of the other continents. Of those, at the end of our study of the western countries, we had already found 984,000. Here we must add 984,000 to 1,472,760 for a total of **2,456,760** survivors.

The next stage is an examination of **Russia**. The situation here is not involved; everything is very clear. Mr. Raul Hilberg, who finds 3,020,000 Jews there in 1939, concludes that 420,000 were exterminated, and 2,600,000 survived. Mr. Arthur Ruppin gave 3,000,000 Jews in 1926. Between 1926 and 1939 Jewish emigration probably corresponded to their natural rate of increase because the Russian Jews have always been in an endemic state of migration. And, if we accept David Bergelson's evidence, we can calculate the number of sure survivors as follows: $\dfrac{3,000,000 \times 80}{100} = 2,400,000$, which leaves 600,000 missing in 1945. Mr. Raul Hilberg gives only 420,000 as exterminated, which can mean only one thing: if 600,000 Russian Jews fell into German hands, 180,000 were not exterminated — perhaps they were not even arrested and deported, or, if they were, they came back from the camps where they were interned. The percentage of those exterminated in the latter case is seventy per cent (420,000 out of 600,000) and of survivors, thirty per cent. That is still a fearful number. The *World Center of Contemporary Jewish Documentation* finds that 1,500,000 were exterminated (in the German zone, none in the Russian zone) which means there were 1,500,000 survivors, but to make it sensational, it gives 600,000 for the German zone in such a way that the reader thinks it applies to both zones. On the same data, the *Institute of Jewish Affairs* of New York finds 1,000,000 exterminated and 2,000,000 survivors.

But, Mr. Raul Hilberg charges the *Institute of Jewish Affairs* with an exaggeration of 580,000, figured by subtracting 420,000 from 1,000,000 deportees who it lists as being exterminated in its statistics, and the *World Center of Contemporary Jewish Documentation* with having made an exaggeration of 1,080,000 (figured by subtracting 420,000 from 1,500,000) in its statistics. It is in the statistics of the latter that we have calculated this exaggeration. Thus, we come to this conclusion: the 1,080,000 Jews who were incorrectly listed in the exterminated column, and who were quite alive in 1945, if they are no longer in Russia, nor elsewhere in Europe, must be living — with their offspring since 1945 — in another country on another continent. Our study of the Polish Jewish population brought us to 2,456,760 survivors. To this number we can add 1,080,000 for a total of 3,536,760 survivors.

The case of the Jews of the **Baltic** countries is as clear as that of the Russian Jews. To my knowledge no one has ever taken into account the number of Finnish Jews exterminated. For the three other countries, Mr. Arthur Ruppin gave the following figures for 1926: Esthonia, 5,000; Latvia, 80,000; Lithuania, 160,000; total, 245,000. By moving 10,000 to 15,000 individuals around from one country to another, the *World Center of*

Contemporary Jewish Documentation comes to the same total, and Mr. Raul Hilberg gets 244,500 for 1939. What about the natural increase from 1926 to 1939? He does not consider this. Perhaps he felt that emigration compensated for it. But we are within 500, so let us call it 245,000. According to David Bergelson, the survivors can be calculated as follows: $\frac{245,000 \times 80}{100} =$ 196,000. And, 196,000 subtracted from 245,000 yields 49,000 missing in 1945. The *World Center of Contemporary Jewish Documentation* finds 219,000 exterminated and 26,000 survivors. As for Mr. Raul Hilberg, he gives us a higher figure: 244,500 exterminated, and no survivors. It is hard to see why, if the Russians evacuated the Jews all along the front lines — and, Mr. Raul Hilberg subscribes to that fact if not to its significance — they should have deliberately made an exception in the Baltic countries. Mr. Raul Hilberg claims this, but does not give an explanation. Here once again, 196,000 minus 26,000 (from the official statistics) gives 170,000 Jewish survivors, carried over into the column of exterminated, who, since they are no longer in the Baltic countries, are somewhere else in the world together with their offspring born since 1941-42. The total of survivors at this stage: 3,536,760, plus 170,000 or 3,706,760.

Let us proceed by returning to the West: First, we shall examine **Czechoslovakia**. We have seen that 260,000 Jews counted in 1926 by Mr. Arthur Ruppin could, at the most, have become 293,800 by 1939 and not 315,000 as is claimed by other Jewish sources. We have also seen that 131,600 among them had surely fled into Hungary through Slovakia, and that when the deportations began, 162,200 remained in the country, according to the German statistics of Mr. Korherr who had a tendency to exaggerate what he called the "Jewish danger" rather than to lessen it. (For example, for Europe he gave eleven million Jews in 1941!) The *World Center of Contemporary Jewish Documentation* found 55,000 survivors in 1949. Logically, then, 107,200 only could have been deported from Czechoslovakia. Even if one insists on taking "Exhibit 83" of the Eichmann Trial in Jerusalem seriously, which takes account of the deportation, very much disputed, of 15,000 Jews of the Protectorate of Lodz on October 15, 1941, that would still give a total of only 122,200 deportees. After October 15, 1941, the

Jerusalem court made no further case for any other deportation from the Protectorate of Bohemia-Moravia except to give an overall total, without any justification whatever of 35,000. And even if one accepts it, the total is still only 142,000. Except for this, all the other Jews of the Protectorate are listed as having been victims of the forced emigration that was organized by Eichmann from Prague before the war. (See, "Exhibit 66" which gives no figures.) It is only for Slovakia that the Jerusalem Court gives an estimate of Jewish losses: for the whole, "more than 70,000 out of 90,000" ("Exhibit 104"); 58,000 up to the end of May 1942, and more than 12,000 from September 1944 to March 1945. If we refer to that Court for an estimate of Jewish losses for all Czechoslovakia, we find 70,000 in Slovakia plus 35,000 in Bohemia-Moravia which gives a total of 105,000. And, that means that, when it claims to have found only 55,000 Jews still alive there in 1945, the *World Center of Contemporary Jewish Documentation* attempted to promote a truth which the judges of the Jerusalem Tribunal did not admit, since it was on documentation officially supplied by the *Center* that they based their conviction. But, the significance of this disavowal is seen with regard to the number of Czechoslovakian Jews announced in the general statistics given by this group as having been exterminated since it fixed the number at 260,000, figured by subtracting 55,000 from 315,000. Actually, the balance should be as follows:

1. Czechoslovakian Jewish population in 1939: 293,800

2. Those Jews who crossed into Hungary (where the discount of the deportees and those found again alive are included in the totals resulting from calculations made for Hungary, since it is impossible to do otherwise[18].): 131,600

3. Those Jews who remained in Czechoslovakia prior to the deportation program: 162,200

4. The number of deportees as determined   by   the   Jerusalem
Tribunal: 105,000
5. Those Jews who were not de-
ported from Czechoslovakia: 57,200
6. The number of those not de-
ported, as determined by the
World Center of Contemporary
Jewish Documentation: 55,000
                                                   2,200

And, here we have 2,200 European Jews listed among the
dead who were quite alive in 1945, and who — since they are no
longer in Europe, officially — must be on the lists of those living
in another country on another continent. In the study of the
Jewish population of the Baltic countries we found 3,706,760
for the whole, in the same situation. Now, we have 3,706,760
plus 2,200 or 3,708,960.

Next, we shall study **Hungary**. There, the Jewish situation
was as complicated as in Poland. Mr. Arthur Ruppin had counted 320,000 Jews in 1926, and we have seen that they probably
increased to 361,600 by 1939. The *World Center of Contemporary Jewish Documentation* gives 404,000 and Mr. Raul
Hilberg 400,000[19], Dr. Kasztner, as we have also seen, gives
800,000 Jews as continuously living there since the beginning of
the war[20], including — according to him — 205,800 Czechoslovakians, 215,000 Poles, and 17,500 Yugoslavs and, apparently,
361,700 Hungarians. The question is, how many of those
800,000 Jews were arrested and deported? And, here we have a
hopeless muddle. It is over the deportation and the fate of the
Hungarian Jews that the divergencies in the accounts of the pro-
Zionist witnesses and the interpretations given to them by those
who, since the end of the war, have made it their business to
dramatize the Jewish tragedy, are the most numerous, the most
serious, and the most contradictory. Of these divergencies the
reader has already had a taste from the analysis made of the
Hoess testimony, commandant of the Auschwitz camp, and of
Miklos Nyiszli, the pertinence of which my references to the
Kasztner Report and the book of Joël Brand have confirmed on
all points. These divergencies make the contentions of the Zionist movement so vulnerable, on the whole, that it was on the

deportation of the Hungarian Jews — in the hope of promoting an official truth around which the whole world could be rallied — that the Jerusalem Tribunal was most precise. It is quite obvious, for example, that the five trains a day containing 4,000 or 5,000 persons was a piece of stupidity which absolutely had to be eliminated, because during the 52 days while the deportation of the Hungarian Jews lasted, that number would yield 260 trains and between 1,040,000 and 1,300,000 deportees from a country in which, at the maximum, there were only 800,000 Jews, of whom, moreover, it has been clearly said that 200,000 were not deported[21].

The Court of the Jerusalem Tribunal therefore decided that from May 16 to July 7, 1944, "in less than two months, 434,351 persons were deported in 147 freight trains, at about 3,000 persons per train, men, women, and children, or an average of 2 to 3 trains a day" ("Exhibit 112"); that "12,000 were killed at Kamenetz-Zodolsk during the summer of 1941;" that "45,000 to 50,000 died while working in Galicia and in the Ukraine in 1941-42" ("Exhibit 111"); that "1,500 in the camp at Kistarzca were deported on July 20, 1944," (Exhibit 113"); that "50,000 left Budapest on foot for the Austrian frontier (220 km. away) after November 10th," ("Exhibit 115"); and, finally, that "15,000 [were] sent to Austria to the Vienna-Strasshof camp to be kept in the ice-house," ("Exhibit 116"), on a date given without further detail as "after June 30, 1944." That total accounted for varies between 557,851 and 562,851. "Exhibit 115," which mentions the 50,000 Jews who left Budapest on foot, does not say it, but the *Report* of Dr. Kasztner makes it clear that this march was interrupted on Himmler's orders about the 17th or 18th of November, that 7,500 persons were saved and brought back to Budapest, and that 38,000 only[22] reached Germany. If account is taken of the 200,000 survivors given in the statistics of the *World Center of Contemporary Jewish Documentation*, there must have been, in Hungary, 757,851 or 762,861 Jews in all on March 19, 1944. And, likewise, Mr. Raul Hilberg estimated the number to be about 750,000. But, see how our methods and approaches differ: I draw the conclusion that out of the "800,000 souls in the Hungarian Jewish community," ("Exhibit 111"), there were 40,000 to 50,000 that the Jerusalem Court could not account for. As for Mme. Hannah Arendt, with her maximum of

"476,000 Hungarian victims," (and we shall never know how she got the number) we are struck by the fidelity with which she reports what she sees and hears when she is sent out to write a story. And, we can understand why it is that Mr. Robert W. Kempner has publicly expressed his dissatisfaction with her work. (*Die Aufbau, op. cit.*).

Now we shall take up the whole business in detail:

1. **The number of trains.** We may be richly informed about the arrival of these trains at Auschwitz-Birkenau, but we have much less detail about their departure from Hungary. So I shall begin by saying that to gather together 3,000 persons in a station and load them into 40 cars is not a minor undertaking, and, to make it clear to those who are not specialists in transportation, I know of no better way than to cite from my own experience during the departure, from the camp at Compiègne, of the train in which I was deported to Buchenwald.

Camp Royallieu where we were first assembled could hold about 10,000 persons. Every week, at the end of 1943, about 1,500 arrived, and as many left. The transport in which I was included was composed of 1,500 able-bodied persons and about 50 sick.

Awakened at six in the morning, collected on the parade grounds, grouped in fives, and by fives in hundreds, we finally left the camp a little before eight o'clock with the 15 squads of 100 each in the lead and with a truck following slowly behind that carried those who were sick. A procession of 15 squads of 100 persons, marching five abreast, is long; armed soldiers were stationed at the head and in a single line along the sides; a space of 350 to 400 meters was maintained between each squad; and a special guard followed at the rear of the column.

A little before nine o'clock, we found ourselves lined up along the station platform with each group of 100[23] facing a train car into which it must climb. The train: it was a long line – it seemed immense to us – of freight cars. How many? I did not count. Probably, there was a car for each group (making 15) plus a special car for the 50 sick persons. I noticed that on the roof of every third car were soldiers armed with a machine gun and something else which those of us in my squad decided was a floodlight. At the head and at the rear were two passenger cars in which additional guards travelled to reinforce, if necessary en route, the other guards who were stationed among the cars. In addition, there were freight cars which carried supplies. In all, 25 to 30 cars — 25 at a minimum. And, a train of 25 to 30 cars is very long. Even so, such a train carried fewer than 1,600 prisoners with 100 per car.

A little after 10 o'clock the train seemed to be about ready to depart. No one was left on the platform, we were told by those who could see from the skylights at the head an'. end of the car. Nevertheless, the train did not move. A railwayman explained: a train that is not in the timetables cannot just simply depart; all of the stations along the way have to be notified, and that can only be done at the moment when it is about to start. Another long hour of waiting: a little before noon the train got under way.

In all, our departure took a good half day. And we heard plenty of *"Los!"* and *"Schnell!"* On our arrival at Buchenwald, we were unloaded a little faster; but each car was brought to the platform separately, since the unloading platform was not as long as the train. It took at least two good hours to empty all the cars, so they could go to Weimar.

I do not mean to say that what took place at Budapest was exactly the same as Compiègne, but only that, whether here or there, the job was the same in varying degrees. Everywhere, for example, people had to be collected together, the cars loaded, and so forth; all these things took about the same amount of time no matter where they happened.

From reading the *Kasztner Report* and Joël Brand's book, one gets the impression that there were 200,000 to 250,000 Jews in Budapest, although a more precise estimate, which neither gives, cannot be stated. The organizations of which they were the heads seem, indeed, to have tried to avoid too great a concentration of Jews in the capital and to have tried to spread out over the whole country the 400,000 odd Poles, Czechoslovaks and Yugoslavs who were continually arriving in a steady flow. Where they could not avoid this concentration was in the Hungarian and Rumanian frontier regions which they were all trying to reach, and that is why, except for Budapest, one or two centers for these areas (east of the Theiss) were chosen as assembly points for which trains could leave directly for Auschwitz without going through Budapest. At Budapest itself, the Jews seem to have been first directed to an area fairly far from the station, which Dr. Kasztner and Joël Brand designate with the name "brick-works," and where, although we cannot give an exact figure here either since they do not, it can be guessed that at a maximum it was possible to gather together about 10,000 persons. The official thesis: from there to the station, in columns of 3,000 men, women, children and the aged – and baggage, as mentioned by all the witnesses who claim that the Jews took with them everything they could – they were marched.

In any case, on this or that side of the Theiss, they had to be collected: by trucks or on foot to the nearest station and by rail from the nearest station to the assembling area. Oddly enough, at Budapest it was not the Jews of the city, for the most part Hungarian, who were rounded up at the "brick-works," but those from other regions who were fetched from 100 to 150 kilometers away. The "brick-works," moreover, could not hold more than 10,000 at a time – officially deported in batches of 3,000 who were replaced by a similar number. In short, whether at the "brick-works" of Budapest or elsewhere, railcars had to be assembled, and these cars had to be drawn from the lot of 1,000 which, Kasztner tells us, were at the disposal of Eichmann. The two operations took place at the same time, because, at the assembly points, the Jews being deported could only be replaced by an equal number, so if they had to go as far to collect them as to deport them, each operation would have required an equal number of rail cars. But they were deported 500 to 550 kilometers away, at the most 600, and they went only 100 150 or 200 kilometers away to get them.

Therefore, only two-thirds of the cars could have been used for deporting, very few more. Let us say 700. And, we reason as follows: it took four days to get to Auschwitz, four days to get back, and at least half a day to load and unload the 3,000; consequently, each train could not return empty to its point of departure to be ready to take off again, loaded, until the evening of the ninth day after its initial departure. At the rate of three trains of 40 cars each per day, the system must have bogged down after the sixth day, following the departure of the second train. At the rate of two trains a day, the operation would not be stopped for want of additional cars until the ninth day after the departure of the first train; the evening after the return of the first from Auschwitz, the second could leave again. Moreover, the system was able to function only on condition that it worked like a clock[24].

Indeed, in what he recounted to Willem Sassen, and from whom *Life* (November 28 and December 12, 1960) drew the abominable stuff that was presented to its readers as authentic memoirs, Eichmann said that he only rarely succeeded in getting two trains per day out of Hungary. Is his statement not to be believed because it was to his interest to minimize? Of course, but to judge by the exhibits that were attached to the verdict which was handed down by the Jerusalem judges, his testimony is to be believed no less than that of the prosecution witnesses who, in the opposite sense, plainly did not deprive themselves of dramatizing it beyond all measure.

2. **Number of persons per train.** As with almost all facts from Jewish sources, the Court of the Jerusalem Tribunal is in flagrant disagreement with itself: it tells us, in "Exhibit 112," that the Jews were deported from Hungary at the rate of "about 3,000 per train;" in "Exhibit 127" it states that there were no more than "on an average of 2,000 Jews per train." And, on this point, more than one oversight shows up this contention: it is not clear why — if Eichmann, who was presented as eager to deport the greatest possible number of Jews, was in the habit of crowding together "about 3,000 persons per train" with "70 to 100 persons and even more per car," as is stated in "Exhibits 112 and 154" — he only put 1,500 as "Exhibit 113" states, in the fully laden train to the camp at Kistarzca.

I recall that at Nuremberg Hoess told Professor Gustave Gilbert that the convoys consisted of 1,500 persons, and, at the bar of the Tribunal, that they averaged 2,000 persons. Moreover, in his confession he spoke of "5 trains of 3,000 persons per day" but also that they "never carried more than 1,000 persons." But, Eichmann, still in what he told Sassen, claimed that he deported in all a maximum of 200,000 Jews from Hungary, but he gives no exact details about the numbers for each convoy. He noted the five trains per day that were mentioned by Hoess, and on that occasion he said that he did not often achieve more than two at the most. He noted also the 3,000 per convoy and protested against that figure no less vehemently. But the 2,000 that Hoess spoke about at Nuremberg did not startle him: he only said that it was quite a lot.

My opinion is, on the contrary, that the transportation of 2,000 persons in a single train of forty cars was quite possible.

What is not possible was the transportation of 3,000 persons. How many less, then? Let us think about it a little: it is about 500 kilometers from Budapest to Auschwitz, and the trains took at least four days to cover this distance, at about 124 km per day. There were two reasons for this slow pace: first, they were not scheduled in the timetables — "off the track" as railroad people say — and they had to make long stops all along the way to let the regular trains through; second, the war was on, and during the months of May and June 1944, they were frequently halted by air attacks and were threatened also with partisan attacks. They needed to be protected the whole way by both the stationary forces spread out at regular intervals from one end of the route to the other, and guards who had to travel with them. We have seen that to transport fewer than 1,600 persons in 16 cars from Compiègne to Buchenwald no less than 25 cars were necessary. Out of the 40 cars in a train leaving Hungary, it would very well be that a minimum of 10 were needed to carry more than two dozen people each along with their arms and their supplies for eight days. One hundred and fifty armed men for a convoy of 40 cars would be a minimum. In all that I have read about the deportation of the Hungarian Jews, I have never seen the slightest mention of this aspect of the problem. It is, however, well known that no convoy of that sort was ever sent off *unescorted* on any railway line by the Germans during the war. However resigned the Jews may have been to the fate that was in store for them and however sealed the cars may have been, at a speed of 125 kilometers per day, every unguarded train would have arrived at Auschwitz practically empty. Considering all that they were allowed to take along with them, they surely had whatever was necessary to saw, cut, and tear up all the boards of all the cars. And, that could be done without any risk, if there were no surveillance. But, 147 trains with about 150 guards for surveillance per train means that about 22,050 Hungarian gendarmes must have been employed since Eichmann's *Kommando* had only 150 men. Never anywhere has it been mentioned that S.S. units, the *Wehrmacht* or any other German army or police groups were sent to help him with this job.

I repeat my question: how many Jews? The answer: a maximum of 30 cars, loaded with Jews, per train — 2,400 persons at 80 per car at the most. It is thus only the figure of 80 per car that is questionable. Once again, my personal testimony: I refer to a group of Hungarian Jews whose convoy, originally bound for Auschwitz, had arrived at Dora at the end of May 1944. Of the 1,500 or so people of this convoy, a certain number were sent to satellite camps around Dora as soon as they arrived. How many remained with us, I do not know; maybe they filled an entire block. Because of the racist policies of Nazism, they were to be completely isolated from the other prisoners. That block was surrounded with barbed wire. And from that protected block they went to work like everyone else, but as a separate *Kommando*. For them, assembly took place within the block, before their leaving for work and on their return. We envied them. Fifteen days after their arrival, if your clogs had been stolen in the night, if you wanted more bread, or if you required some tobacco or something else, you had only to make a quick dash to the Jewish block in the morning between reveille and roll-call, or in the evening before lights out, and, in exchange for something else, you could get just about anything you wanted: it was a regular market. We admired them; at the gate of the camp they had been made to undress completely, and had been sent to be disinfected; they went in completely naked, their contact with other prisoners was limited, and, all the same, they had succeeded in procuring a little of everything that could be gotten in the camp only with the greatest difficulties and at a very high price.

After a little while, the special surveillance over them became hardly more than a facade: once in a while we could exchange a few words with them, and even have short conversations. Thus it was that we learned about their odyssey. They told us about what they had had to leave behind when they came into the camp[25], and, since we were old hands in their eyes, they asked if they would get it back, when, how, and so on . . . They had been transported from Hungary to Dora, 70 to 80 persons in a car, with all of their baggage. They had made a long periplus of six to seven days before arriving. They had been told when leaving that they were being taken to Auschwitz, and when they learned that it was at Dora that they would be unloaded, they were pleased. They told the most appalling things about Auschwitz. There were neither women nor children among them. The latter had been separated out on departure, and at the moment it did not surprise us since that is what happened to us.

From my personal observation, I have come to the following conclusion: the "70 to 100 persons and even more per car" of which "Exhibit 154" of the Jerusalem Court speaks, meant an average of 80 per car, the dividing up of the Jews having taken place in the cars or on the platform of the departure station on the basis of what they were carrying with them: more in one and fewer in another. With those "3,000 or so persons per train" we have, assuming that all the cars were occupied by Jewish deportees, an average of 75 per car, a fact to which "Exhibit 112" attests.

Not all the trains, however, had the same complement of Jews: the one destined for Kistarzca, which is mentioned in "Exhibit 113," was officially carrying only 1,500. It was probably also a train of 40 cars, with ten or so for surveillance and security, like all the others, or about 50 per car on the average . . . What is probable on the whole is that the human cargo, in reality, lay between the minimum of 1,500 indicated by Hoess, and the possible maximum of 2,400. So that the average of 75 per car of "Exhibit 112" could be the general average, about 2,200 per train. In any case, that figure is plausible.

If it is true, as it is claimed, that Eichmann managed to deport about 200,000 Hungarian Jews in all, then this figure assumes that 32,000 Jews were deported on foot, and that the remaining 168,000 were deported by rail. About 77 trains would have been required during the 52 days that the deportation of Hungarian Jews lasted. This thesis — in addition to supporting the 200,000 deportee figure — has the advantage of being within the realm of technical possibility — the very limit of what is possible with 1,000 cars. Since Eichmann said that he only rarely succeeded in getting two trains off per day, one could think that this is only the impression of a zealous employee who did not achieve the objective set him and who exaggerates his failure even to himself: 77 trains in 52 days, is still two trains per day, every other day. And, under the circumstances it was a fifty per cent success.

3. General Schedule of the Deportation of the Jews in Hungary:

March 19, 1944:	800,000 Jews
End of November 1944, deported:	200,000 Jews
Not deported:	600,000 Jews
"Exhibit 111" of Jerusalem Trial refers to 57,000[26] dead in Hungary, and no others are found in the Judgment:	57,000 Jews
Survivors among those not deported:	543,000 Jews

The official statistics of the *World Center of Contemporary Jewish Documentation* mention only 200,000 survivors in 1945; the other 343,000, who were alive and who were without any doubt not all Hungarian, are listed in the statistics of those dead either in Hungary or in the other countries from whence they came. For those people not listed anywhere in any statistics of the living in Europe, and who are therefore not in Europe — officially at least — we had arrived at a total figure of 3,708,960, at the end of our study of the Czechoslovakian Jewish population. Hence, we now add the Hungarian Jews: 3,708,960 plus 343,000 gives us **4,051,960** who are living elsewhere — with their offspring since 1945 — if they are not in Europe. And of course we should add, as everywhere all those who returned alive from deportation, and are themselves in the same case.

Closely bound to Hungary is Yugoslavia, because of the stream of Jews who came from there, and Rumania, to which they were going. Yugoslavia herself is bound to Italy through the Jews who fled there.

Yugoslavia: we have seen that the *World Center of Contemporary Jewish Documentation* said there were 75,000 Jews there in 1939, of which only 20,000 were found still living in 1945. In April 1941 Yugoslavia was invaded by German troops and was cut into a number of pieces. Two states were created by the diplomacy of the Rome-Berlin Axis: Croatia was declared independent, and Serbia remained under German occupation. Italy received, besides Slovenia which she occupied, a large part of Croatia, where she systematically counteracted the anti-Jewish policy of the Pavlevich government, which was more Hitlerian than Mussolinian. Toward the East, the region of the upper Vardar, with Skoplje and Monastir, was handed over to Bulgaria. Within this puzzle, this is how the Jerusalem Tribunal ("Exhibits 105 and 106") divided up the Yugoslavian Jews: 30,000 in Croatia and 47,000 in Serbia, or a total of 77,000. No comment: we are accustomed to discrepancies in the Jewish sources. Another discrepancy: the Court of the Jerusalem Tribunal found that, according to "Exhibits 105 and 106," in 1945 there were still living only 1,500 Jews in Croatia and 5,000 in Serbia for a total of 6,500. From the preceding it would appear that the entire Jewish population of Slovenia, where — because of the proximity of Trieste — it has always been dense, must have fled into Croatia and into Serbia in order to be either closer to the Germans or right under their fist. After all, the Tribunal apparently found none there in 1945. In addition, it would seem that — according to the Tribunal — not one went to Hungary, where Dr. Kasztner found quite a large number of them, enough to note them in his *Report*. One might even be tempted to believe that 2,000 (the number that the Jerusalem Court found in excess of that number that was noted by the *World Center of Contemporary Jewish Documentation*) came from areas where there were no dangers, in order to be more certain of being exterminated. It has often been commented that the European Jews accepted their fate with great resignation; from the way the Jerusalem Tribunal told it, the Yugoslavian Jews were not only resigned, they were masochists.

Until the Jerusalem trial, Yugoslavia presented an enigma: an official spokesman of the *World Center of Contemporary Jewish Documentation*, Mr. Poliakov, explained to us (in *Bréviaire de la Haine* and *le Troisième Reich et les Juifs*) that in Yugoslavia "the Jews took refuge by the thousands;" that in Croatia where Krumey had arrived on October 16, 1943, he did not succeed in deporting more Jews than did his colleague Alois Brunner, who managed to send 10,000 from Nice to the concentration camps[27]; and that after the *coup d'etat* of Badoglio (September 1943) the Jews had followed the Italian troops as they left Croatia. All this does not sit very well, as we see, with "Exhibits 105 and 106" of the Jerusalem judgment. They are in complete contradiction, in any case, both with the way the Jews were divided up among the various zones after the dismemberment, and with the number of deportees in Croatia, which "Exhibit 105" tells us numbered 28,500, all charged to Krumey except for 2,800.

Mr. Poliakov was just about mute on the subject of Serbia as to details: with the stamp of approval of the *World Center of Contemporary Jewish Documentation*, he declared, "No deportations in Serbia, all the Jews exterminated right there." He limited himself to stating that there were 20,000 survivors and 55,000 exterminated for the whole of Yugoslavia (*Bréviaire de la Haine*, p. 180). In order to get more precise details, other writers had to be turned to: Michel Borwicz, Joseph Billig, and others . . . But, unfortunately, in making a total out of all the details picked up, a figure of 30,000 was barely reached. And, hence, I came to the conclusion that the estimates of Mr. Poliakov were without any basis, and therefore pure fantasy. On the other hand, the figure of 30,000 could be supported by plausible proofs. However, Mr. Poliakov was surely correct concerning the Jews in Croatia, and so it was the Jews of Serbia who had paid the heaviest toll in deportation and death. Furthermore, it was logical: the Germans had been hunting them down since 1941, and even if they did not deport them until 1942 they were all set to, the minute the order was given.

By following the events in the order in which they took place, another discovery was made: the statistics drawn up at the end of 1941 for the Wannsee Conference by Mr. Richard Korherr — therefore before deportation steps were taken in Yugoslavia[28] — mentioned 40,000 Jews at that time in the whole of Yugoslavia. One could only conclude that 75,000 minus 40,000 or 35,000 had fled to Hungary and Italy since they were no longer there and had not been arrested. And, if we deduce that it was out of those 40,000 that the 30,000 or so mentioned as having been arrested had been taken, it is logical. And, in Serbia — since, with the exception of about 10,000 — the Croats had followed the retreating Italian troops since September 1943; that is logical, too.

The *World Center of Contemporary Jewish Documentation*, then, had no factual basis for putting more than 30,000 Jews in the column of the exterminated — assuming that they all were, after having been arrested — in their statistics. They placed the number at 55,000, or 25,000 too many. Given the fact that the number of Yugoslavian Jews who were arrested and who are dead, beyond the justified figure of 30,000, has already been

included in the results of the calculations on the Hungarian
Jews and that the remainder will be included in the calculations
which will be made for Italy, it can be said that here are another
25,000 living European Jews to add to the 4,051,960 Jews who
we found to be living at the end of the study of the Hungarian
Jewish population: Thus, the total now amounts to **4,076,960**.

Italy: Mr. Arthur Ruppin says there were 50,000 Jews there
in 1926, and the *World Center of Contemporary Jewish Documentation* gives 57,000 for 1939. The latter figure is very possible: figuring a natural rate of increase of thirteen per cent, we
get 56,500. Let us accept 57,000. We have, however, to add the
16,500 Yugoslavian Jews who fled there, so we have 73,500.
In 1945 the *World Center of Contemporary Jewish Documentation* found 15,000 deportees exterminated and 42,000 living.
Logically the *Center* should have found 58,500 survivors, and
the overstatement on the number of deaths should have been
16,500. Actually, the overstatement of deaths was even more
significant since even Mr. Rolf Hochhuth, who recently distinguished himself with that fraudulent writing on the theme of
the Gerstein Document, *Der Stellvertreter*, found only 8,000
Jews arrested and deported in Italy and since the judges at Jerusalem found only "7,500 deportees of whom no more than 600
survived" ("Exhibit 109"), or 6,900 exterminated. In this case,
the number of survivors should be 73,500 minus 6,900 or
66,600. And, the overstatement of the *World Center of Contemporary Jewish Documentation* is 66,000 minus 42,000 or
24,600. To be added to the total of 4,076,960, whom we
found to be still living after we completed the study of the
Yugoslavian Jewish population and who are no longer − at
least, officially − in Europe, is this 24,600 which yields
4,101,560.

Rumania: Mr. Arthur Ruppin counted 900,000 Jews in
1926, and the *World Center of Contemporary Jewish Documentation* found no more than 850,000 in 1939 (a figure with
which the *Institute of Jewish Affairs* agrees, but for which Mr.
Raul Hilberg gives only 800,000). There is nothing unusual in
that since the Jewish population has always emigrated from
Rumania in large numbers. Concerning the number of deportees exterminated and the number of survivors, the *World
Center* says half and half, the *Institute* agrees except for 5,000
each, and Hilberg is, naturally, in total disagreement; there

were 380,000 survivors and 420,000 exterminated, he says. Another thing that points up how conscientious all these people are: the writer of the statistics for the *World Center of Contemporary Jewish Documentation* is, as we know, Mr. Poliakov, and, commenting on the figures of his own statistics (*Bréviaire de la Haine,* p. 186), he tells us that in 1939 there were 700,000 Jews in Rumania, and in 1945 only 250,000 (*op. cit.* p. 188). "Exhibit 110" of the Jerusalem Court summing up the story of the Rumanian Jews is very prudent: "In this way about half of Rumanian Judaism was saved from extermination," it states, basing its decision on the written deposition of Dr. Safran, Chief Rabbi of Rumania, but without any reference to what that deposition contained.

For the rest, if the one who drew up that document was attempting to show that no Rumanian Jew had ever been deported by the Germans, he could not have succeeded better. In fact, only one deportation project for 200,000 Jews is cited, decided upon for the first time on July 26, 1942, to start on the following 16th of September; it was discussed a second time on September 17th; then on the 26th and the 28th of September, the Germans and the Rumanians finally reached agreement on the details of the project. But on the 22nd of October, when the deportations were not yet under way, the Rumanian government changed its mind and told the Germans that it would take charge of the Jewish problem in Rumania by itself.

Until then, the German policy had been precisely that the Rumanians should themselves take charge of their own Jews, and the whole of the diplomatic correspondence between the two governments attests to the fact that the Rumanians had not ceased proposing to the Germans that they turn the Jews over to them, but without success; the Germans did not want them. And, when the time came when they did want them, the Rumanians no longer were willing to turn them over.

The Chief Rabbi of Rumania claims in his deposition — at least according to the writers of the press reports of the Jerusalem Trial — that until August 1942 the Rumanians, who did not succeed in getting their Jews accepted by the Germans, exterminated them. He cited massacres of Odessa Jews by the Rumanian army (60,000 victims), pogroms at Bucharest, Ploesti, Jassy, Constanza, and "victims by the tens of thousands," but he gave no other details. On the whole he estimated that from February 1941 to August 1942 ("250,000 to 300,000 Jews were exterminated" by the Rumanians and *not* by the Germans.

This idea is highly contestable. At Paris during the same period, everyone with whom I was associated and who was familiar with the system of escape lines for European Jews during the war knew — from the Jews themselves, with whom they were in contact — that in Rumania, although the government did not show any particular sympathy, they were at least given tourist passports for a fee of $1,000 each with which they could move on. The Chief Rabbi affirms that it was only after October 1942 that this policy was put into practice. This date corresponds precisely with the change of policy of the Antonescu government which, suddenly, after having for so long begged the Germans to take the Jews that they wanted to turn over to them, refused to do so when the Germans were ready to accept. Mme. Hannah Arendt echoes this fact (The *New Yorker,* March 16, 1963). The information that we in Paris had about this was out of line in only one detail: the price for the passport was, it seems, not $1,000, but $1,300.

This contention that half of Rumanian Judaism (or 425,000 out of 850,000) was exterminated due to the deportation by the Germans reveals a difference between "250,000 to 300,000" and 425,000 of some 125,000 to 175,000 Rumanian Jews. It is most questionable for another reason too: the territorial changes that were made in Rumania between 1939 and 1945.

In August 1939, the Russo-German Pact forced Rumania to pay a heavy tribute to the contractants and to their allies, namely to turn over northern Bukovina and Bessarabia to the USSR (June 1940); a significant part of Transylvania to Hungary; and Dobroudja to Bulgaria (August 1940). The movement of the Jewish populations from these areas, when the transfers took place, has never been studied, to my knowledge. The generally held contention is that they stayed where they were or that few moved away. There were, moreover, agreements about moving people which were not all settled when the German-Russian conflict began in June 1941. I refer those readers who are interested in these agreements to the excellent work of the *National Institute of Statistics and Economics* of Paris, which came out in 1946, (*Presses Universitaires de France*), with the title, *Les Transferts Internationaux des populations.*

Naturally, Rumania had been waiting since 1940 for a chance, as the relations between Germany and Russia deteriorated, to get back the territories which she had lost, particularly Bessarabia which was more likely than others to be obtained. In June, 1941, she went into the war against Russia on the side of the Axis, and as a result, she got back not only Bessarabia but was also given an occupation zone which was called Transnistria and which extended out from the 1939 frontier and from the Dniester to the Bug. Germany took for herself the zone beyond, from the Bug to the Dnieper.

Naturally, too, in evacuating Bukovina and Bessarabia, the Russians also evacuated as much of the population as possible, which, of course, was fleeing in all directions before the German troops. At any rate, from the 11th to the 21st of December 1943, the International Red Cross sent one of its delegates, Mr. Charles Kolb, to Rumania. He stayed there from December 11, 1943, to January 14, 1944. On his return he drew up a report in which he noted that 206,700 Jews were missing in Bessarabia-Transnistria, and 88,600 in Bukovina. Otherwise, he observed nothing abnormal. From this report it is possible to assume that all of these 295,300 Rumanian Jews, now Russian, who found themselves on the Russian lines, had fled before the German troops just as their Polish co-religionists did in 1939 and were saved from deportation at the hands of the Germans. One can assume it, but it cannot be stated with certainty. In any case, Mr. Poliakov, who cites this report (*Bréviaire de la Haine*, p. 371) concedes "that just before the German attack, a portion of the Jewish population may have been evacuated by the Russians." Anyway, since this report was based on investigations made in 1943-1944, at a time when the Jews were no longer in any danger in Rumania, and since he does not record one missing elsewhere, it can be assumed with certainty that at that date 800,000 minus 295,300 or 504,700, were still living, and were neither arrested, deported, nor massacred afterwards. One can assume this with all the more assurance since it is more or less supported by "Exhibit 119" of the Jerusalem court, which mentions no deportation of Rumanian Jews by the Germans; even if it had, such a deportation could only have taken place before October 22, 1942, which is to say that it could not have taken place, since until then, the Germans had consistently refused to give in to the pleas of the Rumanian government to take its Jewish population.

It is an odd coincidence that these 295,300 Jews, which Mr.
Charles Kolb said were not in Rumania, are numerically within
the limits of the "295,000 to 300,000" claimed by the Chief
Rabbi to have been exterminated by the Rumanians. One is led
to the thought that they are the same, and that in order to hang
Antonescu, the Russians who saved them claimed he had exterminated them.

As for Mr. Raul Hilberg, he is even more subtle. After having
examined the misdeeds of the *Einsatzgruppen* in Russia and
after having integrated into the statistics on Russia the Jews
they allegedly exterminated in cities such as Odessa, Chisinau
and Cernauti, he counts those who were missing in Transnistria,
which is where Odessa was between 1941 and 1944 and in
Bukovina where the other two were, by putting them in with
the statistics for Rumania (p. 485-509); that is, he counts them
twice.

Conclusion on Rumania: in order to know exactly how
many Jews should be reported as missing in 1945, we should
know just as exactly how many of the 295,300, counted as
missing by Mr. Charles Kolb at the end of December and the
beginning of January 1944, were evacuated by the Russians,
and how many remained under the yoke of the Germans or
Rumanians. However, we do not know this. We should also
know how many emigrated, and there must have been quite a
number because of all Jews the Rumanian Jews were in the best
position, having the least distance to go, with the least effort, to
get out of Europe. But, if the Russians had saved half of those
counted as missing by Mr. Charles Kolb, and if the other half,
fallen into the hands of the Rumanians, had been massacred in
the pogroms in Odessa, Bucharest, Ploesti, Constanza, and other
places, the Rumanian Jewish population of 1939 might be ap-
portioned as follows:

a. massacred:		147,650
b. saved by the Russians:		147,650
c. emigrated, or found living in 1945		
(800,000 - 295,300):		504,700
d. total number of survivors:		652,350
e. officially found still living by the		
World Center of Contemporary		
Jewish Documentation:		425,000
f. overstatement of those exterminated:		227,350

These 227,350, although still living in 1945, have been improperly added to the column of exterminated by the *World Center of Contemporary Jewish Documentation*. Consequently, we have 227,350 more European Jews to be added to the 4,101,560, in the same situation, who were found at the end of our study of the Italian Jewish population. At this point of our work, the total should read: **4,328,901**.

Bulgaria: The statistics which appear on page 300 mention that the Jewish population of Bulgaria in 1939 was 50,000. And, the *World Center of Contemporary Jewish Documentation* has accepted this figure as representing the pre-war Jewish population. The World Center claims that 7,000 Bulgarian Jews were exterminated during the war. Mr. Raul Hilberg found only some 3,000 missing, and "Exhibit No. 108" of the Jerusalem Tribunal mentions 4,000 deportees from Thrace and 7,000 from Macedonia, for a total of 11,000, but nothing is said about losses. This claim of 11,000 deportees is not supported by any exact facts; it is not known when they were deported or where they were sent. As for Mr. Poliakov, commenting upon the World Center figures of which he is the author, he cannot even cite them correctly: he claimed some 13,000 deportees out of a total Jewish population of 20,000. In addition, he says nothing about survivors. Returning to the statistics of the World Center, there is no problem in determining the number of survivors: 50,000 Jews in 1939 less 7,000 of them who were exterminated leaves a total of 43,000. Giving the World Center the benefit of the doubt and accepting its estimation of losses, there is no exaggeration of casualties to be added to the total that was found at the end of our study of Rumania.

Greece: At one time the official statistics took separate note of Macedonia where some 7,000 Jews were supposedly deported, but there was no mention of how many were there in 1939. Since then, this particular contention has disappeared from the official statistics, and Greece alone remains with 75,000 in 1939, with 60,000 deportees exterminated in 1945, and, therefore, with 15,000 survivors. Mr. Raul Hilberg gives the following figures: 74,000 in 1939, 62,000 exterminated, and 12,000 survivors. "Exhibit 107" of the Jerusalem Tribunal mentions 80,000 in 1939, 70,000 exterminated and 10,000 survivors. Finally, Mr. Arthur Ruppin had already taken a census of 75,000 Jews in Greece in 1926. Could Jewish emigration equal the natural rate of increase? It is possible.

Greece was divided into two zones of occupation: to the north were the Germans, who had their general headquarters in Salonika; to the south were the Italians who had theirs at Athens. The Jews were proportioned like this: 55,000 to to 60,000 persons concentrated around Salonika in the German zone and 15,000 to 20,000 in the Italian zone concentrated around Athens. All the Jewish sources are in agreement in saying that the Germans did not do anything about the Greek Jews until July 1942 when they made them wear the yellow star and this only in the German zone. In the Italian zone, nothing changed. It was only in February 1943 that the policy of collecting them into the ghettos of Salonika and the surrounding areas began. These steps were taken by Dr. Max Merten – administrator of the zone, with the help of two men sent from the R.S.H.A., Wisliceny and Günther – from the 15th of January 1943 on. Mr. Poliakov claims (*op. cit.* p. 182) that the first deportation began on March 15, 1943, and ended on May 9th; 43,000 Jews in convoys were deported to Auschwitz (with 2,700 persons per convoy, one convoy every 3 or 4 days, means that here, where the Jews were massed, the work of deportation did not go on as fast as in Hungary where the ungrouped Jews were allegedly deported at the rate of 2 to 3 convoys of 3,000 per day). The remainder, or at least about 12,000, were deported from July to August 1943 in three convoys. At that rate, there must have been about 4,000 persons per convoy at the least. The trip from Salonika to Auschwitz lasted an average of 10 days, and, as Mr. Poliakov claims, on arrival the Jews were sent directly in a group to the gas chamber, without any prior selecting out of the able-bodied since they were in so bad a state. This is, in fact, what Wisliceny, taking the theme from Hoess, commandant of the camp, claimed at Nuremberg, but Hoess did not confirm it! "Exhibit 107" of the Jerusalem Tribunal is not in agreement with this aspect of the deportation of Greek Jews: "The 56,000 Jews of the Salonika region were all deported from March 15th to the end of May 1943," it says; therefore, there were no convoys in July-August, but it does not state precisely the number of convoys nor the number of persons per convoy. The attorney, Max Merten (who was sentenced to 25 years in prison in 1946, but set at liberty almost at once, and who was a witness for the defense at the Jerusalem Trial) claimed that thanks to Eichmann, and in spite of Wisliceny's efforts to thwart him, about 20,000 Jews escaped deportation.

Furthermore, he claimed that between the time that they were forced to wear the yellow star (July 1942), and the beginning of their concentration into ghettos (February 1943), many Jews in the German Zone went over into the Italian zone. He added that, since he was not in harmony with the deportaion measures envisaged because the Jews were giving him no trouble, he not only saw no objection but he even helped their flight as much as he could without attracting the attention of Wisliceny and Günther. That is why, after having been sentenced to 25 years in prison, he was freed almost immediately.

In the Italian zone, the Jews were not alarmed until after Badoglio's *coup d' etat* in September 1943. Then, deportation operations were assigned to Wisliceny and Günther. Before the Bratislava Tribunal which sentenced him to death, the former claimed (June 27, 1947) in a written deposition that 8,000 to 10,000 of the Jews in that zone had been deported. For the city of Athens, according to "Exhibit 107" of the Jerusalem Court, "a large number were nevertheless warned in time to hide themselves and to flee, so that no more than 12,000 remained." So all the others had to be looked for and gathered together in the first place. In order to deport 8,000 to 10,000 Wisliceny had to apply himself in earnest, and we see that he did not try to mitigate his guilt. Let us accept the figure and reason thusly: we do not know how many Jews succeeded in passing from the German into the Italian zone, but we do know that those in the former zone were deported in 19 convoys, and that after that there were no more. At an average of 2,200 per train of 40 cars, an estimation that was established and used in our calculations for Hungary, we come to a total of 41,800. This means that there were 14,200 who had fled into the Italian zone, figured by subtracting 41,800 from 56,000 (the figure given by the Jerusalem Court for the number deported from the German zone). Consequently, the Jewish population of that zone should have been 33,200 figured by subtracting 56,000 from 75,000 and adding 14,200 to the remainder. If Wisliceny did deport 8,000 to 10,000, there must have been left over 33,200 minus 8,000 to 10,000, or 23,200 to 25,200 survivors for the whole of Greece.

Therefore, the *minimum* overstatement of the *World Center of Contemporary Jewish Documentation* is 10,200. (This figure allows for the 15,000 Jews who were already in the Italian zone.) And, that only on condition that the 19 trains really did leave Salonika, each carrying about 2,200 persons, which is possible, but not likely. By adding this 10,200 to the total at the end of the study of the Rumanian Jewish population, we get **4,339,110.**

The following countries remain to be looked into: Germany, Austria, Denmark, and Norway.

Germany was already mentioned in connection with the Jewish population of Holland, Belgium, Luxemburg, and France. It will be remembered that at the time of the invasion of France by German troops, figures from Jewish sources showed that there were 252,000 foreign Jews in France whose nationality it was impossible to determine, except to say that outside of the thirty or, at the most, forty or so thousand who were German, the rest were all Polish. By looking only at the European survivors, there was no objection in stating that they were all Polish (or all German) because they could not be allotted. But now we must take into account the fact that 40,000 German Jews were already counted, unless we want to count them twice.

So, in 1939, this was the structure of the German Jewish population: 210,000 remained in Germany because 300,000 out of 510,000 emigrated, according to the *World Center of Contemporary Jewish Documentation.* Mr. Raul Hilberg says: 240,000 remained in Germany and 300,000 out of 540,000 emigrated. Taking account of the natural rate of increase this ought to be closer to the truth, but there is another factor to be considered: from 1926 to 1933, Mr. Poliakov tells us (*Bréviaire de la Haine*, p. 11) that the demographic curve of Jewish communities, worried about their fate in the face of the rise of Hitlerism, was on the decline. Therefore, let us say that there were 210,000 Jews in Germany in 1939. Officially only 40,000 should have been found still living in 1945, which would mean that 170,000 were exterminated.

To the support of the details which he brings forth to justify these 170,000 exterminated and these 40,000 survivors, Mr. Poliakov refers to the statistics compiled at Himmler's request, on April 17, 1943, for the date of December 31, 1942, which he speaks of as having been "prepared with great competence" (*Bréviaire de la Haine,* pp. 383-384). I am of this opinion: the German demographer Korherr seems to have been a competent man and that is why I, too, have come to refer to his data; however, he has a troublesome tendency to see a few too many Jews everywhere. But, except for this, if I accept the picture of German Judaism as he saw it for December 31, 1942, I really do not see how Mr. Poliakov, who also accepts it, has been able to draw from it the conclusions he does. This is what we find in the recapitulative table about the German Jews:

Arrested up to December 31, 1942:	100,516
Not yet arrested:	51,327
Total:	151,843

It is true that this total is shown as concerning the "former *Reich* and the Sudentenland," but that is without significance: on May 17, 1937, there were only 2,649 Jews in the Sudentenland, the rest having fled to Bohemia-Moravia, then to Hungary, or elsewhere. Except for about a thousand, the figure pertains only to Germany. I repeat: Mr. Poliakov accepts these figures. But if there were only 151,843 in Germany on December 31, 1942, (free or in concentration camps) and if they had been able to arrest in all only 100,516, then 210,000 minus 151,843 or 58,157 had been able to emigrate after 1939. That also means that after December 31, 1942, it had not been possible to arrest more than 51,327. The following July 1st, it was finished: the law declaring Germany *"Juden frei"* (free of Jews) was promulgated, and Mr. Poliakov tells us, "not a single Jew remained at liberty except those married to Aryans," (p. 68) and these, Mr. Richard Korherr tells us in his report, numbered 16,760. We know that later they were in their turn arrested and deported — officially, at least.

Now let us correct the error which we deliberately made, when the problem had to be solved by the elementary process of the false supposition, in stating that the 40,000 European Jews who were found living in Holland, France, Belgium, and Luxemburg were Polish, although we knew that they were not. It is among the 58,157 Jews who left Germany after 1939 and before December 31, 1943, that they are to be found, and they were included in the study of the Polish Jewish population. If we do not want to have them counted twice, they must be withdrawn from the number of German emigrants, and we must only count among the number of the latter: 58,157 minus 40,000, or 18,157.

Next, we can figure the maximum number of German Jews who were arrested and who were deported and never came back. If out of the 151,843, the *World Center of Contemporary Documentation* found 40,000 survivors in 1945, then that means that 151,843 minus 40,000, or, 111,843 never returned, or had not returned by 1945. And, since the *World Center* shows 170,000 Jews in the column of the exterminated, that figure is an overstatement of some 58,157. Consequently, the total number of German Jews who were considered dead, who are no longer officially in Germany, nor in Europe, but who are alive, and who should be included in the column of the living in other countries and in other continents is 76,314. The addition of this 76,314 to the total at the end of the study of the Greek Jewish population gives us 4,415,424, who must be added to the survivor column.

I hope that I shall be excused for having considered the German Jews without any reference to the Jerusalem Trial: Exhibits 56, 57, 75, 77, 83, 90 and 91, which provide the calculations, barely account for 10 to 15 thousand who were allegedly arrested and deported. It would be ridiculous even to take them into consideration[29].

Austria: for 1939 the *World Center of Contemporary Jewish Documentation* speaks of 60,000 Jews as still being there (with this figure based on an emigration of 180,000 after Hitler came to power in Germany, out of 240,000) and of 20,000 survivors in 1945, or 40,000 exterminated. Mr. Arthur Ruppin counted 230,000 Austrian Jews in 1926 − the same situation as for the German Jews in relation to the demographic curve and the natural increase.

The Zionist writing concerning the drama of the Austrian Jews is not very abundant. The Austrian Jews were also neglected by the Jerusalem Tribunal. Studied together with the Jews of Germany and Bohemia-Moravia, and in the same Exhibits, this Tribunal said that there were 5,000 arrests and deportations on October 15, 1941, and 3,000 more on the 25th and 28th of November and December 2nd of the same year. In 1943-1944, the *Kasztner Report* and Joël Brand take note of a clandestine Jewish community, relatively little disturbed. They do not give the number of individuals in this community, but, judging by the way in which it is referred to, it must have been significant. "Exhibit 97" of the Jerusalem Court mentions that, in Austria, arrests and deportations were not within the competence of the R.S.H.A. as everywhere else, but of the *Jewish Emigration Center*, which was set up in Vienna in 1938 by Eichmann and which existed throughout the war. That certainly explains why they were tracked and persecuted less zealously and with less brutality. Dated December 31, 1942, the statistics of Mr. Korherr say that in all 47,655 Jews were arrested and that 8,102 remained at liberty. As a total, and all during the war, then, there were 55,757 Jews in Austria, which means that there were only 4,243 emigres after 1939. That also means that if only 20,000 out of these 55,757 Jews were found living in 1945, the overstatement of the *World Center of Contemporary Jewish Documentation* would only amount to those 4,243 who emigrated after 1939, but who are incorrectly listed as dead. I emphasize: if only 20,000 were found still living. However, I have already shown that the balance of Jewish losses was determined between May and October 1945 — Mr. Poliakov says it is dated August (*Le Troisième Reich et les Juifs*, p. 196) — in order to be available to Justice Jackson in time, and, in the jungle of displaced persons which central Europe was then, many Jews who had been deported and who were living had not gotten back to their former domiciles in time to be counted. All these were accounted for as dead, and since then, if they have been found still living in their domiciles or elsewhere (many never went back), no corrections were ever made in the statistics.

My conclusions for Austria are that 4,243 European Jews *surely* must be reintegrated into the column of living in the statistics for 1945, and must be added to the preceding total, giving a new total of **4,419,667**.

And, to finish up, we shall examine **Denmark and Norway:** There were 7,000 Jews in Denmark and 1,500 in Norway in 1939, according to the *World Center of Contemporary Jewish Documentation*, or a total of 8,500 for the two countries. The same source gives the total number of exterminated as being 500 in Denmark (since in the days just before the day fixed for their arrest, the Danish government, which knew about it, forwarned the national Jewish community), and 900 in Norway for a total of 1,400. The Jerusalem Court gives the losses down to the last person: 737 in Norway and 422 in Denmark, or, 1,159.

The exaggeration of the *World Center of Contemporary Jewish Documentation* is 241. This exaggeration can be attributed to rounding out the figures, and is not intentional. But still it must be added to the preceding total, of which it can be said (with the exception of the 480,000 German and Austrian Jews who emigrated before 1939 and who were accounted for and considered living in 1945) that it is the general total of European Jews *improperly* inscribed in the column of exterminated in the statistics of the *World Center of Contemporary Jewish Documentation:* 4,419,667 plus 241, or, **4,419,908**.

FOOTNOTES

[1] *Die Welt* does not say so, but these estimates are taken from a study which was put out a few days before by the *Jewish Communities of the World*, official organ of the World Jewish Congress. They were published by the *Jerusalem Post Weekly* on April 19, 1963, and after that on various dates by the entire world press. It may be pointed out that for the year 1962, the *World Almanac* of 1963 (p. 259) gives the world Jewish population as 12,296,180. In other words, compared to 1959, not only did the world Jewish population not increase, it decreased.

[2] Arthur Ruppin was in charge of the course in Jewish Sociology at the Hebrew University of Jerusalem. His major work, *Les Juifs dans le Monde moderne*, from which the *Menorah Journal* got its figures, was not published in France until 1934.

[3] Actually in the above statistics, the World Center for Contemporary Jewish Documentation had question marks in place of losses for Bulgaria, and had omitted Luxemburg. It was only later that exact information concerning these two countries were given officially, and I was not able to take them into account in *Ulysse trahi par les siens*.

[4] They are derived from the statistics on page 670 of his book, but on page 767, they are given as 5,100,000, as has already been noted.

[5] In that version of the genealogy of peoples, the Arabs, who are also descended from Noah — like everyone in the world, to be sure! — but via the relations of Abraham with Agar, servant of his wife Sarah, are considered the illegitimate branch, and we who are only descended from Japhet, as well as those descended from Chanaan, cursed by the Old Man, are considered only as side branches, the last of the line of descendants, degenerated, and in addition forever discredited for having fallen into the heresies. That is the basic justification for the qualification "chosen people," as Israel claims — thank you, no for us! — and this is taught as an historical truth in all Hebrew universities on the threshold of the 21st century!

[6.] [The precise figure which is cited in *Religious Bodies*, Vol. II, Part 1 (Washington, D.C.: U.S. Government Printing Office, 1941) for the American Jewish population in 1926 is 4,081,242 persons.]

[7] Before this date, the Visigoth King Siebrut had chased them out of Spain (613) along with all who were of oriental origin, and King Dagobert of France (629), had done the same, but these banishments were of short duration.

[8] They were banished and forced out of England in 1220, from France in 1394, from Spain in 1492.

[9] The *Jerusalem Post Weekly* (April 19, 1963) gives 2.3 million. On the

other hand, in his book, *Le Peuple et l'Etat d'Israel,* Mr. Ben Gurion gives 2 million for 1958 (p. 66). If there were only 2.045 or 2.05 million in 1962, it shows that not only was the normal population increase of 1 per cent per year not reached in Israel, but also that immigration had been halted. Perhaps one could even speak of emigration.

10.[Here, Professor Rassinier takes the rate of natural population increase of one per cent per year and computes the entire increase over the given term in a single calculation (e.g., the sum of 174,610 is multiplied by 31 per cent to yield the natural growth over a period of thirty-one years). This method is used throughout the entire study. Although this simplified method produces adequate approximations, the estimation of the natural population growth would be more precise if the one per cent increase for each year were added to the figure for the preceding year with one per cent then taken of the new total, with the procedure being repeated for each year of the given term. For example, the natural growth from 1931 to 1962, as figured in item "a" is 63,091 (or an increase of about 36 per cent) when the latter method is used. Likewise, a natural increase of 101,249 (or 16 per cent) is achieved instead of 94,350 for item "b." Because it is felt that Professor Rassinier's "shorthand" method of calculating population growth resulted in approximations which are of sufficient accuracy for the purpose of this study, his calculations have not been changed.]

11 If the figuring were done on the basis of the natural increase rate of 1.25% (or 20% every 16 years) of Professor Shalom Baron, the global increase for the period of 1931-1962 would be carried to 523,308 individuals, or an increase of 92,046, and the number of immigrants actually living in the country diminished by as much, or 1,444,128 minus 92,046 equal 1,352,082.

12 In a work intended for students of the college for Higher Economic Studies (*Principles et tendances de la planification rurale en Israel*, Paris, (1963) Professor Albert Meister claims that "one immigrant out of ten in Israel (or 10%) would return into the Diaspora" after a brief sojourn.

13 When the airplanes in many trips brought them back to the Promised Land, which they no longer hoped to see, and whose location most of them no longer knew, as Leon Uris just about says in *Exodus*, they at first thought it was the end of the world as proclaimed in the Scriptures, "The day when men shall fly." And they arrived in Israel to discover such other unsuspected things as a table, a chair or a fork, etc . . . but at the same time they came with the conviction of being "the Chosen People," destined in the twentieth century to take the future of the world in charge.

14 In order to spare the reader, the steps in this calculation do not appear. If he feels the need of verifying it himself, he can make use of the method which appears earlier in this chapter.

[15] [If Arthur Ruppin's figure of 4,500,000 Jews living in the United States in 1926 had been used instead of the official census figure, a total Jewish population for 1962 — exclusive of immigration — of 6,120,000 persons would be had, using the natural growth coefficient of one per cent annually. If Shalom Baron's coefficient had been used, the 1962 figure would be 6,804,000 persons, once again exclusive of immigration.]

[16] However, the *World Almanac* of 1945 takes note of only 240,000, p. 494.

[17] It was another one of the machiavellianisms of Nuremberg that every time that the prosecution brought forth an accusation for which they would not or could not give the source they used the expression "in full cognizance" or "from an assured source" — that was generally the case when the source was Jewish — and it was up to the *accused* to prove their innocence. At Nuremberg it was not up to the prosecution to prove guilt since the Allies recognized early that their adherence to the Anglo-American jurisprudential presumption of "innocent until proven guilty" would deny them the "convictions" which they sought.

[18] The Czechoslovakian Jews who went into Hungary were arrested there together with their Polish and Yugoslav co-religionists without any nationality distinctions being drawn. The survivors and the deportees as listed in the calculations concerning Hungary cannot be distinguished either, since there are no records. This could be significant with regard to losses by nationality, but is not for losses of a general European nature, and that is what we are investigating.

[19] The Jerusalem Tribunal has 480,000 in its "Exhibit No. 111."

[20] This figure is confirmed by "Exhibit No. 111" of the Jerusalem Tribunal.

[21] Dr. Kasztner says 300,000 ("800,000 of which 500,000 were deported," page 1 of his *Report.*)

[22] Figure given by Dr. Kasztner as coming to him from Eichmann himself.

[23] In France and in Germany, freight cars are larger than in Poland, Czechoslovakia and Hungary. I learned this by experience when we were evacuated from Dora in April 1945, with 80 per car in a train composed at least half of such cars; we were just as crowded with 80 in a Polish car as we were with 100 in a French car.

[24] We can see then what would have happened under Joël Brand's system: "Every day," he told the Jews in Constantinople, when he met with them towards the 18th of June, 1944, "12,000 Jews are thrown into the cars." (*Histoire de Joël Brand*, p. 125). Conclusion: four trains per day, and the system exhausted the supply of empty railroad cars before the evening of the 5th day!

[25] At Auschwitz, the "baggage" collected in this manner by the administration of the camp was gathered into a corner of the camp which, according to the official plans produced at Nuremberg and other trials, was composed of 30 blocks separate from each other and heavily guarded: "Canada" they were called by the deportees. The official view was that on the approach of the Russian army, the S.S. tried to set fire to them but did not succeed. On their arrival, the Russian troops found in the six blocks set aside for clothing: 348,820 outfits for men, 836,525 outfits for women, but only 5,255 pairs of shoes for men, and 38,000 pairs of shoes for women. There were also 13,694 rugs. (*Auschwitz, Official Communication of the Museum of the Auschwitz Commission* — Panstwowe Museum W. Oswiecimiu — published in Cracow in 1947). That gives an idea of all that the Jews brought with them. Women remained women even in the worst circumstances: compare what was found on them with what was found on the men. Other barracks contained objects of all sorts of value. The commission does not give an enumeration, or an estimate of the market value, but trains and trucks were required to transport it all. All these things must have taken up a great deal of space in the cars "of 70 to 100 persons and even more" mentioned in "Exhibit 154" of the Jerusalem trial. Conclusion: in the cars of the Jews who carried with them the most goods, there were fewer persons, and in the others more than expected.

[26] Actually, it said: 57,000 to 62,000.

[27] In the *Bréviaire de la Haine*, he even specified "3,000 deportees in all from Croatia." (p. 181.)

[28] Deportation of the Jews from Yugoslavia was decided upon on January 19, 1943, for Croatia, but was not seriously begun until after the arrival of Krumey, on October 16, 1943; deportations were begun in March, 1942 in Serbia.

[29] Still, the method of the judges at Jerusalem must be emphasized: the case of the German Jews is treated in their verdict — in the aggregate — together with Austrian Jews and those of Bohemia-Moravia. To cover up the ridiculous aspect of the number of German Jews which they were taking into consideration, and contrary to the system they used for other countries, they did not total them. In order to give the impression that there was a great number, they included among the German Jews, the 55,000 Polish Jews who were in Germany, when on October 7, 1938, the Polish government decided to deprive them of Polish nationality by not renewing their passports. By this act they were depatriated, and the Germans at that time did not want people without passports on their land. Nor, did the Poles, who had depatriated them. Since no other country wanted them either, it was a very bad state of affairs. It was the origin of the assassination of Counsellor vom Rath in Paris on November 7, 1938, by Grynszpan, a son of one of these 55,000 Poles, and of the "*Kristallnacht*" of November 9th and 10th in Germany.

Chapter Fifteen

Conclusion: Six Million Exterminated Jews—
Fact or Fiction

Logic demands that this demographic study end with general statistics which include the following four items for each of the European nations which I have surveyed:

1. The number of Jews who were living there just before Beck's accession to power in Poland (1932) and Hitler's accession to power in Germany (1933);
2. The number of Jews among them who, to escape persecution, emigrated between 1932 and 1945;
3. The number of Jews who remained in Europe and who were still alive there in 1945;
4. The number of Jews who cannot be accounted for and who, hence, are presumed to be dead.

In order to give the exact truth of this dark story, these statistics should be accompanied by others giving the structure of the world Jewish population at the end of 1962. And, in four sections also, for each of the nations of the other continents:

1. The number of Jews living there before the rise to power in Poland of Beck, and in Germany of Hitler;

2. The natural increase in the Jewish population from 1932 to 1962;
3. The census of the Jewish population at the end of 1962;
4. The number of Jewish immigrants calculated from the difference between the total figures of Items 2 and 3. (There is no doubt that this difference comes near the 4,419,908 figure that is mentioned in the preceding section.)

This was my intention at the beginning. Now, this double labor turns out to be impossible; the second statistics cannot be determined unless and until the leadership of international Zionism agrees to undertake a census of the world Jewish population, and we have seen that Zionist leaders are not about to accept this idea. As for the first statistics, there is a long series of other difficulties that still present obstacles in spite of all the specific data that the preceding study has produced.

The most insurmountable of these difficulties, and which sums them all up, is the following: if we now know that a *minimum* of 4,419,908 Jews succeeded in leaving Europe between 1931 and 1945, we are much less well informed on their nationalities. For countries like Denmark, Norway, Germany, Austria, Bulgaria, and one or two others — the Baltic countries for example, even Greece — there is no problem; they were not on the route of the Jewish migration; the Germans found only national Jews in those countries and everything is clear. But it is not the same in the other countries — Holland, Belgium, France, Italy, Hungary, Rumania — which were countries into which to escape, or to go through, before they became occupied by German troops. There, the Jews were arrested and deported pell-mell, and it is impossible for us to determine accurately the nationalities of those who managed not to get arrested as well as those who were. Hungary is the archetype of this difficulty: there, we did succeed in determining that out of the 800,000 Jews who were living there on March 19, 1944, 543,000 had not been deported; that about 200,000 had been deported; that 57,000 had very probably been massacred in police operations; and that 343,000 had managed to emigrate. But, in each of these categories, it was impossible to determine who was Hungarian, who was Yugoslavian, who was Czechoslovakian, and who was Polish. The same questions hold for Rumania, where we found 147,650 massacred, and 652,350 survivors, 227,350 of whom emigrated. The same questions are found again for Holland, for Belgium, for Luxemburg and for France. In France, we found that only 81,000 Jews of one nationality or the other could have been arrested and deported; we know also that there were no Belgians among them, that the number of French was necessarily between 6,000 and 11,999, and that the number of the Luxemburgers was between 0 and 2,000, the others being Dutch. But these are, all the same, figures which are insufficiently exact to be called statistics. In Poland, we know that 729,040 Jews were arrested, either on their national land or on the emigration route toward the west; but of the 289,300 who tried to emigrate by the Danubian route, how many were arrested in Hungary and how many in Rumania? So many questions for which there are no answers and which can equally be applied to the Czechoslovakians who fled to Hungary and the Yugoslavians who fled to Italy.

In the final analysis, rather than to circulate statistics based on nationalities, every datum of which might have been open to question, and to add to the confusion created by the historians and the statisticians who voice the line of international Zionism, I have preferred to draw up these statistics on the only plane where we are sure of ourselves, that is in Europe. Here, no serious debate is possible: we have affirmed that a minimum of 4,419,908 European Jews managed to emigrate early enough to escape arrest and deportation to concentration camps, and we can add them to those that the historians and statisticians who support the Zionist "genocide" fiction, found living in Europe in 1945.

Here then, on information from the *World Center of Contemporary Jewish Documentation*, are our statistics on the European scale in four sections, with the integration, for 1931, of the 300,000 German Jews and the 180,000 Austrian Jews who are admitted to have left Europe to flee from Hitler together with the million Jews who were in the part of the Russia that was never occupied by the German troops:

Description	1931	1945	Official Losses	Emigrants Traced	Actual[a] Losses
Statistical totals from page 302	8,297,500	2,288,100	6,009,400	---	---
Known German emigrants	300,000	300,000	---	---	---
Austrian emigrants acknowledged	180,000	180,000	---	---	---
Russian Jews saved by Soviet authorities	1,000,000	1,000,000	---	---	---
Actual totals from the *World Center of Contemporary Jewish Documentation* statistics	9,777,500	3,768,100	6,009,400	---	---
Actual totals as arrived at in this study	9,777,500	3,768,100	---	4,419,908	1,589,492

[a] The figure in this column actually represents the number of European Jews who were not accounted for in the preceding study. Consequently, this figure must be viewed with the following caveats: first, this figure represents a *maximum* figure which doubtless would be considerably smaller if a census of the world Jewish population were taken today since whenever a question has arisen pertaining to the propriety of some statistic, it has been resolved in a manner which has favored the proponents of the Zionist line. Second, not every person who is included within this figure can be said to have died at the hands of the Germans. The mere fact that a person is not accounted for does not necessarily mean that he is deceased. These comments also hold true for Mr. Hilberg's statistics which are outlined on the following page.

Here again are the same statistics, but this time based on the information of Mr. Raul Hilberg who did not divide Russia into the two zones, but who, too, acknowledged that there were 300,000 German and 180,000 Austrian Jewish emigrants:

Description	1931	1945	Officials Losses	Emigrants Traced	Actual Losses
Statistical totals from page 302	9,190,000	3,782,500	5,407,500	---	---
Known German emigrants	300,000	300,000	---	---	---
Austrian emigrants acknowledged	180,000	180,000	---	---	---
Actual totals of Mr. Raul Hilberg for 1945	9,670,000	4,262,500	5,407,500	---	---
Actual totals as arrived at in this study	9,670,000	4,262,500	---	4,419,908	987,592

On the basis of the proceding analysis, this is where we stand now: First, out of the study of the statistics of the *World Center of Contemporary Jewish Documentation* and from its own data, we find 1,589,492 European Jews dead or missing as a consequence of Nazi persecutions in concentration camps or in some other way. Second, out of the study of Mr. Raul Hilberg's data we find only 987,592 dead or missing Jews.

Twice I took up this problem: first in *Ulysse trahi par les siens,* published in France in 1960, and, second, in an article for the German review *Deutsche Hochschullehrer-Zeitung* (Tübingen, 1/2, February 1963). Each time that I reviewed the problems, I did it in terms of the data from Jewish sources that had been published at the time. But, the first time, neither the judgment of the Jerusalem Tribunal, nor, more significantly, the study of *The Jewish Communities of the World* of February 1963 had been brought out. And, in terms of what was already known, my conviction had been that the number of Jewish victims of Nazi persecution, in concentration camps or otherwise, should be placed at about 1,000,000, more or less. The second time, I had in my hands the Judgment of the Jerusalem Tribunal, and I had followed day by day the hearings of the Trial, but I still was not acquainted with the study of the *Jewish Communities of the World,* then not yet published. As a conclusion to my writing for the *Deutsche Hochschullehrer-Zeitung* (pp.61, 62) I had claimed that if the number were greater than 1,000,000 it could not by any means exceed 1,655,300 victims. Today, with all the documents at hand which were lacking then, it can be said that, based on data prior to that of the *World Center of Contemporary Jewish Documentation,* the number of victims is 1,589,492. On the other hand, the figure is 987,592, based on Mr. Raul Hilberg's data. To achieve greater exactness, we must wait for the new Zionist leaders like Shalom Baron, Leon Poliakov, and Michel Borwicz, among others, to give new avowals, or for another trial like the Jerusalem one, to bring us new light on the question. As well as we know these Zionist circles, neither one nor the other of these hypothesis is excluded, but, rather, both are more likely than not to occur. In those circles, indeed, neither talkers without conscience, seeking cheap publicity, nor, alas, judges looking for vengeance, are lacking. I shall bet a good deal on two other things: the latent and continuous dissensions which exist between Mr. Ben Gurion and Mr. Nahum Goldmann, and the fracas between Khrushchev and Mao Tse-tung.

For a long time now Mr. Nahum Goldmann has been showing signs of fatigue and impatience with the policies of Mr. Ben Gurion with regard to Germany. For example, he had stated publicly that he was not enthusiastic about the arrest of Eichmann and the trial which followed. Through various indiscretions we learn that he does not place much value on all the trials in Germany, aimed at former members of one or another of the Nazi organizations of Hitler's time. In Israel itself, there is a very serious divergence between his group and that of Mr. Ben Gurion, each time the latter finds a German minister stupid enough to accept an invitation sent him with the sole object of having him publicly insulted in Israel by his partisans, and thus of making an issue that attracts the attention of the whole world to the debt which Germany, because she rallied to Hitler in 1933, assumed with regard to Israel. Everything takes place as if, not daring publicly to take a position in opposition to Mr. Ben Gurion with regard to his policy toward Germany, Mr. Nahum Goldmann were trying behind the scenes, to silence him on his main theme. And, the fact that, with regard to the Jews who were exterminated, the statistics which we have from the American partisans of the Zionist line are generally more moderate than those which come from the European branch (as is illustrated by the figures of Mr. Raul Hilberg compared with those of the *World Center of Contemporary Jewish Documentation*) could very well reflect the dissentions between the two men. This would then explain the divergencies and contradictions revealed in the Jewish sources in their statistics.

As for the quarrel between Khrushchev and Mao Tse-tung, it could be of consequence in that, along with that of the United States, the Jewish population of Russia is one of the greatest enigmas weighing on the problem. The *Institute of Jewish Affairs* of London and the *Jewish Communities of the World* both told us clearly in 1962 that there were 2.3 million Jews in Russia. But Mr. Raul Hilberg revealed to us that there were 2,600,000 in 1946, and that estimate, which can be considered to be confirmed by the journalist, David Bergelson (in *Die Einheit,* December 5, 1942), can also be considered closer to the truth. In that case, it is not 2.3 million Jews that were in Russian in 1962, but 3,016,000, adjusted for a natural increase at the rate of sixteen per cent. If we take Professor Shalom Baron at his word, that figure would be even greater: 3,120,000. But, let us not be tempted. However, we could justify the use of a larger figure, all the less, because in reality there are surely many more than 3,016,000, since the Jewish journalist, David Bergelson, also told us, let us not forget, that eighty per cent of the Baltic Jews, the Poles, and the Rumanians, who found themselves behind the Russian lines as they fled before the German troops in 1941-1942, were saved and sent on their way toward Central Asia by the Soviet authorities. At the end of 1942, Bergelson estimated that there were about 5.2 million Jews on Soviet territory, 3 million of them Russian, and in that he agrees with the statistics of April 17, 1943, of Mr. Richard Korherr, which have already been referred to. Question: what happened to those 2.2 million non-Russian Jews? Answer: some of them managed to escape and reach either the American continent or Israel; the rest of them did not. How many were in each group? We cannot tell. But, we can be sure that as long as Khrushchev and Mao Tse-tung were getting along together it surely was not easy for Jews who had been transported to Central Asia during the war, to make it to the American continent via China; those who have been able to manage the trip in the post-war period must have managed it clandestinely. The subsequent quarrel between these two grand men of Bolshevism could result in Mao Tse-tung aiding the Jews to leave Soviet territory, just as the China of Chiang Kai-shek aided them before World War II, and for the same reasons. In that case, it could happen that one day a very significant number of Jews might turn up suddenly in all of the countries of the American continent, and perhaps also in Israel. And, unless it is kept hidden in the dark, a new light will be shed on the statistics of world Jewry. Neither is this hypothesis excluded. And, if the United States should adopt a rational policy toward Russia, the truth would come out very fast.

But to return to the problem as it exists in the data that we actually have: we know that the number of European Jews who died as victims of Nazi persecutions is either 1,589,492 persons, established on the basis of data from the *World Center of Contemporary Jewish Documentation* compared with the Exhibits of the Tribunal at Jerusalem and the study, *The Jewish Communities of the World*, which came out in February 1963, or is 987,952 persons, based on the data of Mr. Raul Hilberg compared in the same manner. It still remains to be discovered how the 4,419,908 Jews, who were living in 1945, were divided among the other countries of the world, and who, not being listed as living in the European statistics of Jewish sources, are necessarily thought to have left Europe between 1931 and 1945. That is the problem for the second statistical analysis, which, in my opinion, should present by country the structure of the world Jewish population in 1962. And, as is pointed out in a preceding paragraph, these statistics are impossible to establish at the present time.

We already know one thing which was revealed to us in the study of the Israeli Jewish population, and that is that it includes 1,048,368 European Jews who immigrated to Israel between 1931 and 1962. It remains to be seen how the remaining 3,371,540 European Jews are distributed around the rest of the world.

It is in this latter matter that the Jewish sources are the most secretive. Rarely do we find, for example, in the study of the *Jewish Communities of the World* and in the *World Almanac* of 1963, non-European countries where the admitted Jewish population is greater than it would have been by natural increase based upon the statistics of Mr. Arthur Ruppin for the period of

1926-1928. There are some places where even the natural rate of increase has not been reached; that is the case with the United States, where, if we can believe the aforementioned publications, the population has not risen more than from 4,461,184 in 1936 to 5,500,000 in 1962. However, we have seen that at the natural rate of increase of one per cent there cannot be fewer than 5,550,489 Jews in the United States, and that, at the natural rate of increase which Mr. Shalom Baron gives, there should be 6,170,837. The few countries on continents other than Europe, where the Zionists concede that there is a Jewish population greater than what it would have been by natural increase, based on the Ruppin statistics, are the following: Argentina, Canada, Brazil, and South Africa. For these four countries, these are the statistics that can be drawn up:

Country	1926 Population	Natural Increase, 36%	1962 Population		Immigration[b]
			Natural	Conceded	
Argentina	240,000	86,400	326,400	450,000	123,600
Canada	170,000	61,200	231,200	254,000	22,800
Brazil	40,000	14,400	54,400	140,000	85,600
South Africa	60,000	21,600	81,600	110,000	28,400
TOTAL	510,000	183,600	693,600	954,000[a]	260,400

[a] The total allows one to admire once again the seriousness of the statistics from Jewish sources. For Argentina, Canada and Brazil, the total is 844,000. However, there are, in addition, a few Jews in the other countries of the American continent, notably in Mexico, 70,000; in Uruguay, 60,000; in Chile, 15,000, and so on. The total, therefore, for these six countries is 989,000. And for the whole Western Hemisphere, the same statistics give a total of 6.3 million, which the *Jerusalem Post Weekly* (April 19, 1963) brings forward. If, from this total for the two American continents, we subtract these 989,000 persons, there remain for the United States 5,311,000 and not 5.5 million as is claimed by the official statement of the *Institute of Jewish Affairs* of London and the *World Almanac* of 1963 (p. 159). That is what you come to when you want to conceal the actual total of the Jewish population of the United States.

[b] These estimates for immigration include natural increase.

By making an allowance for the natural increase, we get close to 200,000 immigrants of European origin for these four countries, assuming that the figures published in the aforementioned authorities for 1962 are exact, and it would by astonishing if they were. If they are, we still have 3,171,540 European Jews to locate. To do that we would have to be able to draw up figures for all of the countries of the world in the same manner as we did for Argentina, Canada, Brazil, and South Africa. But we cannot, since the latter are the only ones given by the Zionists which concede any immigration.

Still, something must be done, since, if they are not in Europe and not in Israel, these 3,171,540 Jews who were certainly living in 1945 must be somewhere else — together with the additional number that they have accumulated at the natural rate of population expansion. Where? In order to say that with any real certainty we shall have to wait once again for new revelations that the publicity-seeking Zionist movement will not fail one day inadvertently to produce. Until then we can only conjecture, and that is not my method. I shall, therefore, limit myself to stating my basic principles which have defined the direction that my research has taken, and which I continue to pursue.

1.   It is not probable, but it is possible—that in August 1945, the date when Mr. Poliakov told us (*Le Troisiéme Reich et les Juifs*, p. 196) that the European Jewish communities had begun to make an inventory of their losses for Justice Jackson and had come up with only 3,768,100 survivors according to the *World Center of Contemporary Jewish Documentation*, or 4,262,500 according to Mr. Raul Hilberg — that they gave figures considerably understated for reasons of propaganda. I say it is possible, for two reasons: there was such a chaos of displaced persons in Europe at that time that any serious census was out of the question; and the method used in the Jewish communities, which everywhere counted only Jews of the nationality of the country, might have distorted the results.

2.   Even if the result of this Jewish census of 1945 was not out of line (which is not admitted), it is certain that, if all the Jews who had left Europe between 1931 and 1945 had not returned by 1945, many of them came back later, at least to Western Europe, since we can assume that those who returned to the other side of the Iron Curtain were the exceptions. France, in this case, is typical: 300,000 Jews in 1939 and between

450,000 and 500,000 at the end of 1962, with about 130,000 Algerian Jews and about 20,000 Moroccan and Tunisian Jews who came seeking refuge, after the granting of independence to those three countries. 300,000 to 350,000 French Jewish nationals is a normal figure in relation to the entire French population in 1962. But the statistics of the *World Center of Contemporary Jewish Documentation* continue to claim 180,000 in 1945 plus the natural increase rate of 16 per cent, or 208,000 (216,000 if we use the natural increase rate of Mr. Shalom Baron). It is very probable that if one went to the trouble, one could make similar statements for Belgium (where, in addition, 20,000 to 25,000 Jews returned from the Congo), Holland, Austria, and perhaps even Germany. However, all of the Jews who returned to Europe after the month of August 1945, whose number we cannot know exactly as long as the Zionists refuse to give it to us, since official census-taking will "bring down the wrath of God," surely must amount to several hundreds of thousands and must belong with those 3,171,540 which no Jewish source allocates to any place.

3.   The problem of the Polish, Baltic and Rumanian Jews, who in the years 1941-1942 were evacuated to Central Asia and who, if one can believe the Jewish journalist, David Bergelson, should have numbered between 2 and 2.2 million in 1942, since there were 3 million Jews in Russian in 1939, and at the end of 1942, there were about 5.2 million. How many of these Jews are still living in "Central Asia" (read, Siberia) with their offspring? How many have succeeded in escaping in the past 16 years? Where have they gone? Everything points to the fact that those who managed to escape secretly from the U.S.S.R. reached the American continent, which was for them the easiest to get to. Concerning that supposition, a hypothesis, for what it is worth, and which I do not offer as a certainty, runs through my mind: in 16 years, it is possible that half of them, at a cost of immeasurable difficulties, managed to leave Central Asia for the American continent. If that is so, and since the Zionist demographers have not located them in Canada, Brazil, or in any other country in the Western Hemisphere, they must be in the United States. Thus, the following statistics could be drawn up for Russia and the United States:

A. *Russia*
1. Jews found still living by
   Mr. Raul Hilberg in 1945:   2,600,000
2. Jews still living in Central Asia,
   according to Mr. David Bergelson: 2,200,000
3. Total Jewish population in
   Russia in 1945:   4,800,000
4. Jews who succeeded in in
   leaving Cetnral Asia for the
   United States: 1,100,000
5. Jews who were left in Russia;   3,700,000
6. Jewish natural increase of
   16% since 1947:   592,000
7. Total Jewish population in
   Russia in 1962:   4,292,000

B. *United States*
1. Jewish population for 1926
   (official figure):   4,081,242
2. Jewish natural increase of
   36% since 1926:   1,469,247
3. Total Jewish population in
   1962:   5,550,489
4. Jewish immigrants from
   Central Asia since 1946:   1,100,000
5. Their natural increase of
   16% since 1946:   176,000
6. Total Jewish population
   from Asia together with
   progeny: 1,276,000
7. Total Jewish population in
   the United States in 1962:   6,826,489

But, this total of 6,826,489 includes only immigration from
Central Asia, and, therefore, it excludes all of those who, like
Mme. Hannah Arendt and Mr. Robert W. Kempner, came to the
United States by some other route from Europe. We can surely
say that they number more than two, but, how many we do not
know, or, at least, not yet. All that can be said is that they are
there and that surely the Jewish population of the United States

is greater than 6,826,489 persons. It can also be stated that the claim of the *National Observer* (July 2, 1962) that there were 12,000,000 Jews in the United States in 1962 may be an exaggeration toward the other extreme, but, I would not be astonished if one day soon a Zionist leader inadvertently reveals that there were about 8 million Jews in the United States. The estimate of 12,000,000 in the United States has been repeated several times with an attempt at numerical documentation by the *Economic Council Letter* published in New York City.

I repeat that the preceding analysis is only conjectural and is not a fact; it is, however, the hypothesis that is necessary to every work as a basis from which to conduct further research; it is the hypothesis which orients mine. To my mind, it is plausible and it expresses, all the better, my profound conviction which, until now, has not led me to any impasse or error and which has made it possible for me to state some ten years ago the conclusions that were to be drawn later from the Jerusalem Trial and the study of the *Jewish Communities of the World.*

The actual Jewish population of the world in 1962 is very close to being the following, at least in the order of magnitude of the figures. By using statistics for each country of the world dated for 1926, or 1927, or 1928, as the case was, Mr. Arthur Ruppin estimated that world Jewry had reached a total of 15,800,000 persons as of that date. We have seen that the *World Almanac* of 1951 estimated the world Jewish population at 16,643,120 for 1939. The natural rate of increase having considerably dropped between 1926 and 1939 (Poliakov *dixit*, *cf.* p. 295), but when it is compared with that of Mr. Arthur Ruppin, this estimate is allowable. Here, then is the Jewish population of the world in 1962, calculated on the corrected data of the *World Center of Contemporary Jewish Documentation.*

1.	World Jewish population in 1939:	16,643,120
2.	Jewish victims of Nazism:	1,589,492
3.	World Jewish population living in 1945[1]:	15,053,628
4.	Jewish natural increase of 16% since 1946:	2,408,580
5.	Total Jewish population on 1962[2]:	17,552,208

And here is the same as calculated on the corrected data of Mr. Raul Hilberg:

1. World Jewish population in 1939:   16,643,120
2. Jewish victims of Nazism: 987,592
3. World Jewish population living in 1946:   15,655,528
4. Jewish increase of 16% since 1946:   2,504,884
5. Total Jewish population in 1962:   18,160,412

And, here we are at the end of this study. It remains for me only to make an apology to the reader: this study has clearly been very long, and difficult to follow, like all that is technical by nature. But a demographic study can only be of such a technical nature. What the reader must recognize is that, until now, the proponents of the Zionist line – whose "official" contentions on the horrors of the war I have been following – have never been faced with arguments other than those from journalists, which have been often vague and specious, factors that have been the main reason for their lack of success. The only way to shatter their arguments was to set up against them the arguments of a specialist. And, that is what I have tried to do.

FOOTNOTES

[1] "Between 15 and 18 million in 1947," as Hanson W. Baldwin has said (*cf.* p. 294 above).

[2] It must not be forgotten that this total comes out of the study of Jewish sources, that is, those which have been published under the sanction of the Zionist movement or by the Rabbinate, after investigation of the synagogues. But, if it is true, as claimed by Arthur Koestler (*A l'ombre du Dinosaure*), that not more than two-thirds of the world's Jews are registered in the synagogues, then there is room to wonder if this figure should not be augmented in the same proportion.

Appendices

Index

Appendix A:

Four Descriptions of Prison Life in French Penal Institutions

The following are four descriptions of prison life in penal institutions which were operated by the French government at about the same time that Buchenwald and other German concentration camps were functioning.

Discipline in the Maison Centrale in Riom in 1939

"Three notable elements must be remembered about disciplinary methods.

"The first is the institution of an internal hierarchy of prisoners who cooperate with the wardens in maintaining proper order. I have often heard the French become indignant over this institution in the Nazi prisons, over these gratuitous assistants to the gang wardens; they are the same persons who cannot admit that the Germans were ignorant of what was going on in their country, and yet who do not know what is happening in France. For the *Kapos,* the *Schreibers,* the *Vorabeiters,* the *Stubendienst,* etc. . . there are however, precedents. The workshop bookkeepers, the foremen (although there were civilians too), the entire administration are made up of prisoners, and obviously enjoy certain advantages. Quite apart from this are the provosts explicitly in charge of keeping order. That goes for the dormitory provost, who has next to his bed an alarm button to alert the wardens in case that something abnormal occurs (smoke, reading, conversations, etc. . . .) and which, happily, is little used. However, its use is up to the official executioner, the provost of the Ward.

"Now I must say what a Strong-Ward is: the special prison within the prison, and in fact a torture chamber (I can attest that the word is not an exaggeration). This second element of discipline, like Dante's Hell, includes various circles. It begins in the discipline room, where — in principle — the convicts are marched around in a circle with very short pauses, at a pace maintained by giving a special ration to the pace-setter, while smaller rations are given to the others; the fact is that blows rain down. I was lucky enough to escape this myself, but I can attest to having often seen the poor beggars coming back from the 'room' with obvious signs of recent blows. Then, there was solitary confinement — in principle — up to 90 consecutive days, practically equivalent to a death sentence, with a tin of soup every four days. Finally, there were some refinements of cruelty which are particularly repugnant. In particular was the torture called the 'shirt,' a straight-jacket that tied the arms to-gether behind one's back; very often, then, the arms were brought up as far as the neck. I attest, after having collected numberless testimonies all in agreement, that some wardens struck the men with various instruments, including the poker, until death resulted. I attest that the Nazis only added some de-tails in perfecting the art of slowly killing men.

"Now, and this is the third instrument of discipline, these 'accessory' sentences, which sometimes meant a death sentence, were not pronounced by tribunals established by law, but by a jurisdiction which to my knowledge was ignorant of the law, the *Prétoire.* It is a tribunal within the prison presided over by the director, assisted by a sub-director (in penitentiary slang, the *'sousmac'*) with the head warden acting as clerk. At the *Prétoire,* there is no pleading, no defense, no intelligible indict-ment, and no reply except for the ritual *"Merci, Monsieur le Directeur,"* following the sentence. I was always able to get off with a simple fine, which meant only cutting down my right to buy things in the canteen; income was limited to salary, since help from the outside was very much reduced; in those days, no package was allowed to be received by a prisoner except for underwear. But heavy sentences were constantly handed down even for a simple non-fulfillment of a job." (Pierre Bernard, *Révolution prolétarienne*, June 1949.)

In the Prisons of the "Liberation"

"All the French wanted this," say our 'patriots.'

"Edouard Gentez, printer at Courbevoie, sentenced in July 46, not as a criminal, but as a printer, was transferred from Fresnes to Fontevrault in September 46. As a result of beatings, privations and cold, he contracted pleurisy, which caused him to be struck from the list to be transferred to Fontevrault.

"An hour before the departure, the condemned of the S.P.A.C. who were on this list were struck off on an order; they were still needed. They were replaced, and Gentez was among those newly inscribed.

"He arrived at *Centrale*, two and a half hours standing, in the sun, then eight days shut up in a hole called the '*mitard*:' after this, Gentez was admitted to the infirmary, ruled over by a butcher assassin, Ange Soleil, a mulatto who had cut to pieces and walled up his mistress, which prepared him for the functions of prison provost-nurse-doctor, far more powerful than the young civilian doctor, a dandy named Gaultier or Gautier.

"Soleil admitted those sick men into the infirmary who shared with him two thirds of their parcels, and rejected those whose parcels were too small, by a very clear and simple system.

"Gentez, having neither parcel nor funds, could not pay, and in spite of the seriousness of his sickness, was put into the '*inoccupés*,' those forced to three quarters of an hour fast march, one quarter of an hour rest, from morning to night, every day, Sundays included.

"Gentez, who was too weak, was let off that torture, but for all that was not permitted to lie down or even to sit down; he had to remain standing, without moving, hands behind his back, without coat, during the marching.

"The cold aggravated his pleurisy and Gentez went each week to the medical office where he was given aspirin, cod liver oil, and where cupping glasses were applied to him, but he was never admitted to the infirmary.

"He groaned without stopping all night long. The two prisoner doctors, the surgeon Perribert and Doctor Lejeune, sounded his chest Saturday morning, and discovered double bronchial pneumonia.

"When Gentez fell down in the yard, the nurse who was called, went to find Ange Soleil, who began to shout, called him a faker, and had him thrown in a dungeon, along with Doctor Perribert, who was guilty of having made the examination without authorization.

"Gentez was stripped naked and thrown into the cell, where the temperature was five degrees above zero (-15° C.) He knocked all night for help, but no one came. The next morning, January 14, 1947, he was found dead.

"Finally, he was carried to the infirmary, where he was pronounced dead there, of a heart attack. He was buried simply under a number, 3479.

"But there was an embarrassing witness, Gentez' son whom I knew in prison and next to whom I lived out the vicissitudes of this stark drama. He obtained an investigation. This was properly conducted. Ange Soleil was transferred to Fresnes, but was set free by a procedure of amnesty [sic]. The Directors Dujour, Vessiéres, and Guillonet were removed.

"Andre Marie had promised to reduce Gentez' son's sentence to three years, as a result of this tragic business. Since then more than three years have gone by, and, if I am well informed, he is still in prison." Signed: Benoit C. . . .

"This is an extract of a letter sent to me from X prison . . . somewhere in France. (My discretion is due to the fact that I do not to want to expose the author to the legal process mentioned in the above document.)

"Benoit C. . . has not read *Valsez, saucisses*, which he is not acquainted with, but *Vertiges.*

"He informed me about the percentage (10%) of social workers gabbling around — not at all to reproach them for it — and describes without too much complaint the curious ways of certain *'messieurs de l'oeuvre de Saint-Vincent-de Paul'* [gentlemen of the Society of . . .] with fingers heavy with signet rings.

"This testimony is all the more conclusive, as it comes from someone obsessed with sex and not at all with politics." (Communication from A. Paraz.)

At Poissy

"In February 1946, head shaved, in clogs and coarse cloth, Henri Béraud found himself in Workshop 14 on the second floor of the jail at Poissy. Under the eye of an overseer whose duty it was to enforce 'the rule of silence,' a rule that weighed on the prison night and day, he made tags with cord or twisted wire, averaging .95 francs per thousand.

"Typical prison stupidity: the table chief was a burglar who had under him, besides Béraud, General Linsard, a colonel, two Justices, an advocate general, the editor-in-chief of the *Journal de Rouen*, a university professor, and some Paris journalists.

"In his book, *Je sors du bagne*, one of his prison companions at Poissy, as on Ré island, brought out how much the convict Béraud earned during the month of April 1945: labor, 15 Fr. Deduction for the prison administration, 12 Fr. left, 3 Fr. Set aside, 1.50 Fr. left for the prisoner, 1.50 Fr.

"And this was for work for more than seven hours a day." (*La Bataille*, September 21, 1949.)

German Prisoners in France

"La Rochelle, October 18, 1948. Informed of the scandalous acts of which former officer Max-Georges Roux, 36, assistant to the commanding officer of the German prison camp at Chatel-aillon-Plage was guilty, the examining magistrate of La Rochelle referred the matter to the military tribunal at Bordeaux where Roux had been transferred. The ex-officer was then serving an 18 months prison sentence which had been given him the preceding August at La Rochelle for breach of trust and for swindling various associations[1].

"Infinitely more serious were the crimes committed by Roux in the prisoner-of-war camp. It was a matter of real crimes, and so great that it seems difficult to believe that Roux could be the only one found guilty before the judges. At Chatelaillon this base person had, among other things, made several [P.O.W.] strip and had beaten them with a leaded whip. Two of the unfortunates had died during these sessions with the knout.

"One overwhelming testimony was that of the German doctor Clauss Steen, who was interned at Chatelaillon. Interrogated at Kiel, where he lives, Mr. Steen stated that from May to September 1945, he had verified at the [P.O.W.] camp the deaths of fifty of his compatriots. Their deaths had been brought about by insufficient food, heavy labor, and by the perpetual fear they lived in of being tortured.

"The food given out in the camp, which was under the orders of the commanding officer Texier, consisted, in actual fact of a plate of clear soup with a little bread. The rest of the rations disappeared in the black market. There was one period when the number of those with dysentery amounted to 80 per cent.

"Texier and Roux, with their subordinates, proceeded, besides that, to loot their prisoners, taking away from them everything of value. The thievery of these gangsters with military braid, was estimated at one hundred million; they had so well organized their business that bank notes and jewelry were sent directly to Belgium by automobile.

"Let us hope that with Roux the other guilty persons will soon be incarcerated in the fortress of Ha, and that an exemplary punishment will be meted out to these real war criminals." (*Les Journaux,* October 19, 1948.)

FOOTNOTES

1. At present this Roux holds a high administrative office in the southeast of France. As a reward for his fine deeds no doubt!

Appendix B:

The Two French Versions of the Gerstein Document

The following is the French version of the Gerstein Document as presented by L. Poliakov in 1951 (*Brévaire de la Haine*, pp. 220-24), with this comment: "This account was written down as is, in a halting French; the style has, in essence, been respected." And eleven years later in his book the *Procès de Jérusalem*, Mr. Poliakov presents it again in the form of Exhibit No. 124 of the Judgment, with this comment: "This document was written down by Gerstein directly in French. We present it here just as is." These two versions are reproduced on the following pages in parallel columns, with the first printed on the left side, and with the second printed on the right side, so that the reader may see for himself to what extent Mr. Poliakov merely "in essence, respected the style." What is one to think of a document which, after an interval of eleven years, can be presented in two such contradictory versions? It will be noticed that the Jerusalem Tribunal retained neither the daily extermination figures of the camps cited, nor the visit of Hitler to Belzec. And, what is one to think of a man like Mr. Poliakov who, after an interval of eleven years, presents these two versions of the same text?

From this same Mr. Poliakov we have a third version of the Gerstein Documents in *Le Troisième Reich et les Juifs* (1955, pp. 107-119) and a fourth version in *Le Terre Retrouvée* (April 1, 1964). These third and fourth versions include whole paragraphs which do not occur in one or the other of the first two. Moreover, they include material which is contradictory on many points, when compared with the former. And, like the former, they both bear the assurance that they were "reproduced as is," but with an additional notation. "From the German historical review, *Viertel-Jahreshefte für Zeitgeschichte*, no. 2, April 1953." There is no doubt that at this rate Mr. Poliakov could soon be the impresario of a multitude of "Gerstein Documents," all different and all contradictory, but somehow all authentic. Incidentally, not one of these versions mentions the estimates which appear in the original in which the number of European Jewish victims "reaches 25 million."

Lastly, to conclude this discussion of the proliferation of Gerstein documents, I want to mention that a small volumn has just come out in German with the title *Kurt Gerstein* (E.V.Z. Verlag, Zurich) and with the signature of a certain Helmut Franz, who was, he says, an intimate friend of Gerstein. Mr. Franz gives us a second German version of the Document that is very different from the one offered by Hans Rothfels.

So that none of these alarming manipulations lose any of their flavor, there might be some interest in giving a little free publicity to the latest news which has reached us concerning this famous "Document:" in offering his fourth version in the French tongue in *La Terre Retrouvée*, Mr. Poliakov informs us that his original version (which of the four?) "has disappeared from the central depository of the archives of the French military court," and also that "the dossier of the proceedings begun against the man in 1949 by the *Spruchkammer* of Tübingen" was gone. Since these "two essential items" – and how essential! – "were lacking," he says that he was "prevented – from undertaking a serious study." It is remarkable that he is aware of this after having given three versions already and that this fact does not prevent him from giving the fourth.

We are forced to conclude that no one will ever be able to consult this document removed forever in this way from the scrutiny of historians. So I ask this question: in whose interest was it that this document should disappear? I propose to make an inquiry into this disappearance which is a criminal outrage to historical truth.

The Gerstein Document

First French version attributed to Gerstein by Poliakov in 1951, in *Bréviaire de la Haine.*

A.   Poliakov's Introduction:

The victims are no longer here to give testimony before the world; their executioners, too, have disappeared, or gone underground. Among the rare testimonies which have come down to us on the functioning of the camps, here is one from the tragic hero of the German Resistance, the chemical engineer Kurt Gerstein. His account was written down directly in halting French and we have in essence kept his style.

B.   Text of the Document:

. . . in January 1942 I was made chief of the technical disinfection services of the *Waffen-S.S., including also an extremely toxic gas section.*

In this capacity I was visited on June 8, 1942, by S.S. *Sturmbannführer* Günther of the R.S.H.A., in civilian clothes. He was unknown. He ordered me to get for him immediately, for an ultra secret mission, 100 Kg of Prussic acid, and to bring them to a place known only to the driver of the truck.

A few weeks later, we left for Prague. I could more or less guess what purpose the Prussic acid was to serve, and what kind of an order this was, but I accepted because it gave me the chance I had long been waiting for to get to the bottom of all these things. Moreover, as an expert on Prussic acid, I had such authority and jurisdiction that it was easy for me to state under some pretext or other that the Prussic acid was not usable, decomposed or something like that, and thus to prevent its being used for extermination. We took with us, pretty much by chance, Professor Doctor of Medicine Pfannenstiel, *S.S-Obersturmbannführer*, holder of the chair of Hygiene at the University of Marburg-on-the-Lahn.

The Gerstein Document

Second French version attributed to Gerstein by the Jerusalem Tribunal in 1961, offered to the public by Poliakov in *Procès de Jérusalem.*

A. Tribunal's Introduction:

Exhibit 124. Here now we have a description from the pen of a German of the extermination method at the camp at Belzec, which very much resembled the one at Treblinka. The author is an officer of the S.S. by the name of Gerstein, whose conscience gave him no peace, and who, after 1942, tried to unveil to the world what was going on in the extermination camps.

Immediately after the war he drafted the document which we are about to cite, and handed it over to allied officers. Later we will return to Gerstein's comments about that. For the moment we will only say that the statements of Gerstein are supported on all points by the depositions we have heard, so that the proofs are mutually backed up. We consider that the description given by Gerstein is a description of what he actually saw. Here is what he wrote (T/1309 (1)):

(N.B. This document was drafted by Gerstein directly into French. We offer it as is.)

B. Text of the Document:

[That part of the document that appears on the page at the left is omitted by the Jerusalem Tribunal.]

Then we left with the truck for Lublin (Poland). *SS-Gruppen-führer* Globocnik was waiting for us there. At the factory at Collin, I purposely let it be understood that the acid was to be used to kill human beings. In the afternoon a man showed a great deal of interest in our truck. He went off in a great hurry when he saw he was observed. Globocnik told us: "This is one of the most secret of all secrets there are, even the most secret. Anyone speaking about it will be shot at once. Just yesterday, two gabbers were shot." Then he explained to us:

"Actually (it was the 17th of August 1942) there are three installations in existence:

1) Belzec, on the Lublin-Lwow road. Maximum per day, 15,000 persons.

2) Sobibor, I do not know exactly where it is, 20,000 persons a day.

3) Treblinka, 120 Kilometers NNE of Warsaw.

4) Maïdanek, near Lublin (in preparation)."

Globocnik said, "You will have to disinfect a very large quantity of clothing coming from Jews, Poles, Czechs, etc. Your other duty will be to improve the working of our gas chambers, functioning on the exhaust of a Diesel motor. A more toxic gas is needed, and one that works faster, such as Prussic acid. The *Führer* and Himmler — they were here the day before yesterday, August 15th — ordered me to go myself with all those who are to see the installation."

Professor Pfannenstiel asked him. "But what does the *Führer* say?" Globocnik answered, "The *Führer* orders that all operations be accelerated. Dr. Herbert Linden who was here yesterday asked me, 'But wouldn't it be more prudent to burn the bodies instead of burying them? Another generation might judge these things in a different way.'

"I answered, 'Gentlemen, if ever after us there is a generation so cowardly, so soft that it cannot understand our so good and so necessary work, all of National Socialism will have been in vain. On the contrary bronze tablets should be buried stating that it was us, we, who have the courage to carry out this gigantic work.' Then the *Führer* said, 'Yes, my good Globocnik, you are right."

[That part of the document that appears on the page at the left
is omitted by the Jerusalem Tribunal.]

The next day we left for Belzec. Globocnik introduced me to SS¹ . . . who showed me the installations. That day we did not see any dead, but a pestilential smell pervaded the whole region. Next to the station there was a large barracks "wardrobe" with an office-window "valuables." Farther on a hall with about a hundred chairs, "hair-dresser." Then a corridor 150 meters long in the open air, with barbed wire on both sides and with a sign "To the baths and inhalations." In front of us a house of the bath establishment type; on the right and on the left large concrete basins with geraniums and other flowers. On the roof the star of David. And on the building the inscription "Heckenholt Foundation."

The next day, a little before 7 o'clock, they announced to me: "In ten minutes the first train will arrive!" Indeed, a few minutes later a train did arrive from Lemberg: 45 cars with more than 6,000 persons.

Two hundred Ukrainians detailed for this service, tore off the doors and with leather riding whips chased the Jews out of the carriages. A loud-speaker was giving instructions: Take all clothing off, even artificial limbs and spectacles.

Turn all valuables and money in to the window marked "Valuables." Women and girls are to have their hair cut in the "Hair-dresser" barracks. (An *Untersturmführer-S.S.* told me, "It's to make something special for submarines.")

The other day we left for Belzec. A small special station with two platforms sloping up the hill of yellow sand immediately to the north of the road and the railway. To the south, near the roadway, with a few service houses with the sign "Service area Belzec of the S.S. army." Globocnik introduced me to *S.S.-Hauptsturmführer* Obermeyer of Pirmasens, who showed me the installations with great *retenance*. That day no dead were seen, but the smell of the whole region, also of the highroad, was pestilential. Next to the little station there was a large barracks "Wardrobe" with a window "Valuables." Then a room with 100 chairs "Hair-dresser," then a corridor 150 meters long in the open air, barbed wire on both sides and with a sign "To the baths and inhalations!"

In front of us a house like a bathing institution; to the right and left, big concrete tubs with geranium or other flowers. After having gone up a small stairway, to the right and to the left, three and three rooms, like garages, 4 x 5 meters, 1.90 m. high. Going back, but not visible, wooden openings. On the roof, the star of David in copper. In front of the building the inscription "Heckenholt Foundation."

More — that afternoon — I did not see.

Other morning, a few minutes before 7 o'clock, I was told, "After ten minutes, the train will arrive!"

Truly after a few minutes the first train arrived from Lemberg, 45 cars with 6,700 persons, 1,450 already dead on arrival.

Behind the little sky-lights with barbed wire over, children, youngsters, full of fear, women, men.

The train arrived: 200 Ukrainians, coerced to this service, tore off the doors and with leather riding whips chased the people out of the cars. Then a big loud speaker gave instructions: "In the open, some in the barracks, take off all clothing, also artificial limbs and spectacles. With little piece of string, offered by a little Jewish boy 4 years old, tie the shoes together. Turn in all valuables, all money to window." Valuables without voucher or receipt. Then the women and the young women to the hair-dresser — to have cut, one or two cuts, the hair which disappears into large potato sacks "to make something special of it for submarines, padding etc. . . . " the *S.S.-Unterscharführer* of the service told me.

Then the march began. On the right and left the barracks, behind, two dozen Ukrainians, guns in hand. They approach. Myself and Wirth, we find ourselves in front of the death chambers. Completely naked, the men and women, babies, the mutilated, they go by. In the corner, a big S.S. with a loud pastoral voice says to the wretched people, "Nothing terrible will happen to you! Just breathe very deeply, it strengthens the lungs, it is a way of preventing the spread of contagious diseases, it's a good disinfectant!" They asked him what their fate was to be. He told them, "The men are to work, build houses and lay streets. The women will not be made to; they will be occupied with housekeeping and in the kitchen."

It was for some of these poor people a last little hope, enough to make them march without resistance toward the death chambers. Most of them know everything, the smell gives it away! They go up a small wooden stairway and go into the death chambers, most not saying anything, pushed by the others coming behind them. A Jewess of about 40 years with eyes like torches, curses the murderers; getting a few blows of the whip from Captain Wirth himself, she disappeared into the gas chamber. Many say their prayers, others ask, "Who will give us water for death?" (Israelite rite.) Into the chambers the S.S. shove the men, "Fill up" Wirth has ordered, 700-800 in 93 sq. m. The doors are closed. At this moment I understand the reason for the sign "Heckenholt." Heckenholt is the driver of the Diesel, whose exhaust is to kill the unfortunates. *S.S. Unterscharführer* Heckenholt tries to get the motor started. But it doesn't go! Captain Wirth arrives. It is noticeable that he is afraid because I am present at this disaster. Yes, I see everything and I wait. My stop watch clocked everything, 50 minutes, 70 minutes, the Diesel doesn't go!

Then the march began: to the right and left barbed wire, behind two dozen Ukrainians with whips. Led by a young girl, extra-
ordinarily beautiful they came on. Myself with Captain Wirth,
Police, we found ourselves in front of the death chambers.
Completely naked, men, women, young girls, children, babies,
those with only one leg, all naked went by. In the corner a
husky S.S. who, in a loud, pastoral voice, said to the poor things:
"Nothing will happen to you except that you must breathe
deeply, it makes the lungs strong, this inhalation, it is necessary
to counter contagious diseases, it is a very good disinfectant!"
When he was asked what was to become of them, he said to
them, "Truly the men are to work making roads and houses.
But the women do not have to. Only, if they want to, they can
help with the housekeeping or in the kitchen." For some of
those poor people a little hope once more, enough to make
them march without resistance to the death chambers, most
of them know everything, the smell indicates what their lot will
be! Then they go up the little stairway and – seeing the truth!
Mothers, nursing, babies at the breast, naked, many children of
all ages – naked – they hesitate, but they go into the death
chambers, most of them without saying a word, pushed by
those behind them who are hustled by the whips of the S.S.
A Jewish woman, about 40 years old, with eyes like torches,
calls the blood of their children down on their murderers. Getting
five blows of the whip on the face from Police Captain Wirth
himself she disappeared into the gas chamber. Many say their
prayers, others say, "Who will give us the death water?" (Israelite rite.) Into the rooms the S.S. push the men. "Fill up good,"
Captain Wirth has ordered. The naked men are standing on the
feet of the others. 700-800 in 25 square meters[2] and 45 cubic
meters! The doors close. Meanwhile the rest of the train, naked,
are waiting. I am told, "Also in winter naked," "But they might
die!" "That's what they are here for," was the answer. Then I
understood what "Foundation Heckenholt" meant. Heckenholt
is the driver of the Diesel "the exhaust of which is destined to
kill the poor people!" *S.S. Unterscharführer* goes to some
trouble to get the Diesel motor running. But it doesn't start.
Captain Wirth arrives. I can see that he is afraid because I am
observing this disaster. Yes, I see everything, and I wait. My
stop watch has fixed everything. 50 minutes, 70 minutes, the
Diesel engine does not go!

The men are waiting in the gas chambers. In vain. They are heard crying "like in the synagogue" says Professor Pfannenstiel, his eye to a window fitted into the wooden door. Captain Wirth, furious, gives a few lashes of the whip to the Ukrainian who is Heckenholt's helper. After two hours and 49 minutes – the watch recorded everything – the Diesel begins to run. 25 minutes go by. Many are already dead, that can be seen through the little window, since an electric lamp lights up the interior from time to time.

After 32 minutes, finally, all are dead! On the other side, Jewish workers open the wooden doors. They have been promised – for their awful work – their lives, as well as a small per cent of the valuables and money found. Like pillars of basalt, the men are still standing, there not being the smallest space for falling or leaning. Even in death can be seen families holding hands. It is difficult to separate them, as they empty the rooms for the next load. They throw out the bodies, blue, damp with sweat and urine, legs covered with fecal matter and menstrual blood. Two dozen workers are busy going through the mouths, opening them with iron hooks, "Gold on the left, not on the right!" Others examine the anus and genital organs looking for money, diamonds, gold, etc. . . Dentists take out with the help of hammers, gold teeth, bridges, crowns. In the midst of them stands Captain Wirth. He is in his element, and, showing me a large can full of teeth, he says, "Look for yourself at the amount of gold! Just from yesterday and day before yesterday! You can't imagine what we find every day, dollars, diamonds, gold! You'll see yourself!" He leads me to a jeweler, responsible for all these valuables. They show me one of the heads of the great Berlin store "Kaufhaus des Westens," and a little man to whom violin music was being played, the heads of the gangs of Jewish workers. "He is a Captain of the Imperial Austrian Army, Chevalier of the German Iron Cross!" Wirth tells me.

Then the bodies were thrown into great ditches about 100 x 20 x 10 meters in size, situated near the gas chambers. After a few days the bodies began to swell up and the whole thing raised up about 2 to 3 meters because of the gas forming in the corpses. After a few days, when the swelling was over, the bodies sank down. Then, I was told, on the tracks of the railway the bodies were burned with the use of Diesel oil, so as to make them disappear . . . . "

The men wait in their gas chamber. In vain. We listen to them crying "like in the synagogue" says *S.S.-Sturmbannführer* Professor Dr. Pfannenstiel, ordinarius of Hygiene at the University of Marburg-Lahn, with his ear to the wooden door. Captain Wirth, furious, gives 11 to 12 lashes of the whip across the face of the Ukrainian, who is assistant to Heckenholt. After two hours, 49 minutes — the stop watch has recorded everything — the Diesel starts. Until this moment the men in the four chambers already full are living, living four times 750 persons in four times 45 cubic meters! Again 25 minutes go by. Many, it is true, are dead. That is what can be seen through the little window, through which an electric lamp lights up for a minute the inside of the room. After 28 minutes, still a few alive. After 32 minutes, finally, all are dead! From the other side, Jewish workers open the wooden doors. They have been promised — for their awful labor — their liberty and a few percentages of whatever the value of the valuables and money found. Like pillars of bassalt the dead are still standing, there not being the smallest space to fall or to lean.

Even dead, one recognized families with their hands still clasped. It was difficult to separate them, in order to empty the rooms for the next load.

C.   Poliakov's Conclusion:

There is much to add to this description, valid for Treblinka or Sobibor as well as for the camp at Belzec. The installations were conceived more or less in the same manner, and carbon monoxide, produced with a Diesel motor, was the method used for administering death. At Maïdanek, which was created later and which lasted until the last days of the German occupation, the method of asphyxiation with Prussic acid (Zyklon B) was introduced, as it was in Auschwitz; we have pointed out, on the other hand, that Maïdanek was not a camp for immediate extermination.

The researchers of the Polish War Crimes Commission have established that the total number of victims was close to 600,000 at Belzec, 250,000 at Sobibor, more than 700,000 at Treblinka, and 300,000 at Chelmno (300). They were more than 90% Polish Jews; but there was no European nationality not represented in the remaining 8 to 10%. In particular, out of the 110,000 Jews deported from the Netherlands, at least 34,000 were exterminated at Sobibor (301).

After nine months of intensive activity, the Belzec camp stopped functioning in December 1942. In the fall of 1943, once the "final solution" was for all practical purposes achieved in Poland, Sobibor and Treblinka were also closed down, and as many traces of them as possible were effaced, buildings torn down or destroyed, and the grounds carefully re-wooded. Alone, the camp at Chelmno, the first in place, kept on operating without interruption until the month of October 1944, and was not completely eliminated until January 1945.

C.   Conclusion of the Jerusalem Tribunal:

It is evident from the report of the Polish commission enquiring into Belzec (T. 1316) that this camp served above all for the extermination of Jews from southeast Poland; but Jews from Czechoslovakia, Austria, Rumania, Hungary and Germany were also killed there. The Commission estimated at 600,000 at least the number of people who met death there.

125. Testimonies given on Sobibor camp have given us a picture similar to that of Treblinka and Belzec camps. The Jews who were exterminated there came from Poland and the territories which the Germans occupied in Soviet Russia as well as Czechoslovakia, Slovakia, Austria and Germany. This camp was destroyed following a revolt of the Jewish prisoners which broke out there in October 1943. According to the estimates of the Polish Commission, 250,000 persons at least perished there.

126. Maïdanek camp, a large concentration camp near Lublin, likewise served as an extermination center for Jews. They were killed there by shooting and by gas. Witness Joseph Reznik described to us (Session 64) a massacre of Jews by shooting that took place in November in "Field No. 5 of Maïdanek." In the report of the Polish Commission is found the number of victims who were killed in the open in a single day, November 3, 1943: 18,000 Jews. Gas chambers were also installed at Maïdanek. Jews were deported to this camp from Poland, Slovakia, Czechoslovakia, and western and southern Europe. The Commission estimated that 200,000 Jews perished there. Maïdenek camp had branch camps, such as Travniki, which has already been mentioned as the destination for Jews from Germany.

Author's Postscript

The manuscript of this work was being printed when the shocking business of the *Vicaire* hit Paris. In the newspaper, *Le Monde*, which supported the play, I wrote that the Gerstein Document was an historical forgery, so false that the Nuremberg Tribunal itself had ruled it out as not proof of evidence, on January 30, 1946. *Le Monde* (December 26, 1963) published the information I gave them, with the following editorial comment:

"It is true that during the Nuremberg Trial the President set aside this part of the proof brought by the French Prosecution. Taken from the documents of the American delegation, it had not yet been authenticated under oath. This took place January 30, 1946, during the morning session. When the proceedings were resumed in the afternoon, the British Attorney General Sir Maxwell-Fyfe, explained that this report as well as all those of series PS had been authenticated by American officers. The Court then decided to take it in consideration."

I wrote again to *Le Monde* to point out to them that "authenticated by American officers" and "taken in consideration" did not mean "retained for the prosecution." I pointed out:

1. That during the afternoon session in question what had above all been decided (Report of the Hearings, p. 377) by common consent of the President of the Tribunal and Mr. DuBost was that Document P.S. 1553 was composed solely of 12 invoices for Zyklon B and that the Gerstein statement was not part of it. The Gerstein statement had only been introduced as a foundational reference to the aforementioned invoices: "To document P.S. 1553 [sic] attached the deposition of Gerstein and the explanations of the American chief of service who obtained this document . . . ."

2. That all the P.S. documents "authenticated by American officers" had not necessarily been authenticated by the Tribunal − far from it! − and had not all been retained for the prosecution. All of those documents that had been authenticated and retained for use as evidence appeared either in one of the books reporting the hearings or in the list (Volume 24) of the documents retained, and in one or the other of the 18 volumes of documents, which was not the case with the Gerstein

statement. In fact, all that was retained from P.S. 1553 by the prosecution at the Tribunal appears in volume 27, pp. 340-42. Two invoices for Zyklon B are found there (out of 12), but of the Gerstein statement there is not a word.

On December 30, 1963, Mr. Jacques Fauvet answered that the statement of Gerstein had, indeed, not been "taken in consideration" but that "he hesitated to prolong the controversy."

In a word, I was right, but the readers of *Le Monde* were not to know it. The controversy remained open in their columns, but only to those who supported the merits of the argument of the play. Such are the mechanisms of conditioning public opinion. I need not comment further.

FOOTNOTES

[1] This name is not legible. Wirth?, Poliakov says in a note.

[2] In other versions of this document, the dimensions of these rooms are given as 4 x 5, or 20 sq. meters, not 25; note also that the Poliakov version of 1951 does not give the dimensions of the rooms, but only their ground area, or 93 square meters.

Appendix C:

The Wolfgang Grosch Statement and A Report of a Second Lieutenant to a Lieutenant

1. The Wolfgang Grosch Statement

The following is the statement of Wolfgang Grosch which is quoted from *Le Pitre ne rit pas* by David Rousset:

> The undersigned Wolfgang Grosch attests and declares that the following is true:
>
> . . . Concerning the construction of the gas chambers and their crematory ovens, the people of office C were responsible for the construction, after office D sent the order. The chain of command was this: office D got in touch with office C. The C.I. bureau laid down the plans for these installations, in so far as it concerned just the construction alone, then sent them to bureau C. III which took care of the mechanical aspects of these constructions, such as, for example, getting the air out of the gas chambers, or the fittings for the gassing. Then bureau C. III turned over the plans to some private company, which was to supply the special machines, or the crematory ovens. Always in channels, bureau C. III notified bureau C. IV which sent the order on via the Inspection Division of West, North, South and East Constructions, to the Board of Directors of Constructions. The Board of Directors of Constructions then transmitted the construction order to the respective directive offices of concentration camp construction, who

then had the construction proper built by the prisoners which the D. III office put at their service. Office D gave the orders to office C. and the instructions concerning the dimensions of the constructions and *their purpose*. Fundamentally, it was office D which gave the commands for the gas chambers and the crematory ovens. signed: Wolfgang Grosch. (Emphasis added.)

This deposition was given to the Nuremberg Tribunal. If it was not entirely Grosch's doing, the gibberish in which it was drafted seems to have been scrupulously respected by the translator, obviously to keep up the confusion. The following points, however, cannot escape the reader:

1. It is only a question of the *construction* of gas chambers, and not of their intended purpose or their use;

2. The witness refers back to facts whose materiality could easily be established, and to "instructions" which could be published, but which, nevertheless, seem to have been carefully avoided, particularly concerning the purpose of the gas chambers, to which an allusion is made.

3. Out of all the construction projects for the camps (living quarters, infirmaries, kitchens, workshops, factories, and the like), whose planning and building were consigned to office D, the gas chambers and crematory ovens were picked out and, in a singular manner, juxtaposed, with the object of better impressing upon public opinion the idea that the crematory ovens were designed as instruments of genocide for the specific use in the concentration camps; such a conclusion is unwarranted since cremation is a common practice — just as common as burial — all over Germany. For all these reasons, no historian can ever accept this deposition as reliable historical data.

2. Report of a Second Lieutenant to a Lieutenant

David Rousset also cites the following report in his *Le Pitre ne rit pas:*

501 P.S.

Kiev, April 16, 1942

(*Reich* Secret Business)

No. of postal sector: 32,704

B.N. 40/42

    To S.S. *Obersturmführer* Rauff

Berlin, Prinz Albrechts, 8.

The overhauling of the vehicles of D groups and group C is completely finished. Although the vehicles of the first series can be used, even in bad weather (nevertheless it must not be too bad) the vehicles of the second series (Saurer) bog down *completely in rainy weather*. When, for example, it has rained, if only for half an hour, the vehicle cannot be used. It simply slides. It is not possible to use them except in perfectly dry weather. The only question that arises is one of knowing whether the vehicle can be used right at the place of execution when it is stopped. First of all, the vehicle must be brought to the place in question, which is only possible if the weather is fine.

The execution place is usually 10 to 15 km. away from the main roads, is chosen ahead of time, and not very accessible. It is completely inaccessible if the weather is damp or rainy. If the persons are brought on foot or by car to the execution place, they see right away what is going on, and become restless, which is to be avoided as much as possible. The only solution left is to load them in the trucks in the assembly area, and then take them to the place of execution.

I had the vehicle of group D. disguised as a gypsy wagon, and to do this I had one little window put on each side of the small cars, such as are often seen on our peasants' houses in the country, and two of these little windows on each side of the large cars. These vehicles were caught onto so quickly that they got the name "death cars." Not only the authorities, but even the civilian population, called them by this name, as soon as they were seen. In my opinion, even the disguise will not long keep them from being recognized.

The brakes of the Saurer vehicle which I drove from Simféropol to Taganrog proved to be defective en route. The S.K. of Mariupol found that the brake handle worked on both oil and compression. Persuasion and bribery on the part of the H.K.P. did the trick, so that a form was made from which two handles could be cast . . . . When I arrived a few days later at Stalino and Gerlowka the drivers of the cars complained of the *same defects*. After an interview with the commanding officers of those *Kommandos*, I went at once to Mariupol to have two other handles made for each of the vehicles. According to our agreement two handles will be cast for each car and six more will be sent to S.S. *Untersturmführer* Ernt for the cars of group C. For groups B. and A. handles can be got from Berlin, since their shipment from Mariupol northward is too complicated and takes too much time. Little defects in the vehicles are repaired by the technicians of the *Kommandos* or groups, in their own workshop.

The bumpy ground and the unbelievable condition of the

roads and highways, little by little wear out the connections and the waterproofing. They asked me if we then had to have the repair work done in Berlin. But this would cost too much and would require too much gasoline. In order to avoid these expenses I left an order to have small soldering jobs done on the spot, and in case this should prove impossible, to tele-graph at once to Berlin, saying that vehicle P.O.L. No. . . . was out of service. In addition, I gave an order that all the men should step away at the moment of the gassing so as not to have their health affected by any possible emanations of these gasses. I would like, on this occasion, also to make the follow-ing observation: several *Kommandos* have their vehicles un-loaded by their own men, after the gassing. I drew the atten-tion of the S.K. in question to the damages, as much moral as physical, which these men were risking, if not immediately, at least a little later. The men complained to me of headaches after each charging. The regulation, however, cannot be modified[1] because it is feared that the prisoners[2] used for this work might be able to seize a favorable moment to flee. To protect the men against this disadvantage, I beg you to issue ordinances in accordance.

The gassing is not accomplished as it should be. In order to finish the job as soon as possible, the drivers always press the accelerators to the bottom. This chokes the persons to be executed instead of killing them by putting them to sleep. My directives are to open the throttle in such a way that death is more rapid and peaceful for those concerned. They do not then have such disfigured faces, do not leave behind them so much elimination as we have seen until now.

Today I am going to the station of group B. and further news can reach me there.

Signed: Dr. Becker
S.S. *Untersturmführer*

This report comes as support for an affirmation of Eugen Kogon who writes in his *Enfer organisé*:

> . . . they (the S.S.) also used traveling gas chambers: they were autos which on the outside looked like police vans, and which on the inside had been adequately equipped. In these cars, asphyxiation by gas does not seem to have taken place very fast, since they usually rolled along for a long time before stopping and unloading the dead bodies. (Page 154)

Eugen Kogon, who does not tell us if any of these death vehicles have been found, does not cite this report either.

In any case, the translator is to be congratulated, for although he failed to satisfy one's curiosity about certain things, he at least gave the text an extraordinary Latin cast in the expression of thoughts. And it must be noted:

1. That it is easier for the present researchers to uncover documents about what went on at Mariupol than about what happened at Dachau;

2. That, instead of an order that was issued by a ministry, being placed in evidence, what we have is the simple letter *between a second lieutenant and his lieutenant* concerning the matter;

3. That even if this letter is a genuine document, it does not seem that any of the vehicles were found; at least, if any were found, very little publicity was made about the discovery.

The matter is still at issue, but, as we have seen from the proceedings of the Chelmno trial at Bonn, March 6, 1953, another version has been brought forward: it is no longer a question of Saurer vehicles. It was discovered in the meantime that the Saurer firm had not been making that type of vehicle since 1912! Rather, now it is claimed that the vehicles were American-made trucks that were designed for the disinfecting of troops while on campaign. These trucks, it seems, were furnished to Germany by the United States at the time of the Spanish Civil War. Further, it is claimed that vehicles of a similar nature were built by the Germans.

Verily, witnesses to anything can always be found!

* * * *

FOOTNOTES

[1] It is curious that this report of a second lieutenant was found, but not the written order with which it is concerned; or at least, it is curious that the one was published and not the other.

[2] What prisoners?